Poetics and Ethics of Anthropomorphism

Poetics and Ethics of Anthropomorphism: Children, Animals, and Poetry investigates a kind of poetry written mainly by adults for children. Many genres, including the picture book, are considered in asking for what purposes 'animal poetry' is composed and what function it serves. Critically contextualising anthropomorphism in traditional and contemporary poetic and theoretical discourses, these pages explore the representation of animals through anthropomorphism, anthropocentrism, and through affective responses to other-than-human others. Zoomorphism – the routine flipside of anthropomorphism – is crucially involved in the critical unmasking of the taken-for-granted textual strategies dealt with here. With a focus on the ethics entailed in poetic relations between children and animals, and between humans and nonhumans, this book asks important questions about the Anthropocene future and the role in it of literature intended for children. *Poetics and Ethics of Anthropomorphism: Children, Animals, and Poetry* is a vital resource for students and for scholars in children's literature.

Christopher (Kit) Kelen is a poet and painter, resident in the Myall Lakes of NSW. Published widely since the 1970s, he has a dozen full length collections in English as well as translated books of poetry in Chinese, Portuguese, French, Italian, Spanish, Indonesian, Swedish, Norwegian, and Filipino. A Greek bi-lingual volume is in preparation. His latest book of poetry in English is *Poor Man's Coat – Hardanger Poems*, published in 2018. Kit's *Book of Mother* is forthcoming in 2021. Emeritus Professor at the University of Macau, where he taught for many years, Kit Kelen is also a Conjoint Professor at the University of Newcastle. With Björn Sundmark, Kelen has edited two large-scale Routledge anthologies in the Children's Literature area: *The Nation in Children's Literature* (2013) and *Child Autonomy and Child Governance in Children's Literature: Where Children Rule?* (2017). In 2017, Kelen was awarded an honorary doctorate by the University of Malmö, Sweden.

Chengcheng You is an assistant professor in the Department of English, Faculty of Arts and Humanities, University of Macau. Her articles appeared in *Children's Literature in Education*, *Mosaic: An Interdisciplinary Critical Journal*, *The Lion and the Unicorn*, *International Research in Children's Literature*, and *History of Education and Children's Literature*. Her publications also include book chapters published in the anthologies: *Child Governance and Autonomy in Children's Literature* (2017), *Debatable Lands: New Directions in Children's Gothic* (2017), and *Posthumanism in Fantastic Fiction* (2018). Currently her research interests include critical approaches to children's literature, interdisciplinary studies in animals and literature, adaptation of Chinese classics, and the translation of Children's Literature.

Children's Literature and Culture
Jack Zipes, *Founding Series Editor*
Philip Nel, *Series Editor, 2011–2018*
Kenneth Kidd and Elizabeth Marshall, *Current Series Editors*

Founded by Jack Zipes in 1994, Children's Literature and Culture is the longest-running series devoted to the study of children's literature and culture from a national and international perspective. Dedicated to promoting original research in children's literature and children's culture, in 2011 the series expanded its focus to include childhood studies, and it seeks to explore the legal, historical, and philosophical conditions of different childhoods. An advocate for scholarship from around the globe, the series recognizes innovation and encourages interdisciplinarity. Children's Literature and Culture offers cutting-edge, upper-level scholarly studies and edited collections considering topics such as gender, race, picturebooks, childhood, nation, religion, technology, and many others. Titles are characterized by dynamic interventions into established subjects and innovative studies on emerging topics.

Rulers of Literary Playgrounds
Politics of Intergenerational Play in Children's Literature
Edited by Justyna Deszcz-Tryhubczak & Irena Barbara Kalla

Antarctica in British Children's Literature
Sinéad Moriarty

Dust Off the Gold Medal
Rediscovering Children's Literature at the Newbery Centennial
Edited by Sara L. Schwebel and Jocelyn Van Tuyl

Sexuality in Literature for Children and Young Adults
Edited by Paul Venzo and Kristine Moruzi

Poetics and Ethics of Anthropomorphism
Children, Animals, and Poetry
Christopher (Kit) Kelen and Chengcheng You

For more information about this series, please visit: www.routledge.com/Childrens-Literature-and-Culture/book-series/SE0686

Poetics and Ethics of Anthropomorphism
Children, Animals, and Poetry

Christopher (Kit) Kelen
and Chengcheng You

NEW YORK AND LONDON

First published 2022
by Routledge
605 Third Avenue, New York, NY 10158

and by Routledge
2 Park Square, Milton Park, Abingdon, Oxon OX14 4RN

Routledge is an imprint of the Taylor & Francis Group, an informa business

© 2022 Taylor & Francis

The right of Christopher (Kit) Kelen and Chengcheng You to be identified as authors of this work has been asserted by them in accordance with sections 77 and 78 of the Copyright, Designs and Patents Act 1988.

All rights reserved. No part of this book may be reprinted or reproduced or utilised in any form or by any electronic, mechanical, or other means, now known or hereafter invented, including photocopying and recording, or in any information storage or retrieval system, without permission in writing from the publishers.

Trademark notice: Product or corporate names may be trademarks or registered trademarks, and are used only for identification and explanation without intent to infringe.

Library of Congress Cataloging-in-Publication Data
A catalog record for this title has been requested

ISBN: 978-1-032-11311-1 (hbk)
ISBN: 978-1-032-11312-8 (pbk)
ISBN: 978-1-003-21933-0 (ebk)

DOI: 10.4324/9781003219330

Typeset in Sabon
by Newgen Publishing UK

Contents

Acknowledgements		viii
Introduction		1
1	Dear Little Man: Who's Talking to Whom?	17
2	How Practical Are These Cats? Animal Poetry at Large	58
3	The Little Dog Laughed to See Such Sport: The Childish Appeal of Humanimal Ambivalences	103
4	Beware the Jubjub Bird: Cautionary Verses Revisited	140
5	If You Go Down to the Woods Today: Wild and Domestic Textuality	172
6	Carnivorous Companions: Anthropomorphic Food in 'The Walrus and the Carpenter' and Elsewhere	202
7	This Little Piggie Went to Market: A New Humanimal Politics for Poetry	239
Index		265

Acknowledgements

We gratefully acknowledge the 2018/2019 fellowship offered by the International Youth Library, which gave us access to the collection of the library that is necessary for completion of the book. Special thanks to the library colleagues and fellowship holders of the year for their invaluable support and help in the writing process of this book.

Thanks are due to University of Manitoba Press for granting the permission to use parts of an article titled 'Liminal Encounters: Ethics of Anthropomorphism in the Poetry of Levertov, Szymborska, and Fulton'. The article originally appeared in *Mosaic: An Interdisciplinary Critical Journal*, 52(2) (2019): 147–165. We also acknowledge that Chapter 6 is derived in part from an article published in *English Studies*, 2021, copyright Taylor & Francis, available online: www.tandfonline.com DOI:10.1080/0013838X.2021.1952529.

We are grateful to University of Macau for the grant support (Grant No. SRG 2019-00169-FAH).

Introduction

Imagine a fairytale forest, a place where strange creatures meet, a place where familiar things (such as your own name) *become* unknown. Through Looking-Glass Land, Lewis Carroll's Alice finds herself in just such a curious fairytale wood. Having crossed a border akin to that which the sleeper crosses when entering into a dream, Alice finds herself in a kind of Carrollian *selva oscura* (twilight forest). In this a-semiotic space where everything forgets itself, we find an apt metaphor for the situation of the foreigner who, entering a new culture, has lost the name for everything he/she knows. It is in this wood 'where things have no names' that Alice meets a Fawn with whom she has a curious conversation. There is immediate rapport between these creatures who can identify neither themselves nor each other. They do not know who they themselves are, they have no names to offer now, but each has empathy for the other, in a place uniquely equipped to facilitate empathy. Pressed by Alice to divulge his identity, the Fawn promises to do so if Alice will come along with him a little further. 'I ca'n't remember *here*', he says (Carroll 2009, 156). The two progress together lovingly, Alice's arms around the soft neck of the Fawn, until they come out of the woods and, in the moment of recognition, the Fawn flees at top speed. Terror for the Fawn is in the truth that words convey to the visible world. Between Alice and the Fawn is a dialogue that notionally cannot begin because no one knows who or what his/her interlocutor may be. Yet there is a dialogue, there is rapport, and there is even affection. The circumstances of Alice and the Fawn are exemplary for those of us who work with poetry today, and particularly in the fleeting space between languages – a place where Alice has already found herself in her early encounter with the poem 'Jabberwocky'.

Beyond the storybook, there is something uncanny – something upside down – in this reported encounter between child and fawn. It is only *in* the story that we expect the human child and the other-than-human animals to know, each, who the other is. Only *in* the storybook do we expect conversation between them. So, *in* the story, it is not only the rapid departure of the fawn on recognising a human that conforms to a child's worldly

DOI: 10.4324/9781003219330-1

reality; as well, the lack of understanding, each, of whom the other is, likewise feels real for its witness. So that the border of the woods we have said and will encounter in this book is akin to one between waking and dreaming, is in turn akin to a border between the story, for instance in which animals might speak, and what we think of as the 'real world' – the world outside of the storybook.

The meeting of Alice and the Fawn raises all kinds of questions about human identity, child–animal affinity, animal anxiety, and the possibility of a land where animals and humans live in harmony on the basis of an equal rapport. There is a perhaps messianic echo here of the biblical prophecy of wild and domestic creatures getting on rather well in a notional utopic [post-apocalyptic] future [Isiah 11: 6–10].

In an age now known as the Anthropocene, questions about human–animal relations and questions about extinction are of growing importance. Are lambs who lie down with lions likely to get up again? That may well be a question about symbols, but the term 'Anthropocene' alerts us to the devastating consequences of human actions, in terms of worsening ecology, rapid disappearance of wild species, climate change, and the attendant catastrophic weather events the world has begun recently to witness.

There has been a long journey in ideas to dismantle the centrality of humans in the universe humans perceive and understand, a long journey to see past the necessity of the human domination of nature. In the realm of ideas, the projection of human agency – through anthropomorphism – has accounted humans and their proxies as authors of their own story and the story of all life, of everything that is, was, or could be. We can trace the process of de-centring of the species doing the talking – from Copernicus' debunking of the Ptolemaic geocentric system in the heavens, through Darwin's recognition of the human species as descended from other and earlier (and now extinct) animals, to the advent of the Freudian unconscious, and the bringing into doubt of very many assumptions and dogmas about the human mind (and where it had been and what it could know about itself).

Now digital technology marks another turning point in dissolving the boundaries between human bodies and those of other creatures and organisms. The late twentieth century and early twenty-first century is a juncture in which conceptualisations of the human being vis-à-vis animals, and their respective boundaries, are undergoing critical revision, along with child–animal, human–animal relations. A hundred and fifty years after Lewis Carroll, we return to Alice and the nameless fawn in the wood where things have no names. These sympathetic creatures, in their unexpected moment together, provide a touchstone image for those poems in which we encounter children and animals and all their various conjunctions and all the questions these raise.

Animal Voices and Poetic Language

The idea of animals (of literary animal characters) as others with kinship with children seems to have been taken for granted by generations of children's authors. Academic readers have argued a child–animal nexus in children's literature to be 'so common that it is easy to forget the figurative nature of the alliance' (Rudd 2009, 242). It has become perhaps an automatised metaphorical idea that children be regarded as little animals ('rug rats' and the like); or as John Morgenstern suggests, children are 'talking animals' (2000). Of course these little human creatures are not talkers to begin with but human company takes them step-by-step in that direction. Frequently regarded as non-dualistic and even animistic in orientation, children's thinking may be suggestive of an affinity with other small creatures, one much observed and encouraged by adults, for instance in terms of 'cuteness'. To meet children's reading needs as well as adult assumptions of a romanticised child–animal affinity, children's literatures have located a felicitous space to shelter anthropomorphic daydreams.

Before we are carried away with this cute affinity of animals for children and vice versa, we should perhaps not omit to mention the great ambivalence attendant on the analogy; we should not forget how abused and endangered children and animals often have been and often are by the activities of adult humans, who, we must remember are by-and-large the producers of culture for children and of beast fables as well. Let us also not forget how – as part of their general enculturation – children are taught to view and to understand animals: *Don't be a pig/a dog/a rat, don't follow like a sheep, don't monkey about, follow them over the cliff like a lemming* and so on. A catalogue of negative and fairly specific connotations suggests that everything that could be wrong with a human has a particular animal antecedent in mind, one of which children should be warned to beware. Even those traits of animals we find the most useful are certainly not what adults like to see in their offspring, even if at times they tell those same children that they are cuddly bunnies and little lambkins and snuggly baby ducks.

One might hypothesise that an unconscious motive for presenting so much in the way of animal, albeit anthropomorphised, antics for children is simply to keep them in line, by positing the virtue of human behaviour over that of other-than-human animals. Asserting a difference between human and animal behaviour is a way of insisting on human superiority and a way of keeping animal others excluded from the better treatment to which humans believe themselves entitled. It is likewise a way of dividing wild and dangerous behaviour from tame and acceptable behaviour. The analogy with racism, and with class and gender, as means of excluding difference, is irresistible here. But perhaps it is only the twenty-first-century urban mind that needs to rationalise why cultures for children should be so thickly populated with animal analogy. The fundamental reason may simply be that this proximity of human for other-than-human is traditional; traditional in the sense of being the norm for most humans most of the time over the course of homo sapiens' existence.

In this book, we explore questions of for whom and for what purpose animal poetry is composed. The focus of this work is on poetry because poetry is our particular interest, because the area of children's poetry has been neglected and because the role of poetry in children's literature, as for example, in the texts of picture books, has come to be underestimated, if not indeed ignored. We argue that for poetry, for children as for any audience, to be worth preserving, it needs to have epoch-to-epoch resonance for the adult reader. This is why we deal, in this book, largely with well-known works of literature. Concomitant with this claim, we note that resonance of poetry from childhood will have great importance for those adults to whom poetry remains a vital source of rhythm and meaning in life. Nor need 'animal interest' be a boutique industry for poets. In the Japanese tradition, where poetry prizes communion with nature, many of the most famous haiku are populated with animal characters, in texts widely accessible to, and loved and remembered, by children.

We focus, in this book, on the ethics in poetic relations between children and animals, humans and nonhumans, and we consider which rhetorical strategies are employed in spelling out the nature of relationships with other-than-humans and corresponding human responsibilities. For this purpose, we have devised a typology for the classification of texts of interest in theorising relationships between children, animals, and poetry. Our objective in classifying texts for this study is to understand the relationship between anthropomorphism (as rhetorical strategy) and anthropocentrism (as ideology); further, to explore whether it is possible, through poetry, to make sense of a world of others, and of the process or struggle involved in the representation of others.

Our taxonomy of relevant texts is built upon the following assumptions:

> First, humans produce texts. There is no doubt that animals communicate, and that they may sometimes communicate with animals of other species, for instance humans. Animal communication has been extensively studied and is often complex and fascinating, but these things are not within the remit of the present study. There is no doubt that animals make things, and that likewise making may be a cross-species endeavour. That other-than-human animals may be said to create what we humans consider cultural artefacts; we regard as an assertion based on powers of analogy. Claims, for instance, that 'animals make texts' (Moe 2014, 11) are only understood by humans through analogy

with human cultural production. This is not to deny what one might think of as animal 'story telling' (the dances of the bees), or animal lyricism, on the wing, or feelings analogous to human love and human awe. Animals may do all sorts of things humans might never succeed at, but they do not write, or more generally, produce culture in the way that humans do. Our point here is not to assert some great-chain-of-life human pinnacle exceptionalism; it is rather to suggest how little we know of animal thought and action. Human claims of animals doing as we do may generally be accounted as anthropomorphisms.

Second, our over-riding rhetorical category in these analyses is prosopopoeia – the putting on of masks, the making of illusions. In relation to this, a question worth asking is – how far is it possible to write/speak about animals without exploitation or sentimentality? With the imitative powers of many species in mind, we observe that, though many animals have faces and that humans can indeed put on animal masks, nevertheless (and despite the imitative, even 'deceptive', abilities of a wide range of animals [the lyre bird is a famous example]), the putting on of masks, as such, is a human activity. It is humans who put on human or animal masks and make voices in ways that express putatively vicarious pleasures of the animal mind, or that express concerns of animals, or for the natural environment.

Third, we propose that anthropomorphism and zoomorphism are essentially the one rhetorical strategy. To some degree, to make animals human is to make humans animal (and vice versa). It is often possible to apply to a particular character in a story a 'sliding-scale' analysis revealing how human or how animal that character is purported to be. Certainly, the projection of a spectrum from animality to humanity has historically had strongly moral, especially class and race-based and gender-based, connotations.

A broad context of culture for our investigation is suggested in the Gaia concept, as developed from James Lovelock's original formulation (1979, 1988) and in the anthropological approach to anthropomorphism proposed by Stewart Guthrie in *Faces in the Clouds* (1993). Other key theories we invoke to commence our journey include the 'biology watching' of Lewis Thomas, George A. Kennedy's proposition of animal rhetoric (1992), John S. Kennedy's approach to anthropomorphism (1992) and posthuman thoughts. Notable among these human–animal thoughts are Levinas' ethnical encounter with an animal (1969), Deleuze and Guattari's conception of becoming-animal (2005), Derrida's coinages of '*animot*' (2008), Haraway's posthuman vision of 'cyborgs' and 'contact zone' (2003, 2008). Each of these terms opens up a new interpretive trajectory for the understanding of human–animal relationships. Each also points towards a discovery of multiplicity and heterogeneous affect in human–nonhuman symbiosis. And each suggests leaving the dominant human self behind to embrace the middle of difference in the relation to the other. As cultural phenomena with relation to other-than-human animals, these theoretical revisions resonate with human perception of the worldwide ethical predicament that faces the animal world. They open new venues of thought and help promote new theoretical outlooks for human–nonhuman relations.

A System for the Classification of Texts

This book is interested in poetic texts for children and for adults that involve animals or relationships between humans (and especially children) and animals. In Chapter 1 we deal largely with poetry that would be considered as aimed at an adult readership. In the next few chapters, focused on popular verse, picture books, and nursery rhymes, we deal with poetry aimed at principally at a child audience. We note the variety and complexity of poems about animals and child–animal relations, in order to propose a typology of texts. Texts that interest us in this study typically deploy classical rhetorical strategies we can collectively name as *prosopopoeia*, especially personification and anthropomorphism. As well, narrative modes conventionally applied in fiction have been helpful for our categorisation of poetic texts, namely, first person, second person, and third person, with varying degrees of omniscience, narrative delivery. The difference between first- and third-person narrative mode in these cases is, we might say, essentially one of framing, determined by whether an animal or other nonhuman is seen to be quoted or paraphrased (third person), or speaking directly for themselves (first person).

We propose a specific text classification based on an assessment of the extent to which a text diverges from what we could call a notionally 'pure' dialogism – an equal discourse in which one party speaks *with* another. Accordingly, we have, as below, devised a prepositionally based system for understanding differences among acts of speech for/to/with/over/about animals and children. In particular, we identify:

1 Poetic texts that speak *to* animals – the text is specifically addressed to an animal (or other nonhuman) in particular, for instance in the form of apostrophe, as in odes, for example, John Keats' 'To a Nightingale', Percy Bysshe Shelley's 'To a Skylark', W.H. Auden's 'Address to the Beasts', and Pablo Neruda's odes to common things.
2 Poetic texts in which there is speech *with* animals – in conversations/ dialogues, either inclusive or exclusive, as in many children's picture books where children and animals speak with each other, adults being, case by case, included or excluded from the conversation.

Examples can be found in Carroll's Alice books, Ted Hughes' *The Cat and the Cuckoo* (1987) and *Collected Poems for Children* (2008), picture books, such as Maurice Sendak's *Where the Wild Things Are* (1963).
3 Poetic texts in which there is speech or narration *for* or on behalf of animals (or other nonhumans). Assuming the voices of others may draw attention to the situation of animals through deliberately empathic techniques, or it may effect a changed perspective for the reader (aesthetic, embodied, critical) through the effort to convey another point of view. Ted Hughes' 'View of a Pig', Wisława Szymborska's 'View with a Grain of Sand' fall into this category.
4 Poetic texts that speak *over* animals – with a noted anti-empathic tendency, particularly in landscape poetry, colonial poetry, or happy zoo poems. In these poems, agency of animals is ignored, and the alterity of animals is taken for granted. John Donne's 'The Flea' would be a convenient example, where the animal in question, in the poem purely for the purpose of argument to persuade the reluctant lover, nevertheless must die in order that the argument be demonstrated.
5 Poetic texts that speak *about* animals – in discussing others, to describe, through observation, animal behaviour as it 'actually' or 'factually' is in the here-and-now, in a documentary style, equally a haiku style; or to use the animal narrator or hero as an observer of, and commentator upon, human behaviour (e.g. Farid ud-Din Attar's *Conference of the Birds* [1177/1984], Don Marquis' *Archy and Mehitabel* [1927]).

In each case there is an apparent possibility of reversibility, that is, that animal characters might speak for/to/with/over/about humans or adults. And it is easily shown that every instance of apparent reversibility is an illusion facilitated by framing, as an animal appearing to address humans may be no more than a textual act of human empathy for other-than-human others, or perhaps a sham show of such. Is the textual framing and re-framing of animals undertaken for their benefit or for that of humankind? How is motion from frame to frame achieved? By way, for instance, of detachment, distance, or defamiliarisation? Here we admit that however poetry succeeds in articulating voices that are unheard or easily ignored, nevertheless, anthropomorphic/zoomorphic texts will not be rid of ideological illusion. We note the apparent contradiction that the mode most apparently empathic – speaking for animals (or assuming the animal's mask, as in animated TV series *Bojack Horseman* [2014–2020]) is also the mode most disempowering to actual animals; or, to return to our sliding scale of human–animal character quality – here the apparent animal is in fact almost entirely human (the mask is in such cases most easily seen through). In other words, the illusion of an animal speaking is an ambiguous presence in an exchange between human and hybrid human–animal sensibility. In Paul Wells' terms (2009), we find here a 'bestial ambivalence' that results from different levels of interaction among the pure 'animal' (animal character represented with known animal traits), the aspirational human (animal character that demonstrates favourable human qualities), the critical human (animal character as a critique or commentator of humankind), and hybrid humanimal character combining the abovementioned traits, and which directs us to a human–animal world, parallel to the imagined animal world in the text.

This book situates animal poems in different subgenres of children's poetry, such as nursery rhymes, cautionary verses, nonsense poetry, and animal poetry. After the first, our chapters mainly follow an ontogenetic-chronological order considering how different forms of poems are presented to their readership: young children in ascending age brackets, YA, dual audience, and adults. It is noted that cross-generational themes are frequently woven into children's books. Quite often, the popularity of classic books among both adults and children attests to the text's ability to transcend a generation gap. Besides, the child–adult dichotomy that has been at the core of children's literature has been to some extent dissolved, with the crossover phenomenon becoming a part of contemporary cultural reality (Postman 1982; Beckett 2009, 2012; Falconer 2009). This book embraces the possibility that great poems have 'ageless' appeal to various groups from epoch to epoch, as well as potential lifelong appeal for individuals.

Besides the age scope, we emphasise that assigning a text to a given generic category does not necessarily exclude it from another generic possibility. What kind of text is Carroll's 'Jabberwocky', for example? A nonsense poem? A beast fable? A poem about fantastic animals? A textual rite-of-passage? Where and how are human/other-than-human relations in this poem? The obvious answer is that animal others in this text are objectified to the point of being unknowable – they are just names, however suggestive (until, for instance in the case of 'Jabberwocky', we see the Tenniel or other illustrations of them).

Determinations of genre thus imply differences in points of view (re-framings) that will impact on our understanding of human/other-than-human relations, as these are presented, text by text. As to the question of what ought to be considered a poem, this book considers that a significant majority of picture book texts should be able to be regarded as poems in-their-own-right or as 'accompanied poems'. Obvious examples to bring to mind include Dr. Seuss' *The Cat in the Hat* (1957) and Sendak's *Where the Wild Things Are*. These are poems with pictures, where the juxtaposition of text and image has *inter alia* the function of implying particular readerships. For our purposes then a picture book contains a poem unless there is reason to think otherwise.

This study is intended neither to be exhaustive nor encyclopaedic. Rather, working through the thematically focused chapters, we visit well and less known specimens of poetry in order to better elucidate the imagination, and likewise the right/wrong sense, of one particular animal – the human animal, the 'us' in the story.

We aim in these pages, neither to historicise particular text types or genres, nor to engage reception or reader response theory. Our interest is, through analysis, to understand texts of contemporary relevance for both child and adult readerships, and to understand what these texts tell us about the relationships between animals and human animals (and particularly children).

Our hope is to understand the ways in which we humans imagine ourselves as animals or imagine other animals in our shoes. Likewise we wish to understand the ways in which we conceive of textual artefacts or conversation to, with, for, over, and about animal others. Such acts of communication help to explain, and indeed are constitutive of, the ethical-aesthetic being of the animal we are. Understanding the poetry in question will help to answer questions as to the justness of our being as we are. Such understanding should help us to decide who and how we want to be.

Overview of the Chapters

The book is organised into seven chapters, each exploring an aspect of anthropomorphism as related to poetry and animals. Chapter 1 of this book considers the relationship between poetry and animals, in a range of text types, from various cultures. It explores various speaking positions in terms of the prepositional typology we have proposed in our introduction. Poetry about animals draws our attention to questions, ethical and otherwise, as to the possibility of writing and speaking for others. That kind of investigation in turn suggests questions as to whether human thinking can take us beyond the limits of a literary construction of animals. We focus, in this chapter, on the ethics in poetic relations between children and animals, humans and nonhumans, and we consider which rhetorical strategies are employed in spelling out relationships with other-than-humans and corresponding human responsibilities.

Main poems dealt with in this chapter include:

- Theodore Roethke's 'The Bat' and 'The Meadow Mouse' (cited in Sword and McCarthy 1995)
- Czeslaw Milosz's 'With Trumpets and Zithers' (1969/2003)
- Wisława Szymborska's 'In Praise of Self Deprecation' (1981)
- Ted Hughes' 'Thought Fox' (1957/2019)
- Les Murray's 'The Gods' (1992/2006)
- Rainer Maria Rilke's 'The Panther' (1903/1989)
- Shaun Tan's 'Cicada' (2019)

Chapter 2 focuses on nonsense in poetry for children, its rhetorical means, and its ideological effects. The likening of dissimilars (we know as the principle of metaphor), which Aristotle considered essential to the art of poetry, is shown by Horace in his *Ars Poetica* to present a clear danger of excess: poetry can result in the creation of monstrous hybrids. It is just this art of the absurd nexus we find historically characteristic of poetry in the category of 'nonsense', as intended for children, from Edward Lear, through to Dr. Seuss and beyond. 'The Owl and the Pussycat' (1871/2001) provides a fine early example. It would appear that poetic texts for children, involving animals, tend either to the absurd – where the fun is made by connecting what cannot be connected, for instance animals too dissimilar or antagonistic to plausibly coexist (as in the idea of a romance between an owl and a pussycat); or else to articulate a plausibly complex social reality for a certain animal, imagined by way of behaviours, recognisably both human and animal, as in T.S. Eliot's *Old Possum's Book of Practical Cats* (1939/2009).

By turning humans into animals, one gives animals powers of awareness and self-awareness. We investigate whether it could it be so as to suggest that humans behave without reflecting on or thinking about their, or whether it is that making the whole of the world subject to what appear to be the rules of nature – the rules which apply to every and any animal – may have the effect of making the world of humans and its patterns or rules seem as if it were natural. It is our argument in this chapter that naturalising the world of human relations through an appeal to naturalness supported by evidence of a concocted nature is an ideological inversion *par excellence*. The child reader is expected to believe that social relations presented by talking animals provide cultural norms of relevance to the child in her/his own growth to maturity. Don Marquis' early twentieth-century text *Archy and Mehitabel* (1927), and subsequent books in the series, subvert various stereotypical assumptions about both animal behaviour and its accessibility to fairytale motives. One could see the kind of challenge we meet in Marquis' Archy as forerunner for much more recent texts, drawing attention to ontological dimensions of human–animal relations, such as in Dr. Seuss' variously indeterminate anthropomorphised animal characters, or in Shaun Tan's postmodern picture book, *The Lost Thing* (2000). In different ways, the poems with which this chapter deals originate in doubts of an ontological/epistemological kind, as also expressed by Denise Levertov in 'The Cat as Cat' (1962/2002).

Chapter 3 is principally concerned with nursery rhymes, mainly selected from Iona Opie and Peter Opie's *The Oxford Dictionary of Nursery Rhymes* (1997), and focuses on the roles and relationships that these canonical (print-assisted) survivors of oral tradition propose for animals. It is in nursery rhymes many of us as individuals first encounter anthropomorphised animals. Coming from the era before the advent of children's literature, nursery rhymes are full of hidden meanings, nevertheless a model for texts with a joint child–adult readership – as evidenced in the much-argued allegorical content of many nursery rhymes (e.g. 'Three Blind Mice'). In this chapter, we are interested in the manner in which knowledge of and dissemination of nursery rhymes via parents and other adults connects those parent figures and the children in their care with a putative 'traditional knowledge' and so a popular wisdom about various aspects of life and society, much as is the case with proverbs and aphorisms more generally.

Several themes for analysis include the implication of the unknowability of animals, parameters of non/human identity ('Bye, baby bunting'), nature–culture conflicts, eco-phobia ('Ladybird, ladybird'), and the celebration of human kindness/unkindness towards animals. In particular, we note that nursery rhymes embrace the aesthetics and ethics of human–animal interaction in various manifestations of anthropomorphic nonsense and humanimal ambivalence. This chapter explores the source of ambivalences, either adult–child, human–animal, nature–culture, as in the nursery rhymes, 'Pussy cat, pussy cat, where have you been?', 'Let's go to the wood, says this pig'. There are many nursery rhyme examples of animal characters portrayed as outsmarting their predators, as in 'Six Little mice sat down to spin' and 'A fox jumped up one winter's night' and 'A carrion crow sat on an oak'. Different degrees of sympathy and empathy are suggested in these texts, where innocence and 'wild extravagances' (Opie and Opie 1997, 2), human and animal identity are integrated through nonsense and play into a special affect, a textual sport, intended at least in part for a young readership. This chapter is an attempt to make sense of how nursery rhymes, as an originary crossover genre, generate ambivalences for the child.

Chapter 4 deals with cautionary verses, with a particular emphasis on the most famous nonsense poem of all time, Lewis Carrol's 'Jabberwocky'. The nonsense of cautionary verses is anchored in the contradictory norms of absurdity established in nursery rhymes. The interest in this chapter, as in nonsense poetry more generally, is in understanding the method in the madness. Based on the similar vicariousness of children's literature and animal-concerned poetry, this chapter examines how ambivalences arise from a history of writing children and animals as proxies for humans of various stripe. In Carroll's 'Jabberwocky' we meet the apparent didacticism of nineteenth-century poetry intended by adults for children. The animals in this story poem (the Jabberwock, the Jubjub bird, and the Bandersnatch) teach not by talking but by being available as fearsome fauna of the potentially hunt-able kind. It is the tale that is instructive; once 'into' the poem we see that it for the telling of the tale that the poem is presented. We analyse how the performance and the dialogic encounter are necessary to the exegesis the text here demands. But, just as there is an outside in the poem to the story it contains, so there is an outside of the poem in Alice's first encounter with it – it is in a book and on a page she merely happens upon. Nonsense, irony, and portality are key themes in our investigation of this most famous of all nonsense texts.

If we read the Alice books as a series of parodic cautionary verses set up to call into question apparent common sense, these verses become the standard for subsequent self-parodic cautionary tales in the English and often in other languages. This chapter re-examines didacticism, as it concerns power and especially gender relations, human–animal relations and adult–child relations. In Lear's rambling bird-obsessed bestiary (2001), and in the cautionary tone we find in Hilaire Belloc's 'Jim, Who ran away from his Nurse, and was eaten by a Lion' (1941, 5–10), and like works, we find a creaturely didacticism that challenges received wisdom and common sense by stressing imagined animal voices, and that plays with the indeterminacy of animal meaning.

Chapter 5 investigates the wildness and domestication problematics in children's literature, with particular reference to Jimmy Kennedy's lyrics to 'The Teddy Bear's Picnic' (cited in Boulton and Ackroyd 2004, 17). As in Bakhtin's carnival more generally (1968), childhood is also reckoned as a possible venue for turning things upside down or inside out. Our aim in discussing a number of carnivalesque poems and picture books concerned with humanimal ambivalence is to consider how ideas of wild justice, domestic bliss and child-adult/human-animal power relations figure in texts concerned with tame-and-wild liminalities. This chapter proceeds from Zanni Louise's and David Macintosh's picture book *Archie and the Bear* (2017) and Sendak's *Where the Wild Things Are* to A.A. Milne's *Winnie-the-Pooh* (1926/2013), a text that plays with the pretend-animality of the child entering culture, a figure embodied in that 'bear of very little brain' whom 'long words bother' (45), who just happens to exercise impressive poetic skills. As the analysis of these texts offers a glimpse of how poetry appeals to ethical concerns regarding the treatment of animals, wild and otherwise, in a material culture, the chapter further investigates how the interplay of empathy and defamiliarisation guides poetic trajectories for the staging and retrieval of fabulous virtues and vices, by involving anthropomorphic animals.

Our close reading of Jimmy Kennedy 'Teddy Bears' Picnic' is with a view to understanding what this song suggests about symbol and reality in human–animal relations, and in particular about relationships between children/childhood and animals/animality. The position of the (adult or child) reader/listener in this text – like that of the foreigner in a new culture – is one we might see as foreshadowed by Carroll's Alice, in her experience of the wood where things have no names. In and about the *topos* we name 'the picnic woods', things become what they touch – are brought to life – a toy is a bear is a child is asleep and could wake to be anything. Nor is wakefulness protection from the vicissitudes/of play – here is Johan Huizinga's (1980) *homo ludens* unfettered. Play is performance and, as with 'Jabberwocky', the play and performance take place on various interacting planes – some more textual, others more or less practical. We sing to play to be ourselves, in order to know who we are. But can we know who we are when we encounter animals, when we meet our bears, even as vaguely as we do in the picnic woods? Ambivalence, like irony, is catching. The encounter with the inscrutable other makes us mindful of Levinas' dictum – 'the absolutely foreign alone can instruct us' (73).

Chapter 6 surveys the ethics of anthropomorphic food in literature, focusing on a crucial and under-examined aspect of Carroll's 'The Walrus and the Carpenter', that is, the relationship between euphemism and atrocity in the dealings with less powerful but sentient others, those anthropomorphised entities that are – or are in danger of becoming – food. Situated at the intersections of anthropomorphism studies, animal ethics, and Carrollian scholarship, this chapter explores how aesthetics and ethics work in considerations of form and courtesy, which impact the lives of such anthropomorphised entities. With a close reading of 'The Walrus and the Carpenter', Chapter 6 examines that Alice's interpretive discussion with the Brothers Tweedle, following the recitation of 'The Walrus and the Carpenter', re-frames the ethical dilemma of eating sentient speaking animal others, in the context of a larger ontological enquiry. We note that consideration of food anthropomorphism as both rhetorically and ethically invested compels us to participate in contradictions between aesthetic forms of society and the grisly truth of power relations among animals, especially of the power humans exert over human others as well as animals from the imperialist context to the contemporary situations of meat eating.

Chapter 7 develops the themes of cannibalism and Holocaust introduced in Chapter 6 and goes on to engage poems in which conscience and consciousness are negotiated in response to environmental ethics. We consider activist poems, in this chapter, such as Alice Fulton's poem 'Some cool'(2004, 111–114), a poem that appropriates nursery rhymes, such as 'This Little Piggie went to market', to explore ethical dimensions of human action and experience. Thinking and feeling are faculties of the one body – that hungers, that sates itself, that reads its own affect in the eyes of a sometimes unspeakable other. It is uncomfortable to discover, through the silence of the wilderness or of domestication, questions that had gone unasked in the slaughterhouse and in the kitchen, especially when we have, for better or worse, gone so far as to anthropomorphise those we later decide to eat. Cannibalism and Holocaust are the psychopathologies brought to mind here. This concluding chapter engages poems in which conscience and consciousness are negotiated and represented, as response to environmental ethics, as in Rilke's *The Eighth Elegy* (1922/1977), in the poetry of Wisława Szymborska and Alice Fulton. Poems that enlist the imagination of childhood and child/animal presence are selected to discuss what we have already introduced as 'humanimal sensibility', that mode of subjectivity structuring a human-perceived affinity among living things. It is not, however, simply the 'old joy' about animals that 'returns in holy presence' (Levertov 2002, 19), such as has been considered a key generic characteristic of texts for children across a range of cultures. New humanimal sensibility works as an ecological advocacy 'felt' in contemporary poetry about children and animals. In this chapter, paradoxes of presence and absence return to the fore in our witness of the world and its literature, as these concern non-human animals today. Real animals are – species by species – vanishing from our world in the here-and-now. Yet more and more animals – from beastly machines to posthuman creatures – are witnessed and imagined in poetry, in philosophy and the media. In a world where humans and their animal victims are ever more numerous, the diversity of other-than-human life is vanishing at a rate humans have less and less difficulty in measuring.

Entering Planet Earth's Sixth Great Extinction, also known as the Anthropocene Extinction, the question is what can be done to reverse the course of the current catastrophe. How can there be justice for the creatures and peoples wronged by greed driven human induced climate change? Children, such as Greta Thunberg and her followers, have already begun taking things into their own hands with their own protest movement. The question is what can culture, more broadly, and literatures in particular, contribute to the debate and the solution. What will the role of poetry be written as it is mainly by adults in a Green New Deal for the children and other animals of this world?

References

Attar, Farid ud-Din. *The Conference of the Birds*. London: Penguin, 1984.
Bakhtin, Mikhail. M. *Rabelais and His World*. Cambridge, MA: MIT, 1968.
Beckett, Sandra L. *Crossover Fiction: Global and Historical Perspectives*. New York, NY: Routledge, 2009.
Beckett, Sandra L. *Crossover Picturebooks: A Genre for All Ages*. New York: Routledge, 2012.
Belloc, Hilaire. *Hilaire Belloc's Cautionary Verses*. New York: Alfred. A. Knopf., 1941.
BoJack Horseman. Produced by Lisa Hanawalt and Raphael Bob-Waksberg. Netflix, 2014–2020.
Boulton, Jo and Judith Ackroyd. *The Teddy Bears' Picnic and Other Stories*. London: David Fulton, 2004.
Carroll, Lewis. *Alice's Adventures in Wonderland and Through the Looking-Glass and What Alice Found There*. Oxford: Oxford University Press, 2009.
Deleuze Gilles & Guattari Félix. *A Thousand Plateaus*. Minneapolis: University of Minnesota Press, 2005.
Derrida, Jacques. *The Animal That Therefore I Am*. New York: Fordham University Press, 2008.
Eliot, T.S. *Old Possum's Book of Practical Cats*. 1939. Illus. Axel Scheffler. Boston: Houghton Mifflin Harcourt, 2009.

Falconer, Rachel. *The Crossover Novel: Contemporary Children's Fiction and Its Adult Readership*. New York: Routledge, 2009.
Fulton, Alice. *Cascade Experiment: Selected Poems*. New York: Norton, 2004.
Guthrie, Stewart E. *Faces in the Clouds: A New Theory of Religion*. New York: Oxford University Press, 1993.
Haraway, Donna Jeanne. *The Companion Species Manifesto: Dogs, People, and Significant Otherness*. Chicago: Prickly Paradigm Press, 2003.
Haraway, Donna Jeanne. *When Species Meet*. Minneapolis: University of Minnesota, 2008.
Hughes, Ted. *The Cat and the Cuckoo*. Devon: Sunstone Press, 1987.
Hughes, Ted. *Collected Poems for Children*. London: Faber & Faber, 2008.
Hughes, Ted. 1957. *The Hawk in the Rain*. London: Faber & Faber, 2019.
Huizinga, Johan. *Homo Ludens*. London: Routledge and Kegan Paul, 1980.
Kennedy, George A. "A Hoot in the Dark: The Evolution of General Rhetoric". *Philosophy and Rhetoric* 25(1) (1992): 1–21.
Kennedy, John. S. *The New Anthropomorphism*. Cambridge: Cambridge University Press, 1992.
Lear, Edward. *The Complete Verse and Other Nonsense*. Harmondsworth: Penguin, 2001.
Levertov, Denise. *Selected Poems*. New York: New Directions, 2002.
Levinas, Emmanuel. *Totality and Infinity: An Essay on Exteriority*. Trans. A. Lingis. Pittsburgh, PA: Duquesne University Press, 1969.
Louise, Zanni. *Archie and the Bear*. Illus. David Mackintosh. Sydney: Little Hare, 2017.
Lovelock, James. *Gaia: A New Look at Life on Earth*. Oxford: Oxford University Press, 1979.
Lovelock, James. 1988. *Ages of Gaia*. Oxford: Oxford University Press, 1995.
Marquis, Don. *Archy and Mehitabel*. Garden City, N.Y.: Doubleday, 1927.
Maurice, Sendak. *Where the Wild Things Are*. New York: Harper and Row, 1963.
Milne, A.A. *Winnie-the-Pooh*. 1926. Illus. E.H. Shepard. London: Egmont, 2013.
Milosz, Czeslaw. *New and Collected Poems, 1931–2001*. New York: Ecco, 2003.
Moe, Aaron M. *Zoopoetics: Animals and the Making of Poetry*. Toronto: Lexington Books, 2014.
Morgenstern, John. "Children and Other Talking Animals". *The Lion and the Unicorn* 24(1) (2000): 110–127.
Murray, Les. *Collected Poems*. Melbourne: Black Inc., 2006.
Opie, Iona and Peter Opie. *The Oxford Dictionary of Nursery Rhymes*. Oxford: Oxford University Press, 1997.
Postman, Neil. *The Disappearance of Childhood*. New York: Delacorte, 1982.
Rilke, Rainer Maria. *Duino Elegies and The Sonnets to Orpheus*. Trans. A. Poulin, Jr. Boston: Houghton Mifflin Company, 1977.
Rilke, Rainer Maria. *The Selected Poetry of Rainer Maria Rilke*. New York: Vintage, 1989.
Rudd, David. "Animal and Object Stories". *The Cambridge Companion to Children's Literature*. Eds. M. Grenby and A. Immel. Cambridge: Cambridge University Press, 2009. 242–257.
Seuss, Dr. 1957. *The Cat in the Hat*. Boston: Random House, 2007.
Sword, Elizabeth Hauge, and Victoria McCarthy, eds. *A Child's Anthology of Poetry*. New York: Ecco Press, 1995.

Szymborska, Wisława. *Sounds, Feelings, Thoughts: Seventy Poems*. Trans. Magnus J. Krynski and Robert A. Maguire. Princeton: Princeton University Press, 1981.
Tan, Shaun. "The Lost Thing". *Lost & Found*. New York: Arthur A. Levine, 2011.
Tan, Shaun. *Cicada*. New York: Arthur A Levine, 2019.
Wells, Paul. *The Animated Bestiary: Animals, Cartoons, and Culture*. New Brunswick: Rutgers University Press, 2009.

1 Dear Little Man
Who's Talking to Whom?

In a world age now beginning to be called the Anthropocene, we see that human action is taking an increasingly heavy global toll on the natural environment. Perhaps thought (or mindset) as we know it takes a toll as well? It might be time for humans to think again about their place in a world age they have decided to name after themselves.

A key stake in the re-think now called for is an often taken-for-granted anthropocentric point of view. This is what Alfonsina Storni's poem 'Hombre pequeñito' challenges. The challenge comes through a little role reversal. The poem speaks from 'a canary that wants to fly', a subaltern's perspective to pose a question as to the possibility of cross-species understanding:

> I was in your cage, little little man,
> little little man who gave me my cage.
> I say 'little little' because you don't understand me
> Nor will you understand.
> (Storni, 27)

Endowing other-than-human and notionally non-agential creatures with a capacity to speak and reason might broadly be read as countering a dominant human-centred world view. Characteristic of children's literature in general, this offering of our speech to others has become a common tropical device to foster empathy for those lacking this capacity. As the chained persona utters a desperate protest against the fate of imprisonment, any 'little man' (or woman) who reads this poem might empathise with the subaltern voice here heard.

But what are animals doing in poetry anyway? And what are we doing with them there? In one of Emily Dickinson's most popular poems 'I'm Nobody! Who are you?' (1976, 133), the persona identifies herself as a non-entity who runs the risk of being banished if she asserts herself too much in public. As if celebrating the joys of obscurity, Dickinsonian rejection of being 'somebody' suggests – through the frog figure – that existential angst might come with social status. The poem is 'about' human society, but the anthropomorphic suggestion on which it depends

DOI: 10.4324/9781003219330-2

raises questions humans might wish to ask about frogs. If, in this poem, a human analogy is invested in the presence of a frog, a spontaneous image of the tail-less amphibian as a noisy and unpleasant creature leaps to mind. This analogy alerts us to questions about the representation of animals in the poetry: How aware are we of the frog? How aware are we of the human-frog analogy implied? Do we think in terms of human-animal relations reading this poem or do we merely accept a fabulous premise in the aptness of the analogy purposed to re-consider human activity?

Poetry about animals has drawn our attention to questions, ethical and otherwise, as to the possibility of writing and speaking for others. Perhaps writing and/or speaking for others (including the other-than-human ones) is part of the general mission of poetry. As Susan Stewart notes in *Poetry and the Fate of the Senses* (2002), 'poetry making is an anthropomorphic project: the poet undertakes the task of recognition in time – the unending tragic Orphic task of drawing the figure of the other – the figure of the beloved who reciprocally can recognise one's own figure – out of the darkness' (2). In this book, we wish to ask whether poetry, especially for, or involving children, ought to be regarded as a form of expression apt for the purpose of de-familiarising human-centred territory with other-than-human perspectives.

That prospect in turn suggests questions as to whether human thinking can take us beyond the limits of a literary construction of animals as humans-in-some-other-form. To briefly historicise the human/other-than-human relationship in Western modernity, we may read a reaction to the Cartesian mechanical view of animals in Romanticism and its revival of a link with nature, its glorification of the natural environment, and its giving a voice to animal others and their haunts. While the advent of the Anthropocene signifies a (probably) irreversible environmental crisis today, Western discourses again find new means to articulate, re-examine, and renew understandings of human-nonhuman relationships.

Awareness of unequal power plays in human-animal relations is to the fore in recent years. Scholars and critics concerned with representations of otherness have formulated new terms to situate and to deal with relationships gone awry between humans and the world of animal others they inhabit. Those marginalised and mute in a biopolitical network of justice, have been named as Richard Doyle's 'postvital life' (2003), Donna Haraway's 'companion species' (2003), Agamben's 'bare life' (2004), Judith Butler's 'precarious life' (2004), Deleuze and Guattari's 'becoming-animal' (2005), Eric L. Santner's 'creaturely life' (2009), Jane Bennett's 'vibrant matter' (2009), and Melinda Cooper's 'surplus life' (2011). These expressions seek to define idiosyncratic ethics on various scales of ontology, epistemology, biopolitics, and literary representations of interspecies interaction. To different degrees, the attempts to refresh understanding of human-animal relations stress the role of anthropomorphism. Jane Bennett, for instance, voices her political ecology by elevating the role of anthropomorphism:

> I will emphasize, even overemphasize, the agentic contributions of nonhuman forces (operating in nature, in the human body, and in human artifacts) in an attempt to counter the narcissistic reflex of human language and thought. We need to cultivate a bit of anthropomorphism – the idea that human agency has some echoes in nonhuman nature – to counter the narcissism of humans in charge of the world.
>
> (xvi)

The ethical imperative of some contemporary discourses has come to extol the virtues of anthropomorphism in interpreting the presence of nonhuman animals in the moral domain. Yet this is a mode of thought and of making culture that has more readily be regarded as toxic to human understanding of other-than-human conditions.

Donna Haraway has coined the term 'significant otherness' for pets, horses, and other companion species, and implicitly promotes manifold benefits of anthropomorphism in the treatment of animals. 'I am who I become with companion species', as Haraway describes it, 'who and which make a mess out of categories in the making of kin and kind' (2008, 19). If we choose to empathise with animals, then inevitably we tend to invite a further projection or mapping of our mind on other minds. Minding animals might lead us to more sound ethical judgements concerning the treatment of nonhuman animals.

Poetry, in particular, has come to engage with 'animal thinking'. George A. Kennedy's surmised 'rhetorical energy' in animal gesticulation and vocalisation suggests a new rhetorical angle on the human-animal continuum and how 'minding' animal ways of being has enriched human rhetoric (1992). Kennedy's argument is expanded in Debra Hawhee's 2006 essay 'Language as Sensuous Action: Sir Richard Paget, Kenneth Burke, and Gesture-Speech Theory', Donna Haraway's monograph *When Species Meet* (2008), Diane Davis' 2011 essay 'Creaturely Rhetorics', and Tobias Menely's monograph *The Animal Claim* (2015). Aaron M. Moe, continuing this line of considering animal influence in poetry, elicits a 'zoopoetics' from human–animal interaction in poetry, his argument being that great poems are 'inextricably bound up with the intensity of animal *poiesis*' (2014, 5, emphasis in original). Onomatopoeia, for instance, is popularly reckoned to translate animal sound into language. The vocal approximation of the calls of other animals' growls, meowings, buzzings, and cooings cues a human consciousness of animality, allows we humans to recognise, and so in a sense *live*, the animals in ourselves. Likewise, Onno Oerlemans, in his book *Poetry and Animals: Blurring the Boundaries with the Human*, dismisses earlier allegorical animal poems as 'purely anthropocentric' (2018, 34), as totally obscuring the presence of actual animals. Following the trend of 'animal-oriented criticism' in contemporary animal studies, he believes in an 'inherent playfulness' in poetry that can allow it to 'break out of ideologies and categories, to be at once anthropomorphic and antianthropocentric' (18).

In all of these negotiations, we face the contradiction that anthropomorphism, while possibly means to the expression of empathy for other-than-human others, must nevertheless be a rhetorical strategy or mode of human perception integrally bound up with the problem of anthropocentrism, or one might say 'human imperialism'. If it is not possible for humans to avoid an anthropocentric position in their relations with other-than-human others, is it yet plausible that an anthropocentrism might be reconfigured so that human–animal boundaries and relationships are more fairly drawn? Or at least so that the boundaries may be seen? Conversely, is it the case that anthropomorphism is a means of obscuring such boundaries? Does anthropomorphism, as a rhetorical strategy, serve to conceal an anthropocentric world view?

It may be that the answers to these questions already lie in the doctrines and practices of other-than-Western ethical systems; for instance, in those of Daoism or Buddhism or in the animisms of non-literate cultures. Whether or not we countenance this possibility, there is a compelling need for anthropomorphism to be re-contextualised and re-evaluated in contemporary theoretical discourse, as more than, in Hank Davis' words, 'a form of intellectual laziness' which results from 'the failure to make species differentiations' (1997, 336). This needed re-examination is currently underway, which builds on the aesthetic-ethical groundwork of Levinas' encounter of alterity (1969), Martin Buber's 'I-Thou' relationship (as opposed to 'I-It') (1958), Patrick Murphy's idea of 'nonhuman speaking subjects' (1995), of Adorno's conception of art and literature as participants in the suffering and making muteness eloquent (2002), of Josephine Donovan's aesthetics of care (2016), and of posthuman thinkers such as Cary Wolf, Rosi Braidotti, and Donna Haraway. It is from such groundwork, this book examines the interrelations of children, animals, and poetry, considering anthropomorphism as trope and as a liminal zone in which different rhetorical imperatives are obeyed or disobeyed. Our use of the word 'trope' is to suggest that anthropomorphism is not only a conscious rhetorical strategy, but also a mode of human perception, one which exists in everyday speech as much as in literary works or in hortatory discourse.

Un/Consciousness of Anthropomorphism

Etymologically, anthropomorphism, from the Greek *anthropos* (human being) and *morphe* (form), denotes the attribution of human form or traits to other-than-humans. The world is seen by humans through the anthropomorphic lens, whether by design or not, and whether consciously or not. Do we know who or what we are talking about, just in our everyday language? Or could all these utterances be a sort of hallucination as conveyed in the psychological terms 'pareidolia' and 'apophenia'? The former was introduced by Victor Kandinsky in 1885 while the latter was introduced by Klaus Konrad in 1958, both employed to refer to involuntary conditions in which the familiar is misperceived among random phenomena (cited in Blom 2010, 32; 389).

Numerous examples in our quotidian life present what we might think of as low degrees of anthropomorphism that are sometimes too subtle to be noticed. We may hear the eagle 'whistle a song' above a little town that 'huddles against' the exposed cliff or see the salmon leaping with a splash, 'a fish-dance' in the 'calm' water. Bees, we think, 'dance' to tell a story. And while all of this may be true in a way, we need to acknowledge that it is true for us, and in our way.

Once we move from unconscious uses of anthropomorphism in words, images and ideas to higher degrees of anthropomorphism, the eagle can be animated with a proud look, or the curious salmon might be given a name in token of some human quality, for instance the resolution shown in travelling all the way back up the river from the sea – a feat that would be arduous for a human. The literary imagination takes as a frequent starting point an unconscious empathic tendency to imagine ourselves in another skin.

Anthropomorphism appears pervasive in every culture. As a mode of human perception, the scope of unconscious anthropomorphism might be thought to encompass the human sense of reality. The Chinese characters for ginseng, involving a pictorial reference to human shape, provide a perfect illustration of how humans, since ancient times, have calibrated the likeness of the nonhuman world to the human mind. Documented in Tao Hongjing's *Root and Herbal Classics* (505–507), ginseng, named after its resemblance to human body and limbs, was discovered by a mythic ruler Shennong. Its importance was further established by its ascertained medical value for human kind (Park et al. 2012). We not only search for human biological form to draw us near to the natural world (think of Pygmalion's sculpture), we also attribute symbolic human qualities to plants, flowers, and trees. Orchid in spring, bamboo in summer, chrysanthemum in autumn, and plum blossoms in winter – these are widely acknowledged in Chinese culture as 'The Four Gentlemen', symbolising exemplary qualities of the ideal gentleman, of noble mind, great strength and resilience, and unyielding heart. Besides, anthropomorphic representations such as seeing, in chance images, such phenomena as Buddha's smile or an animal shape, in clouds, portraying 'musical instruments as people', and drawing 'parallels between edifice and body' have a popular appeal across various cultures (Guthrie 1993, 133–150). It is tempting to say that to anthropomorphise is only human. According to Protagoras' famous dictum 'man is the measure of all things'. Taking into account the frequent unconsciousness of anthropomorphism, it might be better to say that 'the human is the creature who cannot help but measure everything against him/herself, and usually without noticing that that is what s/he is doing'.

Despite the obvious enrichment of culture and art that has come from un/conscious anthropomorphism, there is a long history of criticism directed at this particular trope, as mis-attribution, as a mistake that should be warned against and hopefully corrected. Spinoza critiqued the anthropomorphising of God as human, and in his *Ethics* (1677) regarded the act of anthropomorphism itself as appropriating the whole world to suit human arrogance. An oft-cited passage in David Hume's *The Natural History of Religion* (1957) derides philosophers who employ anthropomorphism with an innate but mistaken propensity to humanise all other nonhuman objects and animals:

> There is a universal tendency amongst mankind to conceive all beings like themselves, and to transfer to every object, those qualities, with which they are familiarly acquainted, and of which they are intimately conscious. We find human faces in the moon, armies in the clouds; and by a natural propensity, if not corrected by experience and reflection, ascribe malice and good-will to everything, that hurts or pleases us ... Nor is it long before we ascribe to them thought, and reason and passion, and sometimes even the limbs and figures of men, in order to bring them nearer to a resemblance with ourselves.
> (1957, 29)

Why do we speak as we do of the world and all that is in it, as if it were mainly consisting of human activities and attributes, human shapes, and moods and motives? There can be no doubt that anthropomorphism is, in this sense, from a moral point of view, closely tied to anthropocentrism. In *Genesis*, Adam 'gave names to all cattle, and to the fowl of the air, and to every beast of the field' (Genesis 2: 20). Here, the human power of naming is an act of authority and mastery, and a first step towards the bringing of other-than-human others into the human fold. The animal's is a face as is ours (at least this is true in the case of mammals, among other creatures), the animal's pleasures and pains as ours. If the animal cannot express these things, then we humans take them as read. A culturally determined hierarchy of names and functions resolves where each animal is in the human world – as friend or enemy, slave or supper. The more words we may associate with an animal in particular, the more important that animal has been to a particular human culture.

Here we call into play anthropomorphism's corollary in zoomorphism. We can easily divine how important particular animals have been to us through their idiomatic presence in our everyday language – through the degree and frequency with which humans liken themselves and other humans to particular animals – cunning as a rat, slippery as an eel, Wile E. Coyote.

But do we know who we ourselves are when we speak or perceive? Stewart Guthrie complicates this question in his (1993) monograph *Faces in the Clouds: A New Theory of Religion* by suggesting that we humans are, in fact, 'as mysterious to ourselves as is the world in general' (185). In Guthrie's view, we rely on anthropomorphism to shape our perception of the world, not in the light of our familiarity with ourselves, but in terms of 'our interests, which usually involve humans' (185). Arguing from a radical interdisciplinarity, Guthrie asserts that religion could account for 'an even broader, more diverse, and more pervasive phenomenon, anthropomorphism' (202). He posits that the origin of religion inheres in human perceptual process and imagination involving anthropomorphism. When 'primitive' people attribute human form, behaviour, intelligence, and emotional content to nonhuman animals, events (volcanoes, thunder, fire, etc.), or inexplicable beings, such transference of human attributes and emotions engenders manifold and illusory forms of spirits, divinities, and other supernatural beings. In all likelihood, anthropomorphic or theriomorphic imagination is a starting point for religions the world over, and as varied as Shinto, pantheism, and monotheism. Guthrie claims, 'There is no religion without relationship, no relationship without significant communication, no significant communication without language, and no language without likeness' (244). Thus the ubiquity and generality of anthropomorphism in almost every field and every culture are camouflaged in different forms. Religions, as all human creations, depend in their origins on a close relation to human likeness and its projection into a wider-than-human world.

The 'universal tendency' anthropomorphism summons forth, John S. Kennedy tells us, is a habitual thinking mode that is 'dinned into us culturally from earliest childhood' and 'presumably programmed into our hereditary make-up by natural selection' (1992, 5). Invariably embedded in human consciousness, anthropomorphism pursues humans from one realm of thought and feeling to another. In many instances, conscious and unconscious forms of anthropomorphism are at work at once.

In Theodore Roethke's 1938 poem, 'The Bat', we find an anthropomorphic mapping of an imagined 'bat world' onto relationships as humans know them. In this poem, we meet an ambiguous effort to see a bat in human terms. The bat as 'cousin to mouse', and the use of the gendered pronoun 'he', rather than 'it', in the first stanza, immediately blur the otherwise rigid human-animal boundary. Bat is surely an opposite of a human collectivity? It is a close kind of enemy; it sleeps when we wake and vice versa. Then the bat in human-built space goes on to be placed in the human field of objects – 'attic' 'hat' 'screen'. The bat's 'fingers' make a 'hat'. So this bat in the house has what humans have and makes what humans might make. We know that this is a human way of seeing a bat, that this is a bat seen humanly. But we also know that the bat seen closely, like the mouse, has much in common with humans – what we call fingers for instance.

What is a bat to the human observer? It can be a mouse with wings, because the flightless rodent is something closer to human experience, more in the mind of humans. (The German *fledermaus* shows how serviceable this idea may be, for other than poetic purposes.) The mouse, present in the poem only by analogy, offers a bridge to the bat-ness of the bat (something further from human experience). But mouse-ness is only half the bat. The flighted bat is fearful, because irrational – 'loops in crazy figures half the night'. 'Figures' provides an unconsciously human measure for the action of the bat – as if an effort at deliberate shape (of a kind we could understand) is a sign of the bat's failure at humanity, or a failure at humanness at least. 'Crazy figures' seems an oxymoron in this context, but it sets up the close encounter with the bat as something frightening, never wished for. Fearful because of the bat's human face, its status here is almost-us. The encounter is uncanny because it is a view into a distorting mirror, where humans glimpse their 'bat-selves' with at least a little horror:

> But when he brushes up against a screen,
> We are afraid of what our eyes have seen:
>
> For something is amiss or out of place
> When mice with wings can wear a human face.
> (cited in Sword and McCarthy 1995, 228)

In his celebrated essay 'What Is It Like to Be a Bat' (1974), Thomas Nagel asserts that we would never be able to access the mental perceptions of the bat, while too much assumption of what it feels like for a bat to be a bat may only expose the anthropomorphic fallacy. Roethke's poem brings Nagel's speculation to the fore, approaching the complexity of efforts at empathy and likewise efforts humans make to keep their distance from creatures with whom they have so much in common. The complications are achieved by bringing into question distances we take for granted between humans and the animal others with whom we humans have kept unintended company down through the ages. These proximal relationships – and particularly in the case of the bat – take on new resonance with the advent of COVID-19.

The work of Roethke's poem is 'ambiguously' anthropomorphic because it calls its own rhetorical basis into question. The poem does this by playing on the unconscious knowledge its reader has of where and how we are vis-à-vis animal others, like bats and mice. Nowhere does the poem ask us how animal we are, or how we are of an animal world, where we are just one species among many. Still, flipside of the question as to how human the other animals are or can be is the question as to how animal we humans are and/or can be. We shall return to zoomorphism shortly.

The bat never gets to read the poem about the disturbing quasi-human-ness of bats. Is the bat's understanding of the unwanted encounter with the bat-ness of humans therefore any less profound, any less disturbing? We will never know. We do though get from the poem a sense that our unconsciousness of the encounter has something in common with that of the bat's.

The Seeking of Forgiveness

Looking to another end of a spectrum in awareness, in Czeslaw Milosz's long poem 'With Trumpets and Zithers' (1969/2003), a persona addresses his human consciousness in a range of settings. This is a poem full of presence and – and as suggested in the mock triumphalism of the title – a wide-ranging cognisance of world historical time, of relevant Bakhtinian chronotope. It is full of deliberate confusions of human and animal other, of landscape and what animates it, of sentience and 'a herd of islands', 'quiverfuls of buildings touched by a ray'. The reader must work to connect these images, to find a narrative joining the dots here. Sven Birkerts writes of Milosz's poetics, 'brevity is a kind of shorthand for the enormity of the unspeakable' (1983, 115).

The poem engages reflexively with what it offers the reader's senses, likewise the reader's conscience. Aleksander Fiut notes that Milosz's poetry 'returns again and again to the questions of what institutes human nature, what marks its limits, and how it manifests these' (1987, 67). The haecceity of its substance in words is to the fore of the self-examination in this work: the poem is concerned with how it can be here for us to read. And so it is concerned with who we readers are, where we are, in the poem's presence. To be in – to be with – a poem is to suspend some disbelief. The seventh section of the poem begins: 'From a limbo of unbaptized infants and for animal souls let a dead fox step out to testify against the language' (2003, 228).

This is a poem about many things, but perhaps above all it is an exploration of the limits of language and empathy as these relate to the boundaries humans take for granted between themselves and 'the rest of creation'. The apparent paradox of one without language testifying *against* language is belied by the fact that we the readers are witness to the whole scene – paradox and fox and the work of understanding what is testified. Survival can be testimony, as can the particular foxness of a fox. More of this later in the chapter when we come to Les Murray's fox in his poem 'The Gods' (1992/2006).

The Levinasian encounter with the absolutely other (for Levinas 'the only one who can instruct me' [73]) – in this case with one whom we know to have no words – suggests that we desire to be known, to be touched, to be the objects of an encounter, the potentials of which and the significance of which are larger than language. In the ninth section of Milosz' poem, 'I was sitting before a mirror but no hand reached out of darkness to touch me on the shoulder' (2003, 229). Here we witness thwarting of the expectation of meaning as something solemnly given, as for instance by the one in whose image we might imagine ourselves having come to be.

Rather than encountering the deity in any expected form, the persona is met by the flashing vision of flocks of birds 'taking off from the banks of spring ice'. This vision culminates in an expression of animal creativity: 'Fanning with their four wings storks stood on their nests in a majestic copulation' (Milosz 229). Where are humans situated in relation to this sublime, if not Nietzschean, vision of brute nature, unsullied with our mindfulness and self-knowledge, not to mention prudery? The persona cannot trust his own 'dishonest memory' to preserve anything, 'save the triumph of nameless births' (229). The stanza ends with this portent: 'When I would hear a voice, it seemed to me I distinguished in it words of forgiveness' (229).

Whose forgiveness and for whom? One returns to the language-less testimony of the dead fox. We can imagine the cause of the fox's demise. If they can come this far down a road of redemption, what humans imagine of nature's language – of the speech of nature to them – is that they might be forgiven. Surely though, humans, however, well meaning, kid themselves if they believe that they approach a putative sentience of nature through such human abstractions as redemption and forgiveness, not to mention language?

Yet along with the limits and boundaries revealed by means of transgression, in this poem we find an urgent need for humans to admit their animality. The tenth section of the work begins:

> The dream shared at night by all people has inhabitants, hairy animals.
> It is a huge and snug forest and everyone entering it walks on all fours
> till dawn through the very thick of the tangle.
>
> (229)

'All are quadrupeds' (230), we are told. And it is through the night these creatures come, whose 'rosy tongues lick each other's fur'. Later in the stanza the two-legged come into the picture, so that we recognise their place in the story in relation to the mammalian collectivity preceding and from which humans come:

> The two-legged, some to the left, some to the right, put on their belts, garters, slacks, and sandals.
> And they move on their stilts, longing after a forest home, after low tunnels, after an assigned return to it.
>
> (Milosz 2003, 230)

The coming of the human animal is prefigured by the advent of consciousness – in particular, of ego, and of the language it implies: 'The "I" is felt with amazement in the heartbeat, but so large it cannot be filled by the whole Earth with her seasons'. Here is Milosz's admitted 'Whitmanesque temptation' (Franaszek 2017, 398) – a powerful 'I' that contains a multitude of voices, 'many long dumb voices … with the twirl of my tongue I encompass worlds, and volumes of worlds'. These liberating lines call attention, particularly to 'rights of the others … of the trivial, flat, foolish, despised' (Whitman 1902, 42–43). The self-coming-to-consciousness cannot help but regards itself as bigger than all it takes in. But what is the status of this so apparently essential abstraction, contained in a body but bigger than the world? 'Nor would the skin guarding a different essence trace any boundary' (Milosz 2003, 230). 'Animals are like us', as John E. Becker comments on the paradox of animal being in this poem, 'yet they are not us: and so it is that they furnish enough mystery to satisfy our most desperate desire—to find our true selves at a deeper level than mob rhetoric and hard reason' (1990, 395).

The perceiving self is world-containing but cannot tell itself apart from everything beyond its skin. It is animality and a 'forest home, after low tunnels' humans long for a return to, and far from being a much vaunted escape from such, religion is what offers humans their rightful former place in 'creation' – a place among and not apart from, in harmony with and not at odds with, the world of nature. Nature is then ironically that sphere against which humans appear to have been struggling in order to discover themselves. It is only to essences language gives access. It is only of types and archetypes we're made mindful in words. Again, Les Murray's fox in 'The Gods' will be instructive. Is language then the kind of curse of which Caliban complains? Milosz's dead fox doesn't curse; s/he testifies.

In the last (11th) section of this long poem, humans are de-centred from the action and life on earth finds its cosmic centre in a coelentera – the 'all pulsating flesh, animal-flower', described in the following terms: 'All fire, made up of falling bodies joined by the black pin of sex' (Milosz 230). Milosz's cosmic view is revealed as, ideally not anthropocentric, but biocentric. His coelentera 'breathes in the centre of a galaxy, drawing to itself star after star' (230). Where are humans, where is the human 'I' in relation to this traffic? Milosz's persona's 'I' is 'an instant of duration, on multi-laned roads which penetrate half-opened mountains'. Man is the wrecker, but one whose power as such is (as yet) incomplete. Not everything has yet been wrecked.

The poem is future-oriented, closing with the line: 'I thought that all I could do would be done better one day' (231). What category of action should we take as intended here? Is this about finding harmony with nature? Getting over ego so humans can see who and where we are? Is this about transcending the limits of language so as to recover our animality? Is this about understanding that such transcendence is impossible? But we already have an answer. This is about *all* that I could do. It is in the context of an immense (because unknowable) duty, the title of the poem ironises the triumphalism of organised religion (likewise philosophy, politics, economics) and its claims on truth and categories and a world where the place of our species is understood.

Uncanny Encounters in the World Where Nothing Is Still

If it is urgent for humans to admit their animality, this is because now, living as we do in the planet's Sixth Great Extinction (or, as it is sometimes known, the Anthropocene Extinction), this may be the way people can come to understand the stakes in the games our species plays with all others and with the finite resources we and they share. Encounters with animal others, such as Roethke's bat that is almost but isn't a mouse, are uncanny because we see ourselves in them. And we see our seeing in the eyes of these others. And we see how our seeing, likewise our feeling, may well be mistaken. 'Mice with wings can wear a human face'? We have no way of seeing faces but the way we see our own. If this fact of our seeing has not yet saved the world, it may nevertheless be the last remaining hope that the world we inhabit can be saved.

Poetry is a means of pointing out the uncanny facts of existence, human and otherwise. As with Roethke's human-faced mice with wings, neither poets nor readers need to find themselves comfortable with such facts.

In Roethke's description of the bat as a mouse that can fly with a 'human face', it is through the purposeful extension of human self-regard, we see the animal subject as humanlike. Unwitting anthropomorphism shapes our perception of the world. Let us consider another poem, 'The Meadow Mouse', in which Roethke, whom the poet John Berryman calls 'Garden Master', 'a lover found needing a lower into friendlier ground to bug among worms' (1963), makes an effort *not to* anthropomorphise the animal on which the work is focused. The poem begins with the persona's description of meadow mouse found in a shoe box stuffed with nylon stocking, with his 'absurd' whiskers 'sticking out like a cartoon-mouse' and 'feet like small leaves' shaking. Although the mouse struggled to wriggle away, using his whitish and wide spreading feet, his great sense of comfort was sense after the persona provided it cheese and drinking. The mouse then slumbered peacefully and soundly with its bulging belly:

> His tail curled under him, his belly big
> As his head; his bat-like ears
> Twitching, tilting toward the least sound.
>   (cited in Sword and McCarthy, 231)

The persona's relationship of care with the vulnerable creature entails a domestication – in the poem, by way of language mainly – that is destined to be short-lived. The mouse is known by way of analogy and association, as 'a little quaker', 'a cartoon-mouse', and 'a minuscule puppy' (231). As the persona may settle on the thought of protecting the little mouse, he was scared to find the empty shoe box: 'Where has he gone, my meadow mouse/My thumb of a child that nuzzled in my palm'? (231). When the mouse is gone (of its own volition) it is gone as a lost child would be gone. Where? And why? To what? These are the questions the persona begs. He was alarmed at the thought that the meadow mouse will be easily victimised as it comes around the bottom of the food chain and can easily fall as prey to the predators, as the persona imagines, the hawk, the great owl, the shrike, the snake, the tom-cat.

> I think of the nestling fallen into the deep grass,
> The turtle gasping in the dusty rubble of the highway,
> The paralytic stunned in the tub, and the water rising,—
> All things innocent, hapless, forsaken.
> (cited in Sword and McCarthy 1995, 231)

The mouse is gone presumably because the attention of the domesticating human – the otherwise God-like omniscience in the piece – could not be maintained. Ironically this comes after the (presumably human-fearful) trembling has stopped. The mouse in the poem wished to go elsewhere, and for reasons, we may suppose, not accessible to us. Assuming, as we mustn't, is just to assign reason and volition to a mouse. So we would fail to understand that a meadow mouse, however, seemingly vulnerable, is capable to adapt or find a sense of comfort in its natural habitat, no matter how brutal its looks to human spectators.

Pathos accruing to the creature's diminutive size and place in the wilds of brute nature is all to do with its now well-developed status, as anthropocentrically determined – the mouse as quasi-pet, the mouse as cultural artefact, the mouse as capable of feeling, fear, perhaps of something approaching Quaker fervour. The mouse/child is gone to dangers of which it cannot know, but of which the adult human persona is well aware.

A central theme of this book will be the ways in which children and animals stand, we may say, in each other's shoes – from the adult poet's point of view, and so from a reader's point of view. In the poetry that interests us, frequently children and animals are arranged metonymically: one is associated with, one suggests, the other. This association is made by adults, and, in the case of children's literature, for the heuristic benefit of children. Animal and child are each a category of at least lesser sentience. Less than adult human sentience, the animal like the child, the child like the animal, each is ideally the object of adult care, concern, and love. Indeed, in human-animal relations, an aesthetic of care has been proposed, to entail 'attentiveness to each individual organism' (Donovan 2016, 80).

Harold Bloom remarks that the 'implied anthropomorphic claim' in Roethke's poetry helps establish 'a new order of understanding: that such (anthropomorphic) qualities, precisely as they are human, are derived from the natural order' (1988, 67). The act of perception, which leads to 'a more-than-analogical relationship between perceiver and things perceived', Bloom continues, 'when it is expressed, is one with the growth, the vital principle, of the things perceived' (67). Close to care, concern, and love, lie cuteness and pathos and charm, these each of a kind that must be deeply instinctual, of a kind that allows the human species to survive and to thrive, to make up stories to show and tell and for passing on. 'Cuteness and pathos and charm' are big abstractions, but each as evocative of animality as of the cerebral human world.

If the relationship of adult humans to animals and children was purely and reliably one of care and love, one might imagine various problems the world could go without. Importantly, the child like the animal, is each ideally the object of adult control – of stewardship and mastery, entailing the comprehension of what others, cared for, are presumed not to be able to understand. This ignorance of the other is a vast category; we might say it extends up to and including the nature of children and of animals – of their shared animality.

Roethke's 'The Meadow Mouse' ends with an (albeit passive voice) reminder of the plausible limit of adult, human love *cum* control: that 'All things innocent, hapless/are at risk of being forsaken'. Richard Katrovas considers the penultimate line of the poem, 'a rip in a canvas on which has been an idyllic landscape', from which 'we see a small part of a horrific depiction of one of the inner circles of Dante's Hell' (1986, 420). While this account might overstate the horrors of life on the planet's surface, the ambiguous resolution nevertheless invites us to what Katrovas terms 'a sense of lingering suspension' (420). Adult human cerebration might not be able to save you (for instance, as an other-than-human pet-sized animal) – from the wicked ways of the world, from humans, and their built systems ('turtle gasping in the dusty rubble of the highway') and (in the case of 'the paralytic stunned in the bathtub') even, perhaps, from yourself.

Consider the ambiguous quality of brute nature as it presents to those who might be ours but who stray beyond the human pale, to 'live by courtesy of the shrike, the snake, the tom-cat' (cited in Sword and McCarthy 1995, 231). The meadow mouse's status, at poem's end, as one strayed from human care, offers an adequate point of reference to Barbara Creed's proposition of 'stray' as 'human-animal ethics in the Anthropocene' (Creed 2017, 8). According to Creed, stray creatures 'potentially trouble the conscience, and haunt the unconscious, of many of those who are not homeless and acutely aware of the deprivation the *unheimlich* stray is suffering, or of the instabilities that constantly threaten their own sense of self' (78). There is nothing courteous in the attentions of shrike or snake or tom-cat for any meadow mouse they might meet. It is only our human way with words that allows the dark humour here. It is humans who might extend courtesy beyond their own species. Beyond the human sphere of consideration, such ironies will be lost on the mouse, as on the animals for which the mouse is prey.

A poetic trajectory has been noted, in Roethke's poetics, that involves 'conscious imitation', 'sympathetic imitation', and 'a widening sensibility' in understanding neglected voices and echoes (La Belle, 1976). Careful, conscientious, and self-conscious as the persona in 'The Meadow Mouse' is, this is not primarily a poem about care for animal others; rather it is about limits of the human qualities empathy and understanding. 'Do I imagine …'? 'seems' – these phrasings point to what the persona cannot know about the meadow mouse. 'Hapless' and 'innocent' – these kind words are adult human projections onto the lot of others at least in part beyond our understanding. 'The Meadow Mouse' depicts a world that is not merely anthropocentric; it is a world in which efforts *not to* anthropomorphise must fail.

Questions Raised by a Clear Conscience

Humans furnish the world around them with their own attributes – out of kindness or concern, for reasons of greed or viciousness, or perhaps simply because they cannot help it. On the other hand, humans see the animal in themselves for perhaps as wide a range of motives and reasons, often for instance because 'instinct' may be claimed as self-justification. Anthropomorphism and zoomorphism are, to some extent, flipsides of the one coin – the coin of anthropocentrism. For those with language to deal with the world, the world appears to be all about *us*. The moral and intellectual failure of this way of seeing and being in the world is matched poignantly by the failure of efforts to think or feel a way around it. We face a simple contradiction that every intellectual effort to see or express the world we inhabit from other-than-a-human perspective shows us further from that possibility than we were before we started thinking about it. Is the problem here our thinking and speaking for others who cannot speak? Or is it simply too much thinking and speaking more generally (as for instance in a book like this)?

It is true that we humans have a vast and growing store of knowledge about animals, knowledge of a kind the other-than-human animals cannot have about us or indeed about each other or themselves. Presumably though, other animals have instincts (or instinctual 'knowledge') about themselves and other creatures, humans may never share.

Our scientific understandings of animals extend well into the workings of their brains (Bekoff et al. 2002; Roitblat et al. 2014). Nevertheless, it remains reasonable to ask whether it is just to assign reason or volition to a mouse. Though clearly mice do things for reasons, though clearly they choose courses of action and so decline other ways they might have gone, to express all of this about them is to put them in our rather over-sized shoes. Perhaps though the question hardly matters because we cannot think of the mouse without giving it at least this much of ourselves. Our observer's paradox is not limited to investigations one might think of as scientific. It is in general a hall of mirrors we look out to in the effort to see beyond ourselves. Wittgenstein has told us that the limits of our language are the limits of our world. Mice in a poem then are of the human world, and only more mysteriously so when they have absented themselves from that world. Perhaps all perception and cognition are likewise implicated in the manner Wittgenstein claims for language? So we have borrowed from Protagoras to say that humans are creatures who cannot help but measure everything against themselves, and usually without noticing that that is what they are doing. Homo sapiens are, we may say, the solipsist species. Is it for us to know if other species are as well?

The point of human solipsism made very forcefully in Wislawa Szymborska's poem 'In Praise of Self-Deprecation' – a touchstone poem for our study, and one to which we will return. In this poem, Szymborska's idea of 'self-deprecation' draws a sharp line between the lack of apparent 'humanity' characterising the little bestiary she has chosen and the moral torments that are brought by the ethical imagination of human beings. Ironically belied by the matter-of-fact reporting, it is by virtue of these particular animals that the particular inhumanities of humans are known:

> The buzzard has nothing to fault himself with.
> Scruples are alien to the black panther.
> Piranhas do not doubt the rightness of their actions.
> ...
> There is nothing more animal-like
> than a clear conscience
> on the third planet of the Sun.
> (Szymborska 1981, 189)

The first thing to ask about this work is simply who is it about? And if one answers that the poem is not really about buzzards, piranhas, rattlesnakes, jackals, locusts, alligators, trichinas, horseflies, or killer whales, then precisely *how* is it about humans? Negatively, of course. It is about qualities we see ourselves, but not them, as having. The principle of human-directed zoomorphism is under challenge here.

The challenge comes by way of the *sub specie aeternitas* point of view only revealed in the last line of the poem. The endorsement of 'a clear conscience' in Szymborska's poem problematises the animal-like lack of conscience (inhumanities) for which certain humans are known to see beyond the anthropocentric perspective. We are not told who is watching, but whether alien or God or gods, or some objective future human/animal, activity, and the order of things on the only known living planet is now seen from an imagined outside. Still the poem is at least partly about what it is to be animal. It is about the relationship between human ideas of how we and others ought to be/think/feel/doubt/reason/ be glad; it is about the relationship of these to animality – theirs and ours. This is a poem about the manner in which humans are animals.

As earlier noted, we humans endow ourselves with the supposed qualities of animals (sly fox, subtle serpent) but reflection reveals these to be anthropocentric projections. It is what each animal means for us that gives us the hypostasising clue we apply through folklore to take each creature for granted, to put it in its box (or perhaps better said, cage or refrigerator). If snakes never bit humans, if foxes never ate the chickens humans keep, then we would not speak of either creature as treacherous. There is however no objective basis for endowing snakes or foxes with the putative qualities of theirs we recognise in fellow humans we distrust. Every zoomorphism is an anthropomorphism, and vice versa.

Szymborska's poem turns on the flawed assumptions that fuel anthropomorphism and zoomorphism, and by bringing these, not into focus but into question, it problematises human self-regard and human superiority over animal others. We think we know what the problem with each of these animals is, but none of them has a problem. We humans are the ones with the problem. Perhaps ours is, as suggested by Nietzsche in *The Gay Science*, the problem of consciousness:

> Consciousness is the last and latest development of the organic and consequently also the most unfinished and weakest part of it. From consciousness there proceed countless errors which cause an animal, a man, to perish earlier than necessary ... If the preservative combination of the instincts were not incomparably stronger, if it did not in general act as a regulator, mankind must have perished through its perverse judgements and waking phantasies, its superficiality and credulity, in short through its consciousness.
>
> (1977, 158)

Szymborska's poem cuts through the thinking/not-thinking we humans routinely do about how animals are, how we're like them, and how they're like us. The force of the poem goes to what's lacking in the equation, and so witnesses a *via negativa* by way of which anthropomorphism may be refused. Yes, the buzzard has no means with which to fault himself, because fault is something only humans can find. The poem tells us, animals 'live as they live and are glad of it'. The claim that ends the poem takes us to consider moral responsibilities seriously and human motives lightly. What is a 'clear conscience'? If it is indicative of a guilt-free subjectivity, why is its absence so often associated with animal ways of being as perceived, as assigned, by humans? The animals in Szymborska's poem seem particularly to underline the dangers anthropocentric moralism might pose for the will to power, in the hope of restoring an amoral innocence. Without consistently resisting the morality that denies animality as a source of humanity, Szymborska's poem embeds a nuanced critique of the habitual metaphoric tendency in truth-making Nietzsche famously problematised. In the famous essay 'On Truth and Lies in an Nonmoral Sense' (1873), he writes:

> nature is acquainted with no forms and no concepts, and likewise with no species, but only with an X which remains inaccessible and undefinable for us. For even our contrast between individual and species is something anthropomorphic and does not originate in the essence of things; although we should not presume to claim that this contrast does not correspond to the essence of things: that would of course be a dogmatic assertion and, as such, would be just as indemonstrable as its opposite.
>
> (1990, 83–84)

Pointed, along these problematic Nietzschean lines, towards a transcendence of anthropomorphism, Szymborska's animal menagerie recalls the oscillation of Dickinson's frog between connotation and physical being. Both poets employ an 'animetaphor', to borrow Akira Lippit's term, in establishing an 'originary topography shared by human beings and animals' (1112), as well as conjuring up figurative animals as extra-textual.

In Szymborska's poetry, the perspective of the relatively powerful, for instance the human, is frequently de-emphasised, while the insignificant and otherwise silent are offered the opportunity of a voice. Justyna Kostkowska points out that Szymborska's nature poems de-centre the 'patriarchal standards of expertise, objectivity, and absolute truth' once prescribed by Cartesian schools of thought (2004, 185). Szymborska critiques overweening human pride to celebrate a creaturely existence, a way of being in which sentience extensively endorses an 'aesthetic-recreational environmentalism' based on a kind of 'preferential valuing' (Embree 2003, 43). Achieving an agreeable intersubjective valuing of the minor requires experiencing of the interplay between consciousness and conscience.

If, as for Danté, metaphors are beautiful lies in the *Convivo* (cited in Bowe 2020, 199), we should acknowledge the rhetorical trickery that makes a poem like 'In Praise of Self-Deprecation' go. It is true that the self-critical jackal does not exist but this and like facts need not lead us to the conclusion expressed in the last stanza of the poem. A little reflection suggests it isn't a clear conscience the animals on our planet are frequently possessed of; the other-than-human animals have no conscience at all. Certainly they do not self-deprecate.

Then again if we consider 'clear conscience' the plausible attribute of a particular animal on our planet – the animal of the 'we' speaking and listening/writing and reading here representative of which species produced the poem, the animal which does not rate a mention in the poem – perhaps it is this quality of 'clear conscience' above all others that characterises human activity on the third planet from the sun. With clear conscience all kinds of atrocity may be justified, and routinely gone on with.

The lesson? We humans must own and live up to our qualities, and to the fact that those qualities we habitually claim to be borrowing from other animals, in fact are qualities of ours we have imposed on them. This represents an ideological inversion along the lines of Sartrean 'bad faith'. The circle of Sartrean *bad faith* is one in which 'I flee in order not to know, but I cannot avoid knowing that I am fleeing' (Sartre 1998, 43). Authenticity and consciousness each thus function as obstacles for the other.

Whether we read in Polish or English or any other language, the materiality of the poem gives the lie to the illusion of a supra-human view of activity on our planet. But it is this beautiful illusion that allows us to weigh the clear conscience of humans who have done wrong by behaving in ways they attribute to conscience-less animals.

If we are right in saying that Roethke's 'Meadow Mouse' is not a poem about care for animal others but about limits of the human qualities empathy and understanding, then 'In Praise of Self Deprecation' is a poem about the baselessness of one particular animal's assumption of moral superiority over others. We know it is mostly to other-than-human animals that humans are doing what would be wrong were it done to other humans – what we would, in that case, call murder and cannibalism, for instance. We know that humans are doing these things today on a hitherto unimaginable industrial scale and that these activities are growing exponentially. We know that this is mostly done with a 'clear conscience'.

The striking thing about Szymborska's poem is that it challenges a presumed human superiority over those creatures with whom we share so much but for whom conscience and self-deprecation are meaningless. It is we humans, with our consciousness of atrocity and genocide and crime more generally, who do not resile from what objectively might be considered our 'crimes against animality'. So far are we humans from such a collective recognition, the formulation 'crimes against animality' rings humorously, if not impiously.

And yet, as Roethke has shown us there is, for humans and perhaps not only for humans, such a thing as empathy beyond our own kind. It is possible to look into the eyes of animal others and find, beyond words, a place of meeting, perhaps of cooperation, or of mutual aid. We may be murderers and cannibals, we may have invented cruelties on a scale no other animals could match, yet many if not most of us can still feel for animal others. We can, as Milosz has dreamt, do better one day the all we can do.

Anthropomorphism as a Rhetorical Strategy

Negative impacts of human civilisation result from the imposition of human-centred understanding, and the imposition of human traits onto animal others. The conscious acceptance of animal traits among humans, may however allow humanity to see itself in the light of a problem to be solved, and for the common good. Beijing National Stadium, built for the use of 2008 Olympic Games, is also known as the Bird's Nest. The exterior design is apparently drawn from nest-building in birds. Chinese martial arts are another illustration of how humans also learn from animals and zoomorphise themselves for various health benefits. The movements of the five animals, tiger, crane, leopard, snake, and dragon are imitated by Chinese martial arts practitioners to either zoomorphically enhance their speed, agility, and other combative techniques, or to activate yin/yang balances. Trained with the instinctive reflexes they observe in animal fighting and self-defence, Chinese Kung Fu masters are able to incorporate the animals' ways of beings in the world with the momentum of their bodies. The traditional names of yoga *asanas* are likewise frequently derived from ancient observations of animal behaviours.

If anthropomorphism, concomitant with zoomorphism, is a universal tropic strategy, embodying a universal feature of meaning making (in natural languages), then what cultural differences are there in its realisation? Are there equivalents, or variants, or opposed ideas, in other-than-Western cultures, to compare with the predominantly Western treatment we have been giving anthropomorphism so far? Pamela J. Asquith in a 1997 essay, investigates cross-cultural differences between American and Japanese primate studies. She finds that 'a most distinctive characteristic of the human/animal divide for Japanese is the inability of animals to cry or laugh' (28–29). She argues that this conception is an ancient one in Japan. As early as in Aristotle's *On the Parts of Animals*, he also asserted that humans were the only animals that laugh (2004, 69). The idea of human beings as *homo ridens* (the laughing species) or *homo risibilis* (the laughable animal) was pursued by Boethius, Alcuin, Rabelais, Voltaire, Baudelaire, and other thinkers (Amir 2014, 262–263). Their accounts asserted or accepted laughter as a distinguishing human emotional response, once animals were found inferior for lacking. As with laughter, in the international discussion of animal behaviours, the capacity for emotionality, second to language and ability to reason, becomes another indicator of a putative human-animal divide.

The study of the emotionality of animals saw a breakthrough in Charles Darwin's observational research in late nineteenth century. In 1872, Darwin provided a detailed account of emotional expressions across species in his *The Expression of the Emotions in Man and Animals*. In this evolutionary framework study of animal behaviours, Darwin asserts that no human mental function was unique as animals exhibit similar emotional and facial expressions to those of homo sapiens. His study highlights the importance of observing animals in natural settings. Not only are nonhuman primates claimed to share the emotions of grief, they have joy, anger, and other complex emotions. For instance, when delicacies were given to a monkey during its meal time, 'the corners of its mouth were slightly raised; thus an expression of satisfaction, partaking of the nature of an incipient smile, and resembling that often seen on the face of man, could be plainly perceived in this animal' (Darwin 2009, 140). Orientation to questions as to whether animals feel pain, disgust, anger, love, and sadness has resulted in different focuses for anthropomorphisms across cultures. Charles Darwin's research may so be considered to constitute what Derrida later called a 'second trauma' (after the Copernican one) inscribed in human history, the Darwinian observations that make human-animal distinctions 'subtle and fragile' (2009, 136).

Our language-wielding species has justly been named 'anthropos polytropos'. This is the first epithet that Homer applies to Odysseus in *The Odyssey*, which we may translate as the man of many tricks, or the man of twists and turns. Michele Le Doeuff in her book *The Philosophical Imaginary* points out that the necessity of a landscape as ground or place of passage is inherent in all philosophies. 'There is no thinking that does not wander', she writes (1990, 12). The self-presumed 'break with myth, fable, the poetic, the domain of the image', in the philosophic mind is, in fact, a disciplined self-deception. For Le Doeuff, a way of seeing the world is realised and defined in an imagery and unconscious rhetoric as given, which renders the complete departure of rhetorical landscape hardly justifiable. What Le Doeuff witnesses in the case of philosophy is true, in general, of investigations thought of as scientific. We can see the tropic rambling likewise in James Lovelock's hypothesis of the Mother Earth Gaia (e.g. biosphere, oceans, and geological eco-systems) (1979, 1988). Anthropomorphised, the Earth is built to be a self-regulating and nurturing image. Though mixing the mythological with the scientific, the very image is also connotative of the interactions among the Earth's living organisms, and at the same time, draws our attention to hard facts about how human activities can impact the Earth as a totality. Le Doeuff's rhetorically problematic philosophical imaginary and Lovelock's Gaia hypothesis together provide us with a framework in which we can consider relationships among the rhetorical and the real, the arbitrary and the motivated, the human point of view and the possibility of another, as these relate – on the grand scale, and likewise on the miniature scale, to the planet that is home to all the life we know.

Oscillating between the poetic and the scientific, Miroslav Holub's poem 'In the Microscope' illustrates the anthropocentric perception of the microscopic world. Under the microscope, what first appear to be 'dreaming landscapes, /lunar, derelict' turn out to be full of 'tillers of the soil' and 'fighters/who lay down their lives/for a song' (cited in LaCombe and Hartman 2008, 4). Holub's analogy of what one captures after gaze down an ocular lens of a microscope becomes more anthropomorphic as the smudges become 'cemeteries', 'fame and snow', and 'murmuring' estates (4).

Holub, like the Biology Watcher Lewis Thomas, gives us a glimpse of the world below the natural capacity of human vision, the world we must assist ourselves to see. In Lewis Thomas' notes about cells, he muses over the probability that 'we derived from some single cell, fertilised in a bolt of lightning as the Earth cooled' (Thomas 1978, 3). His philosophical and poetic excursion to the scientific world in the microscope of mitochondria leads him to consider himself as 'a very large, motile colony of respiring bacteria, operating a complex system of nuclei, microtubules, and neurons for the pleasure and sustenance of their families, and running, at the moment, a typewriter' (70).

The 'here too' in the opening of Holub's poem suggests that it will not matter where humans look, we will always see the same things. Farms and battles and snow and cemeteries are what we humans (perhaps one should add, of a certain era and tradition) are able to see wherever we look, and no matter how deeply we look. Human motives, human perceptions, and abstractions are wherever we cast an eye. Are we humans able to see beyond our own frames of reference? Stewart Guthrie tells us, 'perception is interpretation, interpretation is the provision of meaning, and the form with the greatest meaning is that of humans' (1993, 240). If we do not succeed in avoiding anthropomorphism, then we may ask – what are the terms and conditions under which we exercise what appears to be a rhetorical necessity.

If, as Le Deouff has suggested, there is no thinking, philosophical, or poetic or otherwise, that does not wander, then perhaps we need to look more deeply at our rhetorical, and other, necessities in dealing with a world that includes animals other than us. What in fact are the most fundamental strategies for meaning? Nietzsche suggests that what we know as truth is in fact 'a movable host of metaphors, metonymies, and anthropomorphisms' (1990, 84). Ruskin dismissed as a 'pathetic fallacy', the 'romantic' or 'naïve' wandering caused by anthropomorphic thinking: 'it is only the basest writer who cannot speak of the sea without talking of "raging waves", "remorseless floods", "ravenous billows"' (Ruskin 1918/2013, 122).

Our efforts at empathy equip some animals with cloying, nostalgic sadnesses, as in Robert Hillyer's 'Moo!' (Cole 1963, 170–171). It is a bitter monologue of an old cow whose 'backbone sags like an old roof tree', who is exhausted of being milked, of ploughing the field, of being confined to the shed, and of mourning over his calves.

> Old cow
> For whom
>
> There's no more grass, there's no more clover;
> Summer is over, summer is over.

Ruskin's criticism is a sharp denial of overabundant use of anthropomorphism in Western poetry prior to and in his own time, when Romantic poets invested much human affect in entities that could not exercise human prerogatives of feeling. We find a twentieth century rendition in Ruth Stone's depiction of a roaming mare, in her poem, 'Orchard'. The feminine qualities are accentuated deliberately with her rump like 'a dancing girl's', her curly, tawny forelocks, womanly eyes, and the 'patient stare that grieves'.

> And when she moved among the trees,
> The dappled trees, her look was shy,
> She hid her nakedness in leaves.
> (cited in Barnstone 1996, 82)

In the end of this tetrameter song, the mare shakes 'the hills with trumpeting' – so she is not so purely demure as her highly gendered description here would suggest. There is a clear-cut structure of feeling animated by 'an ironic and entirely original use of pathetic fallacy' (Gross 1972, 97). The observer's self is assimilated into what is rhythmically felt: dancing women, stamping horse, twittering song, trumping hills. 'All the poem's erotic suggestiveness – a mixture of shyness and longing, shame and desire, terror and resignation', as Harvey Gross praises, 'moves toward a nearly perfect climax and resolution of tensions' (98). But what is the point of this kind of poetry, of trying so hard to say that animal others are like us? The pathetic fallacy arrived at, by the time we get to the horse hiding her nakedness, seems overblown and yet a logical conclusion to the project of showing animals to be possessed of what can only be socialised human characteristics. The face-value ideological impact of the poem is to hypostasize socialised human characteristics, to suggest that sex/gender is like this with us because this is what sex/gender universally is like: one sees it even in the animals. If, in such a text, we reach a self-parodic point because the idea of a horse hiding her nakedness in leaves is laughable, and opens the whole of the hypostatic project to critique, then one recognises this would be so despite an author's intention. Responding critically, and in some detail, to Nietszche's 'mobile army' analogy, Paul de Man in 'Anthropomorphism and Trope in the Lyric', writes:

> 'anthropomorphism' is not just a trope but an identification on the level of substance. It takes one entity for another and thus implies the constitution of specific entities prior to their confusion, the taking of something for something else that can then be assumed to be given. Anthropomorphism freezes the infinite chain of tropological transformations and propositions into one single assertion or essence which, as such, excludes all others. It is no longer a proposition but a proper name, as when the metamorphosis in Ovid's stories culminates and halts in the singleness of a proper name, Narcissus or Daphne or whatever. Far from being the same, tropes such as metaphor (or metonymy) and anthropomorphisms are mutually exclusive. The apparent enumeration is in fact a foreclosure which acquires, by the same token, considerable critical power.
> (1983, 241)

If we read anthropomorphism as an act of naming that forecloses figuration, then perhaps rhetorical necessities will press us to view it in a different light from that in which we see key tropes, such as metaphor and metonymy. These are perhaps very different structures of meaning, that have long been entertained as if one, for the sake of convenience.

Stewart Guthrie writes, for instance, that:

> The myriad forms of anthropomorphism range continuously from literal to metaphoric. The most literal anthropomorphism in daily life is mistaking some nonhuman thing or event for a human. We may hear a door slammed by wind or a branch tapping at a window as human action, or hear water in a brook or gurgling in plumbing as a voice.
>
> (105)

'If the first metaphor was animal, it was because the essential relationship between man and animal was metaphoric', writes John Berger (7). Legends are the efforts to understand what such first and essential relationships must have been like. *Genesis* is a good example, as is Dylan Thomas' 'Fern Hill'. It is a poem about the persona's recollection of childhood in his uncle's farm as Fern Hill, described as a world of fantasy, primordial nature, and innocence and Edenic bliss. Time is anthropomorphised as having 'the heydays of his eyes' while the farm is 'like a wanderer white/with the dew', both hailing the persona to embark on a journey of romantic revisit of childhood wonder:

> So it must have been after the birth of the simple light
> In the first, spinning place, the spellbound horses walking warm
>   Out of the whinnying green stable
>   On to the fields of praise.
>
> (2003, 226)

Still, perhaps we need to remind ourselves that there are real animals humans have encountered and still encounter, and without them there would be no allegories or anthropomorphism or zoomorphism at all. As Otto Oerlemans reminds us, 'even early allegories are concerned with, and reflect, something of the actual animal ... readers of animal poems of all kinds need to resist the easy strategy of reading through the poem to find the allegory, to see language as always solipsistic' (30). However well-articulated, we believe Ruskin's critique of the pathetic fallacy, it remains (as may be seen in many poems discussed in this volume) a strategy, if anything, gaining in popularity. Consider its prevalence in children's picture books today.

Perhaps one antidote for anthropocentrism is in the poem that observes the animal encountering us, as in for instance Lydia Gibson's 'Goats'.

The persona passed a green shade in which four white goats lied and silhouetted against the grass, 'leaf-shadows lilac':

> When I came by they were not a bit afraid:
> Never a quiver of ears nor a flip of tails:
> Only four proud little sculptured heads
> Turned slowly in unison to watch me pass.
> (Cole 1963, 162)

Even though we objectify the voiceless others of the piece, their sentience, and their observation of us is undeniable, is notable, is the point of the poem. To see their seeing is a beginning.

Not every animal in a poem can be awarded a specific rhetorical mode of being, and yet textual entities must always be more and less than the actual – in this case animals – they represent. The animal in a poem, however closely encountered, always has some tropic dimension, and this needs to be discussed.

There is in much animal poetry, a guessing at what or how the creature might mean for us; through what lens we might see our characteristics in the animal, the animal's in ours. If Szymborska's 'In Praise of Self Deprecation' is rhetorically an opposite of Roethke's 'Meadow Mouse', then Ted Hughes' 'Thought Fox' in his 1957 collection *The Hawk in the Rain* represents another opposed mode of consideration for humanimal relationships. Much has been written about how Hughes' shamanistic spirit or predilection announces itself unmistakably in the poem, which ambiguously binds him to the fox as either a purely nominal subject or an actual one (Sagar 1975, Dickie 1983, Sweeting 1983, Webb 2013, Piskorski 2020). In particular, Laura Webb develops Keith Sagar's (1975) view of the poem as an allegorical construct and considers this fox of Ted Hughes' 'a metaphor for an endurance that transcends animality and extends towards the human' (2013, 45). While Ted Hughes scholars attend to the synchronisation of the poet and the animal in the creative moment, or in Piskorski's words, "the arche-animality of the fox in its constitutive role in the functioning of linguistic meaning" (120), concerned here is the relationship between animality and creativity as humans – more particularly, as poets – express it.

> I imagine this midnight moment's forest:
> Something else is alive
> Beside the clock's loneliness
> And this blank page where my fingers move.
> (Hughes 2019, 7)

The mind of the poet/persona requires for its creative activity a moment out of time. Such timelessness may be re-conceived as place – as a midnight moment's forest, a kind of blank (starless) wilderness in which the unexpected becomes possible. The making of a poetic text is then as the fox's making of its way through trackless space. What the poet does on paper is a kind of track-making. For the poem to come about, the animal has suddenly, unexpectedly, to be in the mind of the maker.

That we have come out of the timeless moment of the poem's making, back to the place of composition, is indicated by the resumption of the ticking of the clock. This return to the 'real-world' demonstrates that the text has come into being, that the poem is made. Here creativity is romanticised as animal, instinctual – something that can neither be explained nor helped. The creative process is shown to be something deep in the animal, connecting with its wilderness, much older than human categories or the human-defined procession of time. Poetic thought is like the fox, it comes from somewhere beyond the page and comes into its shape 'of a body that is bold to come' and a sharp focus with 'an eye, /A widening deepening greenness, /Brilliantly, concentratedly, /Coming about its own business' (Hughes 2019, 7). Not art for art's sake, but poetry as a process in its own right, one requiring forms of attention that set aside human norms.

Suggested here is a spiral dynamism of a zoomorphic effort – human consciousness mirroring animal instinctual being in the world, per Nietzsche's assertion of humans as animals with powerful instincts that shall not be vented, which should 'strive to survive harmlessly inside in conjunction with the imagination' (1964, 299). If we ask why the poet writes about a thought fox, rather than a feeling fox, we may be able to grasp a sense of joint human-animal agency that Hughes fuses into the poem. So as to make sense of freedom, the poet discharges his 'powerful instincts', as animals do.

So this is a poem about the animal in us, the animal-we-are-that-can't-help-being-there, the animal that must stinkily enter the head and scratch a way out in tracks, if ever we are to make a poem. Hughes' 'Thought Fox' is, in this sense, a reversal of Roethke's anthropocentric projection in the 'Meadow Mouse'. This is the animal arrived unannounced, and to whom the poet must attend; Roethke's mouse – for whom the persona expressed attention and care – ends the poem unexpectedly departing. Whether from culture or from nature (imagined or real), and no matter how unexpected, the thought fox is nevertheless from somewhere. In the reading of the poem we have to imagine it, have to let time stop in its image.

Through an attentiveness towards animals, the poet opens himself to a wide emotional spectrum of receptivity, empathy, sensitivity, and imagination. Attention, according to Simone Weil,

> consists of suspending our thought, leaving it detached, empty, and ready to be penetrated by the object ... [and] holding in our minds, within reach of this thought, but on a lower level and not in contact

with it, the diverse knowledge we have acquired which we are forced to make use of.

(2001, 58)

What eventually 'enters the dark hole of the head'? (Hughes 2019, 7) Is it a sign or a totem of natural energy? The attention demanded by the making of poetry depends on an animal transcendence of time as we have lived it, in favour of being 'now, and now, and now'.

Re-Negotiating Animal Archetypes

As with the fox in Ted Hughes' 'Thought Fox', Les Murray's fox in his poem 'The Gods' has an ambiguously inward and outward aspect. It is a fox of culture and nature. It is an individual with a voice like a human's and it is a voiceless collectivity of foxes. As with Ted Hughes' thought fox, Les Murray's reminds us by smell of its foxness, of its other-than-human characteristics.

> There is no Reynard fox. Just foxes.
> I'm the fox who scents this pole.
> As a kit on gravel, I brow-arched Play? to a human.
> It grabbed to kill, and gave me a soul.
>
> (2006, 359)

Les Murray's 'The Gods' leads us on a particular journey that is invested – infested – with all that allows an animal to be read. Perhaps a complexity of points of view and subject positions is implied by the title of the collection in which the poem was first published (1992) *Translations from the Natural World*. According to Michael Cronin, translation in the Anthropocene extends the ethical dimension of 'translation among humans' to 'other species', so as to enable 'the rehabilitation of the animal subject' and 'cross-species agency' (2017, 77–83). Les Murray's 'translations' are a striking example of Cronin's proposition. Murray remarks that these human translations tend to engage with the natural existence of animals with 'not much metaphor or sense of time, no consequences, no mercy, but no vindictiveness either', but instead, embody

> the new senses and powers, such as flight, the ability to see thermals in the air, to hear and talk in infrasound (the elephants do this), to see heat when I am a snake, to detect scents beyond the human range, to live forever until you die.
>
> (quoted in Bouttier 2019, 158)

As such, the manner of anthropomorphic insight into thinking and writing about a particular animal helps the poet to 'come into animal presence' (Levertov 2002, 19).

We already know this fox of the poem, even if we have never met a 'real-life' fox; because 'fox' is a collection of attributes which we get from story books, old tales, wild life documentaries, and the encyclopaedia. It is all very well to say that there is no archetypal fox, there are only foxes; the fact is that words already designate types before we even consider whether the categorisation is scientific or cultural or literary. True, no two foxes are the same. But without the word 'fox' we have no call to conjure for ourselves an image at all. Are we talking of actual animals, of the category of the animal as antithesis of the human and therefore other, or of symbolic animals? The questions we face reading this text are just as Derrida muses, considering a cat's gaze:

> the cat I am talking about is a real cat, truly, believe me, *a little cat*. It isn't the *figure* of a cat. It doesn't silently enter the bedroom as an allegory for all the cats on the earth, the felines that traverse our myths and religions, literature and fables. The cat I am talking about does not belong to Kafka's vast zoopoetics, something that nevertheless merits concern and attention here, endlessly and from a novel perspective. Nor is the cat that looks at, concerning me, and to which I seem – but don't count on it – to be dedicating a negative zootheology, Hoffmann's or Kofman's cat Murr.
>
> (2008, 6)

With 'The Gods', we begin reading a poem about foxes, but is a poem ever *just* about foxes? That 'Reynard' makes us wonder about ourselves and our wondering. So there are foxes beyond those we archetypally imagine. In just the second line though we come to realise that this is fox as described by fox – a rhetorical play we will find echoed by Shaun Tan's cicada protagonist in *Cicada*, below. Which fox then? 'I'm the fox who scents this pole'.

So why is this poem apparently about foxes, titled 'The Gods'? Perhaps because gods, like foxes, are similarly ambiguous in terms of their cultural construction, and ontological status. Perhaps because this poem is, more ambiguously than Hughes', about creativity, about that from which the perceived world is really made, and about who does the making. The poem asks us about whom we worship, about whom we take for types, exemplary, or otherwise?

The poem is strewn with subject-object and identities confusing ambiguities. 'Who scents the pole' – should we read this as *scents*, as in detects by smell, or *scents*, as in leaving one's own odour (perhaps marking territory)? Or are both meant at once? This fox in the poem is telling we-who-read, 'You think there's a typical one of me, but it's just me here. I'm the fox in question. I smell what's all around me, and I leave my own mark to say I've been here'.

It's from here the story of the poem commences, like in the manner of Craig Raine's 'A Martian Sends a Postcard Home' (1978). Written through the eyes of a Martian who attempts to describe what he observes on earth to his fellow Martians, the poem employs a series of metaphors to draw connections or account of both natural phenomena and technology: caxtons are 'mechanical birds with many wings'; a dim world is like 'engravings under tissue paper' and mist appears when the sky is a bird weighed down by flight (1). Frequently through a posthuman or dystopian lens, the Martian describes nature or culture futuristic and mechanic:

> Mist is when the sky is tired of flight
> and rests its soft machine on ground:
> ...
> Rain is when the earth is television.
> It has the property of making colours darker.
> (1)

The story is naturally inscrutable because it is the story of someone who does not speak our language, and yet speaks our language. As the Martian knows no precise terminology such as 'tear' and 'laughter', he says that books can 'cause the eyes to melt/or the body to shriek without pain' (1). Through the narrator's de-familiarising eyes, we the earth people are transported from the familiar homeland into another familiar foreign land. The conceptual boundary is challenged, which is the first and important step to empathising with others.

In Murray's 'The Gods', the fox tells us that it has gone for a slide on some gravel and then come unexpectedly into human company. At which point, the fox has asked the human whether it wanted to play, but learned instead that the human wanted the fox dead. That relating – that wishing the fox dead – ironically gave the fox life – made it another sentience in the story, made it an adversary for the human. And we remember that the 'games' foxes and humans play are of the life-and-death kind. From now on the poem is about the fox's survival in the human world.

In a next scene, the fox is in a gully looking out for some chicken dinner. The soul the fox has been given has a life of its own, and it sits up inside and, because of that, this 'I' of the fox is addressing us now. And just in the middle of this philosophical speculation, the fox, wishing not to be a target for humans, stops dead still and hopes to go unseen.

At that point, as in Ted Hughes' 'Thought Fox', the moment out of time is evoked. But unlike Hughes' moment we might say the thought fox brings from within to the human poet, this moment is for the benefit of the fox the poem imagines beyond itself. The moment is a kind of reverie and basking for the soul. In that reverie the fox can smell what is in the shadows, it can hear honey working up in the trees. In other words, the finding of things is not how one could ever expect, but nevertheless efforts can be made to help one understand.

From reverie to romance. Other foxes, another fox, a fox is attracting this one in the poem. This fox is with that other and they are urgent, making love. This is all about what one can smell. Or perhaps this is just memory, a memory this fox is having now? The journey proceeds by way of smell; it's smell that is remembered. It's as if any single smell has its little history. The first whiff shatters into time. The way one might think of this is as if skin were something that could be thought, as if that first sniff of the thing was settled on a fox, light as its own fur.

It is night now and the humans have torches to find the foxes. The humans come down the gully with their awkward careful motion, they are hunting with dogs, hunting for foxes, and they come closer and closer. The dog smells of a gunshot, and it comes in a circle around the fox in the poem.

That gunshot smell is sickening for the fox. The nausea comes in waves. The fox is where the dog could see and so make itself quite still. It is the ears of the alert dog that turn to point faster than the movements of a little bird. Though the fox is a proud animal, in order to live, it must play now at not existing. The fox is just a heartbeat now, in other respects it is not there.

So now the fox must be ambiguous, the way things are in words and dreams. *Spring*, for instance is a season, is a thing, is a verb made noun but cannot pounce. Or perhaps *spring* is a failed source of water. The fox does not get away with the ruse of being otherwise than fox-smelling. It is that pretence though that connects the foxness of the fox with gods above. The fox has been already known the way one knows one's hands, or what a colour is. These and the fox we know are examples of gods in and out of the machine.

The gloss of the riddle remains a riddle. This is a radically open text. The achievement of Murray's 'The Gods' is to maximise empathy for what the reader imagines to be a real fox, an actual fox, just at the point where the actuality of foxes is called most into question. On Murray's *Translations from the Natural World*, Michael Malay comments that the text 'juggles two imperatives at once: ethically engaging with the non-human other, by putting oneself into the other's world, while acknowledging the other's irreducibility to human ways of knowing' (165). This effect, of at once maximising empathy and ontological doubt, is achieved to some degree by mysterious means – by making inscrutable (as they must be) fox-ways and the foxness of a fox. But this first-person fox of the poem has a never-failing reflexivity with which to contend – the kind of consciousness of which Nietzsche complained on behalf of we humans. Thus while this fox is aware ('I must be Not for a while'), s/he is also able to recognise what we can take for the futility of that effort ('*a scentless shape I have not been*').

Contrast this questioning of unknowable foxness and how it is for us, with Dylan Thomas' spellbound horses who walk warm from the stables we have provided them, onto the 'fields of praise' for a deity provided.

The challenge of Thomas' poem is to go along with a gospel of all things made eternal in the naturalness of their beginnings.

The contrary challenge of 'The Gods' is to understand the nature of what is unknown between and of ourselves and foxes. The poem demonstrates how, in approaching the actual animal 'between analogy and nonsense, clarity and opacity' (Malay 2018, 166), we pass beyond understanding. As Malay writes, 'By imagining different forms of life, his translations "get out into nonsense" in order to retrieve, not so much clarity or comprehension, but an apprehension of otherness' (197).

Following Murray's 'wild translation', we also notice that today's wild animals are mostly enclosed in nature reserves, or zoos with invisible bars. J.K. Rowling's 2016 film *Fantastic Beasts and Where to Find Them* suggests that the animal menagerie seems only available in a magical suitcase or under the spell of witches and wizards. Then what is worth asking about actual wild animals today will be unsettling: where are wild animals gone? Early in John Berger's essay 'Why Look at Animals', he points out that since the onset of industrialisation, animals have been commoditised, and gradually become a 'spectral' spectacle. Berger laments that 'Everywhere animals disappear' particularly in zoos as the sites of 'enforced marginalization' (1980, 26):

> The zoo cannot but disappoint. The public purpose of zoos is to offer visitors the opportunity of looking at animals. Yet nowhere in a zoo can a stranger encounter the look of an animal. At the most, the animal's gaze flickers and passes on. They look sideways. They look blindly beyond. They scan mechanically. They have been immunised to encounter, because nothing can any more occupy a central place in their attention.
>
> (28)

Berger argues against the dominating, one-sided human gaze at marginalised animals, since animals are deprived of the ability to return their gaze to human subjects. To the extent they 'look' at all, it is but a spectral and hollow look that they wear. So how does the poetic imagination of zoo animals respond to this apparently impossible or non-encounter? Rainer Maria Rilke's 'Panther' offers an example of how a poet's creaturely sensibility may meet with an effort at depicting animals as they are and test the potential for communion with animals behind bars:

> His vision, from the constantly passing bars,
> has grown so weary that it cannot hold
> anything else. It seems to him there are
> a thousand bars; and behind the bars, no world.
>
> As he paces in cramped circles, over and over,
> the movement of his powerful soft strides

> is like a ritual dance around a center
> in which a mighty will stands paralyzed.
>
> Only at times, the curtain of the pupils
> lifts, quietly--. An image enters in,
> rushes down through the tensed, arrested muscles,
> plunges into the heart and is gone.
>
> (Rilke 1989, 25)

It is a fox that enters the mind of Ted Hughes' poet persona. Rilke's panther has a mind entered into by the image of its prison. Yet the panther is in the mind of whoever reads this poem. This panther can see nothing but bars. Caged, much as is Alfonsina Storni's little bird, this panther seems beyond any dream of freedom or escape. It is a spent force. This isn't Hughes' fox 'body that is bold to come'; this is the will wearied, cramped to the point of paralysis. Nor has it the privilege of Murray's untamed fox that knows when not to be. Yet even in this most degraded and abject of subject bodies there remains a heart into which the image may go, if only to immediately vanish. Storni's human addressed in 'Hombre Pequenito' is small because he cannot understand. Rilke's panther has no one to address, has no means of address. Who are we then to read this animal? By what means do we understand it? This is not an allegorical panther but one in whose skin we can imagine ourselves. The heart plunge of the poem's close is ambiguous but in general the empathy the poem demands is of the zoomorphic kind. The panther must have been tricked into the zoo, and we readers have been tricked into the panther's cage, to see what the panther sees – that is, the image of the bars of the cage.

Images of zoo and prison challenge and confuse the empathic potentials of zoomorphism and anthropomorphism, and even when there are no bars or cages visible (Acampora 2010; Braverman 2012; Malamud 1998). What are zoos (?), we must ask ourselves, confronted with this poem. Historically, they were instituted as citizen-building projects showcasing imperialist triumph through the exhibition of exotic animal creatures (Baratay and Hardouin-Fugier 2002), and so-called 'animalized humans', such as hunchbacks, savages, and dwarfs (Braverman 2012, 73). Today zoos around the world remain popular anthropocentric institutions for both intraspecies persecution and interspecies oppression. It is against this background that a maximum degree of intersubjective sensibility, as anthropomorphism and zoomorphism would warrant, would invite us into a possible space full of embodied understandings and make a difference. Consequently, readers and writers alike are absorbed into this de-familiarised space under the intersecting gaze that is affect-driven, as the persona gradually gains awareness to interplay with our conscience. The process of engaging with animal alterity existentially as such is well illustrated in Shaun Tan's cicada story.

Tok! Tok! Tok! Fly Back to Forest

In Shaun Tan's (2019) picture book *Cicada*, the eponymous (yet unnamed) protagonist fits a stereotype of the exploited migrant worker, who is neither understood nor ever taken seriously. This character is the prisoner of a certain economic system, and the position to which he is assigned in it. Shaun Tan's Cicada inhabits a greyed-out world of work in which his is the only (though self-denying) voice.

> Cicada work in tall building.
> Data entry clerk. Seventeen year.
> No sick day. No mistake.
> Tok Tok Tok!
> (N.p.)

This ungendered avatar of unassimilable difference has a voice in the story simply through the fact of inadequate grammatical resources. That is to say, though the story is delivered through an apparently omniscient third person narration, in fact the non-native grammar lets us know that this is really self-description by the migrant worker/cicada. Generically, we are in allegorical territory. It feels to us that this text is spoken from the position of the Asian migrant worker in Australia – the one struggling, but failing, to fit in, the drone who can never come out of his/her shell, who can never be the colourful complete personality his/her co-workers are. This character is the diligent worker, the one who gets the dull job done and so makes up for the inadequacies of those enjoying a superior position in the workplace.

> Human never finish work.
> Cicada always stay late. Finish work.
> Nobody thank cicada.
> Tok Tok Tok!
> (N.p.)

The self-deprecating, self-objectifying third person narration of the cicada is as much as to say 'this is how I am seen', 'this is how little I matter', 'even when I speak for myself, I speak as if I were other, nor can I ever speak properly; and this is, as you see, because of who I am'. Conversely, as suggested by the collective form, 'plague of cicadas', we step outside the story to remind ourselves that this is not a human treated like vermin – this creature is the vermin-in-person.

The reader's capacities for prejudice on the one hand and for empathy on the other are tested by this particular anthropomorphism, which is clearly a zoomorphism too. In this book we are reading the story of a cicada who behaves as a certain human does, who finds him/herself in the circumstances of a certain human. But the allegory is letting us know that the lot of certain humans is effectively the lot of a cicada – cicadas are dull, colourless, kept in the dark for years, unable to see their world, unable to come out of their shells. Marginalised, discriminated against, always risking persecution, the cicada's dire situation is one that would be unacceptable to the story's child or adult readers.

The hybridity figured in this picture book, simultaneously being human and animal or simultaneously neither, as also exhibited in Hughes' 'The Thought-Fox', reveals how human conscience and consciousness are imparted to children by way of an outside that consciousness subsumes and makes ambiguously human and animal. Using anthropomorphism as a boundary-breaking rhetorical strategy, poetic texts that involve other-than-human figures often display what can be called a 'creaturely sensibility', a mode of subjectivity that structures a human-perceived affinity, real or imaginary, among living things, in the service of either creative or critical engagement with animality. Here the animality assumed by Cicada is Kafkaesque. Like Gregor Samsa, the human-become-giant-insect, it enacts a dystopian humancentric world.

> Cicada no afford rent.
> Live in office wallspace.
> Company pretend not know.
> Tok Tok Tok!
> ...
> Human co-worker no like cicada.
> Say things. Do things.
> Think cicada stupid.
> Tok Tok Tok!
> (N.p.)

The critique of contemporary bureaucratic/hierarchic capitalism is poignant.

> No cicada allowed in office bathroom.
> Cicada go downtown. Twelve blocks.
> Each time company dock pay.
> Tok Tok Tok!
> (N.p.)

The grubby brutality of the situation is a stark contrast with the euphemism 'bathroom'. Cicada, of whom we should certainly expect nothing euphemistic, is the character in the piece with no choice but to parrot the euphemisms with which s/he is furnished. This 'Tok Tok Tok' refrain, representation on paper of cicada-speak, comes to carry with it a kind of resignedness, as in 'that's the way it goes' or 'nothing to be done about that'. One also feels that time is ticking, tension is building in the cicada-slave. Is he or she a bomb set to go off? Still the story and the delivery are wry.

> Seventeen year. No promotion.
> Human resources say cicada not human.
> Need no resources.
> Tok Tok Tok!

And of course, the thus demonised human resources are right: cicada is not human and so whatever resources it requires are not of the human kind. This reflexivity, built into the story, is itself a powerful means of critique. We see how things really are if we take circumstances literally, if refuse the culturally imposed tropes of normative solidarity and normative exclusion. We see how things really are for the outsider if we reduce our view to those of a non-native's participation in the language that is necessary to what, in this story, never amounts to what could be called an encounter. And yet presumably as much language as there is from somewhere, and *de rigeur* to the extent of entailing and so limiting the self-description. Corporate power suits itself to think of the character as human, as animal, wherever its advantage lies.

The magic of this poem *cum* story – and perhaps of Tan's oeuvre more generally – is in the insularity of the speaking subject. We readers never meet the co-workers or bosses or anyone else responsible for the mistreatment of the cicada. All the affect, all the empathy, the work musters come from the protagonist's self-distanced self-pity. The narration is matter of fact but we only get the cicada's point of view. The cicada is the victim of all the characters we never meet. And the cicada's lot seems truly hopeless. The nth degree of our protagonist's volition-less-ness comes with the ultimate necessary event in the life of the drone worker – a thankless retirement.

> Seventeen year. Cicada retire.
> No party. No handshake.
> Boss say clean desk.
> Tok Tok Tok!

The worker is a creature commanded, not a party to a conversation. It seems from the pictures now that the brutally unappreciated insect is about to end it all by leaping from the top of the building, or limping off the edge more likely.

> No work. No home. No money.
> Cicada go to top of tall building.
> Time to say goodbye.
> Tok tok tok!

Suicide, it appears, will be characteristically understated as a choice; perhaps not even as a choice – more as an inevitable consequence of circumstances as they are.

It's at this point we see that quite unlike Storni's caged bird, the cicada is able to come out of its shell (and its hell), to fly, to be free, to be itself. And now we know that it was always only ever a matter of time (Tok Tok Tok!) until the cicada (toiling, as it were, in the earth all these years) would be able to transcend the workaday world of its anthropomorphism. The expatriate has a home to go to in the end.

In this story the surprise of liberation comes perfectly naturally just where we would not expect it, just at the apparent nadir of the cicada's career (mock ironically at the highest point in the physical structure of oppression, the building in which the insect has toiled all these years).

And now the poem is in picture form alone. Out of the grey shell a beautiful red creature flies off and joins a multitude (what humans might call a plague) of like beautiful creatures. The individual that was isolated, grey, lonely, is now part of a mass of like creature, at home in the herd. Though the life that was is left behind, this leave-taking event was not a suicide at all. And yet the self-deprecation certainly stands, but now humorously, not tragically.

Joseph Meeker's conception of 'play ethic' suggests an antithesis of the Western work ethic, one that facilitates biological diversity in an open-ended rather than an aggressively fetishised productive way. Following Meeker's thesis, comedy not only 'moderates healthy relations among people' but, more significantly, is a catalyst for conflicts 'between people and the Earth's natural processes' (1997, 11). Whether in terms of humanistic culture or biological stability, 'comedy is a contributor to survival' (11). The Cicada's story is a tale of survival. The transcendence, from numb workaholic to a free forest creature, from the tragic object to the subject with the last laugh, is through what Frans de Waal calls 'animal-centric anthropomorphism', one that 'makes every effort to take the animal's perspective' (2006, 77). Then the resolution of the story is simply that the animal *is* itself. It gets literally out of either the box we have put it in or the shell in which it is naturally stuck. The cicada gets to be the cicada people see and recognise in the end. It simply comes from the book – comes out of the words – in order to be, in order to be itself.

The only way out of anthropomorphism is through flight (in this case literal) from out of the story, from out of the pages up until now, to the extra-textuality of simply being the animal one is and always was. In terms of genre, the flight from textuality is a flight from allegory, certainly, but, as a flight from genre more generally, it takes the reader from what may be guessed through reading clues, into the open-ended unknowable world of the animal who has – like meadow mouse – now simply and anonymously absented itself from our understanding, gone to our unknown.

Cicada, who never had a name, was always a metonym for the collectivity of cicadas. The whole book is a riff on the expression 'coming out of your shell'. And as in the final text offered, it is a joke – a cicada's joke:

> Cicada all fly back to forest.
> Sometimes think about human.
> Can't stop laughing.

Even as the allegory is all but dissolved, one observes the contradictions it entailed. Cicada is indigenous and much more ancient to the place than anything in or associated with an office. It is only in the very short term view of history the cicada can be thought of as an interloper, a blow-in. One is reminded of the 'minority' status of indigenous populations. Unlike Kafka's Gregor Samsa, in *Cicada*, realising animality, an animal identity, enables the liberation of this creature-in-a-book.

What's so funny to the cicadas? It is from the seemingly hopeless lot of the one enslaved we learn that liberation from oppression, from capitalism, is possible and is ultimately just a matter of expressing yourself, simply by being who you are. You're a cicada. You can fly away.

References

Acampora, Ralph R, ed. *Metamorphoses of the Zoo: Animal Encounter After Noah*. New York: Lexington Books, 2010.
Adorno, Theodor W. *Aesthetic Theory*. London: Continuum, 2002.
Agamben, Giorgio. *The Open: Man and Animal*. Stanford, CA: Stanford University Press, 2004.
Amir, Lydia B. *Humor and the Good Life in Modern Philosophy*. Shaftesbury, Humann, Kierkegaard. New York: SUNY Press, 2014.
Aristotle. *On the Parts of Animals*. Trans. James G. Lennox. Oxford: Clarendon Press, 2004.
Asquith, Pamela J. "Why Anthropomorphism is not Metaphor: Crossing Concepts and Cultures in Animal Behavior Studies". *Anthropomorphism, Anecdotes, and Animals*. Eds. R. Mitchell, N.S. Thompson, and H.L. Miles. Albany: State University of New York, 1997. 22–34.
Baratay, Eric and Elisabeth Hardouin-Fugier. *Zoo: A History of Zoological Gardens in the West*. London: Reaktion, 2002.
Barnstone, Willis. "Poet in the Mountains". *The House is Made of Poetry: The Art of Ruth Stone*. Eds. Wendy Barker and Sandra M. Gilbert. Carbondale: Southern Illinois University Press, 1996. 78–100.
Becker, John E. "We Animals: Poems of Our World". *The Literary Review* 33(3) (1990): 395.
Bekoff, Marc, Colin Allen, and Gordon M. Burghardt, eds. *The Cognitive Animal: Empirical and Theoretical Perspectives on Animal Cognition*. MIT press, 2002.
Bennett, Jane. *Vibrant Matter: A Political Ecology of Things*. Durham: Duke University Press, 2009.

Berger, John. "Why look at animals". *About Looking.* London: Writers & Readers, 1980. 1–26.
Berryman, John. "A Strut for Roethke". *The New York Review*, October 17, 1963 Issue.
Birkerts, Sven. "Last Things First: Czeslaw Milosz's Witness of Poetry". *The Agni Review* 19 (1983): 113–129.
Blom, Jan Dirk. *A Dictionary of Hallucinations.* New York: Springer, 2010.
Bloom, Harold, ed. *Theodore Roethke.* New York: Chelsea House Pub, 1988.
Bouttier, Sarah. "Nonhuman Voices in Les Murray's Translations from the Natural World". *Ecopoetics and the Global Landscape: Critical Essays.* Ed. Isabel Sobral Campos. London: Lexington Books, 2019. 157–176.
Bowe, David. *Poetry in Dialogue in the Duecento and Dante.* Oxford: Oxford University Press, 2020.
Braverman, Irus. *Zooland: The Institution of Captivity.* Stanford, CA: Stanford University Press, 2012.
Buber, Martin. *I and Thou.* New York: Scribner, 1958.
Butler, Judith. *Precarious Life: The Powers of Mourning and Violence.* London: Verso, 2004.
Cole, William. *The Birds and the Beasts Were There – Animal Poems Selected by William Cole.* Cleveland & New York: The World Publishing Company, 1963.
Cooper, Melinda E. *Life as Surplus: Biotechnology and Capitalism in the Neoliberal Era.* Seattle: University of Washington Press, 2011.
Crawford, Robert. *The Modern Poet: Poetry, Academia, and Knowledge Since the 1750s.* Oxford: Oxford University Press, 2001.
Creed, Barbara. *Stray: Human-animal Ethics in the Anthropocene.* Sydney: Power Publications, 2017.
Cronin, Michael. *Eco-translation: Translation and Ecology in the Age of the Anthropocene.* New York: Taylor & Francis, 2017.
Darwin, Charles. *The Expression of the Emotions in Man and Animals.* New York: Cambridge University Press, 2009.
Davis, Diane. "Creaturely Rhetorics". *Philosophy and Rhetoric* 44(1) (2011): 88–94.
Davis, Hank. "Animal Cognition Versus Animal Thinking: The Anthropomorphic Error". *Anthropomorphism, Anecdotes, and Animals.* Eds. R. Mitchell, Nicholas S. Thompson & H.L. Albany: State University of New York, 1997. 335–347.
Deleuze, Gilles & Guattari Félix. *A Thousand Plateaus.* Minneapolis: University of Minnesota Press, 2005.
de Man, Paul. *The Rhetoric of Romanticism.* New York: Columbia University Press, 1983.
Derrida, Jacques. *The Animal That Therefore I Am.* New York: Fordham University Press, 2008.
Derrida, Jacques. *The Beast and the Sovereign*, Volume I. Chicago: University of Chicago Press, 2009.
De Waal, Frans. "Anthropomorphism and Anthropodenial". *Primates and Philosophers: How Morality Evolved. Princeton*, Eds. Stephen Macedo and Josiah Ober. NJ: Princeton University Press, 2006. 59–89.
Dickie, Margaret. "Ted Hughes: The Double Voice". *Contemporary Literature* 24(1) (1983): 51–65.

Dickinson, Emily. *The Complete Poems of Emily Dickinson*. New York: Back Bay, 1976.
Donovan, Josephine. *The Aesthetics of Care: On the Literary Treatment of Animals*. London: Bloomsbury Publishing, 2016.
Doyle, Richard. *Wetwares: Experiments in Postvital Living*. Vol. 24. Minneapolis: University of Minnesota Press, 2003.
Embree, Lester. "The Possibility of a Constitutive Phenomenology of the Environment". *Eco-phenomenol-ogy: Back to the Earth Itself*. Ed. Charles S. Brown and Ted Toadvine. Albany: State University of New York Press, 2003. 37–50.
Fiut, Aleksander. "Czesław Milosz's Search for 'Humanness'". *Slavic and East European Journal* 31(1) (1987): 65–75.
Franaszek, Andrzej. *Milosz: A Biography*. Harvard University Press, 2017.
Genesis. *The Holy Bible: Containing the Old and New Testaments*. Salt Lake City: Church of Jesus Christ of Latter-day Saints, 2013.
Gross, Harvey. "On the Poetry of Ruth Stone: Selections and Commentary". *The Iowa Review* (1972): 94–104.
Guthrie, Stewart E. *Faces in the Clouds: A New Theory of Religion*. New York: Oxford University Press, 1993.
Haraway, Donna Jeanne. *The Companion Species Manifesto: Dogs, People, and Significant Otherness*. Vol. 1. Chicago: Prickly Paradigm Press, 2003.
Haraway, Donna Jeanne. *When Species Meet*. Minneapolis: University of Minnesota, 2008.
Hawhee, Debra. "Language as Sensuous Action: Sir Richard Paget, Kenneth Burke, and Gesture-Speech Theory". *Quarterly Journal of Speech* 92(4) (2006): 331–354.
Hughes, Ted. 1957. *The Hawk in the Rain*. London: Faber & Faber, 2019.
Hume, David. *The Natural History of Religion*. Stanford: Stanford University Press, 1957.
Katrovas, Richard. "Mickey Mouse Meets Teddy Human: Sentimental Lyrics as Social Allegory". *New England Review and Bread Loaf Quarterly* 8(3) (1986): 411–421.
Kennedy, George A. "A Hoot in the Dark: The Evolution of General Rhetoric". *Philosophy and Rhetoric* (1992): 1–21.
Kennedy, John. S. *The New Anthropomorphism*. Cambridge: Cambridge University Press, 1992.
Kostkowska, Justyna. "To Persistently Not Know Something Important: Feminist Science and the Poetry of Wisława Szymborska". *Feminist Theory* 5(2) (2004): 185–203.
La Belle, Jenijoy. *The Echoing Wood of Theodore Roethke*. Princeton, New Jersey, Princeton University Press, 1976.
LaCombe, Michael A and Thomas V. Hartman, eds. *In Whatever Houses We May Visit: An Anthology of Poems That Have Inspired Physicians*. Philadelphia: ACP Press, 2008.
Le Doeuff, Michele. *The Philosophical Imaginary*. Redwood City: Stanford University Press, 1990.
Levertov, Denise. *Selected Poems*. New York: New Directions, 2002.
Levinas, Emmanuel. *Totality and Infinity: An Essay on Exteriority*. Trans. A. Lingis. Pittsburgh, PA: Duquesne University Press, 1969.

Lovelock, James. *Gaia: A New Look at Life on Earth*. Oxford: Oxford University Press, 1979.
Lovelock, James. 1988. *Ages of Gaia*. Oxford: Oxford University Press, 1995.
Malamud, Randy. *Reading Zoos: Representations of Animals and Captivity*. New York: New York University Press, 1998.
Malay, Michael. *The Figure of the Animal in Modern and Contemporary Poetry*. New York: Palgrave Macmillan, 2018.
Meeker, Joseph W. *The Comedy of Survival: Literary Ecology and a Play Ethic*. Tucson: University of Arizona, 1997.
Menely, Tobias. *The Animal Claim: Sensibility and the Creaturely Voice*. London: University of Chicago Press, 2015.
Milosz, Czeslaw. *New and Collected Poems, 1931–2001*. New York: Ecco, 2003.
Moe, Aaron M. *Zoopoetics: Animals and the Making of Poetry*. New York: Lexington Books, 2014.
Murphy, Patrick D. *Literature, Nature, and Other: Ecofeminist Critiques*. New York: SUNY Press, 1995.
Murray, Les. *Collected Poems*. Melbourne: Black Inc., 2006.
Nagel, Thomas. "What Is It Like to Be a Bat?". *The Philosophical Review* 83(4) (1974): 435–450.
Nietzsche, Friedrich. *The Will to Power*. Trans. Anthony M. Ludovici. New York: Russell & Russell, 1964.
Nietzsche, Friedrich. (1873). Philosophy and Truth: Selections from Nietzsche's Notebooks of the Early 1870's. New Jersey: Humanities Press, 1990.
Nietzsche, Friedrich. *A Nietzsche Reader*. Trans. R.J. Hollingdale. Harmondsworth: Penguin, 1977.
Nietzsche, Friedrich. "On Truth and Lies in a Nonmoral Sense". *Truth: Engagements across Philosophical Traditions*. Eds. José Medina and David Wood. Malden: Blackwell, 2005. 14–25.
Oerlemans, Onno. *Poetry and Animals: Blurring the Boundaries with the Human*. New York: Columbia University Press, 2018.
Park, Ho Jae, et al. "Ginseng in Traditional Herbal Prescriptions". *Journal of Ginseng Research* 36(3) (2012): 225–241.
Piskorski, Rodolfo. *Derrida and Textual Animality: For a Zoogrammatology of Literature*. New York: Palgrave Macmillan, 2020.
Raine, Craig. *A Martian Sends a Postcard Home*. Ann Arbor: University of Michigan, 1978.
Rilke, Rainer Maria. *The Selected Poetry of Rainer Maria Rilke*. New York: Vintage, 1989.
Roitblat, Herbert L., H.S. Terrace, and T.G. Bever, eds. 1984. *Animal Cognition*. New York: Psychology Press, 2014.
Ruskin, John. *Selections and Essays*. Ed. William Roe Frederick. New York, Chicago: C. Scribner's Sons, 2013.
Sagar, Keith. *The Art of Ted Hughes*. Cambridge: Cambridge University Press, 1975.
Santner, Eric L. *On Creaturely Life: Rilke, Benjamin, Sebald*. Chicago: University of Chicago Press, 2009.
Sartre, Jean-Paul. 1943. *Being and Nothingness: An Essay on Phenomenological Ontology*. Trans. H. E. Barnes. London: Routledge, 1998.
Stewart, Susan. *Poetry and the Fate of the Senses*. London: University of Chicago Press, 2002.

Storni, Alfonsina. *Selected Poems*. Brattleboro, Vt.: Amana Books, 1986.
Sweeting, Michael. "Hughes and Shamanism". *The Achievement of Ted Hughes*. Ed. Keith Sagar. Manchester: Manchester University Press, 1983. 70–90.
Sword, Elizabeth Hauge and Victoria McCarthy, eds. *A Child's Anthology of Poetry*. New York: Ecco Press, 1995.
Szymborska, Wisława. *Sounds, Feelings, Thoughts: Seventy Poems*. Trans. Magnus J. Krynski and Robert A. Maguire. Princeton: Princeton University Press, 1981.
Tan, Shaun. *Cicada*. New York: Arthur A Levine, 2019.
Thomas, Dylan. *The Poems of Dylan Thomas*. Ed. Daniel Jones. New York: New Directions, 2003.
Thomas, Lewis. *Lives of a Cell: Notes of a Biology Watcher*. New York: Viking Press, 1978.
Webb, Laura. *Animal and Human Endurance in Hughes' Poetry. Ted Hughes: From Cambridge to Collected*. Eds. Wormald, Mark, Neil Roberts, and Terry Gifford. New York: Palgrave MacMillan, 2013.
Weil, Simone. *Waiting for God*. Trans. by E. Craufurd. London: Harper Collins, 2001.
Weil, Simone. *Waiting on God*. New York: Routledge, 2010.
Whitman, Walt. *Poems of Walt Whitman: Leaves of Grass*. New York: T.Y. Crowell, 1902.

2 How Practical Are These Cats?
Animal Poetry at Large

The Roman poet, Horace, begins his *Ars Poetica*, with the description of what is for him, a literary monstrosity:

> If a painter had chosen to set a human head
> On a horse's neck, covered a melding of limbs,
> Everywhere, with multi-coloured plumage, so
> That what was a lovely woman, at the top,
> Ended repulsively in the tail of a black fish:
> Asked to a viewing, could you stifle laughter, my friends?
> (cited in Nabergoj 2013, 38)

The likening of dissimilars (we know as the principle of metaphor), which Aristotle considered essential to the art of poetry, is shown by Horace to present a clear danger of excess: poetry can result in the creation of monstrous hybrids. The same is true of the (apparently inescapable) anthropomorphic thinking we humans do, examination of which brings us to the conclusion that the animal world is beyond human grasp. Yet interpreting that world in human terms seems the only possible way to make sense of it.

Here we re-emphasise a point made in the Chapter 1 that a key stake in the anthropomorphic description of nonhuman animals and environment is the strong likelihood of an anthropocentric point of view, or we may say, ideology. As Stewart Guthrie puts it, the anthropomorphic world view is 'coloured and misled by a strong tendency to see the world as like ourselves' (1997, 51). Finding absurd humour in this fact and its entailments may be the most powerful means available of critiquing the ideological construction of anthropocentrism, as it is aided by the rhetorical strategies of anthropomorphism and zoomorphism.

Nonsense and Anthropomorphism

One of the most fundamental, and powerful, kinds of nonsense able to be made in poetry for children, is having the animals do what humans do, and in particular, having animals speak. Likewise, in texts for children

DOI: 10.4324/9781003219330-3

that do not necessarily present themselves as poetry as such (for instance picture books and animations), anthropomorphised animals are a more or less taken for granted stock-in-trade for everyday consumption. The animals need not do much at all in order to amuse. Take for example the nursery rhyme 'Three Young Rats':

> Three young rats with black felt hats,
> Three young ducks with white straw flats,
> Three young dogs with curling tails,
> Three young cats with demi-veils,
> Went out to walk with two young pigs
> In satin vests and sorrel wigs;
> But suddenly it chanced to rain,
> And so they all went home again.
> (Wu 2010, 24)

In these verses we see, somewhat self-consciously, that plot is of little importance. What matters is the manner in which the cast, as cast, is an impossibility. Roderick McGillis demarcates nonsense verse as a 'deeply self-conscious of form':

> It foregrounds such formal features as language, onomastics, rhythm, rhyme, stanza shapes and rhetorical devices – especially paradox, prosopopoeia, repetition, alliteration and paronomasia. In this type of verse, form subsumes subject. Travelling to sea in a sieve, hunting a snark, confessing an attraction to a passing gentleman, slaying a monster with a vorpal blade all become silly subjects in nonsense verse.
> (2002, 156)

McGillis makes a point in defining nonsense as formally and rhetorically bound and drawing the intricate form-subject relation it entails. What he omits in this account of rhetorical devices is anthropomorphism. The surprise and the point of 'Three Young Rats' are the incongruity of the anthropomorphism. We might find these characters funny and harmless mainly because they are humans behind animal masks, who showcase unpredictable, but very human, encounters. Wry and amusing, the nonsense irony points to pretentious, upper-class British manners.

This nonsense rhyme needs also to be read as carnivalesque. Nonsense and carnivalesque construction are commonly related in children's literature. Celia Catlett Anderson and Marilyn Fain Apseloff write, 'Humor is a major ingredient in a healthy childhood, and the extreme type of humor that is called nonsense is especially useful' (1989, 6). Dwelling on the psychological aspects of nonsense literature for children, Leo Schneiderman claims that 'One cannot imagine nonsense literature apart from the spirit of carnival' (96). 'The sensitive ear will always catch even the most distant echoes of a carnival sense of the world', writes Mikhail Bakhtin (1984, 107). Bakhtin's theory of carnival has become central for those critics who focus on the liberating and often subversive use of violations of commonsensical or authoritarian assumptions to evoke laughter. It is praise of folk laughter and, through it, a series of crowning and decrowning rituals make rigid social hierarchies crumble. John Stephens, applying Bakhtin's notion of carnival to children's literature, draws out three types of carnivalesque texts which 'interrogate the normal subject positions created for children within socially dominant ideological frame' (120). 'Three Young Rats' fits Stephens' first type, in imagining bizarre anthropomorphic characters beyond 'habitual constraints' of human cognitive comfort zone, though it still 'incorporates a safe return to social normality' (121). However outlandish or stylish the characters seem, they 'all went home again'.

The nonsense theorist Jean-Jacques Lecercle, insisting on the similarities of detail from 'a comparison between the texts of carnival literature and nonsense texts', believes that 'Carnival is the embodiment of the negative prefix in "nonsense" – it says no, locally and temporarily, to order and hierarchy, not least the hierarchy of the comic and the serious' (2012, 194). It is not our intention here to devote much space to the definition of nonsense and its relationship to carnival literature, from either of the general points of view of poetry or of cultural artefacts intended for children. Still there are some salient themes theorists have investigated to help to understand the intellectual benefits of nonsense verses. First, the thematic incongruity, intertextual contradiction and zaniness, and the humour that arises from these elements are well acknowledged. Elizabeth Sewell, in her *The Field of Nonsense* (1952/2015), describes nonsense 'as a collection of words or events which in their arrangement do not fit into some recognized system in a particular mind' (3). Sewell compares nonsense to game, 'a play of the side of order against disorder', in which the unresolvable tension arises as 'it cannot suppress the force towards disorder in the mind, nor defeat it conclusively, for this force is essential to the mind no less than the opposing force of order' (47). Susan Stewart observes that 'the humor of nonsense often comes from the contradictions that arise when the abstract and systematic nature of discourse is brought to the fore – humor without a context as well as metaphor without a context' (1989, 37–38). The playful subversion of language and epistemology is noted in nonsense. In *An Anatomy of Literary Nonsense* (1988), Wim Tigges defines nonsense as 'a narrative genre in which the seeming presence of one or more "sensible" meanings is kept in balance by a simultaneous absence of such a meaning' (255). To achieve such a balance, nonsense writers often play 'with the rules of language, logic, prosody and representation, or a combination of these' (Tigges 27). In postmodern discourse, more thinkers embrace the co-presence of sense and nonsense. Deleuze thinks that the negation of sense in nonsense 'no longer expresses anything negative, but rather releases the purely expressible with its two uneven halves' (1990, 123). Extracting possibilities between sense and nonsense, Lecercle further draws on psychoanalysis and philosophy to see nonsense in terms of 'the dialectic of excess and lack' (3), which has a central paradox, or contradiction, that 'excess always compensates for lack' (6), or 'Lack of sense ... is always compensated by excess or proliferation of sense' (31). These definitions of nonsense all revolve around the possibility of meaning-making in counterintuitive nonsense.

Our working definition of nonsense, drawn upon the above notions, focuses on its ambivalence and subversive potential. Nonsense is not gibberish or a meaningless construct, rather, either literary or ornamental, it is an active process, in which suspension of sense and coherence has the effect of drawing attention to their normal operation. Anthropomorphism may motivate this process. The attribution of notionally human characteristics to nonhuman entities, often a de-automatisation made conscious, gives the licence to and fosters participation in an anarchic and capricious playworld.

The specific role of anthropomorphism in nonsense, and of speaking animals in general – this particular turning of the world upside down – by giving a voice to the voiceless, may be the most enduring, consistent ridiculous phenomenon in the history of culture. There is plenty of didactic potential in it, as we can see in Bertram Murray's 'I caught a fish'. The persona was startled when the baby fish he caught assumed speech capacity, and 'spoke in just a tiny squeak,/Not loud like you and me'. The fish's demand of another drink angered the persona who dismissed it as a greedy request and would turn the fish into a dish. The fish tended to deceive the persona by spinning an origin tale of its birth:

'My dad's a great big whale,
'And if you put me on a dish
'He'll kill you with his tail'.
    (Cited in Ireson 1983, 65)

The persona was not easily fooled, so was the implied readership. But there was a comic turn when the boy acted on his impulse and threw the fish to the sea, simply because he was angry with 'the tot'. The fish gave a nod to him, thinking that his trick had worked, heartily declared his dad was merely a cod. A fish in the water again, but the boy was still left dumbfounded. It is evident that the anthropomorphic poem, partly for the fun of nonsense, serves for the rhythmic and rhyming effect, partly for the caution against feelings of unresolved and childish anger. Chapter 3 will focus largely on nursery rhymes, but we introduce these poems here as straightforward examples of the kind of nonsense, so logically staged in a story, that we routinely expect children to consume as part of the fun in their education.

In Bertram Murray's 'I caught a fish' we read the drama of humans versus animals, as we have already seen in monologic form in both

Alfonsina Storn's 'Little Man' and in Shaun Tan's 'Cicada'. In this case we have a dialogue, from a human child's point of view – an episode of speaking *with* the fish. The conversation is one from which the implied child narrator learns a happy lesson. The drama resolves as comedy. The little fish survives. The empathic link between child-fisher and fish is strengthened by the diminutive status of the fish – it's little, it's a 'tot', it speaks in awe of its dad. In this poem attention is drawn to the generally otherwise accepted nonsense of the animal speaking. 'It made me jump', 'I didn't know a fish could speak'. Shaun Tan's *Cicada* celebrates a secret victory over the human world. Reminiscent of the fisherman's trickery in the Arabian Nights tale of 'The Fisherman and the Jinni' (Mathers 2004), this fish is an animal that sweet talks its way to survival. We must remember that – despite the lightness and the humour – the stakes here are life-and-death. Joseph W. Meeker shows that comedy is integrally bound to survival in his book *The Comedy of Survival: Literary Ecology and a Play Ethic*:

> We can learn from a grieving mother caribou how to go on with life after terrible losses. Comedy is a strategy for living that contains ecological wisdom, and it may be one of our best guides as we try to retain a place for ourselves among the other animals that live according to the comic way.
>
> (1997, 21)

This poem is not simply a vehicle for didacticism – as in the lesson that one may be tricked by a lie – it is also formally didactic. The anthropomorphising of animals (and the corollary implied zoomorphising of humans) in this kind of text is, in and of itself, a force for both empathy with other-than-human others and for normalising of a de-automatising impulse characteristic of many cultural forms, but particularly of poetry in modernity and later. The turning upside down of the world as we know it really to be, today is, one might say, a key responsibility for poetry and poetic forms of culture. Having the animals speak, when we know that in real life they cannot speak, is a means of introducing children not only to empathy for others but one of its most frequent heuristic vehicles – the imagination of worlds and situations and possibilities other than those known to be the case. We can think of this as the principle of fiction. It is learned by example, in the telling. The more eloquent, and the more surprising, the more convincing the text telling will be.

Worth noting in such a text as 'I caught a fish' is a child–animal alignment and an adult presumption the child will identify with the principal character in the poem. Such mode of identification has been found problematic (Lesnik-Oberstein 1996; Rose 1984; Stephens 1992), as it implies an evident tone of didacticism and immersive identification with characters' perception, emotions, and opinions, without proper judgement. Ursula K. Le Guin observes in a lecture that, it appears we give animal stories to children and encourage them to be interested in animals because we see children as inferior, mentally 'primitive', not yet fully humanized, thus pets and zoo animal stories are 'natural' steps in the child's way up to adult, exclusive humanity – rungs on the ladder from mindless, helpless babyhood to the full glory of intellectual maturity and mastery.

(Le Guin 2004)

Le Guin notes the condescending nature of writing animal stories for children. It also implies children's lack of agency in choosing the reading materials that are typically purchased by the adults, particularly in the earlier stages of childhood. Adults, in choosing such texts, often unwittingly participate in acts of Althusserian 'interpellation'(Althusser 1971), 'hailing' the child into ideologically constructed (for instance class) positions that do not relate (or that negate) his/her objective conditions of life. Lack of child agency and the overattribution of agency to features of talking animals give rise to a phenomenon addressed as 'identification fallacy' (Nikolajeva 2014). Maria Nikolajeva holds that such identification should be discouraged because, for the development of mature reading and growth, readers should be able to liberate themselves from protagonists' subjectivity and be able to evaluate them properly. By contrast, empathy as a result of the proper engagement with fictional protagonists without immersive identification is constructive. This emotion helps generate and assess the understanding of characters from the text to life. With a certain irony, such narrative logic still works in a familiar anthropocentric narratology, that of serving for human purposes of learning, with innocent or good or wicked literary characters.

We may say then that the formal didacticism of a poem like 'I caught a fish' is characteristic of rhymes in which animals are given a speaking voice. These are carnival forces in the world of the child, as of the adult who was once a child, likewise of the adult who was once a child and who now reads the child into the carnival of the imagination. This is what Roni Natov delineates as 'poetics of childhood':

> Through language, the adult can recapture in part what can never fully be reclaimed, what has been twice removed, leaving to empty chambers: in one, the negative space of the first great loss, the body of the mother; in the other – what comes with the growing consciousness and socialization of the child – the loss of the immediacy of a primal response to the natural world.
>
> (2003, 6)

The retrospective gaze at childhood is a search for an ideal child image and for adult, it also represents a creative liberation, a renewed chance to image what could make a difference. What such rhymes achieve in a short space is close, in principle, to the fundamental creativity of culture.

64 *How Practical Are These Cats?*

Chapter 3 of this book focuses on nursery rhymes and in Chapter 4 we deal with the poetry in cautionary tales as these involve children and animals, and look particularly at the most famous of all nonsense poems, Lewis Carroll's 'Jabberwocky'. We have introduced both text types here through this treatment of 'I Caught a Fish', in order to bring nonsense into the larger frame of children, animals, and poetry, and to understand the ideological stakes nonsense brings to them.

Odd Couple

Let us turn now to a much more complex and much more nonsensical text than 'I caught a fish': Edward Lear's 'The Owl and the Pussy-cat', a canonic text for nonsense scholars.

> The Owl and the Pussy-cat went to sea
> In a beautiful pea-green boat,
> They took some honey, and plenty of money,
> Wrapped up in a five-pound note.
> The Owl looked up to stars above,
> And sang to a small guitar,
> 'O lovely pussy! O Pussy, my love,
> What a beautiful pussy you are,
>   You are,
>   You are!
> What a beautiful Pussy you are!'
>
> Pussy said to the Owl, 'You elegant fowl!
> How charmingly sweet you sing!
> O let us be married! Too long we have tarried:
> But what shall we do for a ring?'
> They sailed away, for a year and a day,
> To the land where the Bong-Tree grows,
> And there in a wood a Piggy-wig stood,
> With a ring at the end of his nose,
>   His nose,
>   His nose,
> With a ring at the end of his nose.
>
> 'Dear Pig, are you willing to sell for one shilling
> Your ring?' Said the Piggy, 'I will'.
> So they took it away and were married next day
> By the Turkey who lives on the hill.
> They dined on mince, and slices of quince,
> Which they ate with a runcible spoon;
> And hand in hand, on the edge of the sand,
> They danced by the light of the moon,

> The moon,
> The moon,
> They danced by the light of the moon.
> (cited in Blake 1994, 103)

Consider what Edward Lear has his readers visualise in this canonic poem originally published in 1871. A bird and a cat, in a boat, in love. There are multiple layers of absurdity already in this setting, even before the animals shove off. Cats don't like water and won't like boats. Owls don't need boats to cross the water. Birds and cats are not natural travelling companions, let alone friends or lovers. Quite apart from certain physical incompatibilities and the fact that owls fly around and cats are generally more earthbound, there remains the proclivity of cats for catching and eating birds and a like carnivorous proclivity (for small four-legged creatures) on the part of owls. Allowing for some variation in size, it is possible to imagine either party killing or eating the other. So, considering matrimony from a hyperbolic zoomorphic point of view, they are evenly, perhaps perfectly, matched. In this poem, 'birds, cats, people, and animals all play out the contradictions we feel in their human-like animality and our animal-like humanity. Each species seems whimsical, as if it were an increment of our personal, multiple self', as Paul Shepard remarks (1997, 72).

As suggested, there are various transgressions of expectation in the poem. For instance, when they meet the pig, the owl and the pussycat address him as if in a letter: *Dear Pig, are you willing to sell for one shilling*. There is a strange mixture of formality and informality here. The unknown pig is addressed familiarly, as if already an acquaintance, but the object of the address is contractual: a business proposition. In fact *the land where the Bong-Tree grows* – unknown to the reader – is named in very matter-of-fact way, as if that descriptive title ought to identify it to anyone. This is a common feature of dream imageries and events, and of nonsense poems: things totally unfamiliar present as already known. Overturned expectations are there from the first line of the poem. The next incongruity is a little harder to spot: *went to sea in a beautiful pea-green boat*. *Went to sea* sounds very serious, romantic, adventurous. *Pea-green boat* seems domestic, cute. As an incongruity this is trivial however next to the image of an owl and a pussycat as sailing companions.

The third and fourth lines of the first stanza seem more definitively silly: 'they took some honey and plenty of money wrapped up in a five pound note'. Are they taking the right things with them? Food of course they need. Honey is a good energy source and very portable, good for a journey where space is at a premium. With money they should be able to get whatever else it is they need, provided there are shops along the way, or characters from whom one might need to purchase rings. Five pounds was a lot of money in those days (an 1870 five pound note would be roughly the value of £500 today). So this is all very sensible. In fact having only spent a shilling that we know of it seems quite probable that by the end of the poem this level-headed couple still have their five pound note. But how should you carry your money? And how should you carry your honey? Does it make sense to wrap honey and coins up in a paper banknote? Every transgression seems to point to a common sense goal or procedure. Somehow the idiotic manner in which the owl and the pussycat handle their finances serves to remind us of the fact that they are an owl and a pussycat. The anthropomorphising unravels here, draws attention to itself. It is hard to imagine an owl playing a guitar. But what choice do we have?

The rhetorical object of the poem, one might say, is to maximise possible types of incongruity. Much of this is achieved through overtly striking imagery, some of it through more subtle means. This journey of impossible characters into the unknown turns on making all things strange. There is, for instance, the matter of animating and de-animating the landscape. When they come to the land of the bong-tree, the first thing the owl and the pussycat see is a piggy-wig. *A piggy-wig stood. Stood* seems to imply some kind of a landmark, something inanimate, or possibly a tree of some kind. The reader thinks *ah it's not a pig – it's something else*. But then the thing standing there comes to life as a pig, a personified pig – a male pig – with a ring at the end of his nose. An anthropomorphic pig, of course.

The point is that if you try to follow through the logic of the poem, you would not be able to predict a particular incongruity from the ones preceding it, because in each case there is a different order of craziness operating. The *happily ever after* ending is presided over, sensibly enough, by the embodiment of craziness, the moon.

Nonsense, like every artefact, has a cultural/historical setting. In the late nineteenth century, as European empires (and particularly the British) approached their colonising peak, the idea of strangely mismatched (human) characters going off on a long sea voyage, and making a new life together, would have been relatively commonplace, if still novel. Lear merely presents this novelty in an exaggerated anthropomorphic form. Or, better to say, Lear zoomorphises unlikely characters for a shipboard romance. Of course, these two are very much in love from the outset. Monstrous miscegenators? No, they miniaturise (and make cute) the hybridising common in the British Empire approaching its zenith. And of course, an owl and a pussycat do have certain things in common, as suggested in Lear's unfinished, posthumously published notes for a sequel. 'The Children of the Owl and the Pussy-cat' appeared in Angus Davidson's biography *Edward Lear: Landscape Painter and Nonsense Poet*. It is about the Owl and Pussy-cat's offspring, who are 'partly little beasts and partly little fowls', telling us of the death of their feline mother 'long years ago', and the resulting single-parent upbringing they had 'in the hollow of a tree in Sila's inmost maze' (Lear 1992, 167). The limited success of that sequel, might be attributed to the fact that there is less excitement in reversing the dynamic of the original text; that is, it is less amusing to find the similarities between these otherwise antagonist characters, as opposed to drawing together their monstrous differences.

Lear's rhetorical tricks are exemplary and seminal in the development of nonsense for children. And we see them well exercised for instance in the works of Dr. Seuss, which are littered with nonsense neologisms, of a kind the reader is intended to pretend to take for granted. This is a wonderful textual ride for the child reading, who in any case experiences so much of the strangely worded world as if it were supposed to be already known. The denouement of *The Cat in the Hat* might be thought to face the same problem as Lear's sequel to 'The Owl and the Pussy-cat': putting things back together, however miraculous that may be, is simply not as exciting as taking the world apart in the first place.

A Comedy of Animal Manners

It would appear that poetic texts for children, involving animals, tend either to be absurd – where the fun is made by connecting what cannot be connected, for instance animals too dissimilar or antagonistic to plausibly co-exist (as in the idea of a romance between an owl and a pussycat); or else to articulate a plausibly complex social reality for a certain animal, imagined by way of behaviours, recognisably both human and animal, as in T.S. Eliot's *Old Possum's Book of Practical Cats* (1939/2009), later adapted to the famous West End Broadway (1981) musical, *Cats*. The book may be read as a corrective for the serious bleakness of the disintegrated world presented in *The Waste Land*.

> What are the roots that clutch, what branches grow
> Out of this stony rubbish? Son of man,
> You cannot say, or guess, for you know only
> A heap of broken images, where the sun beats,
> And the dead tree gives no shelter, the cricket no relief,
> And the dry stone no sound of water.
> (1963, 53)

Each of these texts, apparently ahistorical and a-contextual, is interested in, and very much a product of, contemporary events and manners.

Written through the 1930s, Old Possum's cats are there to reveal both the ubiquity of a particular pet and the range of types and relationships in English society. Delivered through the vehicle of the humorous mystery of the life we cannot see being lived among us, the cats in all their antics hold up a mirror to the reader – to show a life as rich and as varied, as adventurous, if not more so, than their own. A putative foreign-feeling inscrutability[1] and lack of logic are keys to the humour. And yet these cat characters prove themselves time and again to be solid British types, thus suggesting an outside from which the manners of empire may be viewed as arbitrary. The inscrutable fussiness of cats is featured – as in the Rum Tum Tugger, of whom it is written, 'If you offer him cream then he sniffs and sneers' (Eliot 2009, 16).

Though all social strata are present to some degree in the collection, the average cat included is middle class, well heeled, conservative, and socially established. This is well developed from the outset with the names cats are given as examples of their naming: Peter, Augustus, Alonzo, or James, and then again Plato, Admetus, Electra, Demeter. Likewise, the notion of names secret to the cats themselves suggests there is an immutable core of Platonic truth to the social order. Such a way of things appears to be beyond any possibility of description, as teased out in the image of the feline in 'profound' meditation, in 'rapt' contemplation:

> Of the thought, of the thought, of the thought of his name:
>   His ineffable effable
>   Effanineffable
> Deep and inscrutable singular Name.
>
> (2009, 3)

The frequent passivity of real house cats provides a blank slate for speculation as to the motives, knowledge, plans, intentions, secrets of the fantasy cats in the book. Old Deuteronomy, 'a cat famous in proverb and rhyme/A long while before Queen Victoria's accession' (25), commands awe and respect. Villagers stop the traffic so that his repose might not be disturbed. Perhaps a generalised gentility is suggested simply because cats are creatures of apparent leisure; house pets, and cats particularly, entailing, in their own right, a leisure class. The ease and jollity of these cats in domestic or urban setting we can find in these poems present also the urban qualities of the 'petit flaneur'. Aneesh Barai connects this book with the 'varied influences of Baudelaire on [Eliot], his personal vision of the city, his class interests in the spectrum of cats presented'. Eliot focuses 'all of these into a text that both officially and subversively maps London as a way of introducing the city to a child audience' (Barai 2017, 15). His own social position and that of his readers are likewise suggested here. In Henry Hart's words, 'Eliot walks through himself in *Old Possum's Book of Practical Cats* and offers a multifaceted self-portrait' (2012, 402).

Old Possum's cats are deliberately mysterious – witness Mr Mistoffelees and Macavity. These cats are ubiquitous or at least great travellers – as in Growltiger and Skimbleshanks. Fantastic criminal exploits (Growltiger and Macavity) make the cats gremlin-like blame-ables for various misfortunes humans (or others) may suffer. And always the silence of cats is a wry testimony to their unseen doings.

Cats themselves (witness Mungojerrie and Rumpelteazer) are frequently the cause of disruption, but importantly often a repository of good order, however fiercely they need to work at it, as in the fearsome case of The Great Rumpuscat. Of course, as all social orders are human orders one way or another, it is human arrangements that such fantasy cats are, literally or allegorically, protecting, promoting, aligning with presumed actual feline interests.

A number of Old Possum's company are involved with culture – as in for instance Gus: The Theatre Cat, or Bustopher Jones, who doesn't haunt pubs but has eight or nine clubs and a coat of fastidious black, not to mention white spats. Bustopher hangs out at the Drones, and so is presumably a chum of Bertie Wooster's. What is it that Jellicle Cats live for? 'They are resting and saving themselves to be right/For the Jellicle Moon and the Jellicle Ball'.

Pretensions of gentility, or at least of established class position, predominate. At the book's end, the self-introduction of Cat Morgan, whose voice 'it aint no sich melliferous horgan' (Eliot 2009, 56) could be thought of as an afterthought towards inclusion, in class terms.

Despite the exciting adventures throughout (for instance with Mungojerrie and Rumpelteazer, for instance in the battle between the Pekes and the Pollicles), the comedy is all about the disruption and restoration of viable, sensible order of a very British kind. Here Molly Best Tinsley reminds us, in concord with Sewell's claim of Eliot as a nonsense poet (1962), that 'The Book of Practical Cats is a receptacle for all the "love and charity" excised from Eliot's serious existential statements – a sort of immersion in the otherwise destructive element, nonsense, as the ultimate way to reach heaven' (1975, 167). This is a book, in darkening times, about the survival of manners. Those manners are organised through unspoken codes of which cats are both secret transgressors and frequent custodians.

Skimbleshanks, for instance, certainly 'doesn't approve/of hilarity and riot, so the folk are very quiet/when Skimble is about and on the move' 'You can play no pranks with Skimbleshanks' (Eliot 2009, 55). Perhaps though, Skimbleshanks is the odd cat out and a delightful anarchy is more prevalent than not, as for instance in the case of the Rum Tum Tugger who 'doesn't care for a cuddle;/But he'll leap on your lap in the middle of your sewing, For there's nothing he enjoys like a horrible muddle' (16). We have no reason to think that we have any comprehensive or representative sample here of cats that might be practical. The book end naming and addressing poems suggest the kinds of problems that might be encountered in efforts to generalise about cats.

From those available to us, it seems wild unpredictability is to the fore among these more and less practical characters, and it is always productive of plot. Still, kindness and care are values receiving some promotion. Consider the Old Gumbie cat, Jennyanydots, who though lazing all day (and so presenting this passive view to her unseen human owners), spends her nights teaching ill-mannered mice music, crochet and tatting, as well as baking cakes for the mice in her care, this with the sole sainted aim of improving their digestion. This Jennyanydots, one notes, is the only female feline worthy of a titled poem in the book (though it should be noted that the gender of the protagonist, in this case, could not be guessed from the title, 'The Old Gumbie Cat'). One might presume that half of the dance-loving Jellicle cats are female, but this is not evidenced in the text. Very few of the names in 'The Naming of Cats' could be female names and the anonymous any-cat-at-all of 'The Addressing of Cats', is normatively male. In saying so, the gender representation of cats is nevertheless indeterminable in the book. Elizabeth Sewell, one of the earliest students of T.S. Eliot as a nonsense poet, considers that 'Cats are images for the body and for woman (so Grishkin) but in appeasable form. It is possible that cats are also images for God, in miniature' (70). For the characteristics that practical cats embody, Jeanne Campbell and John Reesman note from Eliot's response letter that the poet tends to 'allow his characters the right to retain their mystery and power, even in a "simple" nonsense poem' (1984, 31):

> At least, of all the Cats between Mousehole and John O'Groats,
> You can't say, some of them are sheep and other Cats are goats.
>
> For even the nicest tabby was ever born and weaned
> Is capable of acting, on occasion, like a fiend.
>
> And even my toughest characters, who gloat in doing harm,
> Are not entirely destitute (admit it, please) of Charm.
>
> And all my Cats with one accord disclaim the title "pets",
> Which is only suitable to parrots, Pekes and marmosets.

Eliot's defence of his Cats foreshadows the French neologism proposed by Derrida, *animot* (rather than *l'animal* or *les animaux*), to champion against the violence done to the animal that begins with this pseudo-concept of 'the animal'. In Derrida's opinion, 'animal' is a word that fails to canvass the inherent multiplicity in a variety of animals. In a Derridean way that endorses the heterogeneous elements of 'plural animals heard in the singular' to 'envisage the existence of "living creatures"' (Derrida 2008, 47), practical cats are charming and 'entitled to expect/these evidences of respect' (Eliot 2009, 61).

One should note that alongside the above-mentioned Jennyanydots' care and concern, she does have her own militaristic bent, that might have been taken as Hitlerian at the time, or equally as an antidote for Nazi tendencies:

> She thinks that the cockroaches just need employment
> To prevent them from idle and wanton destroyment.
> So she's formed, from that lot of disorderly louts,
> A troop of well-disciplined helpful boy-scouts,
> with a purpose in life and a good deed to do—
>
> (Eliot 2009, 7)

Perhaps all this merely reflects the real imaginative role/s that British cat owners of the time have wished their pets to play in their lives. In the context of the rise of fascism, this is what one might regard as the wishfulness of the work. The world of these cats is like the Hobbiton and the Shire Tolkien is imagining at the same time a world of predictable social stability, where for all the adventures and excitement, one nevertheless knew what is what. If the humour is simply based on the allegorical almost-tautology that our pets are so much like us, it needs to be noted that the animality of cats is seldom allowed to get in the way of either their social position or their narrative function.

For all its conservative limitations, *Old Possum's Book of Practical Cats* is an open text. Its characters are of the round variety; of interest because, for the most part, we do not know what they will do next. The success of the text may be measured through the delighted ambivalence named-and-so-known (anthropomorphic cats) provide by being as confusing as we humans are.

It is worth noting that 'them as us' reading has been problematised by critics. Stacy Rule dismisses an allegorical reading of the book. She detects 'a desire for equitable relationship' in the poet's insistence on the addressing of cats (154), rather than seeking an 'obedient, predictable, and unproblematic' pet companionship that often characterises dog–human ties. Without losing the sight of enigmatic nature of cats, 'Eliot calls for an equalization of the two species based on singular personalities' instead of 'prompting us to see cats as symbols for humans' (Rule 2011, 156). Rule's view somehow echoes Paul Douglass' earlier observation that 'Neither a sermon nor an aberration, the book expresses Eliot's love for dog-, cat-, and mankind, and his desire to keep alive in himself the irreverent child' (1983, 110). As suggested above, these poems also subtly capture feline traces and represent them as both catlike and humanlike:

> That Cats are much like you and me
> And other people whom we find
> possessed of various types of mind.
> For some are sane and some are mad
> And some are good and some are bad
> And some are better, some are worse.
> (Eliot 2009, 58)

They are practical cats, with a capacity for doing something, not there merely to be stroked and fed, purr and adorn the household. They may also 'be anything but practical' with strange mysteries that dissolve what is commonly regarded as 'wholly good or bad' (Campbell and Reesman 33). If the allegory is too thoroughgoing to notice, then we may say that humans are almost never seen in these poems for the simple reason that humans are always already there, in the cat suits. Humour in Eliot's case is from the conflation of dissimilars; but the humour is, unlike that which Horace described, intended, and there is nothing monstrous about it.

In the case of both *Old Possum's Book of Practical Cats* and 'The Owl and Pussy-cat', an absurd conjunction (making the creature what and where and how it is not) is the basis of the humour. There would seem to be two continua at play in every such instance of anthropomorphism. First, as previously suggested, we may question, at any point in the investigation, how human and how animal any particular character is (?). Second, it needs to be asked, how arbitrary or motivated is the analogy at any point (?). 'The Owl and the Pussy-cat', for instance, is at first glance, along the lines Horace suggested, highly arbitrary in what it throws together, with the difference being that Lear's intention was clearly humorous; *Old Possum's Book of Practical Cats*, seems highly motivated in its detailed delivery of a very British comedy of manners, these played out in feline form.

A Cockroach and a Cat

Don Marquis' 1916 creation, *Archy and Mehitabel* (first collected in 1927), and the sequel volumes *Archy's Life of Mehitabel* (1933) and *Archy Does His Part* (1935), offer the reader the autobiographical observations and storytelling of a cockroach, who is the reincarnation of a *vers libre* poet. Close companion of Archy the cockroach is Mehitabel, the alley cat, who claims to be the reincarnation of Cleopatra. In this (minor) epic storytelling work of decades, class (and class pretensions) and gender (and gendered pretensions) are always to the fore.

Archy is introduced to the reader via the example of Dobbs Ferry's rat, another typing–writing animal (9). Don Marquis' narrative persona tells us that the rat is both ghost and animal. This curious creature is however always interrupted by the night watchman and so never manages to complete a story. The zeitgeist justification for the possibility of a story along these lines is that 'It is an era of belief in communications from the spirit land'. The fact that the Dobbs Ferry rat is putatively known to the public (through print media) helps to normalise the case of Archy, the vers libre cockroach, whose works are clearly on a higher literary plane.

The minoritarian, quotidian, irreverent tone of Archy's whole oeuvre is given special emphasis by the fact that he is unable to create capital letters in his typescript. This is because he types by leaping from key to key and has no means of holding the shift key down (which he would need to do while jumping on another key in order to capitalise a letter). The question of how Archy works the shift to get a new line is soon raised by readers, but the privileges of monologic text are asserted and this very reasonable doubt is quickly dismissed as a distraction by Archy. One notes that this avant-garde poetic activity is seeing newspaper publication (in New York's *Evening Sun*) some years before E.E. Cummings'

How Practical Are These Cats? 73

first volume of poetry was published. The lack of caps suits the view of the underside of life presented throughout. This is the big self-important world of modernity and progress from the point of view of a cockroach, a creature that should not be there. And it is a world turned upside down, along the lines of the Bakhtinian carnival. This point of view reminds us of the survival, among the skyscrapers, of rats and roaches and alley cats, and other unofficial inhabitants of the city – these being quite the opposite in tone of the T.S. Eliot's dramatis personae. The view from under is perennially surprising in Archy's writings. In 'pity the poor spiders':

> I remember some weeks ago
> meeting a middle aged spider
> she was weeping
> what is the trouble I asked
> her it is these cursed
> flyswatters she replied
> they kill off all the flies
> and my family and I are starving
> to death it struck me
> as so pathetic that I made
> a little song about it
> (Marquis, 'pity the poor spiders')

Archy's cockroach humility is outweighed however by his pretensions as a poet (and his competitiveness, evinced in his characteristic dismissal of rival poets). His pretensions as a poet are conversely undermined by his rough diction, which seems to fit nicely with the lack of punctuation (otherwise attributed to technical issues with the typewriter). Of course, we may well ask if at least part of the allegorical purpose of the text is to take the piss out of *avant-garde* poets and poetry. Regardless of intention, many of the poems are in their own right much anthologised classics of *avant-garde* poetry of the first half of the twentieth century.

Don Marquis' magic is in bringing together weighty philosophic, contemporary, and world-historic questions with what appear to be grubby clumsy feelers. A sample of 'archy interviews a pharaoh' shows how sharply attuned the cockroach antennae are. This text serves to place the alcohol prohibition of the time in the long historical context, by means of a discussion with a museum mummy, who is variously addressed by Archy as 'kingly has been', 'old tan and tarry', 'the majestic mackerel', 'my imperial pretzel', 'the royal desiccation', and 'the unfortunate residuum' who 'puts the cough in sarcophagus' (Marquis 2006, 273–276).

The mummy refers to himself as 'a mighty desolation', and finally disintegrates into dust in despair, having waited 4000 years for a beer, and now learning of prohibition from Archy. Up until his demise, the pharaoh's address of Archy is equally playful:

my little pest
says he
you must be respectful
in the presence
of a mighty desolation
little archy
forty centuries of thirst
look down upon you
oh by isis
and osiris
says the princely raisin
by pish and phthush and phthah
by the sacred book of perembru
and all the gods
that rule from the upper
cataract of the nile
to the lower duodenum
I am dry
I am as dry
as the next morning mouth
of a dissipated desert
as dry as the hoofs
of the camels of timbuctoo
thinking …
thinking
of beer
      (Marquis 2006, 275–276)

It is after this speech, Archy tells this 'divine drouth', 'imperial fritter', 'old salt codfish', that there is not yet a law against thinking about alcohol in the U.S. (276). Archy is an animal who speaks for himself and for other animals. He gives voice to all manner of entities lacking voice. In terms of prosopopoeia, several kinds of ventriloquism are involved in Archy's rendition of the world, as in 'mehitabel was once Cleopatra':

I have discovered that
mehitabel s soul inhabited a
human also at least that
is what mehitabel is claiming these
days it might be she got jealous of
my prestige anyhow she and
I have been talking it over in a
friendly way who were you
mehitabel I asked her I was
cleopatra once she said well I said I
bet you lived in a palace you bet

> she said and what lovely fish dinners
> we used to have and licked her chops
> mehitabel would sell her soul for
> a plate of fish any day I told her I thought
> you were going to say you were
> the favorite wife of the emperor
> valerian he was some catnip eh
> mehitabel but she did not get me
> archy
> (Donquis, 'mehitabel was once cleopatra')

Although Archy soon comes to play an ironised version of the role of Johnson's Boswell to Mehitabel, one remembers that he introduced her to the reader by way of a plea to the boss to have her removed because she has almost eaten him, when shouldn't she be chasing rats? We learn that for all her aristocratic pretensions, and for all of Archy's literary pretensions, these are in fact a couple of very practical animals. Their lives, and the cultural artefacts, in song and in and out of rhyme, that they weave around their lives, are very much stories of survival – stories of the survival of animals that have, throughout history – wanted and unwanted – accompanied humans on their way.

How human and how animal are these particular anthropomorphised sentiences, who, for our pleasure, tell what matters to them? In one sense their animal side is limited to clear definition: a cockroach scuttles and jumps from key to key, a cat gets into fights, loves fish. Everything beyond this then can be read as the expression of personality, as human condition writ large. Things are however more complex than this, and while there are poems that could not be distinguished from human-as-human writing, in general it is the imagined animal point of view that informs the under-sided way the world is seen. In 'certain maxims of Archy':

> insects have
> their own point
> of view about
> civilisation a man
> thinks he amounts
> to a great deal
> but to a flea
> or a mosquito
> a human being
> is merely something
> good to eat
> (Donquis, 'certain maxims of Archy')

In terms of the prepositional typology we proposed in our introduction, in *Archy and Mehitabel* we are shown as animals allowed to speak for themselves and for others, particularly those unpopular creatures on lower rungs of the Chain of Being. They are allowed to do so in the way of humans of the class, and gender and cultural positions they each inhabit. In this sense, humanity and animality are intricately bound in these two characters who endorse what Paul Wells describes as 'the hybrid "humanimality"' (2009, 52). It is a term Wells coins in his study of animals in animation, to canvass any animated character that 'operates at the metaphoric and symbolic level, and seeks to show when an idea is shared by the parallel terms that have evolved to define and explain both the human and animal world' (52). This term justifies the humour generated in the case of Archy and Mehitabel as well. Archy is both a downtrodden cockroach and a 'world-weary sceptical and cynical philosopher' while Mehitabel is both a cat and 'a homeless self-centered lady-like *bon vivant*' (McClelland 2010, 24). In E.B. White's words,

> Here were perfect transmigrations of an American soul, this dissolute feline who was a dancer and always the lady, *toujours gai*, and this troubled insect who was a poet – both seeking expression, both vainly trying to reconcile art and life, both finding always that one gets in the way of the other.
>
> (Marquis 2011, 18–19)

They tell allegorically where we are by showing us where animals like themselves are from, and how, for believers in reincarnation, we ourselves might as easily be there. The question is, as Archy ponders his transmigration in 'my naked soul',

> ... will I go
> higher in the scale of
> life and inhabit the
> body of a butterfly
> or a dog or a
> bird or will I sink
> lower and go into the
> carcass of a poison
> spider or a politician
>   (Marquis 2006, 24–25)

Archy and Mehitabel provide us with a nice example of nature and culture met in the allegorical figure of the good-humoured suffering creature, victim of the ways of humans and of their social order, and (increasingly) of their ubiquity. This is by no means an invention of modernity. Apuleius' *The Golden Ass*, for instance, provides an early example. There the accidental metamorphosis into an ass leads the protagonist Lucius on a journey full of revelations.

Why though, we may ask, have all these creatures been talking and scribbling to entertain us, across cultures and down through the ages? Is there any general purpose or function being served by this rhetorical strategy? Is it fair to assume that anthropomorphism and zoomorphism are essentially strategies in the service of anthropocentrism? Could they as easily be empathic strategies in the service of a critique of anthropocentrism. Or are they ideologically neutral tactics, able to serve any ends?

Fairytale Thinking and the Reifying Power of Anthropomorphism

Following Nietzsche's famous dictum about truth as 'a mobile army of metaphors', we argue that poetry about animals, whatever its range of possible inflection, tends to favour what could best be described as fairytale thinking. By 'fairytale thinking' we intend to evoke a kind of moralistic reductionism associated with the fairytale genre (as especially elaborated by Jack Zipes [1983] and many others), where a linear narrative delivers good and evil outcomes, associated with characters able to be classified, likewise, as good or evil. Of interest to us is that many of the characters so involved are anthropomorphised animals, often included in stories on the basis of proverbial (stereotypical) traits – human traits imposed almost as a system of classification on animal others (greedy pigs, wily foxes, sly snakes). This proverbial and fairytale characterisation of speaking animals is a persistent feature of poetry intended for child audiences, from the nursery rhyme (as investigated in Chapter 3) on.

Let us here briefly consider the textual function of anthropomorphism in poetry as it concerns children. By turning humans into animals, one gives animals powers of awareness and self-awareness. And why? Could it be so as to suggest that humans behave without reflecting on or thinking about their behaviour? That would be a possible motive. Or there could be an almost opposite motive. Making the whole of the world subject to what appear to be the rules of nature – the rules which apply to every and any animal – may have the effect of making the world of humans (and its patterns or rules) seem as if it were natural, normal, inevitable. Hypostasising the world of human relations through an appeal to naturalness supported by spurious evidence of a concocted nature is an ideological inversion *par excellence*. The child reader is expected to believe that social relations presented by talking animals provide cultural norms of relevance to the child in her/his own growth to maturity. The rather obvious sleight of hand tends to be overlooked simply because it is so widely practised. It has come to seem to be so naturally true.

Nature and culture meet early in the life of the individual and contradictions between these are faced and teased out and sometimes resolved from an early age. Fables and fairytales show children how to relate to the world and the people around them. They teach children how characters face life crises and so they teach children about decision making. The fairytale, as a story for children, can make its moral teaching obvious. Characters are simply good or simply evil. The child hearing the story can easily see which characters are which. Is it the case therefore that the fairytale teaches children to recognise the difference between good and evil? More fundamentally, the fairytale teaches the child to recognise that there is such a difference. It teaches the child that the advice of her parents, on matters of whom to trust and where to go, is vital, because the child may lack the skill to recognise a wolf in sheep's clothing, or a wolf dressed up as a grandmother. In much the same way, teaching children a fear of the dark (notwithstanding the fact that one might fall over and hurt oneself) is an effective way of keeping them indoors and under supervision. These kinds of teaching are not necessarily bad; they are though easily put to bad purposes, for instance, teaching that certain types of creatures or people, different from your type, are evil or not to be trusted. In pre-literate, as in the ancient and medieval worlds, perhaps this was necessary, if not friendly, advice: the world outside of one's kingdom or even outside of one's village or home may well have been hostile. Children had to be warned about dangerous outsiders. Generalised hostility to others that stops short of accomplished genocide is however self-perpetuating.

Worldwide today, most violence against children is committed by people well known to the children in question; so how useful in general are lessons about 'stranger danger'? To return to the wolf with the grandmother's voice: the animals speak because they are the humans in the story. We are the wolves in sheep's clothing and we are also the sheep in sheep's clothing. In the fable and the fairytale we humans are very often not in our own garb. So, why dress humans up as animals, when you could have humans speaking for themselves? We talk and animals do not.

In his essay 'Fabling Beasts: Traces in Memory' Nicholas Howe writes:

> If animals can speak in human language, and they must if there are to be beast fables, then the most cherished of our modern distinctions between human and animal – that based on language as a creative, recursive faculty – seems pointless, even evasive.
>
> (1995, 642)

Perhaps Howe's assertion ignores a very simple fact: that the speaking animal in the story is most particularly a marker of the fact of being in a story. The child knows that real animals do not really speak, the child does not expect animals to speak as a result of reading the story in which they do. So, far from reading language as pointless or evasive, the child understands through speech what is anthropomorphic of the animal mask the story entertains.

The fantasy world of the story defines itself, as such, by breaking the obvious real-world rule. Excluding the possibility of religion or taught superstition, this is the most fundamental kind of nonsense to which the child is exposed, and usually from a very early age. What does it mean to endow animals with the one power we humans specifically have, and they specifically lack? For one thing, it establishes fantasy for the child as a means of getting through the invisible barrier between what is real and what is not, what can be and what cannot be. This endowment of human speech breaks down the barrier between the human world and the animal world. Or one might say, it breaks down the barrier between the world of nature and the social world.

It should be noted that neither the fairytale nor the telling/writing of stories for children need to be a politically conservative activity. The foregoing remarks are not about genre per se; they are about a style of thought, which, while by no means permanent or 'of the human condition', nevertheless has had currency in very many contexts. The liberatory power of the fairytale (as opposed to the folk tale) has been amply demonstrated by Jack Zipes and others. This is a distinction largely based on mode of delivery; that is, the folk tale is an oral form passed down through tradition, the fairytale is associated with the rise of print culture, with the writing of the Romantic period and its valorising of the imagination. In *Breaking the Magic Spell – Radical Theories of Folk and Fairy Tales*, Zipes makes the contrast in the following terms: 'Imagination and self-realization are celebrated as activities in contrast to the celebration of power, i.e. "might makes right", in the folk tale. The protagonist in the fairytale does not want to rule over other people but over the dualities in his or her own life' (2002, 102). The nub of Zipes' argument as to liberatory power concerns what he describes as a 'continual attraction' of both tale types: 'breaking the magic spell in fairy realms means breaking the magic hold which oppressors and machines seem to have over us in our everyday reality' (46). For the purposes of this argument though, what is at stake is the didactic anthropomorphism central to both genres.

Bruno Bettelheim's studies opened up the psychoanalytic perspective for the reading of fairytales. He firmly believes that it is 'characteristic of fairytales to state an existential dilemma briefly and pointedly', which allows 'the child to come to grips with the problem in its most essential form' (2008, 328). Since Bettelheim, it has almost been a consensus that fairytales teach children how to deal with fear and danger. But they also commonly teach children to be fearful and suspicious of nature and to assert their superiority over it. In 'Goldilocks and the Three Bears' (cited in Tatar 2002), Goldilocks gets away from those three bears after eating their breakfast and breaking their furniture and sleeping on their beds. She can get away with all this bad behaviour because she is only doing it to animals and animals have no recourse. But it is the human situation of these creatures that allows us to develop the empathy with the bears we finally dismiss in favour of our empathy for the scared little girl running all the way home. Those bears fit another category – the ambiguous not-us (as we see ourselves as human) and not-animal-either category. That is the category in which humans have traditionally slotted human others not of their tribe or outside of their civilisation: somewhere in between family/tribe and animal. In a sense all foreigners are able to conform to that category: they can speak but we cannot understand them. In the fairytale they can speak and we can understand them. But that is because we have chosen which of them can speak and we have given them the words which they can speak; we have given them the script. They are not us – they are different from us – but we only know them as we represent them.

It is very easy for those (human, animal, in whatever combination) allowed to speak in that category to slip into the good camp or the evil camp. They are like us and they are not like us, they could be on our side and they could be against us. This ambiguous position is convenient for a society on a war footing, for a society that never knows from where or from whom its next attack will come, or conversely whom or where it must next attack in order to protect or to further its own interests (this being a fine distinction).

It is easy to dismiss certain forms of human behaviour as too tricky or clever or novel or more to the point, unnatural. The behaviour of strangers has often been painted in that way. The behaviour or animals is surely, by contrast, 'natural'. Animals do what they do because that is what animals do. Turn humans into animals in the once-upon-a-time-past – that is, the past you cannot put your finger on – and you have succeeded in making their human actions seem natural. The characters you now have, after this transformation, are – as animals – only doing what animals do. Making the whole of the world subject to what appear to be the rules of nature – the rules which apply to every and any animal – actually has the effect of making the world of humans seem as if it were natural. This reification has the effect of showing what happens in the human world as happening for reasons of necessity, rather than because of the choices of humans.

There are indeed many necessary and also arbitrary events in human affairs. The fairytale makes highly motivated social and familial arrangements (e.g. the relationships between Papa Bear and Mama Bear and Baby Bear) appear to be natural, and so necessary, immutable 'facts of life'. The fairytale shows the child the world as it was once in a mythical past where animals could talk; it does so in order to show how the human world is meant to be. Timelessness in the story implies the eternity of its conditions. By making simply 'normal' arrangements that exist for a reason, the fairytale and fable naturalise and eternalise human behaviour.

In his Old Possum's Book, Eliot establishes 'a surrogate family, imparting to children his vision of beauty and truth, and also delivering cautionary fables of ugliness, evil, and deceit' (Hart 399). Nonsense poetry, to a certain degree, continues 'several tendencies of the fairytale', as Winfried Menninghaus claims. 'The theory of the fairy tale and its Romantic reverberations', he states, 'allow for an understanding of the suspension of "sense" as an integral element of the very genre of the fairy tale' (1999, 9). As in the marriage bliss of the Owl and the Pussy-cat, fairytale and nonsense easily slip into each other.

The tale with the talking animals teaches the child that the way of things in fairytales is how the world has always been because it is even this way with animals. This does not mean that the child believes she is surrounded by witches and castles and giants and talking animals. It means that the roles – in relation to each other – of males and females and parents and children appear to the child as fixed. Good and evil must be fundamental categories, surely, if they apply to the animal as well as to the human world?

But what rational sense could it possibly make to speak of animals as good or evil? If foxes seem evil and sheep seem good to humans, then surely this is only because humans eat sheep and so do foxes. From the foxes' point of view – which foxes cannot express to our satisfaction – surely the roles must be reversed. And from the sheep's point of view: does it really matter by whom one is torn to pieces and eaten? The sheep of the fairytale would have us think so.

One of the most potent illusions of the fairytale can be summed up in the terms of Ruskin's pathetic fallacy (1918/2013, 122) – in this case the impression children receive that the world is naturally ordered in terms of human emotions and human reasoning: a cunning fox, a gullible lamb, a greedy pig. Perhaps it is true that a bear can be fierce and a lion savage but animals act according to their instincts and not so as to conform with human stereotypes of behaviour. This naturalising pattern in the fairytale is as widespread as it is taken-for-granted as it is difficult to notice. It is hard to imagine childhood without these kinds of illusion. But on a planet where many other-than-human species are daily facing extinction, how wise (or fair) can this attribution of human motives to animal others be?

Were it not but one more instance of the pathetic fallacy, one might say that the irony for those facing extinction is that it is only possible for humans to paint animals into the social roles they enjoy in the fable and fairytale because animals cannot speak to defend themselves. In fact, the irony is only available through means of a particular kind of human self-consciousness – that which we associate with empathy and identification. Nor has the animal world generally been able to defend itself by other means from the savagery of the world's number one alpha animal: us. Again, Akira Mizuta Lippit reminds us, following John Berger's observation of animals as hollow and immunised to encounter in zoo, that 'Modernity can be defined by the disappearance of wildlife from humanity's habitat and by the reappearance of the same in humanity's reflections on itself: in philosophy, psychoanalysis, and technological media such as the telephone, film, and radio' (Lippit 2000, 2–3), not to speak of a great many happy animals in children's books.

What happens to the animals in fairytales reflects quite accurately the course of the millennia long struggle of humans to domesticate, consume, or dispense with animal others. The human message for the animal world – for the world of nature – has up until this stage in the human story – been quite simply: domesticate or die. Consider the world's hundreds of millions of dogs today, all descended from the wolf, an animal on its way out, now numbered in thousands. Lippit has written, 'A new breed of animals now surrounds the human populace – a genus of vanishing animals, whose very being is constituted by that state of disappearing' (2000, 3). The history of animals is a haunting memory of animals tamed, transformed, and villified.

There is an important issue for interpretation here, one with which every intelligent child engages, at least unconsciously, when she thinks about fairytales. Is the world presented in the tale really the human world? If the animals are actually people, then the story teaches – courtesy of its cartoon characters – how people behave and how we should behave with them. On the other hand, if the animals are really animals, the world presented in the tale teaches the child how to view the world of nature, how to think of animals, wild and tame and yes, also the humans who happen to resemble them.

Certainly, it would be silly to think humans have not learnt anything from other animals. It is hard to imagine where humans would have got the idea of singing if some birds had not been met in the forest. Are fairytales allegorical representations of the human world or do they present the world of nature from a human point of view? There is a contradiction between these views: on the one hand we are learning about how others are different from us, on the other hand we are learning how they cannot be different from us. Analysis resolves the contradiction in the following form: human strangers, like the animal kind, are to be judged on our terms, in the language of our tribe; and like animals, they end up being unable to speak for themselves.

What is dangerous about the fabulous world of speaking animals is that it shows the child a world in which the contradiction (noted above) comes ready resolved. The child is taught why foxes must be killed at the same time as she is taught why not to trust people who behave like foxes. There is a nasty mind loop here which allows neither foxes nor people painted that way any chance of defending themselves. How sensible is it to teach children that other humans and other-than-human animals are the enemy, or that some animals (i.e. the domesticated ones) are our friends but that some others (i.e. the wild ones) are permanently bad and so deserve to die? The world is too small and too fragile now for this kind of thinking. Humanity cannot afford to go on being on a war footing with nature. The world's present state and prospects call for a new kind of consciousness in which old fairytales (and fairytale thinking) will – among all those metaphors and allegories we live by – be subject to a fundamental and thoroughgoing critique.

Unreal Creatures, Spouting Nonsense

So much for real creatures of the fairytale, or rather for the creatures borrowed from reality for the generically defined cultural purposes of humans. We can see how cats and cockroaches and owls and pigs and rats and ducks and dogs are each able to serve allegorically human purposes, and perform normative behaviours of which only humans are capable.

One might at face value consider the least practical of creatures those that cannot or do not exist at all. Perhaps though these denizens of only the picture book are the most practical of animals from the point of view of both ideological production and its critique? They have no real world to contradict the possibilities they offer on the printed page or on the screen. As we shall see, in Chapter 4, with the Jabberwock and the Jubjub Bird and all of their ilk-if-there-is-one, these absurdities might also be the most instructive of all animals. Just as dream imagery, just as the fantastic imaginations of a Hieronymous Bosch, are always from some real-world somewhere, so the imaginary creatures of nonsense poetry are perhaps more allegorically apt than any simply borrowed existing animal might be.

Consider Christian Morgenstern's (1895) 'The Nasobame':

Auf seinen Nasen schreitet
einher das Nasob?m,
von seinem Kind begleitet.
Es steht noch nicht im Brehm.
Es steht noch nicht im Meyer.
Und auch im Brockhaus nicht.
Es trat aus meiner Leyer
zum ersten Mal ans Licht.
Auf seinen Nasen schreitet
(wie schon gesagt) seitdem,
von seinem Kind begleitet,
einher das Nasobame.

Striding on its noses
there comes the Nasobame,
with its young in tow.
It isn't yet in Brehm's
It isn't yet in Meyer's
And neither in Brockhaus'
It trotted out of my lyre
when it came first to light.

> Striding on its noses
> thereon (as I've said above),
> with its young in tow,
> there goes the nasobame.

Imaginary animals are all nonsensical but some are more nonsensical than others. Competition for the reader's attention frequently takes us further into the realm of the impossible, the absurd, the ridiculous, the sublime (think of the awe inspired by the Jabberwock).

Across the globe we find cultures with rich repertoires of composite monsters and liminal humans. Through the comparison of these taxonomies of human-imagined animality, cross cultural differences and continuities are understood. Animals in arbitrary combinations or grotesque human bodies have their early imagination in the ancient world in Greek and China. We can find imaginary beings readily available in Greek mythologies or eastern bestiaries (e.g. Chinese *Shanhai jing*), for instance, sphinx, mermaid, al-buraq, griffin, minotaur. Boria Sax notes that what we call 'imaginary' 'might have a very palpable reality, but in a cultural environment very different from our own' (2013, 43). The Chinese dragon, for instance, has become an emblem of Chinese cultural reality even though it is not a real animal. The mythical creature has the chimeric physical attributes of nine different animals, some of which include a camel's head, a snake's body, a hare's eyes, a carp's scales, a catfish's whiskers, a stag's antlers, and an eagle's talons.

It needs to be acknowledged though those imaginary creatures have culturally specific purposes. Every aspect of an imaginary creature has some basis in reality, how grotesquely we may view the combination of such attributes. In this way mythical and legendary overtones evoke real world origins, claim the credibility of human experience of animality. The Western conceptualisation of dragon as evil and fire-spouting animal compares interestingly with the Chinese dragon, who is known as the ruler of the sky, who can issue a combination of fire and steam from its nostrils to create clouds and bring timely water to the land. If you meet a dragon in the Bible you may be certain that you are in the wrong place, at least a place ill-advised for humans. The Chinese dragon has, by contrast, been worshipped as an auspicious animal in the long span of Chinese agricultural society, becoming over time an exclusive symbol of imperial families.

Among the most well-known imaginary creatures are also unicorn, thunderbird, phoenix, and mermaid, which may be found in poems or other texts. As creatures with wide currency over considerable time frames, their origins are more amorphous than those of fauna created in and for a specific poem. Despite their evolutionary descent, some of these imaginary creatures are still a popular subject of children's poetry, if, over time, becoming more humane and accessible. In Julie Larios and Julie

Paschkis' *Imaginary Menagerie: A Book of Curious Creatures*, the poem 'Dragon' engages child audiences with a simplified image of a European winged dragon:

> The air around me
> Burns bright as the sun.
> I tell wild rivers
> Which way to run.
> I'm arrow tailed,
> Fish scaled,
> A luck bringer.
> When I fly,
> It's a flame song the world sings.
> But you can ride safely
> Between my wings.
> (2008, 4)

Not a demon of any kind, the dragon in this autobiographicaly framed poem is depicted less serpentine than avian for children. It shows a need for them to have intimate and immediate interaction with the imaginary animal. These animals are at once 'an anthropomorphic projection of human virtues and as well as a fearful vision of violent alterity' (Brown 2010, 6); today they more frequently seem playful and wonderful creatures telling of old human–nature affinities.

Being purely imaginary or nonsensical is what opens an animal-in-poetry to possibility for the reader. Take for instance, Edward Lear's 'The Quangle Wangle's Hat':

> On top of the Crumpetty Tree
> the Quangle Wangle sat,
> But his face you could not see,
> On account of his Beaver Hat.
> For his Hat was a hundred and two feet wide,
> With ribbons and bibbons on every side
> And bells, and buttons, and loops, and lace,
> So that nobody ever could see the face
> Of the Quangle Wangle Quee.
> (cited in Smith 1992, 59)

This Quangle Wangle Quee is inscrutable in the manner of Robert Frost's secret in 'The Secret Sits':

> We dance round in a ring and suppose,
> But the Secret sits in the middle and knows.
> (cited Culler 2009, 76)

Lear's Quangle Wangle Quee could as easily be an abstraction, or represent 'congeries of imaginary creatures so matter-of-factly that you feel in some far corner of the known world they must have always existed' (Willard 1989, 222). The blending of sense and nonsense, the real and the surreal into a miscellaneous assortment of possibilities and things makes the Nasobame and the Quangle Wangle serviceable as floating signifiers. We shall see a sophisticated instance of this rhetorical strategy shortly in Shaun Tan's *The Lost Thing*.

Many nonsense animals are silently observed (although we note the Quangle Wangle does speak, though somewhat inscrutably and to himself, late in the piece). Perhaps just as ideologically serviceable as nonsensical animals is the nonsense animals spout when given the opportunity to speak; though that nonsense might be of a quite uplifting kind, as for instance in James Krüss' 'Spatzen Internationale' ('Sparrows' Internationale') in his book James' *Tierleben* (subtitled as a zoology): a little (untranslatable) treatise on the cultural differences entailed in the 'speech' of various European sparrows:

> Laast uns in verschiednen Ländern
> Einen kleinen Satz verändern,
> Nämlich diesen kleinen Satz:
> Aud dem Dache pfeift der Spatz.
> Laast uns erst nach Frankreich gehen
> Und die Spatzen dort beshen.
> Dann entsteht von selbst der Satz:
> A la dasch pfeiffé la schpaz

Or in his 'Hundesprache':

In Krüss' 'Hundesprache', we meet the general deficiency, from a human point of view, of human-imagined dog speech.

> Ein Hund, der in das Ausland geht,
> Darf gern die Schule schwänzen,
> Weill man ihn überall versteht,
> Ein Hund kennt keine Grenzen.
> »Du« heißt zum Beispiel english »you«
> Und italienisch heißt es »tu«.
> Ein Hund, der sagt nur: Wu!
>
> Ach, ging's uns, wie den Hunden geht,
> Das wäre so gemütlich,
> Weil jeder jeden dann versteht,
> Ob nördlich oder südlich.
> Dann sagt der eine nicht mehr »du«

Der andre »you«, der Dritte »tu«,
Nein, man sagt einfach: Wu!

Doch andrerseits: Mit »wu« allein
Kan man nicht viel berichten.
Zum Beispiel diese Reimerein,
Ich könnte sie nicht dichten.
Drum sag ich liebe einmal »du«
Und einmal »you« und einmal »tu«
Statt unablässig: Wu!

To summarize:
A dog abroad will need no teaching.
His language really is far reaching.
In German, well, we may say *du*.
Italians may address you – *tu*
Your dog makes do with *wu*.

If only we could speak as dogs do!

...

but on the other hand
this *wu* cannot help so much
dogs can't say I love you
    (translation of authors with Jutta Reusch)

Objects and Subjects Lost in Action

Don Marquis' *Archy and Mehitabel,* and subsequent books in the series, subvert various stereotypical assumptions about both animal behaviour and its accessibility to fairytale motives. That is to say, despite its being a comedy of manners along the lines of Elliot's *Practical Cats,* this is a text of interest for the purpose of understanding how assumptions about animals, and the human traits they accrete, may be challenged in poetry. One could see the kind of challenge we meet in Don Marquis' Archy, drawing attention to ontological dimensions of human–animal relations, as forerunner for more recent texts, such as Dr. Seuss' variously indeterminate anthropomorphised animal characters, or those of Tove Jansson, in Moomin Valley, or in Shaun Tan's postmodern picture book, *The Lost Thing* (2000).

    The Lost Thing is, one might say, the affecting tale of a floating signifier, 'who' cannot speak for it/him/herself and whose interests are pursued by someone well-meaning who is nevertheless not adequately equipped to understand this object, its place or purpose or needs. There is a wonderfully subtle and playful indeterminacy to the object of the story – the one understood to have a problem and for whom a solution is sought, the one who cannot be explained or understood but whose lostness and thingness may be dissolved in community, in the discovery that there are like others.

What is this lost thing and what is this story about? The lost thing is a large (perhaps five times the height of the humans in the story) mainly red, teapot-shaped object, with six legs, with tentacles that steam, and other tentacles with bells on. It has doors around its body through which tentacles may protrude at times. It has a lid that lifts on top (apparently for food). The lost thing can bend and tilt and walk. The narrator/persona in the tale begins by telling us that he knew many interesting stories and some so funny 'you'd laugh yourself unconscious', others unrepeatable ... he can't remember any of those, instead he wants to tell about 'the time I found that lost thing'.

There is a wonderful contrast between the extraordinary appearance of the lost thing and its openness to possibility (its cultural suggestiveness), and the flatness of the Gen Y narration, of the youthful bottle top collector, for whom – although his past is full of stories – it seems nothing of excitement or interest could happen in his present. Though it is the story of finding the lost thing we witness in this book, one feels that this can't be of significance precisely because we and the narrator are there to see it. The narrator only encounters the lost thing because he 'stopped to look up for no particular reason'. And at that point he stares at the thing, suggesting how someone different and new might be stared at. The thing itself has a sad, lost sort of look.

At this point in the story one feels there is a missed reciprocity. The thing is looked at the way someone/something strange might be looked at; and it has a particular look – a sad, lost sort of look. It is impossible to say from the pictures through most of the book whether or not there could be eye contact. There is something along these lines in the frame that shows persona and lost thing finally parting. There, the persona is holding out his hands towards what could be some kind of sensor, protruding from the thing. Certainly there is a disjunction between what the pictures show us of this contact and what the narrator tells us about it: 'It was quite friendly though, once I started talking to it'. And then, 'I played with the thing for most of the afternoon. It was great fun'. Though conversation is claimed between thing and narrator, the rest of the story fails to confirm this suggestion, or make it seem likely.

The outlandishness of the newcomer and its apparently language-less state are immediately suggestive of migrant experience. The lost thing is mute and mostly – but not entirely – passive. What kind of a thing is it? Is it animal? Is it machine? Is it alien? Is it a plant that can move? What are its hybrid possibilities? Is it something we cannot see, anthropomorphised, zoomorphised? Is it creature or thing? Its polymorphic status and possibilities lead us to ask various questions. What kind of thing can a creature be? Can a thing be a creature? If we make it so then what have we done?

Our unnamed persona/narrator (Shaun Tan according to the bibliographic material at the front of the book) faces this vicarious identity problem when looking in the newspaper for lost pet notices, but finding only refrigerator repair deals. This is precisely the kind of amalgam the lost thing represents – it is as much like a refrigerator needing repairing as it is like a lost pet. As literalised ambulating signifier it is perhaps above all the elephant in the room – an entity that – not only culturally but – literally does not fit, and which might, for this reason, be in certain social circumstances, unmentionable. The persona's own parents can't see past the filthy feet and worry that the lost thing carries diseases. Their view of it is cursory however and probably doesn't extend beyond those feet because they never look up from the television to see it. It has to be pointed out to them. Once again, nothing is like eye contact. We get a glimpse of how the unfitting is dealt with in the world of the persona into which the lost thing has come. Family interaction does not solve the persona's 'dilemma' with the lost thing, so he resorts to The Federal Department of Odds and Ends (noticed through an advertisement on the last page of the newspaper).

'I have a lost thing', I called to the receptionist at the front desk.
'Fill in these forms', she said.

The lost thing made a small, sad noise.

What kind of a world is it we and the lost thing are visiting here? Someone or something unknown and unseen tugs at the back of the narrator's shirt and a small voice suggests what might be the beginning of a solution to the dilemma. That voice tells the persona, 'This is a place for forgetting, leaving behind, smoothing over'. And then a business card is offered with only a curly arrow on it, an icon now needing to be found by the persona in his quest to help the lost thing.

Finally the arrow leads them to 'the right place' – 'in a dark little gap off some anonymous little street. The sort of place you'd never know existed unless you were actually looking for it'. A buzzer is pressed and when the door opens we see what we must presume to be a collection/a gathering/a zoo or prison for/a haven or an asylum for lost things. Each of the entities is quite different, quite distinct from the others, but collectively they are distinct from the human world otherwise depicted. We straight away know that however misfitted these things are for each other, the lost thing will have a place here and so is presumed no longer lost. That is despite the fact that the persona 'can't say that the thing actually belonged in the place where it ended up'.

In the world into which the lost thing comes, passivity is taken for company and questions are posed on behalf of the unknown, on behalf of the one who cannot be known. The pictures on the page are sharp but indeterminacy is the key to this reading experience. And yet there is communion with this unknowable other of a kind reminding us of Levinas' dictum, 'Only the absolutely other can instruct us'. We shall return to this principle in our analysis of Denise Levertov's 'Cat as Cat' which concludes this chapter. In this, there seems to be a reminder that, however normal our lives are or we make them, we are as selves and as others something of which we cannot be quite sure. Perhaps we are ourselves lost things to someone, perhaps even to ourselves?

Language functions in the story as a pale dividing the knowable from what cannot be known, dividing the dull quotidian world from its outlandish alien outside. Grammatical ambiguity is the key to the objective conditions of the story and the subjective status of its characters. Stories can be known and forgotten. Characters can be named or described or not. A thing can be lost as a person be lost. A thing could be something that a person has lost. Nor are these possibilities mutually exclusive – a lost child may be at once a child who cannot find its way and a child whom a parent has misplaced, is unable to find. And yet these are distinct conditions and attention is drawn to the distinction by the persona's friend, Pete (the only one named in the story).

> 'I dunno, man', said Pete. 'It's pretty weird. Maybe it doesn't belong to anyone. Maybe it doesn't come from anywhere. Some things are like that...' He paused for dramatic effect, '...just plain lost'.
>
> (N.p)

As if there were some primal species of lostness, to transcend the grammatical possibilities of the word. Apparently low in volition, the lost thing has no choice but to leave this grammatical ambiguity unresolved. This is a creature, capable of some telling sounds, but incapable, at least from the reader's point of view, of language as we can know it. Yet we may say, that though assisted, the tentativeness of the narration shows us that the lost thing is not a character spoken for.

This character as problem fallen below threshold of consciousness may be read as simple extension of the ambiguity offered in the title of the story – is this a thing someone has lost or is this thing itself lost? Of course both are and must be true, and the joint solutions to these equally pressing difficulties amount to a finding-oneself of sorts for the reader.

A study of it-ness and of thing-ness, of lost-ness and found-ness, of provenance and of belonging, *The Lost Thing* calls all of these abstractions into question. It calls into question the nature and the possibility of proper attention – attention of the kind that would tell you what is there, or with whom one is dealing.

Suggestive of contemporary crises in both species and language/culture loss, this is also a story about openness to difference, about attention paid to things seen out of the corner of the eye, things that don't 'quite fit'. There is something sadly imponderable about the kind of loss entailed. Such things as the lost thing, which seem to be vanishing from the world, are simply no longer noticed because people are too busy to see them.

People are too busy to see where they are, with whom they are talking. People are too busy to find out who they themselves are or could be. Rather they collect bottle tops.

The Most Impractical of Cats

In contrast with Shaun Tan's lost thing, Dr Seuss' cat in the hat, indefatigable protagonist of the 1957 classic *The Cat in the Hat*, seems the most definite, active, and vocal anthropomorphic creature one could possibly imagine. Who is this cat? He comes from nowhere, but he is an instantly known and named sentience and with a purpose that becomes very clear (if, of its nature, confusing) very quickly. A *deus-ex-machina*, who not only resolves crises, but makes crises to resolve, the Cat in the Hat is an archetypal mirth maker – a carnival character. This animal speaks for himself, but his standing erect gives his mask away, though we need not remember that.

> We looked!
> Then we saw him step on the mat!
> We looked!
> And we saw him!
> The Cat in the Hat!
> And he said to us,
> 'Why do you sit there like that?'
> 'I know it is wet
> And the sun is not sunny.
> But we can have
> Lots of good fun that is funny!'
> (6–7)

Chaos and volition, responsibility and innocence are themes of this work parents buy to read with their children. This book is essentially about children, especially 'the archetypal male child seeking to define himself … in relation to both conventional morality and his own chaotic, anarchic impulses' (Mensch and Freeman 2016, 35). Children and animals, we note, share, if not equally, a proclivity for chaos making in the house. *The Cat in the Hat* creates a world of chaos secret to the children in the story, and it fulfils a parental dream-wish that, after the great rumpus, order might be magically restored.

The contradiction between chaos and order is resolved by the introduction of an animal other, a phantom non-pet who is the most fully human and the only round character in the story. The Cat in the Hat is magical avatar of, on the one hand, mess and trouble, and on the other hand, playtime tidied up. Throughout the story, there is no need for the children to say or do much at all. The fun is all the spectacles going on around them. None of it is of their doing, but their apparent passivity is belied by the inkling we have that imagination is – as its avatar in the Cat in the Hat – supremely confident, preternaturally skilled, extraordinarily whimsical.

What the cat achieves in the way of both creating and of resolving chaos involves whimsical improbable delightful props, and many-handed machinery (Rube Goldberg inspired, no doubt), not to mention Thing 1 and Thing 2. In a 'carnivalesque orientation', as Kevin Shortsleeve remarks on Seuss books in general, Thing 1 and Thing 2 take to 'celebrating the topsy-turvy, the grotesque, festivity, and the travesty of authority' (2011, 197). The genre here is comedy. The Cat in the Hat took the world apart (as children and as pets may do), and then put the former world back together.

> 'Have no fear of this mess'
> Said the Cat in the Hat.
> 'I always pick up all my playthings
> And so …
> I will show you another
> Good trick that I know!'
> Then we saw him pick up
> All the things that were down.
> He picked up the cake,
> And the rake, and the gown,
> And the milk, and the strings,
> And the books, and the dish,
> And the fan, and the cup,
> And the ship, and the fish.
> And he put them away.
> Then he said, 'That is that'.
> And then he was gone
> With a tip of his hat.
> (57–58)

Scholars interpret *The Cat in the Hat*'s commitment to order in the end in different ways. The 'flouting' of parental or authority figures, such as the absent Mother, is the source of anxiety and chaos, as noted by Ruth K. MacDonald (1988), Rita Roth (1989), and Philip Nel (2007b). The historical relevance to the Cold War period and the politics of democratic imagination in *The Cat in the Hat* are further pursued by Richard H. Minear (2001), Henry Jenkins (2002), Philip Nel (2007a), and Kevin Shortsleeve (2011). Through the lens of carnival as a site of resistance, it is possible that the Cat's disruption of domestic order is a reaction against 'the vision of conformist, status-symbol-loving, humdrum suburbia' (Shortsleeve 198). We regard the Cat's capacity to restore the order when the fun is over as emblematic of the bond of trust between parents and children. After the secret madness of imagination, there remains the world that was, but which can never be the same again. The ending question is open and interactive, 'What would you do if your mother asked you?' It leaves us with multiple possibilities – of interpreting the Cat as a 'powerful satanic force in an orgy of joyful self-gratification that will ultimately lead to empty despair' (Mensch and Freeman 117), or as a practical cat both from the point of view of entertaining children and his capacity of cleaning up after his carnival.

The comedy here is of the survival of the domestic order in which children are to grow, from which children are to learn. How human and how cat is this creature? We might say that the allegory turns on the dual character of the story's star. Order is the human side, the unpredictable chaos-making aspect is the other-than-human side, but also the affinity with the other-than-adult side.

This is well-wrought fun that resists being thought too much on, but that nevertheless leads you to take a second look at persons and places and things you might have thought you knew.

The Cat as Cat

Nonsensical animals, animals spouting nonsense, conversations with impossible interlocutors, cross-dressing as others we cannot be – all of these apparently impractical circumstances (these exercises of the imagination), while carrying certain reifying dangers, also allow rethinking of facts of life, of how the world must be, and of relationships taken for granted. Who are we when – like Dr Dolittle – we speak with the animals? Who are we when we remember we cannot? In various related ways, the poems with which this chapter deals originate in doubts of an ontological/epistemological kind, as expressed by Denise Levertov in 'The Cat as Cat' (1962/2002) we now investigate to conclude this chapter.

Denise Levertov's poetry could be categorised as what Muriel *Rukeyser and Carolyn Forché* call 'poetry of witness' (their echoing Jacques Derrida's suggestion that the poem bears witness 'in the manner of an ethical or political act' [*Gift* 35])[1]. Inspiring awe from all presences of life and its attendant myths, pains, and pleasures, Levertov's poems articulate an ethical voice, a voice that speaks to bond with the Earth. The poem 'Come into Animal Presence' (2002, 19) is both an imperative and an invitation to the world of the other-than-human animal, conducted by way of a carefully chosen bestiary (serpent, rabbit, llama, and armadillo). This poem applies a human characteristic (guileless, lonely, disdainful, insouciant) to each of these animals. It pictures an animal world that is independent of 'human approval', existing as its own dignified and innocent entity. There is a powerful appeal in this work to the wild and to lost instinct, as states or conditions to which human animals should be able to relate. The poem is aware of and at play with the contradictions implied in the effort to present the animal point of view. Brought into the animal presence, readers are first asked to abandon the most clichéd of anthropomorphic/anthropocentric animal stereotypes ('No man is so guileless as/the serpent'). It is easy to propose that kind of ideological program but the poem knows that language is both the means and the limit of understanding, of serpents and rabbits and llamas. And it is human understanding with which the poem primarily deals. So that when 'disdain' is attributed to the llama, that disdain stands, like guile, for the whole range of human emotion and attitude with which the animal world is burdened by human understanding.

By means of an understanding language at least mediates, humans, when in Levertov's animal presence, nevertheless approach something beyond words: 'Those who were sacred have remained so,/holiness does not dissolve, it is a presence'. The apparent contradiction here is that, while 'sanctity' and 'holy presence' are human point-of-view abstractions, they are values of a life and being in which humans participate to the extent that they remember their animality, to the extent, that is, that they forget the words that have brought them to this understanding. Abstraction is the key to the contradictions inherent in the human – poetic – effort to understand the other-than-human animal other:

> What is this joy? That no animal
> falters, but knows what it must do?
> That the snake has no blemish,
> that the rabbit inspects his strange surroundings
> in white star-silence?
> (Levertov 2002, 19)

In the case of Levertov's animal joy and presence, the encounter in the place where names may not be spoken is not at all wordless; our only knowledge of it is through the narrative description and through the words reported to us as spoken. It is the sense though of what cannot be spoken that suggests something akin to Levertov's 'sanctity' and 'holy presence' – these are felt in the communion we, as readers, experience in this encountering. Lester Embree in his restatement of Edmund Husserl's 'constitutive phenomenology' emphasises the importance of 'valuing and willing (and objects as valuationally and volitionally encountered)' over that of cognitive encountering (2003, 38). The valuational encounter as a new mode of ecophenomenology can elicit 'enjoyment' that facilitates the appreciation of and respect for the environment authentically engaged. Likewise, the suggestion in this poem is that the encounter with unlanguaged others would be enlightening to human participants ('An old Joy returns in holy presence'). This is not only joy of the animal as known to the human, but also joy of the human that knows its animality.

The space of encountering, reminiscent of what Donna Haraway has termed a 'contact zone' (2008), need not be hierarchically bound. Haraway comments on inter-species relationships, that 'figures help me grapple inside the flesh of mortal world-making entanglements' (2003, 4). Within such Harawayian contact zones, all possible 'others, human cells and not' should be brought into networks of symbiotic interaction and 'subject-and object-shaping dance of encounters' (2008, 4). In the 'contact zone', Haraway hopes for 'current interactions' to change 'interactions to follow' and then to alter probabilities and to morph topologies (2008, 219). What is at stake in the Harawayian contact zone is the finding of techniques to nurture togetherness that allow for differences and connections. In a similar vein, when Levertov extends her cordial invitation to the animal presence, a vision of the dialogic and valued encounter is anthropomorphically enacted, and this allows for a flow of affect we know to be human. Reckoning with the limits of language and human perspectives then gives certain freedom, despite its inevitable constraint, to anthropomorphic writing. The fact that language is ultimately employed to name and interrogate what cannot be named puts us at the intersection of obscured reality and heightened perception. Animals as represented and aptly named through a human lens are inevitably more reified than real. For the similar reason to defy the conventional rhetoric between animality and language, Lippit coins the term "animetaphor", a living metaphor made flesh, which is by definition not a metaphor (2000, 165), but "a trope of animality that is itself profoundly anti-metaphoric" (2002, 10). Suggested is that animals are good to think not because they are "like" us, but because they are also with us everywhere, either directly or not, so that we are embodied into each other at the liminal encounter. Therefore, limits of animal representation cannot be dissolved or resolved in human language, but only blurred and recalibrated through degrees of consciousness, as these occur in moments of encounter.

In her poem 'The Cat as Cat', Levertov problematises the means of representing the cat, as necessarily rhetorical. The persona considers the cat on her bosom, in a way that reminds us of Derrida, as mentioned in Chapter 1, catching the gaze of his cat following him after he comes out of the bathroom naked. 'As with every bottomless gaze', Derrida writes, 'as with the eyes of the other, the gaze called "animal" offers to my sight the abyssal limit of the human' (12). Seeing the contact by eye is a means to resist the rule of the language, as the real and the symbolic, the inner and the outer, the surface and the depths, the luminous and the dark are all dissolved in an enthralling gaze. Derrida's reflection on his cat's seeing him naked brings out his feelings of fascination and fears for the animal encounter and suggests the representation of real animals in particular should go beyond textual understanding. Mysterious resonances between humans and other animals complicate his ruminations on the limits of language and symbolic responsibility for a cat: the philosopher's cat, the poet's cat, or the cat as it is? Levertov's cat is likewise a multiple entity, one rhetorically invested, requiring interpretation as if a work or a fact of nature, but ultimately begging the question of volitional dialogue.

> The cat on my bosom
> Sleeping and purring
> – fur-petalled chrysanthemum,
> squirrel-killer –

> is a metaphor only if I
> force him to be one,
> looking too long in his pale, fond,
> dilating, contracting eyes
>
> that reject mirrors, refuse
> To observe what bides
> stockstill.
> Likewise
>
> flex and reflex of claws
> gently pricking through sweater to skin
> gently sustains their own tune,
> not mine. I-Thou, cat, I- Thou.
>   (51–52)

Does the persona make the cat a metaphor? Is the cat a 'squirrel-killer' or a metaphor? Or both? The character of the communication is verified through the noting of eye contact, of 'looking too long in his pale, fond, / dilating, contracting eyes'. Does dialogue demand language? Other forms of reciprocity and communion are in play here. In 'The Cat as Cat', it is as if the cat's silence on existential questions calls into question the possibility of being a cat's interlocutor, simply because the primacy of the facial encounter here suggests there ought to be a dialogue.

It is the eyes of the cat that reject mirrors. The poem entails both a refusal of those human characteristics we know as reflection or as consciousness, but also a reversal of the arrested image, of hypostasisation – a refusal 'to observe what bides/stockstill'. The cat is a subjectivity interested and invested in movement, change, and a world of becoming. The unavoidable anthropomorphism of a cat's treatment in a poem raises the question of a prosopopoeia: am I the person looking at the cat, or am I now a cat, rejecting the human gaze? Potential for ventriloquism here reminds us of Montaigne's suspicion that 'When I play with my cat, who knows whether she is not making me her pastime more than I make her mine' and further back Descartes' deceiving demon in the *Meditations* (159). Likewise Haraway's cross-species contact zone evokes a respectful access into what her dog thinks. These instances evince a history of speculation – of hope and doubt and of fear – about the possibilities for reciprocity (whether we think of it as dialogic or not) between humans and their un-languaged others.

Nor is there anything peculiarly Western or modern about this kind of speculation. Witnessing all creatures as a classic expression of the embodiment of Dao is reflected in a dialogue of Zhuangzi.

> The earl of the He said, 'Whether the subject be what is external in things, or what is internal, how do we come to make a distinction between them as noble and mean, and as great or small?' Ruo of the

Northern Sea replied, 'When we look at them in the light of the Dao, they are neither noble nor mean' (Zhuangzi, 'The Floods of Autumn').

The hierarchy of all living beings is not explicitly endorsed in Zhuangzi's Daoism. Instead, the freedom and wildness for animal flourishing are valued, whether human or nonhuman. Zhuangzi's appreciation of a fish's joy in the river[2] and his mediation on his dream, revealing that 'I did not know whether it had formerly been Zhou dreaming that he was a butterfly, or it was now a butterfly dreaming that it was Zhou' have been best known anecdotes in classical Chinese philosophy (Zhuangzi, 'The Adjustment of Controversies'). Sax makes the following claim for human–animal relations,

> No animal completely lacks humanity, yet no person is ever completely human. By ourselves, we people are simply balls of protoplasm. We merge with animals through magic, metaphor, or fantasy, growing their fangs and putting on their feathers (2001, XX).

In Levertov's poem, it is a wordless but experiential encounter that suggests dialogic possibilities beyond the pale of language, in which alterity and encountering are equally at stake. As Michael Holquist writes, 'the very capacity to have consciousness is based on *other*ness' (2002, 17). The attention to otherness recreates not a site for alienation but a means to incite participatory engagement. Absorbed into possible space proliferated under the gaze, the persona gradually gains representational awareness that the cat and cat's claws sustain 'their own tune, not mine'. This poem, further modelling the possibility of dialogue through the ironically wordless space of the human–animal encounter, provides a practical instance of our Levinasian leitmotiv dictum – 'The absolutely foreign alone can instruct us' (73). Levinas proposes that through the face of 'alterity' epiphany can be achieved. Respect for the absolute 'other' and imagination of its sensate experience activate the prospect of an infinite neighbouring between human and non-humans. For Levinas, 'The Other precisely reveals himself in his alterity, not in a shock negating the I, but as the primordial phenomenon of gentleness' (150). So Levinas insists on meeting alterity as essential to subject constitution and his ethical philosophy of hospitality. Levertov's last line in this poem revisits the paradox of animality–humanity that persists in human/animal relationships. The subject pairing 'I-Thou, cat, I-Thou' raises a question about how to achieve equity in human/animal relationships. Levertov echoes a proposition of maintaining human relations with the world with the 'I-Thou' attitude, again endorsing a 'subject-to-subject' gaze, one we might place within Harawayian contact zone, a 'naturecultural' spot to meet with companion species and think with those 'significant' others. As Temple Cone argues, Levertov's poems enter into 'I-Thou' relations in a way that acknowledges 'the *presentness* of the other' and a continuum of responsibility (2014, 126). Unlike the 'I-It' relation that objectifies and treats the world with utilitarian morality, the 'I-Thou' relation values reciprocity and intersubjectivity, a merging of experience with animal-as-subject.

Both 'The Cat as Cat' and 'Come into Animal Presence' enact a necessarily frustrated yearning to recover, through words, the haecceity of animals as simply, and wordlessly, being themselves. Acts of reflection are not for the cat, and we, the readers, are stuck in the loop of knowing the situation from the words that paint the picture on which we are to reflect on the reflecting of the human persona. The cat rejects not one but a whole hall of mirrors, and all, of course, because we say so. Beyond the unknowable catness of the cat, we are left with a likewise unanswerable question about subjectivity and the relatedness of 'I' to the other 'Thou'. All that remains to us is to approach the meaning of this encounter in the manner of witness, as Forché puts it: 'the poem makes present to us the experience of the other, the poem *is* the experience ... a living archive' (2014, 26). Poetry creates a naturally dialogic space for the human–animal encounter, which enables the meeting of creatures on common ground. All these seemingly anthropomorphic efforts, however, endow the contact with others with an ethical and philosophical status.

From our point of view, Levertov's is probably the most practical of the cats we have met in this chapter. Personable as the others have been, Levertov's has the virtue of being, more than the others, her own cat – more of an absolute other, who might, by virtue of this absolute otherness, be able to instruct us.

Through poetry, we investigate our differences from and affinities with animal others, and draw the investigation on towards (and beyond) the point of absurdity not simply because we do not know how and whether and to what extent we and they are alike, but because fundamentally humans are animals who know that they are animals, and that animal nature is endlessly fascinating for the human mind. Indulging this fascination is a way of learning about ourselves and the world we so recklessly inhabit at times, the world for which our care is urgently required.

Notes

1. One notes that there are foreigners as such in the text, for instance the Peke 'is no British Dog, but a Heathen Chinese' (33) and of course there are many foreign-sounding names for cats.
2. In this parable from the 'Autumn Water', Zhuangzi and Huizi were strolling along the bridge over the Hao River. Zhuangzi said, 'the minnows swim about so freely, following the openings wherever they take them. Such is the happiness of fish'. Huizi said, 'You are not a fish, so whence do you know the happiness of fish'? Zhuangzi said, 'You are not I, so whence do you know I don't know the happiness of fish'? This conversation about the human capabilities of knowing 'happiness of fish' becomes one of the most famous stories that reflect Zhuangzi's Daoist views.

References

Althusser, Louis. *Lenin and Philosophy and Other Essays*. Trans. Ben Brewster. London: New Left Books, 1971.

Anderson, Celia Catlett, and Marilyn Fain Apseloff. *Nonsense Literature for Children: Aesop to Seuss*. Hamden (Conn.): Library Professional Publications, 1989.

Bakhtin, Mikhail. *Problems of Dostoevsky's Poetics*. Ed. & trans. by C. Emerson. Minneapolis: University of Minnesota Press, 1984.

Barai, Aneesh. "'They Were Incurably Given to Rove': T.S. Eliot's Practical Cats, London and the Petit Flâneur". *The Literary London Journal*, 14(2) (Autumn 2017): 1–15.

Bettelheim, Bruno. "The Struggle for Meaning". *Folk and Fairy Tales* (4th ed.). Eds. Martin Hallett and Barbara Karasek. Sydney: Broadview Press, 2008.

Blake, Quentin. Ed. *The Quentin Blake Book of Nonsense Verse*. Cochin: Viking, 1994.

Brown, Laura. *Homeless Dogs and Melancholy Apes: Humans and Other Animals in the Modern Literary Imagination*. Ithaca: Cornell University Press, 2010.

Campbell, Jeanne and John Reesman. "Creatures of 'Charm': A New T. S. Eliot Poem". *The Kenyon Review* 6(3) (1984): 25–33.

Cone, Temple. "Hasidim in Poetry: Dialogical Poetics of Encounter in Denise Levertov's the Jacob's Ladder". *Poetry and Dialogism: Hearing Over*. Eds. Mara Scanlon and Chad Engbers. Basingstoke: Palgrave Macmillan, 2014. 123–139.

Culler, Jonathan D. *Literary Theory*. New York: Sterling, 2009.

Deleuze, Gilles. *The Logic of Sense*. Trans. Mark Lester and Charles Stivale. London: The Athlone Press, 1990.

Derrida, Jacques. *The Animal That Therefore I Am*. New York: Fordham University Press, 2008.

Douglass, Paul. "Eliot's Cats: Serious Play behind the Playful Seriousness". *Children's Literature* 11(1) (1983): 109–124.

Eliot, T.S. *Collected Poems 1909–1962*. New York: Harcourt, Brace& World, Inc., 1963.

Eliot, T.S. *Old Possum's Book of Practical Cats*. 1939. Illustrated. Axel Scheffler. New York: Houghton Mifflin Harcourt, 2009.

Embree, Lester. "The Possibility of a Constitutive Phenomenology of the Environment". *Eco-phenomenology: Back to the Earth Itself*. Eds. Charles S. Brown and Ted Toadvine. Albany: State U of New York P, 2003. 37–50.

Forché, Carolyn. "Reading the Living Archives: The Witness of Literary Art". *Poetry of Witness: The Tradition in English, 1500–2001*. Eds. Carolyn Forche and Duncan Wu. New York: Norton, 2014. 17–26.

Guthrie, Stewart E. "Anthropomorphism: A Definition and a Theory". *Anthropomorphism, Anecdotes, and Animals*. Eds. Robert. W. Mitchell, Nicholas S. Thompson & H. Lyn Miles. Albany: State University of New York, 1997. 50–58.

Haraway, Donna. *The Companion Species Manifesto: Dogs, People, and Significant Otherness*. Vol. 1. Chicago: Prickly Paradigm Press, 2003.

Haraway, Donna. *When Species Meet*. Minneapolis: University of Minnesota, 2008.

Henry, Hart. "T. S. Eliot's Autobiographical Cats". *The Sewanee Review* 3 (2012): 402.
Holquist, Michael. *Dialogism: Bakhtin and His World*. New York: Routledge, 2002.
Howe, Nicholas. "Fabling Beasts: Traces in Memory". *Social Research* 62(3) (1995): 641–659.
Ireson, Barbara. Ed. *The Faber Book of Nursery Rhymes*. London: Faber, 1958/1983.
Jenkins, Henry. "'No Matter How Small': The Democratic Imagination of Dr. Seuss". *Hop on Pop: The Politics and Pleasures of Popular Culture* (2002): 187–208.
Larios, Julie and Julie Paschkis. *Imaginary Menagerie: A Book of Curious Creatures*. New York: Harcourt Children's Books, 2008.
Lear, Edward. *A Book of Learned Nonsense*. London: Alan Sutton, 1992.
Lecercle, Jean-Jacques. *Philosophy of Nonsense: The Intuitions of Victorian Nonsense Literature*. New York: Routledge, 2012.
Le Guin, Ursula K. *Lecture. May Hill Arbuthnot Lecture Series*. May Hill Arbuthnot Lecture Series, Tempe Arizona, 2004.
Lesnik-Oberstein, Karín. "Defining Children's Literature and Childhood". *International Companion Encyclopaedia of Children's Literature*. Ed. Peter Hunt. New York: Routledge, 1996, 17–31.
Levertov, Denise. *Selected Poems*. New York: New Directions, 2002.
Lippit, Akira Mizuta. "The Death of an Animal". *Film Quarterly* 56(1) (2002): 9–22.
Lippit, Akira Mizuta. *Electric Animal: Toward a Rhetoric of Wildlife*. Minneapolis: University of Minnesota, 2000.
MacDonald, Ruth K. *Dr. Seuss*. Vol. 544. Woodbridge: Twayne Pub, 1988.
Marquis, Don. "Certain Maxims of Archy", *Archy and Mehitabel*, 1927. http://donmarquis.com/home/2011/10/26/certain-maxims-of-archy/, accessed on 8 January 2021.
Marquis, Don. "Mehitabel was Once Cleopatra", *The Life and Times of Archy and Mehitabel*, 1927. https://poetrykeeps.uk/2-mehitabel-was-once-cleopatra/, accessed on 8 January 2021.
Marquis, Don. "Pity the Poor Spiders", *Archy and Mehitabel*, 1927. http://donmarquis.com/home/2011/10/25/pity-the-poor-spiders/, accessed on 8 January 2021.
Marquis, Don. *Archy's Life of Mehitabel*. Garden City, N.Y.: Dolphin Books, 1933.
Marquis, Don. *Archy Does his Part*. New Yor: Doubleday, 1935.
Marquis, Don. *The Annotated Archy and Mehitabel*. Ed. Michael Sims. New York: Penguin, 2006.
Marquis, Don. *The Best of Archy and Mehitabel*. London: Everyman's Library, 2011.
Mathers, Powys. Trans. *The Book of the Thousand Nights and One Night*. London: Routledge, 2004.
McClelland, Norman C. *Encyclopedia of Reincarnation and Karma*. Jefferson, NC: McFarland, 2010.
McGillis, Roderick. "Nonsense". *A Companion to Victorian Poetry*. Eds. Richard Cronin, Alison Chapman, and Anthony H. Harrison. Oxford: Blackwell Publishers, 2002. 155–170.

Meeker, Joseph W. *The Comedy of Survival: Literary Ecology and a Play Ethic*. Tucson, AZ: University of Arizona, 1997.
Menninghaus, Winfried. *In Praise of Nonsense: Kant and Bluebeard*. Stanford, CA: Stanford University Press, 1999.
Mensch, Betty, and Alan Freeman. "Getting to Solla Sollew: The Existential Politics of Dr. Seuss". *Tikkun* 31(3) (2016): 34–35.
Minear, Richard H. *Dr. Seuss Goes to War: The World War II Editorial Cartoons of Theodor Seuss Geisel*. New York: New Press, 2001.
Morgenstern, Christian. (1895). "The Nasobame". Wikipedia. https://en.wikipedia.org/wiki/The_Nasobame accessed on 25 March 2021.
Nabergoj, Irena Avsenik. *Reality and Truth in Literature: From Ancient to Modern European Literary and Critical Discourse*. Göttingen: Vandenhoeck & Ruprecht, 2013.
Natov, Roni. *Poetics of Childhood*. New York: Routledge, 2003.
Nel, Philip. "Children's Literature Goes to War: Dr. Seuss, PD Eastman, Munro Leaf, and the Private SNAFU Films (1943–46)". *The Journal of Popular Culture* 40(3) (2007a): 468–487.
Nel, Philip. *The Annotated Cat: Under the Hats of Seuss and His Cats*. New York: Random House Books for Young Readers, 2007b.
Nikolajeva, Maria. *Reading for Learning: Cognitive Approaches to Children's Literature*. Vol. 3. Amsterdam: John Benjamins Publishing Company, 2014.
Rose, Jacqueline. *The Case of Peter Pan, Or, The Impossibility of Children's Fiction*. London: Macmillan, 1984.
Roth, Rita. "On Beyond Zebra with Dr. Seuss". *New Advocate* 2(4) (1989): 213–225.
Rule, Stacy. "Animal Meaning in T. S. Eliot's Old Possum's Book of Practical Cats". *Making Animal Meaning*. East Lansing: Michigan State University Press, 2011. 145–160.
Ruskin, John. 1918. William Roe Frederick Ed. *Selections and Essays*. Chicago: C. Scribner's Sons, 2013.
Sax, Boria. *The Mythical Zoo: An Encyclopedia of Animals in World Myth, Legend, and Literature*. Santa Barbara, CA: ABC-CLIO, 2001.
Sax, Boria. *Imaginary Animals: The Monstrous, the Wondrous and the Human*. London: Reaktion Books, 2013.
Seuss, Dr. (1957). *The Cat in the Hat*. Boston: Random House, 2007.
Sewell, Elizabeth. "Lewis Carroll and T. S. Eliot as Nonsense Poets". *T.S. Eliot: A Collection of Critical Essays*. New Jersey: Prentice-Hall, Inc., 1962. 65–72.
Sewell, Elizabeth. (1952). *The Field of Nonsense*. London: Dalkey Archive Press, 2015.
Shepard, Paul. *The Others: How Animals Made Us Human*. Washington, DC: Island, 1997. Print.
Shortsleeve, Kevin. "The Cat in the Hippie: Dr. Seuss, Nonsense, the Carnivalesque, and The Sixties Rebel". *The Oxford Handbook of Children's Literature*. Oxford: Oxford University Press, 2011. 189–209.
Smith, Philip. Ed. *Favorite Poems of Childhood*. New York: Dover Publications, 1992.
Stephens, John. *Language and Ideology in Children's Literature*. London: Longman, 1992.
Stewart, Susan. *Nonsense: Aspects of Intertextuality in Folklore and Literature*. Baltimore and London: The Johns Hopkins University Press, 1989.

Tan, Shaun. "The Lost Thing" (2000). *Lost & Found*. New York: Arthur A. Levine, 2011.

Tatar, Maria. "The Story of the Three Bears". *The Annotated Classic Fairy Tales*. New York: W.W. Norton & Company, 2002.

Tigges, Wim. *An Anatomy of Literary Nonsense*. Amsterdam: Rodopi B.V., 1988.

Tinsley, Molly Best. "T. S. Eliot's Book of Practical Cats". *Studies in American Humor* 1(3) (1975): 167–171.

Wells, Paul. *The Animated Bestiary: Animals, Cartoons, and Culture*. New Brunswick, NJ: Rutgers University Press, 2009.

Willard, Nancy. "A Lively Last Word on Nonsense". Eds. Anderson, Celia Catlett and Marilyn, Apseloff. *Nonsense Literature for Children: Aesop to Seuss*. Hamden, Conn.: Library Professional Publishings, 1989.

Wu, Faye-Lynn. *Chinese and English Nursery Rhymes: Share and Sing in Two Languages*. Tokyo: TUTTLE Publishing, 2010.

Zhuangzi. "The Adjustment of Controversies". Trans. James Legge. https://ctext.org/zhuangzi/adjustment-of-controversies, accessed on 2 July 2021.

Zhuangzi. "The Floods of Autumn". Trans. James Legge. https://ctext.org/zhuangzi/floods-of-autumn, accessed on 29 May 2020.

Zipes, Jack. *Fairy Tales and the Art of Subversion: The Classical Genre for Children and the Process of Civilization*. New York: Wildman Press, 1983.

Zipes, Jack. *Breaking the Magic Spell – Radical Theories of Folk and Fairy Tales*. Lexington, Kentucky: University Press of Kentucky, 2002.

3 The Little Dog Laughed to See Such Sport

The Childish Appeal of Humanimal Ambivalences

We are concerned in this chapter principally with nursery rhymes. Not so much interested in their provenance or histories as in the currency and effects they have had and have on what we think of as childhood today, we are interested in the roles and relationships nursery rhymes propose for popular culture and for everyday speech more generally. We focus on the roles and relationships that these canonic (print-assisted) survivors of oral tradition propose for animals. It is in nursery rhymes many of us first encounter anthropomorphised animals. Coming from the era before the advent of children's literature, nursery rhymes are, though often thought to be full of hidden meanings, nevertheless a model for texts with a joint child–adult readership – as evidenced in the much-argued allegorical content of many nursery rhymes. Our interest in this chapter is in the manner in which knowledge and dissemination of nursery rhymes via parents and other adults connect those parent figures and the children in their care with a putative 'traditional knowledge' and so a popular wisdom about various aspects of life and society, as may be the case with proverbs and aphorisms more generally.

Themes for analysis include the implication of the unknowability of animals, parameters of non/human identity, nature–culture conflicts, eco-phobia, and the celebration of human kindness/unkindness towards animals. In particular, we note that nursery rhymes, as selected from Iona Opie and Peter Opie's *The Oxford Dictionary of Nursery Rhymes* (1997), embrace the aesthetics and ethics of human–animal interaction in various manifestations of anthropomorphic nonsense and humanimal ambivalence. We are interested in the source of these ambivalences, and whether these involve relationships between adults and children, between humans and other-than-human animals. The chapter examines, at the more abstract level, what nursery rhymes may tell us about attitudes towards nature and culture, and their relationship.

Some animal characters are portrayed outsmarting their predators, as in 'Six Little mice sat down to spin' (*Dictionary*, 306) or 'A carrion crow sat on an oak' (*Dictionary*, 111). These texts suggest different degrees of sympathy and empathy. Human and animal identities are integrated through nonsense and play in what we might consider textual sports,

DOI: 10.4324/9781003219330-4

of innocence and of extravagance, intended at least in part for a young readership. Nursery rhymes, as an originary crossover genre, generate ambivalences for the child. If nursery rhymes are acknowledged as 'survivals of an adult code of joviality' (*Dictionary*, 3), do these poems that pass to children with adults' approval also generate ambivalence for the adult? Or is it the case that being cast in the role of the knowing one typically deprives the adult of such doubts?

Nursery Rhymes and Nonsense

There would appear to be no entity or idea immune to anthropomorphism. Nursery rhymes provide us with a convenient proof of the efficacy of this proposition, across all ages. Among the collections of nursery rhymes, there are instruction songs, riddles, counting verses, alphabets, lullabies, finger games, ballads, more verse, tongue-twisters, jokes, and more. And in all of these anthropomorphic animals there is a common and commonly nonsensical presence. Take one of the best-known nursery rhymes of all time:

> Hey diddle diddle,
> The cat and the fiddle.
> The cow jumped over the moon
> The little dog laughed
> To see such sport,
> And the dish ran away with the spoon.
> (*Dictionary*, 240)

Many nursery rhymes are, as we see in the case of this specimen, just plain silly – with music from nowhere and for no reason, with jumping animals, improbable distances, laughter, and lots of anthropomorphism. Here, even, the inanimate objects of the kitchen are brought to life, foreshadowing much anthropomorphic nonsense to come (for instance in Lewis Carroll's *Through the Looking-Glass*). Despite its mysterious origin and allegorical possibilities (Foster 2008; Jack 2008), readers of 'Hey Diddle Diddle' are more likely to embrace Sir Henry Reid's joking exegesis that the rhyme 'commemorates the athletic lunacy to which the strange conspiracy of the cat and the fiddle incited the cow' (cited in *Dictionary*, 241).

More seriously though, we can read the fun of this nonsense rhyme as effecting a subversion of an 'animacy hierarchy' (Human > Animal > Inanimate) that is inherent in our conventional repertoire of perception. As Emile Cammaerts puts it in *The Poetry of Nonsense*, 'nonsense steps in gradually, first through the animal story, then through the confusion of all classes and values, finally through the creation of such wild images that they defy all classification' (1925, 25). Such subversion serves no explicit didactic purposes, but is best thought a delightful rendering of topsy-turvydom, purposed to defy the established norms and the attendant rigorous conceptions. As John Goldthwaite puts it, 'Nonsense might be defined more accurately as a flirtation with disorder, a turning upside down of the world for the pleasure of seeing it come right side up again' (1996, 15).

The subversion is also linguistic. The grammatical conceptualization of an animacy hierarchy assigns objects, animals, substances, and spaces within constrained zones of possibility. In this rhyme, the conventional anthropocentric arrangements with regard to agency are transgressed. 'Hey Diddle Diddle' is, on this reading, a carnival play that subverts the bio-category by rejecting 'the cognitive element of truth for the falsehood of exaggerated, because over-imaginative, fiction, its difference from mere wit, are all present, only under a moral cloud' (Lecercle, 181). The transgression of the normal order of things comes with a combination of triviality and fun: the intimate and the cosmic, the near and the far are thrown together in this poem in ways that will not make sense, and yet are seen (in the mind's eye) and so, in a sense, believed. 'The animacy of the non-human world', as per Dominik Ohrem's idea of 'creaturely life', is 'not so much in the somewhat clichéd image of an "observer" or "listener" but by way of an imaginative–affective investment that allows us to render visible the many resonances between and the mutual inter-penetration of human and nonhuman worlds and ways of being' (2017, 10–11). A wide assortment of creatures, given humorous characteristics, appears in nonsense and enter children's lives.

In view of the long-standing bond between nonsense and nursery rhymes, therefore, Hildebrandt classifies the nursery rhyme as an early type of nonsense under the heading of 'Volks-Nonsense' (cited in Tigges 1988, 100), while Carolyn Wells in her nonsense anthology excludes it due to the specific instructive purposes of most nursery rhymes – purposes including literacy, counting, lulling children to sleep – purposes that are other than to present 'nonsense for nonsense sake' (1903, XXII). Different opinions on what is supposedly classified as 'pure' nonsense continue to trickle in the aggregate of nonsense definitions, as in Elizabeth Sewell (1952), Wim Tigges (1988), Susan Stuart (1989), Jean-Jacques Lecercle (1994), and Noel Malcolm (1997).

Despite the fact that many nursery rhymes are relics of meaningful, historical, and allegorical texts, in this chapter, we focus on the nonsensical aspect of nursery rhymes, rhymes that have reached and remained in the nursery after countless retellings. Although nonsense, as we know it, is widely thought to be a British invention, popularised by Lewis Carroll and Edward Lear, its origins in English literature can be traced to the beginning of the seventeenth century, with the work of poets such as Sir John Hoskyns and John Taylor, and even earlier in Geoffrey Chaucer and Shakespeare's oeuvre (Malcolm 1997). The genre finds roots in ancient Greek comedy (Kidd 2014). In tracing the ontogeny of nonsense, broad artistic sources, such as parody (Malcolm 1997, 52–53), the absurd

(Cornwell 2006, 18–19), and the grotesque in Bakhtin's sense (Heyman and Shortsleeve 2011, 35), appear as its close intellectual relations, sometimes offering confusion as to what nonsense is and how is it distinct from these adjacent terms. As a genre, literary nonsense depends on some of the above elements in creating what Lecercle calls 'the dialectic of excess and lack', or there is Tigges' nonsense that 'balances a multiplicity of meaning with a simultaneous absence of meaning' (47). The tension and contradiction between meaning and lack of meaning in an item of nonsense, at the level of semantics, syntax, phonology, context, and representation, engender the odd pleasures. Such pleasures, stemming from reversal and misappropriation of sensible and logical conventions, are of course reader contingent. Michael Heyman reminds us that 'the difference between an educated adult reading and a child reading' is also important in determining whether the 'indeterminacy and multiplicity of meaning' in a text can be well understood (1999, 188). '[T]he pleasure of children', as he further argues against Lecercle's linguistic approach to nonsense's pedagogical scheme of language instruction, 'comes from a reading that avoids symbolic or structural analysis' (188).

Here we recall that Edward Lear, whose nonsense poems are considered as typical incarnations of nonsense poetry and avatars of nursery rhymes, believed that it is 'a *sine quâ non* in writing for children to keep what they have to read perfectly clear & bright, & incapable of any meaning but one of sheer nonsense' (Andersen 1950; Lear 1988, 228; McGillis 2002). In so writing, Lear abandons any of the educational and instructional pretensions of the children's poetry that immediately preceded his. Instead, his writing credo bespeaks the need to take in sound for its own sake, in the anarchical potential of linguistic play, which in itself is illustrative of the nineteenth-century paradigm shift from didacticism to delight. Lewis Carroll's nonsense poems, so often parodic of established nursery rhymes, endorse this change.

While a knowledge of the historical origins of nursery rhymes informs seasoned readers of implications and allusions, it is the play with sound and harmless incongruities that brings joy to novice readers whose ears are mostly sensitive to rhyme and rhythm. At the nascent stage of language development, babbling, repetition, playing with spontaneously created sounds, and onomatopoeia constitute a young child's linguistic repertoire. To augment such sound effects in the form of nonsense is to share the enjoyment with an essentially oral-culture audience. In her monograph *From Tongue to Text: A New Reading of Children's Poetry*, Debbie Pullinger argues that the typologies of nursery rhymes subsume two categories, these being 'rhymes that dull consciousness and calm the body-in other words, lullabies; and rhymes that heighten consciousness and stimulate the body – that is, action rhymes' (2017, 134). The corporeal effect evoked by rhymes is integral to the orality and literacy that children can acquire through poetry. The ingenuity of rhyme that characterises Lear's and Carroll's poems is a case in point, contributing to its enduring appeal among young audiences. On the other hand, the romantic image of the child reader as inventive, playful, and anarchic seems well manifest in nonsense-type nursery rhymes.

For the growing child, for the child coming into culture, the world is in so many ways, yet to make sense. For the thinking adult, capable of critique, broad experience of the world suggests that the world is, in so many ways, yet to make sense. An optimistic adult may hope that sense will come one day, a pessimist may despair of this possibility ever being realised. What better way to test what works in the sense of being sensible, what better way to test what *can* make sense, than by producing and by entertaining the opposite of sense? To make nonsense is a way to find the boundaries of what is sensible, true, and possible. And it is fun.

The Anthropomorphism of an Abstraction

Nursery rhymes frequently feature anthropomorphic relations between humans and animals, likewise between animate and inanimate entities.

> There were two birds sat on a stone,
> One flew away and then there was one,
> The other flew after, and then there was none,
> And so the poor stone was left all alone,
> (*Dictionary*, 97)

The anthropomorphic element here is the stone – made an object of pity for lacking the company of the birds. The bringing of objects to life may introduce allegorical content, sometimes of a profound kind, as in William Blake's 'The Clod and the Pebble'.

> Love seeketh not itself to please,
> Nor for itself hath any care,
> But for another gives its ease,
> And builds a heaven in hell's despair.
>
> So sung a little clod of clay,
> Trodden with the cattle's feet;
> But a pebble of the brook
> Warbled out these meters meet:
>
> Love seeketh only Self to please,
> To bind another to its delight,
> Joys in another's loss of ease,
> And builds a hell in heaven's despite.
> (2002, 66–67)

In Shaun Tan's 'The Lost Thing' we saw how the depiction of an unknown entity might be engaging for the imagination of child and/or adult. It is difficult to say whether the lost thing of Shaun Tan's book is plant or animal or machine, whether it is sea creature or alien, or what hybrid of these it might be. A gliding and ambulant signifier, the lost thing is suggestive of all sorts of allegorical possibilities, and, as such, it allows us to consider the position of the foreigner or migrant in a new place; it allows us to consider the position of the different or other one in a place that takes itself for granted. *The Lost Thing* aids us in considering the relevance of Levinas' proposition that 'only the absolutely other can instruct us'. Can a nursery rhyme inspire a like degree of philosophical reflection?

In contrast with *The Lost Thing*'s plausible range of allegorical reference, Jane Taylor's 1806 rhyme 'The Star' focuses on a single anthropomorphic abstraction:

> Twinkle, twinkle, little star,
> How I wonder what you are!
> Up above the world so high,
> Like a diamond in the sky.
>
> When the blazing sun is gone,
> When he nothing shines upon,
> Then you show your little light,
> Twinkle, twinkle all the night.
>
> Then the traveller in the dark
> Thanks you for your tiny spark;
> He could not see which way to go,
> If you did not twinkle so.
>
> In the dark blue sky you keep,
> And often through my curtains peep,
> For you never shut your eye
> left quotation mark: 'Til the sun is in the sky.
>
> As your bright and tiny spark
> Lights the traveller in the dark—
> Though I know not what you are,
> Twinkle, twinkle, little star.
>   (cited in Sword and McCarthy 1995, 269)

From the polymorphism of a rhetorical object-cum-sentience to the perfectly abstract – apparently unknowable – object of admiration, addressed as if sentient; in either case, the focus of our interest gives rise to questions, to wondering. Wondering – and being full of wonder –

is what each of these texts teaches: the rhyme by way of pure enthusiasm, the picture book by way of a contrast between the outlandishness of what is depicted and the nothing-can-surprise-me flatness of the story's narration.

'The Star' teaches children to question the nature and meaning of things plainly before them; things which the adult world might often overlook or take for granted. It connects children with the long and ever evolving history of science, and of philosophy. This is a poem to start children on a journey of doubt and of wonder and of finding out by asking. Through the device of anthropomorphism, 'The Star' teaches the child to ask of the unknown, and to ask of it as if it were a sentient other. The unknown other, in this case, is a beneficent force, with eternal and omnipresent qualities, the traveller's *sine qua non*. In some senses then, this rhyme is close to a prayer, or may be regarded as a prototype of prayer, acknowledging the unknown-ness (perhaps the unknowability) of the superior force addressed.

Today one might find these arrangements frustrating, even annoying. In Jane Taylor's time too, quite a lot was known about stars, and the quality of the information was such as to undermine the idea that stars were either tiny or unknowable. Newton's celestial mechanics were well established by this time; thousands of stars had been charted. So intensive wondering 'what you are' had borne at least some fruit by this time. Still, from the ontogenetic perspective, the child's knowledge of what a star is or might be, could well commence in the kind of wonder being modelled here in the rhyme – the kind of wonder collectivities of humans (and perhaps the ancestors of humans) would have exercised down through the ages.

The children who hear and sing this rhyme, and engage its questioning impulse, are connected with a common thread of enquiry from the earliest times. As for the anthropomorphism we find in the injunction to twinkle, certainly Ruskin would have to rate it as an egregious instance of his pathetic fallacy. A range of other doubts might be (and have been) expressed about this rhyme.

Timothy Morton's rambling essay '"Twinkle, Twinkle, Little Star"as an Ambient Poem; a Study of a Dialectical Image' (2001) does a very thorough, if at times fanciful, job on the poem, locating it canonically as an important Romantic work. Morton laments:

> it is little-known that one of the world's most famous nursery rhymes is a Romantic poem; not only that, but as I will argue ... a special kind of Romantic-ecological poem that I have chosen to call *ambient*. Furthermore, it is a strong example of a feminine Romantic lineage; though this is a poem by a woman, I hesitate to say that it is 'female', especially insofar as one might note similar poetic phenomena in Keats and Shelley, and for that matter Coleridge and Wordsworth.

A close analysis of this poem will help to reconceive Romantic ecological poetry, which so far has been notoriously both masculine and male.

(2001, n.p.)

Morton notes that Jane Taylor's star is 'both indoors and outdoors, taking apart the difference between feminized interior domestic space and masculinized exterior work space'. According to his reading, 'the comforting implication is that what is outside is also inside – the star peeps through the curtain; the discomforting implication is that what is inside is really just a special instance of the outside – that subjectivity itself is a lonely traveller wandering under the stars'. He goes on to suggest that the poem hesitates between luxury and primitivism, between artifice and nature and that the star, 'being both intimate and alien... is not so much rigidly anti-anthropocentric as it is deconstructively deep-ecological'. So this is a poem to promote ecological awareness, its narrator 'poised between conventional gendered boundaries between inside and outside'. For instance, Taylor's 'like a diamond' makes of nature a fantastic luxury item, handy as jewelled fruit in an interior garden. 'What if technology were exemplified by a lullaby?', Morton's inquiry further leads to his observation about the indigenousness of the poem: 'In Taylor's poem,... the star exceeds human being just as it is caught in it; it is a timepiece and a stile for the traveler; but it is also a wondrous phenomenon, something that opens the mind towards it in itself'. Morton speculates finally that 'The Star' might become 'the nonnational nonanthem' of a certain kind of ecological awareness.

Perhaps this poem of wonder can then help to instil (if not teach) not merely awe in the young, but also respect for the cosmos, and likewise for the objective conditions of nature, as we mysteriously receive these.

Mother Goose as Nonsense Practice

Where do we meet our first anthropomorphised animals or other anthropomorphic entities? In riddles, counting rhymes, lullabies, alphabet books, prayers? The answers might vary from one country or culture to another. In China, for instance, every child is born under an animal zodiac sign assigned to his/her birth year. The traits of agility and shrewd intelligence are thought to accompany throughout life the person who is born in the Year of the Rat, while a practical outlook is foreseen for the child born in the Year of the Cow. The anthropomorphic images of the zodiac animals and idioms related to them may be the first source of a child's perception of human–animal ties.

Attributes are assigned to a birth year in a repeating 12-year cycle (or a 60-year cycle if we include the five elements – earth, wood, metal, fire, and water). Among the 12 Chinese zodiac animals, the rat is the first animal, the sign of which would suggest that the characteristics of quick wit and diligence are inscribed in one's personality. As per our speculation in early chapters it will be a moot point whether the effect of such an institution as the Chinese zodiac is to foster affinities with nature or to hypostasise social attributes as natural through an ideological inversion.

Anthropomorphising the rat is common in a repertoire of anonymous nursery rhymes, some of which are developed from the mythic speculations of why rat comes first and cat has no place in the zodiac system. One of the stories tells that the Jade Emperor sent a cat to notify tigers, sheep, and other animals of their rank. The rat overheard the cat's message and took the first step, hitchhiking across the river with the gullible cow (who thus came second in the race). The Jade Emperor sealed the rat then as the first sign of the zodiac. The cat was squeezed out of the zodiac, and since then had a deep animosity for the rat. The rat wanted to resolve his resentment with the cat, so he asked the weasel to match up and married his most beautiful daughter off to the cat. So the mouse chose the auspicious day of wedding and sent her daughter to the cat's nest (belly). The nursery rhyme 'The rats are marrying off their daughter' as follows is a version of how the rat's parents decided to marry off their daughter to the most powerful figure in the world, which, after a picaresque quest, turned out to be the cat.

> Papa Rat, Mama Rat!
> The rats want to marry off their daughter.
> 'Mr. Sun is powerful, let's wed her to him!'
> Mr. Black Cloud is more powerful than he!
> 'Mr. Black Cloud is powerful, let's wed her to him!'
> Mr. Great Wind is more powerful than he!
> 'Mr. Great Wind is powerful, let's wed her to him!'
> Mr. Standing Wall is more powerful than he!
> 'Mr. Standing Wall is powerful, let's wed her to him!'
> Mr. Gnawing Rat is more powerful than he!
> 'Mr. Gnawing Rat is powerful, let's wed her to him!'
> Mr. Tomcat is more powerful than he!
> 'Mr. Tomcat is powerful, let's wed her to him!'
> But the tomcat ate the bride clean up.
> Thank you Papa-Rat; thank you Mama-Rat!
> Toot toot toot! Bang bang bang!
> The rats have married off their daughter!
> (Jordan 2020)

Like many Western counterparts, Chinese nursery rhymes, as can be seen in the one above, also reflect a simultaneous confusion of candour, cruelty, and comic absurdity. This allows child audiences an access to the dramatic conflicts that could emerge from the imagination of common creatures in our life. The cruelty of a bride eaten is delivered in a ludicrous euphemism – a harmless bit of fun; unless you're a mouse eaten or a bride mistreated. The rat remains popularly conceived as a creature of rampant fertility and equally nuisance, one naturally subject to ill treatment.

Along with hatred of rats and the compulsion to exterminate them, the rat is also considered, as is Disney's Micky Mouse, simply as a wily little animal companion, as the clever underdog:

> He climbed up the candlestick,
> The little mousey brown,
> To steal and eat tallow,
> And he couldn't get down.
> He called for his grandma,
> But his grandma was in town,
> So he doubled up into a wheel
> And rolled himself down.
> (Headland 1900, 38)

This popular Chinese nursery rhyme conjures up the image of a mischievous boy in rat disguise, who, through mischief, learns courage all by himself. The song can be accompanied by a dance which imitates the movement of the rat, or, as the case may be, accompanied by cheerful laughter. It is a song of a simply mischievous and joyful animal-child.

Collectively, we might say that children meet their first imaginary, other-than-human friends, in nursery rhymes, which are teeming with anthropomorphic characters. These rhymes, while in print, are in large part passed on orally, for instance by parents to children. Being in such texts together entails, for parent and child, a passing on, generation to generation, of cultural knowledge and assumptions, of proclivities for nonsense and its borders in experience and knowledge; and a passing on as well of the culturally determined atmosphere and idea of childhood itself.

According to Opie and Opie, nursery rhymes enter a child's life 'at the transitional stage between the picture book pure and simple, and the first story book' (1960, Preface). Despite their earlier origin in Mother Goose rhymes in the mid-late eighteenth century, nursery rhymes had not become a subgenre (nor had the concomitant literary term currency) until the early nineteenth century (Eckenstein 1906, 1–12; Styles 1997, 84–90). As a component of oral literature in the Western tradition, nursery rhymes have received relatively little critical attention, partly because they do not, at first glance, appear erudite or challenging, and partly because of difficulties in tracing the historical origin of nursery rhymes (Foster 2008; Jack 2008).

As Morag Styles notes, 'definitions of nursery rhymes are notoriously come by, because the essence of these rhymes is so difficult to pin down' (1997, 83). For Cammaerts, nursery rhymes reflect the essential musical quality along with the manifestation of 'the working of the mind of the child, his spontaneous challenge to the dictates of Reason, his hostility to the well-ordered world to which "grown-ups" vainly endeavor to introduce him, his suspicion of human laws and restrictions which tend gradually to transform his "play" into "work"' (1925, 18). The root of nursery rhymes is found in the sound, imagination, exuberance, and spontaneity of naivety. To borrow Nicholas Tucker's words, nursery rhymes are 'smooth stones from the brook of time, worn round by constant friction of tongues long silent'. For Sir Walter Scott, this genre exercises the 'imagination-nourishing' power of the wild and fanciful lore of the old nursery (cited in Styles 1997, 84). For this chapter, we consider a nursery rhyme any poem that is aimed at least partly at the youngest of listeners, and employs sensory meaning and sound play calculated to entertain an adult and a child performing the text together.

All sorts of speculation have been directed towards nursery rhymes, largely in the hope of understanding what the apparent nonsense is all about; and particularly with an interest in cracking codes to get to secret underlying, generally-supposed-to-be allegorical meanings (Couchman 2015; Craig 2018; Jack 2008; Opie and Opie 1980, 1997). In this chapter, we are interested in neither historical arguments to attest or counter case-by-case allegorical claims, nor in closely contextualising the historical origins of particular rhymes. As foreshadowed, our interest is in the dissemination of 'traditional knowledge' and 'popular wisdom' through nursery rhymes. Therefore, we show how – through the openness of the genre – nursery rhymes generate ambivalence and school their reader/listener in an openness to the interpretive possibilities of text, to the unexpected qualities of poetry, and to the fractured (and fractious) nature of stories. The nursery rhyme is likewise in general open in terms of its moral and affective potentials. On the one hand, many rhymes promote empathy (and often for animal others), and on the other hand many (if not most) nursery rhymes are firmly anthropocentric, promoting human interests and downplaying animal qualities, if not taking them for granted.

Nursery rhymes frequently deliver a matter-of-fact – sometimes morbid – stoicism to their readers:

> Solomon Grundy,
> Born on a Monday,
> Christened on Tuesday,
> Married on Wednesday,
> Took ill on Thursday,
> Worse on Friday,
> Died on Saturday,
> Buried on Sunday
> This is the end
> of Solomon Grundy.
>   (*Dictionary*, 392)

There is an ambiguous, dark, riddling quality to many rhymes, often bearing on some brutal reality of the world. Take 'Punch and Judy' for instance,

> Punch and Judy
> Fought for a pie;
> Punch gave Judy
> A knock in the eye.
>
> Says Punch to Judy
> Will you have any more?
> Says Judy to Punch,
> My eye is sore.
>   (*Dictionary*, 354–355)

Have any more of what? Knowing what we know of the Punch and Judy 'tradition', it will be reasonable to read this rhyme as a cruel joke to keep women in their place. Violence against children is of course a commonplace in nursery rhymes as well, as in

> Little Polly Flinders
> Sat among the cinders,
> Warming her pretty little toes;
> Her mother came and caught her,
> And whipped her little daughter
> For spoiling her nice new clothes.
>   (*Dictionary*, 354)

Despite the inclusion of Chinese nursery rhymes and those from other non-English countries, we have to admit that this chapter shows some bias towards the best known and most canonic of nursery rhymes, predominantly from the English language; that is towards those with the most resonance for English-language native speakers who grew up with them. This is a book in English and it is perhaps natural that the culture of the language of composition should predominate. Although we largely draw upon those in *The Oxford Dictionary of Nursery Rhymes*, we note with its editors Iona Opie and Peter Opie, that nursery rhymes may be read as 'remnants of ancient custom and ritual', 'last echoes of long-forgotten evil', 'memories of street cry and mummers' play', and the 'legacy of war and rebellion' (1997, 4). These echoes and memories are found resonant in verses for young children all over the world. As with Children's Literature in general, at the core of nursery rhymes is the ambivalence of providing entertainment and inspiration for a dual readership.

As originary crossover genre, nursery rhymes almost inevitably generate ambivalences for the child. They are typically arcane knowledge delivered to one who does not know by one who ought to be in a position to know. Frequently though adults would be in no position to explain the rhymes they offer to their juniors; they merely 'know' them in the sense of knowing which words come next. The knowledge in nursery rhymes may in this way be regarded as arbitrary, the way a spelling rhyme ('I before E, except after C') or a calendar rhyme might be; the difference being that the arbitrary contents of the nursery rhyme constitute apparently useless knowledge. If nursery rhymes are acknowledged as 'survivals of an adult code of joviality, and are in their original wordings, by present standards, strikingly unsuitable for those of tender years' (*Dictionary*, 3), do these adult-made poems *for* children also generate ambivalence for the adult? Or is it the case that, being cast in the role of the knowing, one typically deprives the adult of such doubts? The question here might be asked of arbitrary and of canonic knowledge more generally. Based on such considerations and a thematic overview of key topics of rhymes that involve animal characters, let us focus on (often implied) animal tales in the verses selected and explore conceptual and ethical frameworks that may be at stake in disseminating an ever-evolving set of canonic rhymes from generation to generation.

Human–Animal Relations in the Nursery Rhyme

Nursery rhymes offer child and adult alike a wide range of affective and ethical models for human/animal relations. Let us start with perhaps the flattest.

> Two little dicky birds,
> Sitting on a wall;
> One named Peter,
> The other named Paul.
> Fly away, Peter!
> Fly away, Paul!
> Come back, Peter!
> Come back, Paul!
>   (*Dictionary*, 147)

If we can get past the idea that the poem is either meaningless nonsense, or some deep and important biblical allegory, then, reminiscent of the *fort/da* game Freud describes in *Beyond the Pleasure Principle*, is this nascent existential play? Now it's here, now it's not. Are these simply words to accompany a game played on the fingers for the delight of the child? In that case, there are some questions to be considered. For instance, if we ask of this poem: is this *about* people or is this about birds (?), then we might answer: Yes, this is a poem either about people or about birds. It would be difficult to say if it were more about people or more about birds. Certainly, it is about one or the other. As with our fairytale ruminations in Chapter 2, it will be reasonable to suggest that the anthropomorphism has a reifying effect: that is to say, it asserts the equivalence of human and animal activity – we do what they do, they do as we do. What we can definitely say about this rhyme is that it is not in any tangible way about relations between humans and other-than-human animals.

There are rare cases in nursery rhymes of suggested transformation or of uncertainty between the human and the animal, as in for instance, 'There were three jovial Welshmen':

> And all the day they hunted
> And nothing could they find,
> But an owl in a holly tree,
> And that they left behind.
>
> One said it was an owl,
> The other he said, Nay;
> The third said 'twas and old man,
> And his beard growing grey.
> *(Dictionary*, 422)

We have seen gendered violence in the wholly human Punch and Judy rhyme above. Much of the gender role business of nursery rhymes is conducted with anthropomorphised animals or zoomorphised human characters, depending on how you wish to read.

> Cock, cock, cock, cock,
> I've laid an egg,
> Am I to go ba-are foot?
>
> Hen, hen, hen, hen,
> I've been up and down,
> To every shop in town,
> And cannot find a shoe
> To fit your foot,
> If I'd crow my hea-art out.
> *(Dictionary*, 126)

'Old Mother Goose' suggests, in its nonsensical way, how males might be of practical use to females,

> Old Mother Goose,
> When she wanted to wander,
> Would ride through the air
> On a very fine gander.
> *(Dictionary*, 316)

Nature can be fearful for little Miss Muffet who sat on a tuffet and ate her curds when 'There came a big spider, Who sat down beside her/And frightened Miss Muffet away' (*Dictionary*, 323). This rhyme might be read as teaching arachnophobia. It shows the child that a fear of this kind is common, if not reasonable. And animals, even useful domestic pets, might be wise to entertain a healthy fear of their human companions:

> Ding, dong, bell,
> Pussy's in the well.
> Who put her in?
> Little Johnny Green.
> Who pulled her out?
> Little Tommy Stout.
> What a naughty boy was that,
> To try to drown poor pussy cat,
> Who never did him any harm,
> And killed the mice in his father's barn.
> (*Dictionary*, 149)

In this case, it is Little Tommy Stout who saves pussy. Often though, animals are called upon to save themselves. And often they succeed. As was the case with our little fishie (Bertram Murray's 'I caught a fish') in Chapter 2, where animals are given a voice (that's to say where empathic words may be put in the mouths of animals), they may talk their way out of human-induced dangers. The conflict between humans and animals may be portrayed even-handedly, even if there must always be a winner.

> A little cock sparrow sat on a green tree,
> And he chirruped, he chirruped, so merry was he.
> A naughty boy came with his wee bow and arrow,
> Says he, I will shoot this little cock sparrow;
> His body will make me a nice little stew,
> And his giblets shall make me a little pie, too'.
> Oh, no, says the sparrow, I won't make a stew.
> So he clapped his wings and away he flew.
> (*Dictionary*, 133)

The message to the human adult-in-the-making? Try harder? (Be more determined?) Know why you are doing what you are doing? Do not make your intentions known to your adversary? Have a thought for the creature you would kill and learn to value the lives of others? Perhaps all of the above apply. A text of this kind models an openness to the facts of the story, which have to be read from a point of view. That point of view is potentially mobile, open to contention. You could start the story with one opinion and you could change your mind, not because the story teaches you something in particular, but because your personal experience of it gives you a point of view.

In 'A carrion crow sat on an oak', we see the attack on animal others or nature backfiring, coming back to bite the attacker.

> A carrion crow sat on an oak,
> Watching a tailor shape his cloak;
> Wife, cried he, bring me my bow,
> That I may shoot yon carrion crow.
> The tailor shot and missed his mark,
> And shot his own sow through the heart;
> Wife, bring brandy in a spoon,
> For our poor sow is in a swoon.
> (*Dictionary*, 111)

This rhyme is not necessarily an expression of empathy, just a little cautionary tale in nursery rhyme form, or even counsel against the sinfulness of pride, or exposé of human folly. Other rhymes, however reconciliatory they might seem at points, nevertheless deliver blunt threats from humanity to its others.

> Away, birds, away,
> Take a little, and leave a little,
> And do not come again;
> For if you do,
> I will shoot you through,
> And there is an end of you.
> (*Dictionary*, 83)

We might read 'Away, birds, away' in the light of a compromise offer made to those who cannot understand it, something like a warning in an unknown language, as in the case of Governor Arthur's famous (1830) proclamation to the Aborigines (Wikipedia, 'Governor Davey's Proclamation').

Sometimes, animals, either humans or animals, partake of the same violence against those in the lower rung of evolution:

> What the Old Crow Said
> An old Black crow sat on a tree,
> And there he sat and said to me:
> 'Ho, Mr. Wang, there's a sheep on the hill,
> Which I wish very much you would catch and kill;
> You may eat meat three times a day,
> And I'll eat the parts that you throw away'
> (Headland, 41)

It is a commonplace in the nursery rhyme that the world of animals is useful for human purposes, and that this involves animal deaths. The nursery sometimes also shows animal sufferings and deaths as fundamental for human survival. For instance, in 'Bye Baby Bunting', the unwrapped child might die of cold.

> Bye, baby bunting,
> Daddy's gone a-hunting.
> Gone to get a rabbit skin
> To wrap the baby bunting in.
> (*Dictionary*, 63)

Often however human purposes and attitudes are both more grim, and less clearly motivated, as in:

> Three blind mice, see how they run!
> They all ran after the farmer's wife,
> Who cut off their tails with a carving knife,
> Did you ever see such a thing in your life,
> As three blind mice?
> (*Dictionary*, 306)

This is such an odd story, it feels to be allegorical. First, it has been allegorically explained, and at some length, the most common accounts relating to Catholic/Protestant ructions in the reigns of English monarchs, Henry VIII and Mary I (Jack, *Pop Goes the Weasel* 314). Beyond this, 'Three Blind Mice' encapsulates an eternal human conflict between humans and the animals humans have, but would rather not have, around. It seems to be a tortured death these animals have, a question begged as to whether there is any use to the tails or specific benefit arising from the separation of the rodent from its tail? Should we assume a bounty, with rodents despatched measured by the tail? Is this rather cruelty as sadistic pleasure? That reading fits rather neatly with the allegorical account as well.

In some rhymes, we witness also the strange, perhaps uncanny, cruelty of anthropomorphised animals:

> Let's go to the wood, says this pig,
> What to do there? says that pig,
> To look for my mother, says this pig.
> What to do with her? says that pig,
> Kiss her to death, says this pig.
> (*Dictionary*, 349)

Here ambivalence is demonstrated at the level of purpose or declared intention – love (or putatively loving relationships) and violence are associated. As for Punch and Judy, so for pigs as well. More on pigs shortly.

Many rhymes propose empathy for animal others; sometimes an ethic of care is self-interested or self-protective, and often it is reasoned, as in:

> I love little pussy,
> Her coat is so warm,
> And if I don't hurt her
> She'll do me no harm.
> So I'll not pull her tail,
> Nor drive her away,
> But pussy and I
> Very gently will play.
> (*Dictionary*, 356)

Or there is the more adult workaday rhyme, 'If I had a donkey that wouldn't go':

> If I had a donkey that wouldn't go.
> Would I beat him? Oh no, no.
> I'd put him in the barn and give him some corn,
> The best little donkey that ever was born.
> (*Dictionary*, 153)

Interesting here is the idea of mutual benefit through empathy and resulting kindness. The donkey is presumably the best little donkey ever because of the favourable conditions he experiences, due to the kindness of the master.

There are also stories of revenge on the animal's part. Martin Waddell and Helen Oxenbury's 1991 picture book *Farmer Duck*, offers something along these lines. In a tale emulating the optimistic opening pages of *Animal Farm*, we find the animals of this farm banding together in revolutionary solidarity with a downtrodden duck, who is being worked to death by the farmer. After their successful revolt, they tell the duck all about what they have done on behalf of this creature of undetermined gender.

> The cow and the sheep
> and the hens came back.
> 'Quack?' asked the duck.
> 'Moo!' said the cow!
> 'Baa!' said the sheep.
> 'Cluck! Said the hens.
> Which told the duck the whole story.

Sometimes harmony and reconciliation are promoted, by showing it where it might not be expected, as in the traditional nursery proverb 'little birds in their nests agree'. Edward Strachery, who may be the first to investigate nonsense and consider it as a fine art, remarks that such an art is 'the bringing out a new and deeper harmony of life in and through its contradictions' (206). It is this harmony among all creatures that gives us the access to a wider imaginative world.

> Pussy cat sits beside the fire,
> So pretty and so fair.
> In walks the little dog,
> Ah, Pussy, are you there?
> How do you do, Mistress Pussy?
> Mistress Pussy, how do you do?
> I thank you kindly, little dog,
> I'm very well just now.
> (*Dictionary*, 358)

But Mistress Pussy might not be a little later, once the dog has attacked her? Surely the child would be cynical to ask such a question, when point is to offer a model for peace in our time, suggesting that, if the little birds can agree, then so can we.

Against this image of blissful domesticity, the imagination of what a real animal might do, of how it might not be predicted, is key to the suspense of the animal oriented nursery rhyme and allows it to be memorised and repeated, and to still allow of imaginative novelty. Likewise, with Punch and Judy. We don't know what will happen next but we do know that violence and catastrophe are always on the agenda, as in 'Six Little Mice Sat down to Spin'.

> Six Little mice sat down to spin;
> Pussy passed by and she peeped in.
> What are you doing, my little men?
> Weaving coats for gentlemen.
> Shall I come in and cut off your threads?
> No, no, Mistress Pussy, you'd bite off our heads.
> Oh, no, I'll not; I'll help you to spin.
> That may be so, but you don't come in.
> (*Dictionary*, 306)

Likewise, nature and fate, to which animals as humans are subject, are shown to be fickle and needing to be accommodated.

> Humpty Dumpty sat on a wall,
> Humpty Dumpty had a great fall.

All the king's horses,
And all the king's men.
Couldn't put Humpty together again.
     (*Dictionary*, 213)

Ladybird, ladybird,
Fly away home,
Your house is on fire
And your children all gone;
All except one
And that's little Ann
And she has crept under
The warming pan.
     (*Dictionary*, 263)

'Ladybird, ladybird' presents an empathic confusion between what is of the insect and what is of the human world. Viewed as an incantation by the Opies (1997, 308–310), they write, 'The rhyme is undoubtedly a relic of something that once possessed of an awful significance'. The poem is framed as an empathic directive – telling the insect what to do in order to save itself. The Opies argue that the rhyme originates from the superstition that to kill a ladybird is unlucky. These bugs are possessed of witches and so this rhyme is a kind exorcism. If we think of this rhyme as allegorical, then the circle we follow is something like this – the child warns the insect, which represents a human needing to protect itself from a present danger; so here the child is delivering the kind of warning an adult may give the child. Allegorically then, the child is in *loco parentis* of the littler and lesser sentiences of this world; the one protected is encouraged to model the giving of protection. So a warning turns into a story in order to get to the happy ending. Are things resolved in this story? One senses new perils to face in the not-so-distant future.

 To some extent nursery rhymes parallel the development of the fairytale as a print genre. Like fairy tales, a number of nursery rhymes tell the true tale of some of history's darkest or most tragic events (Jack 2008, 2019). And as with fairytales, the 'unsuitable' or grisly aspects of the rhymes seem to fade over time as tales and rhymes become more anthologised, as generations of judgement filters are applied. Coming from the era before the advent of children's literature, nursery rhymes are full of hidden meanings, nevertheless a model for texts with a joint (child–adult) readership – as evidenced in the (much-argued) allegorical content, as already noted, of many nursery rhymes. It will be fair to say that however much 'fairytale thinking' nursery rhymes evidence, they generally furnish a text of a much more ambivalent kind than we find in the case of a fairytale or even a proverb. Let us return for a moment to 'Six little mice sat down to spin'. Here, the animal-on-animal allegorical warning provides an inkling of ambivalence in the telling of an unexpected tale. The surprise and suspense that come through the threat of – or the likelihood of – violence are a warning to us – not because we are like mice or cats but because things and creatures have their nature and because sometimes offers of help are suspicious. On the other hand, good will has a value. Apart from the threat to life, from the mouse point of view, this nursery rhyme teaches two contradictory proverbs, we might say:

> *many hands make light work*
> but on the other hand
> *too many cooks spoil the broth*

At this point in the investigation, it will be fair to say that a nursery rhyme (just as much of a story as it may be) is typically far more complex than a proverb, and much more open a text than a fairytale. A nursery rhyme can teach a contradiction, and perhaps the resolution of contradiction. A riddle, frequently involving an anthropomorphism (or zoomorphism), teaches us to see the world as made in mystery, and needing work to be understood.

> In Spring I look gay,
> Decked in comely array,
> In summer more clothing I wear;
> When colder it grows,
> I fling off my clothes,
> And in winter quite naked appear.
>   (*The Oxford Nursery Rhyme Book*, 148)

A riddle may teach us to do something as simple as to look up.

> Purple, yellow, red, and green,
> The king cannot reach it, nor yet the queen;
> Nor can Old Noll, whose power's so great:
> Tell me this riddle while I count eight.
>   (*Dictionary*, 355)

Likewise, a well-proportioned chain of cause and effect may teach us to understand how the greatest and the tiniest of things in the world may be connected.

> For want of a nail the shoe was lost,
> For want of a shoe the horse was lost,
> For want of a horse the rider was lost,
> For want of a rider the battle was lost,
> For want of a battle the kingdom was lost,
> And all for the want of a horseshoe nail.
>   (*Dictionary*, 324)

Here, a proverbial inkling of the subtlety of things foreshadows Lorenz' 'butterfly effect'. From little things big things may come. The trick form of a riddle may show that there is nothing to be resolved.

> Riddle me, riddle me ree,
> A hawk sat up in a tree;
> And he says to himself, says he,
> Lord! what a fine bird I be!
> 			(*Dictionary*, 363)

Here narcissism trumps introspection. Of course some mock riddles are simply for the sake of absurdity.

> A man in the wilderness asked me,
> How many strawberries grow in the sea?
> I answered him, as I thought good,
> As many as red herrings grow in the wood.
> 			(*Dictionary*, 284)

Again showing us the anthropomorphism of an abstraction, Jonathan Swift's 'As the World Turns' asks 'who' is the abstract entity to be guessed.

> I'm up and down and round about,
> Yet all the world can't find me out.
> Though hundreds have employed their leisure,
> They never yet could take my measure.
> I'm found in almost every garden.
> Nay, in the compass of a farthing.
> There's not a chariot, coach, nor mill,
> Can move an inch except I will.
> 			(Ireson and Adamson 1958, 53)

Nursery rhymes, like the best poems more generally, often leave their tellers and their listeners with questions, rather than answers – with choices to make rather than certain knowledge of how things are or ought to be. It will be fair to say that nursery rhymes model for the youngest of readers and listeners, the potential complexity of poetry as we know it today. The nonsense in nursery rhymes effectively foreshadows the topical and rhetorical range, and capacity for tangential thinking challenges, characteristic of Modernist and later poetries (Laird 1997; Amiran 2016).

Ethics of Who We Are, Inside and Outside of the Rhyme

One of the key riddling questions posed in nursery rhymes, of all kinds, concerns the relationship of the self-reading to the others-of-the-text. With the distant object in Taylor's 'The Star', with Levertov's close companion in 'The Cat as Cat', and with Tan's 'The Lost Thing', we ask in each of these different cases (each representing relationship beyond language), the extent to which an equal and other sentience has been approached, understood, and justly treated. At stake here is Martin Buber's notion of 'I-thou', as opposed to 'I-it', relationship. Taylor's star is far and yet with us, yet able to be addressed (if only in the manner of prayer), Levertov's cat (like Derrida's) is its own animal despite all we might say, despite how we might choose to address it, and Tan's 'The Lost Thing', whatever closeness or affinity a protagonist/narrator might claim for it, is with us and yet unapproachable. A question in each case remains open as to whether a real meeting has taken place.

Perhaps Taylor has been a little coy on the question of what is and is not known about stars. Nevertheless, the unknown and unknowability are important aspects of our relationship with those beyond our species (and likewise with members of it as well). What kind of attitude does the recognition of unknowability lead to? You can kill what you don't know, you can revere it, worship it, ignore it, hope that it will go away, that it will get to know you, that it will be tamed, or that you will be tamed. To come to terms with the unknown, you can make all sorts of effort or none.

The thing out of place, needing to be explained, or dealt with, such as we see in Tan's *The Lost Thing*, has a long and popular history in nursery rhymes. Mrs Sarah Josepha Hale's 1830 rhyme, 'Mary had a little lamb', was the first utterance recorded on Edison's gramophone in 1877.

> Mary had a little lamb,
> Its fleece was white as snow;
> And everywhere that Mary went
> The lamb was sure to go.
>
> It followed her to school one day,
> That was against the rule;
> It made the children laugh and play
> To see a lamb at school.
> (*Dictionary*, 299–300)

In this poem we meet an opposition between the world of play where we can commune with animals and an adult-ordered world of rules that must be obeyed. There is some softening and understanding in the end of the piece, perhaps to be viewed in the light of a rapprochement between the contrasting worlds of adult and child-with-animal. The world in which the child and animal are free to play together is one with no apparent rules, or else with spontaneously negotiated rules; it is a world motivated by love. The rules of the adult world may seem to be arbitrarily imposed on the child, something like nonsense. A world of rapport, we might say, as opposed to a rule-bound world. The rhyme is necessary then, not just for the fun of it (or for the fun of its nonsense) but because children need to learn these arbitrary rules of the adult world, just as they need to learn to spell or to say, and be able to make use of, their times tables.

Mary's journey is towards understanding what a rule must mean for her. Not knowing leaves us with problems to solve, as for instance in the case Bo-peep.

> Little Bo-peep has lost her sheep,
> And can't tell where to find them;
> Leave them alone, and they'll come home,
> And bring their tails behind them.
> (*Dictionary*, 93)

Our Chapter 4 will focus on cautionary tales. Here we have an example for the young listener, to which we shall return shortly, with a very simple moral – *take care of your sheep or something dreadful might happen to them*. In this case, the calamity is apparently absurd (the theft of the untended sheep's tails), the caution given is not really about a particular real problem worth avoiding. The real lesson is general vigilance – if you don't pay attention and take care then you don't know what kind of weird stuff might befall you – *a stitch in time, saves nine* moral.

There is, in nursery rhymes, much expectation that animals – and especially companion or domestic animals – will serve us (i.e. the human readers of nursery rhymes); and there is punishing them should they fail to do so.

> I had a little dog and they called him Buff,
> I sent him to a shop to buy me snuff,
> But he lost the bag and spilt the stuff;
> I sent him no more but gave him a cuff,
> For coming from the mart without any snuff.
> (*Dictionary*, 105)

The roles in this poem are allegorical for the idea of obedience: the child is in the generalised scheme of power where the pet is, and the child should obey and should know what is expected of it. We can say that the anthropomorphised pet stands, in this kind of rhyme, *in loco infantis*.

Messages of obedience normalise discipline behaviour with an attempt to deliver children from unruly childhoods to administrable adulthoods. Typically in China, Confucianism, the predominant ethical school, endorses five relationships: king–subject, father–son, husband–wife, elder brother–younger brother, and friend–friend. Each of these relationships emphasises the principle of respecting the superior in social interaction.

To adjust to a socially constructed logic of conformity and not to be punished, children likewise have to be obedient to the patriarchal power to fit the social expectations of growth. Reminiscent of 'This Little Piggie Went to Market' (to be encountered shortly), in the following fingerplay poem, a little cow is punished for idleness:

> This little cow eats grass,
> This little cow eats hay,
> This little cow drinks water,
> This little cow runs away,
> This little cow does nothing,
> But just lie down all day;
> We'll whip her.
> (Headland 157)

An Ambivalent Oscillation

There is, we may say, in nursery rhymes, an ambivalent oscillation between the unknowability of animals (who might behave as real animals in the text) and the prosopopoeia presence of allegorical types in the rhymes (of human character types wearing allegorical animal masks). Ambivalence is generated by our frequently being unsure as to which category a character in a rhyme is in – real or allegorical – or whether that character might shift from one to another.

Two pussy-cat rhymes serve as nice examples:

> Pussy cat, pussy cat, where have you been?
> I've been to London to look at the queen.
> Pussy cat, pussy cat, what did you there?
> I frightened a little mouse under her chair.
> (*Dictionary*, 357)

Here the human in the cat suit behaves in the end the way a real cat would and is useful to the queen in the way a house cat might be.

> Pussicat, wussicat, with a white foot,
> When is your wedding, and I'll come to it.
> The beer's to brew, the bread's to bake,
> Pussy cat, pussy cat, don't be too late!
> (*Dictionary*, 356)

Here the dynamic is reversed. The apparently real cat of the first line is fully human by the end of the poem. There are examples too that show very transparently the interchangeability of human and animal characters, as in for instance versions of 'Sing a Song of Sixpence', variously:

> Sing a song of sixpence,
> A bag full of Rye
> Four and Twenty Naughty boys,
> Bak'd in a Pie

and the better known

> Sing a song of sixpence,
> A pocket full of rye;
> Four and twenty blackbirds
> Baked in a pie.
> (*Dictionary*, 394)

The very serious challenge of these rhymes concerns the confusing ethics of who and how to be, with whom to identify, and how to understand the fluid possibilities of identity; these being problems much more pronounced for those growing to be themselves, than for adults.

Between Empathy and Anthropocentrism – Knowing Your Place

It is within the parameters of allegory and prosopopoeia we need to ask why some animal characters are portrayed as outsmarting their predators, as in for instance 'Six Little mice sat down to spin' and 'A little cock sparrow sat on a green tree' and 'A carrion crow sat on an oak'. Different degrees of sympathy and empathy are suggested in these texts, where innocence and 'wild extravagances' (*Dictionary*, 2), human and animal identity are integrated through nonsense and play into a special affect, a textual sport, intended at least in part for a young readership.

Children find consolation in the stories about small animals which are 'a reflection of their diminished power' (Griswold 2006, 53). Size and power are often conflated as a paradox in children's literature, in which child characters often play a bigger role to look 'down' on or take care of figures smaller than themselves. It is by such allegorical means, children learn their place, in both the world of nature and the adult world into which they are growing. Along the way, and in the ambivalent dance between anthropocentrism and genuine *I-thou* engagement, there is plenty of room to exercise both empathy and (sometimes cruel) self-interest.

We find an extended example of the empathic engagement with the lot of a perennial human enemy in 'A fox jumped up one winter's night'.

> A fox jumped up one winter's night.
> And begged the moon to give him light,
> For he'd many miles to trot that night
> Before he reached his den O!

The Little Dog Laughed to See Such Sport

Den O! Den O!
For he'd many miles to trot that night
Before he reached his den O!

The first place he came to was a farmer's yard.
Where the ducks and the geese declared it hard
That their nerves should be shaken and their rest so marred
By a visit from Mr. Fox O!
Fox O! Fox O!
That their nerves should be shaken and their rest so marred
By a visit from Mr. Fox O!

He took the grey goose by the neck,
And swung him right across his back;
The grey goose cried out. Quack, quack, quack.
With his legs hanging dangling down O!
Down O! Down O!
The grey goose cried out. Quack, quack, quack,
With his legs hanging dangling down O!

Old Mother Slipper Slopper jumped out of bed,
And out of the window she popped her head:
Oh! John, John, John, the grey goose is gone,
And the fox is off to his den O!
Den O! Den O!
Oh! John, John, John, the grey goose is gone,
And the fox is off to his den O!

John ran up to the top of the hill,
And blew his whistle loud and shrill;
Said the fox, That is very pretty music; still—
I'd rather be in my den O
Den O! Den O!
Said the fox, That is very pretty music; still—
I'd rather be in my den O!

The fox went back to his hungry den,
And his dear little foxes, eight, nine, ten;
Quoth they, Good daddy, you must go there again,
If you bring such good cheer from the farm O!
Farm O! Farm O!
Quoth they, Good daddy, you must go there again,
If you bring such good cheer from the farm O!

The fox and his wife, without any strife,
Said they never ate a better goose in all their life:

> They did very well without fork or knife,
> And the little ones picked the bones O!
> Bones O! Bones O!
> They did very well without fork or knife,
> And the little ones picked the bones O!
> (*Dictionary*, 173–175)

Three points of view are presented in this rhyme – that of the fox, of the geese and ducks, and of the farming couple who keep them. A fourth character is the moon as presiding deity, who answers the fox's prayer with enough light to make his exploits possible. Even though Mother Slipper Slopper and John are the only named characters in the story (taking Mr Fox to be a fabulous name), empathy clearly is with the fox, suspense in the tale is felt on behalf of the fox and the reader is pleased with his happy ending (with the ending that is happy for the fox).

This is then the classic underdog story as promoted on screen through the twentieth century through such famous anthropomorphised rodent characters as Mickey Mouse and Bugs Bunny, not to mention Roald Dahl's *Fantastic Mr Fox* (1970). There is an anti-humanist agenda by depicting a duel between animals and humans. Humans in general are represented by farmers as empty, lifeless, and inert, in fact, unanimated, while animals on the other side, invincible witty, take the job of beating them successfully. On the one hand, such story could be categorised as what is called 'invasion narrative' as 'a response to the arrogance involved in humankind's separation from nature, from the ecosystem and the food chain' (Gregersdotter and Hållén 2015, 207). On the other hand, if diminutive enemy creatures are allegorically children, then their little victories are victories for the powerless reader who can identify with them as being likewise powerless. These little triumphs (lulls in eternal wars) are carnival moments in Bakhtin's sense (1968), where the 'natural' orders of social hierarchy are briefly overturned. These moments could also serve as Barthesian inoculations for the child. According to Roland Barthes, 'the inoculation' is that figure where 'one immunizes the contents of the collective imagination by means of a small inoculation of acknowledged evil' (1991, 151). What seem minor contingent triumphs are employed to ward off a prospect of the radical overthrow of adult codes.

In many nursery rhymes we find – for the sake of humour or absurdity – unlikely combinations of characters. 'The Marriage of the Frogge and the Mouse' (a 1611 forerunner of 'A Frog He Would a-Wooing Go') foreshadows for instance those we will meet in Edward Lear's 'The Owl and the Pussycat', discussed in Chapter 2. In 'A Frog He Would a-Wooing Go', we see what happens to animals who behave too much like humans. This grisly poem tells the story of a Frog who wears 'his opera hat', with the help of his friend the Rat, is paying court to Miss Mouse. When they come to the door of Mrs Mousey's house, they start drinking beer, singing songs, and merry making. And then danger sets in with the cat and her kittens devouring Miss Mouse and Mr. Rat:

> But while they were all a-merry-making
> Heigh ho! says Rowley,
> A cat and her kittens came tumbling in.
> With a rowley, powley, &c.
>
> The cat she seized the rat by the crown,
> Heigh ho! says Rowley,
> The kittens they pulled the little mouse down.
> With a rowley, powley, &c. (Dictionary, 178)

Where is the Frog now? Is he doing his best to save his friend and future family? We are told that he is escaping like a hypocrite from the scene of murder, but soon gobbled up by a lily white duck as he crosses the pond:

> This put Mr. Frog in a terrible fright,
> Heigh ho! says Rowley,
> He took up his hat and he wished them good-night.
> With a rowley, powley, &c.
>
> But as Froggy was crossing over a brook,
> Heigh ho! says Rowley,
> A lily-white duck came and gobbled him up.
> With a rowley, powley, &c.
>
> So there was the end of one, two, three,
> Heigh ho! says Rowley,
> The rat, the mouse, and the little frog-ee.
> With a rowley, powley, &c.
>   (*Dictionary*, 179)

Although the rat, the mouse, and the little froggy are all eaten up, the story is pictured as a rollicking farce with the sheerly nonsensical refrain. In 'A Frog He Would a-Wooing Go', readers find themselves tricked into an uncertainty and horror as to the 'real' animal credentials of the characters. It is hard to know, in a poem like this, when the masks are being worn, or taken off, or indeed if there are masks under the masks we see. If, as we acknowledge in the case of 'Six little mice sat down to spin', things and creatures have their own nature, then we must expect cats to attack mice, regardless of what they may claim with respect to their intentions. Nursery rhymes show us how animal characters can be undone by their anthropomorphic pretensions, likewise, how anthropomorphisms may be undermined by the putative nature of a certain creature.

Unlike the owl and the pussycat, the characters in 'A Frog He Would a-Wooing Go' come unstuck. Things go awry for them because though they are anthropomorphised creatures behaving with human pretensions, the cat is nevertheless a cat and her kittens are kittens. And as if encouraged by the cat-ness of the cat in the story, the frog meets his fate at the beak of the lily-white duck. That lily-whiteness of the duck, the femaleness of the cat, the youthfulness of her kittens – these softenings are there as red herrings in the plot, and to show that no amount of perceived, or poetic, cuteness makes animals less animal, if indeed they are animals in fact. We might also say of 'A Frog He Would a-Wooing Go' that this is what happens to frogs behaving in such a manner (getting above their station, we might say); and that so this is, allegorically, what happens to children or other persons getting above their station. 'Be who you are', the text tells us, 'Know your place; it's safer'. This rhyme reminds us that, however we feel about our pets and other beautiful creatures we might have about us, they are not human and we will be foolish to expect them to behave according to human norms. Such lessons may penetrate any amount of foolishness and any degree of absurdity.

Some simple jingles seem to survive, not only to remind children of the unmasked presence of certain animals, but also show children how animals may not be predicted. We can expect animals to be not as smart, organised, or logical in their behaviour as we humans are.

> Higglety, piggelty, pop!
> The dog has eaten the mop;
> The pig's in a hurry,
> The cat's in a flurry,
> Higglety, piggelty, pop!
>   (*Dictionary*, 207)

If 'A Frog He Would A-Wooing Go' tests ambivalence by experimenting with anthropomorphic and non-anthropomorphised creatures in the poem, 'Who Killed Cock Robin?', with its emphasis on judicial process, maintains a fully anthropomorphic cast. These characters are animal only in name, and their names are largely seen to be for the convenience of rhyme.

> Who killed Cock Robin?
> I, said the Sparrow,
> With my bow and arrow,
> I killed Cock Robin.
>
> Who saw him die?
> I, said the Fly.
> With my little eye,
> I saw him die.

> ...
> Who'll toll the bell?
> I, said the Bull,
> Because I can pull,
> I'll toll the bell.
>
> All the birds of the air
> Fell a-sighing and a-sobbing,
> When they heard the bell toll
> For poor Cock Robin.
>   (*Dictionary*, 130–131)

Noting a certain amount in common with Farid ud-Din Attar's *Conference of the Birds* (1177) and Chaucer's *Parliament of Fowls* (2015) (possibly composed between 1381 and 1382), and antecedents argued in various languages (including the Norse tale of Baldor), let us put aside the allegorical potential of the rhyme and its supposed origins in eighteenth-century English parliamentary politics. 'Who Killed Cock Robin' does, if we do not simply take it for a joke, have the empathic consequence of suggesting to its reader that human justice might apply to other-than-humans. Here the proposition of sentience among birds and other animals is to the fore and so the humanising of others who are not human suggests for the reader that something along the lines of human justice might be universally deserved. Whatever rules of conduct seem to apply, even to animals, must surely apply to humans. And what clear-headed child will not get a whiff of hypocrisy in the idea that it is a kind of 'justice' humans impose as their law upon on other-than-human animals?

 Still in the 'real world' of nature, what animals do they do for reasons that might be opaque to us, though we can guess at them, as may be shown in the case of 'The cuckoo is a merry bird'.

> The cuckoo is a merry bird,
> She sings as she flies;
> She brings us good tidings,
> And tells us no lies.
>
> She sucks little birds' eggs
> To make her voice clear.
> That she may sing Cuckoo!
> Three months in the year.
>   (*Dictionary*, 139)

With or Without the Masks, One Fate Awaits Us All

When adults physically *play* a rhyme with a child, likewise when children together *play* a rhyme they know, complex negotiations of identity are entailed. Take the example of 'This Little Pig Went to Market', where the little pigs are generally referring to the fingers or toes of the child or the adult or both. One party is identifying a part of the body of the other to identify with the party named in the poem.

> This little pig went to market.
> This little pig stayed at home,
> This little pig had roast beef.
> This little pig had none,
> And this little pig cried, Wee-wee-wee-wee-wee,
> I can't find my way home.
> (*Dictionary*, 349)

The opening line sets the dark tone. Just why would a little piggie go to market? Why make a voluntary act of something a pig, for obvious reasons, would not want to do (if it knew what such an act meant). There is a blaming-the-victim banality to the routinised euphemism here. But then, in the second line, someone seems to have been saved. And then in the third line, the mask is torn away and here is the human having its animal dinner. And then someone misses out on their dinner. Is this the human/animal divide (i.e. is the fed pig the real human; is the unfed pig the real pig?). Of course we cannot know. Nor can we know what it means for the pig of the last line who cannot find its way home. Is this a simple warning not to be lost? Is this a warning not to find oneself at the mercy of arbitrary circumstances, such as for instance, those applying when one isn't sure if one is the diner or the one to be eaten. Much more of this in Chapter 6, where we deal with food anthropomorphism.

Without referring to the implied human–animal relationship, Pullinger treats the rhyme as a situated performance and argues for 'embodied prosody-the process through which meaning is enacted in the body through sound and movement' (2018, 152–153). Emphatic response will be elicited as children participate in the performance of this action rhyme with their body. In her interpretation, the comparison between 'the small, pink, tubby body of the piglet and the body of the child' is so obvious that 'small, anthropomorphised animals acting as child surrogates' (2018, 145). The animal trace is erased. But along the lines of a cognitive shift, it is hard to ignore that ambivalence in 'This Little Pig Went to Market' is between the pig-as-pig, the pig as anthropomorphic character in a pig costume (in a costume irrelevant to behaviour or fate) and the pig as human finger or toe on which the adult counts with the child – flesh that could be fingers holding cutlery, or the body dined upon. There is much at every stage of this rhyme that cannot be definitely known. Certainly the piggy who ate roast beef might have been going to the market to shop, just like anyone else. The ending, as it is, seems unhappy for a pig, but surely being lost is better than going to certain slaughter? In 'This Little Pig Went to Market', absurdity teaches the arbitrariness of life, of fate, of how things are. It also demonstrates the complexity and always potentially surprising nature of relations between apparently well-known things – body parts, dinner, partners in conversation, shopping. Perhaps the ultimate ambivalence a rhyme such as this delivers is concerns the question of how questionable the world's ways are. Delivered as a story needing to be unravelled, 'This Little Pig Went to Market' reveals a world where everything, especially human–animal relations, is open to question. Delivered as fiat or gospel, the rhyme shows the child the arbitrary nature of incomprehensible relationships that simply must be accepted as such.

Empathy may yet win the day among these complex relations. This is certainly the case for Mary and her little lamb:

> Why does the lamb love Mary so?
> The eager children cry;
> Why, Mary loves the lamb, you know,
> The teacher did reply.
> *(Dictionary*, 300)

Returning to Little Bo-peep, though things are somewhat more ridiculous, the stakes are also proportionately higher.

> Little Bo-peep has lost her sheep,
> And can't tell where to find them;
> Leave them alone, and they'll come home,
> And bring their tails behind them.
>
> Little Bo-peep fell fast asleep,
> And dreamt she heard them bleating;
> But when she awoke, she found it a joke,
> For they were still all fleeting.
>
> Then up she took her little crook,
> Determined for to find them;
> She found them indeed, but it made her heart bleed,
> For they'd left their tails behind them.
>
> It happened one day, as Bo-peep did stray
> Into a meadow hard by,
> There she espied their tails side by side,
> All hung on a tree to dry.
>
> She heaved a sigh, and wiped her eye,
> And over the hillocks went rambling,

> And tried what she could, as a shepherdess should,
> To tack again each to its lambkin.
> (*Dictionary*, 93–94)

A cruel joke indeed for the dream to suggest that the lost have been found; in fact a classic wish-fulfilment! But in this poem what is dreamt is more like waking experience and what is waking is more like a dream. Here the child shepherd faces the problem an adult shepherd might face with missing sheep, but in an oneiric form. Those of whom one has a charge of care are a problem to be dealt with and solved, and whether that is in the case of the adult looking after the child, or of the child or adult looking after animals, or in any other case. Still we may say that this poem of responsibility – a cautionary tale – expresses great ambivalence because of the confusions it implies: of waking and sleeping, of knowing and not knowing what to do, of power and powerlessness (for instance against sleep).

Ultimately however, and regardless of volition or degrees of attention and responsibility, *homo propronit sed deus disponit* (Man proposes, god disposes) seems to be the rule (as perhaps in life), universally applicable to all of the denizens of nursery rhymes, regardless of their species or costume status.

> Little Betty Pringle she had a pig,
> It was not very little and not very big;
> When he was alive he lived in clover,
> But now he's dead and that's all over.
> Johnny Pringle he sat down and cried,
> Betty Pringle she lay down and died:
> So there was an end of one, two, three,
> > Johnny Pringle he,
> > Betty Pringle she,
> > And Piggy Wiggy.
> (*Dictionary*, 73)

Nursery rhymes teach us to be kind, to be cruel, to be wise, to be silly, to be concerned (for ourselves and for others), and to be indifferent. We can put the longevity of the genre down to its serviceability for a range of ideological purposes. Nursery rhymes teach us, in short, the wicked and the arbitrary (likewise the good and the motivated) ways of the world. From nursery rhymes we learn that the world and we are as we are and that struggles to make things otherwise, while they may or may not succeed, frequently suggest a good story. We might pause the ambivalence for now, with a *desideratum* from the nursery's best loved avatar of wisdom:

> A wise old owl lived in an oak;
> The more he saw the less he spoke;

The less he spoke the more he heard.
Why can't we all be like that wise old bird?
(*Dictionary*, 340)

Perhaps though this would be too serious an ending for our nursery rhyme chapter? It will be better to mirror the argument we have made here and to capture ambivalence in the shape of pure fun, in the place where nonsense rules and we are lost in the moment:

Round and round the garden
Like a teddy bear;
One step, two step,
Tickle you under there!
(*Dictionary*, 184)

References

Amiran, Eyal. *Modernism and the Materiality of Texts*. Cambridge: Cambridge University Press, 2016.
Andersen, Jorgen. "Edward Lear and the Origin of Nonsense". *English Studies* 31 (1950): 161–166.
Attar, Farid ud-Din. (1177). *Conference of the Birds*. London: Penguin, 1984.
Bakhtin, Mikhail. M. *Rabelais and His World*. Cambridge, MA: M.I.T., 1968.
Barthes, Roland. *Mythologies*. Trans. Annette Lavers. New York: Noonday Press, 1991.
Blake, William. *Collected Poems*. Ed. W.B. Yeats. New York: Routledge, 2002.
Cammaerts, Emile. *The Poetry of Nonsense*. London: George Routledge & Sons Ltd, 1925.
Chaucer, Geoffrey. *Parliament of Fowls*. Scotts Valley: CreateSpace Independent, 2015.
Cornwell, Neil. *The Absurd in Literature*. New York: Manchester University Press, 2006.
Couchman, Marcos R.H. *Enjoying the Moment: Nursery Rhymes and the Nonsense of Living*. Scotts Valley: CreateSpace Independent, 2015.
Craig, Diana. *Ring-a-Ring o'Roses: Old Rhymes and Their True Meanings*. London: Michael O'Mara, 2018.
Dahl, Roald. *Fantastic Mr. Fox*. New York: Knopf, 1970.
Eckenstein, Lina. *Comparative Studies in Nursery Rhymes*. London: Duckworth & Co. Gutenberg Ebook, 1906.
Foster, Sam. *Hey Diddle Diddle: Our Best-loved Nursery Rhymes and What They Really Mean*. Chichester: Summersdale, 2008.
Goldthwaite, John. *Natural History of Make-Believe: A Guide to the Principal Works of Britain, Europe, and America*. Oxford: Oxford University Press, 1996.
Gregersdotter, Katarina, and Nicklas Hållén. "Anthropomorphism and the Representation of Animals as Adversaries". *Animal Horror Cinema*. London: Palgrave Macmillan, 2015. 206–223.
Griswold, Jerry. *Feeling Like a Kid: Childhood and Children's Literature*. Baltimore: JHU Press, 2006.

Headland, Isaac Taylor. *Chinese Mother Goose Rhymes*. New York: Fleming H. Revell Company, 1900.

Heyman, Michael and Kevin Shortsleeve. "Nonsense". *Keywords for Children's Literature*. Eds. Lissa Paul and Phil Nel. New York: New York University Press, 2011. 165–168.

Heyman, Michael. "A New Defense of Nonsense; or, Where Then Is His Phallus? and Other Questions Not to Ask". *Children's Literature Association Quarterly* 24(4) (1999): 187–194.

Ireson, Barbara and George Adamson. (1958). *The Faber Book of Nursery Verse*. London: Faber, 1983.

Jack, Albert. *Pop Goes the Weasel: The Secret Meanings of Nursery Rhymes*. New York: Penguin, 2008.

Jack, Albert. *Children's Nursery Rhymes: The Dark History & Origins of Kid's Nursery Rhymes*. Independently Published, 2019.

Jordan, David K. "The Rats Are Marrying Off Their Daughter". 2020. https://pages.ucsd.edu/~dkjordan/chin/chtxts/RatWedding.html, accessed on 25 March 2021.

Kidd, Stephen E. *Nonsense and Meaning in Ancient Greek Comedy*. Cambridge: Cambridge University Press, 2014.

Laird, Holly. "Laughter and Nonsense in the Making and (Postmodern) Remaking of Modernism". *The Future of Modernism*. Ed. Hugh Witemeyer. Ann Arbor: The University of Michigan Press, 1997.

Lear, Edward. *Selected Letters*. Ed. Vivien Noakes. Oxford: Oxford University Press, 1988.

Lecercle, Jean-Jacques. (1994). *Philosophy of Nonsense: The Intuitions of Victorian Nonsense Literature*. New York: Routledge, 2012.

Malcolm, Noel. *The Origins of English Nonsense*. London: Fontana/HarperCollins, 1997.

McGillis, Roderick. "Nonsense". *A Companion to Victorian Poetry*. Eds. Richard Cronin, Alison Chapman, and Anthony H. Harrison. Malden: Blackwell Publishers Ltd., 2002. 155–170.

Morton, Timothy. "Twinkle, Twinkle, Little Star" as an Ambient Poem; a Study of a Dialectical Image; with Some Remarks on Coleridge and Wordsworth". *Romantic Circles Praxis Series: Romanticism and Ecology*. Ed. Orrin Wang. 2001. www.rc.umd.edu/praxis/ecology/morton/morton.html, accessed on 29 May 2020.

Ohrem, Dominik. "Animating Creaturely Life". *Beyond the Human-Animal Divide: Creaturely Lives in Literature and Culture*. Eds. Dominik Ohrem and Roman Bartosch. New York: Palgrave MacMillan, 2017. 3–19.

Opie, Iona and Peter Opie. *The Oxford Nursery Rhyme Book*. Oxford: Clarendon Press, 1960.

Opie, Iona and Peter Opie. *A Nursery Companion*. Oxford: Oxford University Press, 1980.

Opie, Iona and Peter Opie. *The Oxford Dictionary of Nursery Rhymes*. Oxford: Oxford University Press, 1997.

Pullinger, Debbie. "Nursery Rhymes: Poetry, Language, and the Body". *The Aesthetics of Children's Poetry: A Study of Children's Verse in English*. Eds. Katherine Wakely-Mulroney and Louise Joy. New York: Routledge, 2018. 144–161.

Pullinger, Debbie. *From Tongue to Text: A New Reading of Children's Poetry*. New York: Bloomsbury Academic, 2017.
Sewell, Elizabeth. 1952. *The Field of Nonsense*. London: Dalkey Archive Press, 2015.
Stewart, Susan. *Nonsense: Aspects of Intertextuality in Folklore and Literature*. Baltimore and London: The Johns Hopkins University Press, 1989.
Styles, Morag. *From the Garden to the Street: Three Hundred Years of Poetry for Children*. London: Bloomsbury Publishing, 1997.
Sword, Elizabeth Hauge and Victoria Flournoy McCarthy. *A Child's Anthology of Poetry*. New York: HarperCollins, 1995.
Tigges, Wim. *An Anatomy of Literary Nonsense*. Amsterdam: Rodopi B.V., 1988.
Waddell, Martin. *Farmer Duck*. Illus. Helen Oxenbury. London: Walker Books, 1991.
Wells, Carolyn. *A Nonsense Anthology*. New York: Charles Scribner's Sons, 1903.
Wikipedia. "Governor Davey's Proclamation". https://en.wikipedia.org/wiki/Governor_Davey%27s_Proclamation, accessed on 2 July 2021.

4 Beware the Jubjub Bird
Cautionary Verses Revisited

Human relationships with animals, on the one hand, require caution, and on the other hand, these relations challenge what we think of as sense. Children need to be warned about animals, even the smallest and cuddliest of which might be dangerous in the right condition. The nonsense of cautionary verses is anchored in the contradictory norms of absurdity established in nursery rhymes. Likewise, it is easy to see nursery rhymes, with their frequently menacing tone, as prototypical cautionary tales, sometimes close to fable, though often the menace and absurdity are so entwined that it is difficult to see how the caution is to be read. This is certainly true of 'Jabberwocky', the main text with which we deal in this chapter. The interest here, as in nonsense poetry more generally, is in understanding the method in the madness.

Based on the similar vicariousness of children's literature and animal-concerned poetry, this chapter examines how ambivalences arise from a history of writing children and animals as proxies for humans of various stripes. We consider cautionary verses here as a genre typically written for children, based on three dynamics of equal importance – firstly, didacticism in the form of lessons taught by animal characters; secondly, power relations; and, finally, play within texts.

From Nursery Rhyme to Cautionary Tale

Getting from the wonder of nursery rhyme nonsense to the warnings expressed for young readers in humorous cautionary tales (received as such) typically entails the adoption of a more cohesive narrative structure. Consider, for instance, A.P. Herbert's 'The Spider':

> How doth the jolly little spider
> Wind up such miles of silk inside her?
> The explanation seems to be
> She does not eat so much as me.
>
> And if I never, never cram
> Myself with ginger-bread and jam,

Then maybe I'll have room to hide
A little rope in my inside.

Then I shall tie it very tight
Just over the electric light,
And hang head downward from the ceiling –
I wonder if one minds the feeling?

Or else I'd tie it to a tree
And let myself into the sea;
But when I wound it up again
I wonder if I'd have a pain?
           (Ireson and Adamson 1958, 103)

There would seem to be more or less a straight path here from the funny nursery rhyme, founded in nonsense, to the silly self-parodic warning, nonsensically delivered. Staying with insects and spiders, we need to remember that, along the way, there is a genre directed at children to parody and this is the serious cautionary tale (much in evidence from Aesop on), perhaps the paradigm case of which is in a pre-Victorian artefact, Mary Howitt's 'The Spider and the Fly' that first appeared in 1829:

'Will you walk into my parlour', said the Spider to the Fly;
'Tis the prettiest little parlour that ever you did spy.
The way into my parlour is up a winding stair,
And I have many curious things to shew when you are there.'
'Oh, no, no,' said the little Fly,' to ask me is in vain,
For who goes up your winding stair can ne'er come down again.'

'I'm sure you must be weary, dear, with soaring up so high;
Will you rest upon my little bed?' said the Spider to the Fly.
'There are pretty curtains drawn around; the sheets are fine and thin,
And if you like to rest awhile, I'll snugly tuck you in!'
'Oh no, no,' said the little Fly, 'for I've often heard it said,
They never, never wake again, who sleep upon your bed!'

Said the cunning Spider to the Fly, 'Dear friend, what can I do
To prove the warm affection I've always felt for you?
I have within my pantry, good store of all that's nice;
I'm sure you're very welcome—will you please to take a slice?'
'Oh, no, no,' said the little Fly, 'kind sir, that cannot be,
I've heard what's in your pantry, and I do not wish to see!'

'Sweet creature!' said the Spider, 'you're witty and you're wise;
How handsome are your gaudy wings, how brilliant are your eyes!

> I have a little looking-glass upon my parlour-shelf,
> If you'll step in one moment, dear, you shall behold yourself.'
> 'I thank you, gentle sir, ' she said, 'for what you're pleased to say,
> And bidding you good morning now, I'll call another day,
>
> The Spider turned him round about, and went into his den,
> For well he knew that silly Fly would soon come back again:
> So he wove a subtle web, in a little corner sly,
> And set his table ready, to dine upon the Fly.
> Then he came out to his door again, and merrily did sing,
> 'Come hither, hither, pretty Fly, with the pearl and silver wing;
> Your robes are green and purple—there's a crest upon your head;
> Your eyes are like the diamond bright, but mine are dull as lead!'
>
> Alas, alas! how very soon this silly little Fly,
> Hearing her wily, flattering words, came slowly flitting by;
> With buzzing wings she hung aloft, then nearer and nearer drew,
> Thinking only of her brilliant eyes, and green and purple hue:—
> Thinking only of her crested head—, poor foolish thing! At last,
> Up jumped the cunning Spider, and fiercely held her fast.
> He dragged her up his winding stair, into his dismal den,
> Within his little parlour—but she ne'er came out again!
> (Howitt 1829/1839, 149–154)

Through its dark humour, this rhyme issues an unmistakable (and explicitly made) caution to children:

> And now, dear little children, who may this story read,
> To idle, silly, flattering words, I pray you ne'er give heed:
> Unto an evil counsellor, close heart and ear and eye,
> And take a lesson from this tale, of the Spider and the Fly.
> (Howitt 1839, 154)

Gender is treated in this text as a cross-species absolute, amplified for instance in Tony Diterlizzi's adaptation and illustration of 'The Spider and the Fly'. The lesson may be read as misogynistic, suggesting that unwary men are doomed to succumb to seductive and evil female influences.

Straddling aspects of cautionary and nonsense verse, children's poetry includes witty parodies, biting satire, words of advice and caution. There are, of course, many forms and kinds of nonsense, and if we focus in this chapter on the most famous of all nonsense poems, then we should at least account, along the way, for the kinds of nonsense and the kind of thinking that are relevant to the idea of nonsense that carries a warning. The warning is usually more funny than serious, as we will show later, often involving deliberate hyperbole. It is paradoxical in a way that one would anticipate that the more strictly one adheres to sense, the more it should correspond to sound reason, yet as some cautionary verses would reveal, the very strictness of adhering to didactic logic results in reckless absurdity. The cautionary verse in this respect is paradoxical, involving a co-reliance on nonsense.[1]

Deleuze develops different series of paradox in *The Logic of Sense* (1969/1990) with an opening assertion that 'we present here a series of paradoxes which form the theory of sense. It is easy to explain why this theory is inseparable from paradoxes: sense is a nonexisting entity, and, in fact, maintains very special relations with nonsense' (xiii). Deleuze writes, 'Nonsense is that which has no sense, and that which, as such and as it enacts the donation of sense, is opposed to the absence of sense' (1990, 71). The union of sense and nonsense is investigated by Lecercle who claims that 'lack of sense here is always compensated by excess or proliferation of sense there', which is 'the central paradox, or contradiction, of the genre' (1994, 31). Nonsense, as such, reveals to us that in everyday communication sense and nonsense have no strict boundaries while the most rigorous sense might be the most recklessly nonsensical.

'In common sense, "sense" is no longer said of a direction, but of an organ. It is called "common", because it is an organ, a function, a faculty of identification that brings diversity in general to bear upon the form of the Same' (Deleuze 1990, 77–78). Let us take as given that what we call 'sense' is a socialised phenomenon; that coming to possess this kind of sense is a result of socialisation, and that 'nonsense', seen pejoratively as the state in which sense is either lacking or yet to be achieved, establishes a human flaw-to-be-fixed – something only humans have the potential to achieve. Yet other-than-human animals may be sometimes seen, along with children (and some other adults), as behaving in similar irrational or inexplicable ways and these behaviours may sometimes be thought of as funny (a pattern of observation to which a large proportion of Facebook posts are devoted).

The idea that nonsense has a natural affinity for children and for childish states may appear as a mystery on a par with that of the child-animal nexus we have had the occasion to mention. Perhaps it will suffice, as a shorthand, to link these perplexities by means of the following formula: children, as they are coming into language, are the little animals most productive of nonsense from the adult point of view. Adult retaliation is, in these circumstances, only to be expected. Or one might more generously read adult attempts at nonsense for children as an effort at meeting halfway.

Poetry Directed at Children and the Idea of Childhood

Childhood has been privileged as an ideal state since Romanticism (Natov 2003). To stress the validity of a meta-discursive approach here, one might say, the privileging of childhood as an ideal has been going on ever since childhood was invented, now some centuries ago (Ariès 1962). There is a close relationship between Romantic ideas of nature and the natural state of humankind and the idea of childhood innocence. The flipside of innocence – as per William Blake's schema – is the experience adults have of life and which – however unpleasant – they routinely pass on to children, as in many instances *for their own good*. That passing on of putatively needful knowledge defines our genre of interest here – the cautionary tale. It would be good to understand how poetic texts have reflected and shaped the creation/evolution of childhood as a social construct; conversely, to understand how the idea of the child's way of seeing has shaped a sense of what poetry can or should be, especially through such notions as 'recovered innocence' and de-familiarisation.

Here, we are interested in considering a number of texts which adults speak to children and, in particular, a nineteenth-century post-Romantic artefact – Lewis Carroll's 'Jabberwocky'. In the Chapter 5, we will look at a related twentieth-century artefact, Jimmy Kennedy's 'The Teddy Bears' Picnic'. What interests us in these two texts is the manner in which they embody performative contradictions entailed in the idea of adult conversation for or with children. Before turning to these texts, though, it will be helpful to briefly explore a tradition of texts for children, against which these two poems were written. It is worth noting that such texts might best be thought of as written over or against the voices of children or as a means of pre-empting an anticipated complaint.

Prior to the (more or less co-extensive) golden ages of print capitalism, of European world empire, of nationalism in Europe, and of Children's Literature, poetry ostensibly for children in the English language was largely about ruling them and about helping them to learn how to rule themselves. That is to say, it was didactic in the paternalist and condescending sense as in Geoffrey Chaucer's 'Controlling the Tongue':

> My son, keep well thy tongue, and keep thy friend.
> A wicked tongue is worse than a fiend…
> My son, thy tongue shouldst thou restrain
> At all time, but when they dost thy pain
> To speak of God, in honour and in prayer.
> (1845, 197)

The child listeners imagined by this text are ones who must be ruled because they cannot rule themselves. To learn to rule themselves, they must first learn to rule the tongue. This is the theme of John Hoskyn's seventeenth-century poem 'To his little Son Benedict from the Tower of London':[2]

> Sweet Benedict, whilst thou are young,
> And know'st not yet the use of tongue,
> Keep it in thrall whilst thou art free:
> Imprison it or it will thee.
> (Opie and Opie 1973, 21)

Many poems of earlier ages deliver like messages to the young. There is a reason for this habitual didacticism expressed in Hugh Rhodes' 1545 poem 'Rising in the Morning':

If in youth ye lack virtue,
In age ye shall want honour.
First dread you God, and fly from sin,
Earthly things are mortal;
Be thou not haughty in thy looks
For pride will have a fall.
          (Opie and Opie 1973, 12)

Children should be seen and not heard, as in the anonymous 1858 poem from which the immortal line appears to originate, 'Table Rules for Little Folks': 'I must not speak a useless word, / For children should be seen, not heard'. The today ironic-seeming last lines of that poem are

When told to rise, then I must put
My chair away with noiseless foot;
And lift my heart to God above,
In praise for all his wondrous love.
          (Opie and Opie 1973, 227)

These lines seem to the twenty-first-century reader to express something in the order of a masochist's joy in repression. And there is plenty more of this kind of advice for children. And so we should get up early, thank God a lot, and so on. In case the poetic invocations and examples of good behaviour fail, we may avail ourselves of Thomas Newberry's great merchant:

I have ornaments, implements, fit for the church,
Fine rods for children, of willow and birch.
          (Opie and Opie 1973, 15)

The 'we' here being adults in charge of children, of course. Not all of these child-focused texts are humorous. An anonymous sixteenth-century poem, 'The Unhappy Schoolboy', shows what we might expect were the tables turned:

My master peppered my tail with good speed,
It was worse than fennel seed,
He would not leave till it did bleed.
Much sorrow have he for his deed!
What availeth it me though I say nay?

I would my master were a hare,
And all his books greyhounds were,
And I myself a jolly hunter;
To blow my horn I would not spare,
For if he were dead I would not care!
What availeth it me though I say nay?
          (Opie and Opie 1973, 11)

To get from these serious predicaments to the tongue-in-cheek fun we find in a poem like 'Jabberwocky' involves some table turning, carnivalesque, moves – standing the adult-run world on its head, to show, among other things, that the sensible advice of adults may sound like nonsense in the ears of the innocents to whom it is directed. As we shall soon see, a cautionary tale, in the form of nonsense, has the potential to cast reflexive imaginative doubts on the generic forms in which sense and order are textually enshrined. In the process, there is the opportunity to create a complex and radically open work. From the late eighteenth century, Romanticism in some ways likewise institutionalised a carnival impulse for turning the tables on the generic investments of sense and of social order. William Blake's *Songs of Innocence* (1789/2002) and *Songs of Experience* (1794/2002), as noted by Morag Styles, 'can be seen as cunningly contradicting adult dominance and replacing it with the wisdom of innocence and naturalness, qualities which, in Blake's mind, were associated with the state of childhood' (1996, 191–192).

A legacy of these literary and historical circumstances is that the idea of childhood and an attitude to rationality are important in determining what poetry is for us today. It was William Wordsworth who coined the maxim, 'the Child is father of the Man':

> My heart leaps up when I behold
> A rainbow in the sky:
> So was it when my life began;
> So is it now I am a man;
> So be it when I shall grow old,
> Or let me die!
> The Child is father of the Man;
> And I could wish my days to be
> Bound each to each by natural piety.
> (1882, 260)

Wonder learnt childhood should be sustained through life, and it is the experience of innocent apprehension (a child's empiricism) that the adult world is thought to do well to recover. Now a well-established cliché, the exemplary character of child-wonder is routinely echoed in poetry ever since and still today. As with clichés more generally perhaps, Wordsworth's 'the Child is father of the Man' continues to be echoed because of its engaging insight and the counter-intuitive manner in which it appeals to the primacy of the child's over the adult's experience. This aphorism cuts through received wisdom as to the ways of the world and, in a carnival manner, upends the world so that we see how upside-down our thinking was before we thought again. Appealing also is the idea that the child's thinking is free of ornament and ostentation and so pure in the sense of presenting a reader with a zero degree of connotation. If the poets are, as per Shelley's dictum (1910), unacknowledged legislators, then it will make sense to speak of a child consciousness as having a privileged position as opposed to more prosaic and adult modes of thought. The poet's idea of the child's consciousness proposes an ideal for the manner in which the world is best received.

There are many poetic texts which keep Wordsworth's idea alive to this day. The idea of children's poetic 'legislation' or understanding to the fore (direct or vicarious or of rule/misrule, children but not adults are privileged to understand) is embodied in canonic poetry from Blake to Eliot and in classics such as Dr. Suess' *The Cat in the Hat* (1957) and Maurice Sendak's *Where the Wild Things Are* (1963). In texts like Pixar's *Toy Story* series (1995–2010), we are presented with a temporally bounded world where toys rule in the place of – and for the entertainment of – the child, but only when the human children and adults in the story are not watching or listening.

To historicise the shift in authority, we witness as a result of the invention and idealisation of childhood from the Romantic period onward, we should ask whether children or poets were generally empowered in any socio-political sense by the gaining prevalence of these ideas. And we should note that the kind of generally didactic verse that explained and justified the disempowerment of the young remained popular long after the advent of Romanticism.

Untranslatable Nonsense, Here Be Dragons

The idea of untranslatability, often claimed as characteristic of poetry (Robinson 2010, 23–25), seems to be particularly put to the test in the case of poetry that is intended to be, and regarded as, nonsense. We should not omit to mention the obvious nonsense affinity of foreign words and ways, as per such English expressions, as 'double Dutch', 'all Greek to me'. The perception of nonsense in what is not able to be understood is perhaps a basis for the idea of nonsense literature more generally. Where the known-to-be-there sense in texts is invisible or impenetrable to the reader, humour is a means of overturning what might otherwise be feelings of intimidation.

Take a comparison of humour in different cultures into account, for instance, Chinese literary tradition offers no equivalent genre. Variations of humour, as in jokes, parables, riddles, and wordplay, have been pervasive in everyday Chinese speech as much as in literary works for centuries. Nevertheless, its historical development was overshadowed by Confucianism, the most influential school of thought that instils the doctrine for moderation and decorum and advocates the orthodox literary writings. Against the moral backdrop, nonsensical content in Chinese literature mostly serves adult readers for self-entertaining humour, sarcasm, and intellectual wit. If there is any in children's literature, the content is quite often subject to the onslaught of didacticism and meaning-making overtones. As the Chinese essayist Shi Zhecun aptly comments, 'Even if it is a part of children's literature, a ready-made song of meaningless rhyme will be annotated by the so-called children's literature experts, accompanied by some superficial moral lessons to restrain children's lively imagination' (1986, 88).

While frequently translators take the task of translating nonsense as a challenge (witness the scores of languages into which 'Jabberwocky' has been translated), a question as to the cultural determinants of nonsense remains. Cultural difference, particularly where unexpected, is a source. In translating a nonsense poem like 'Jabberwocky', the overarching difficulty lies not just in teasing the metalinguistic complexity of this deceptively playful form and its rich culture-specific connotations (a nonsense-for-nonsense translation), but also in conveying the communicative effect of the original poem, as Alice says, 'pretty but RATHER hard to understand' (Carroll 2009, 136). Over the time, worldwide translators generally need to decide whether a source-oriented or target-oriented translation should be produced, for that matter, by employing either a domesticating or foreignising translation strategy or a combination of both.

We may ask to what extent are 'translations' of nonsense works better regarded as 'reversionings', in other words, finding equivalent cultural events for other readerships/audiences? Then there are forms of nonsense that require no translation. As Jean-Jacques Lecercle formulates one hypothesis in his essay 'Translate it, Translate it not' that 'You don't need to translate nonsense', which means that 'pure nonsense, being the playful linguistic expression of instinctual drives, is always already translated ... as the text in the target language is already there in the source'(2008, 93). Take, for example, the anthropomorphic child language crow-poem 'Crows' by Uwe-Michael Gutzschhahn:

Krähen
Kra kra
kra kra
Mama kra kra
Ja ja kra kra
Kra kra Mama
kra kra kra kra
Na na na na
kra kra Papa
Kra kra kra kra
Kacka Mama
Na na kra kra
kra kra ba ba
A-a kra kra
kra kra da da
La la la la
kra kra
kra kra

This piece offers a nice contrast with the James Krüss' poems discussed in Chapter 2 – 'Spatzen Internationale' and 'Hundesprache'. In these cases, there *is* something to translate and that translation effort would involve finding equivalent effects for subjects of another idiom, they in turn have differently nuanced attitudes to those who speak languages foreign to them.

In Lewis Carroll's 'Jabberwocky' we find a kind of faux foreignness, an apparent untranslatability that has no immediately obvious source, rather sources that appear to the reader appropriately upon reflection. As Lecercle puts it:

> The semantics of the poem is rather wild (those coinages are words in anticipation of meaning: the English language has since endowed one or two, like 'chortle' or 'galumph', with the meaning they called for), such is not the case for the syntax, which preserves all the grammatical words intact, making the poem a textbook exercise for first-year linguistics; such is not the case for the prosody, which is amazingly regular, or even for the narrative, which, apart from the envoi of the first stanza, cries out for an analysis in terms of Proppian functions.
>
> (2008, 100)

But there is more than this in 'Jabberwocky'. In this poem, we meet the apparent didacticism of nineteenth-century poetry intended by adults for children. The animals in this story poem (the Jabberwock, the Jubjub bird and the Bandersnatch) teach not by talking but by being available as fearsome fauna of the potentially huntable kind. It is the tale that is instructive. Once into the poem, we see that it is for the telling of the tale that the poem is presented. This is one of the almost-too-obvious ways to receive the genre of the text. Inside the frame of the story told by the poem, we see the triumphant success of one beamish boy and as well we see that this rite-of-passage is exemplary for the beamish boy or girl (an Alice, for instance) who is the text's putative listener, the listening subject whom one must imagine will have questions for the tale's teller (questions without which the poem's meaning will remain opaque). Like so much in Lewis Carroll's oeuvre, the text here suggests the performance and the dialogic encounter necessary to the exegesis the text demands. But, just as there is an outside in the poem to the story it contains, so there is an outside of the poem in Alice's first encounter with it – it is in a book and on a page she merely happens upon. Nonsense, irony, and portality are key themes in the investigation of this most famous of all nonsense texts.

If we read the Alice books as a series of parodic cautionary verses set up to call into question apparent common sense, these verses become the standard for subsequent self-parodic cautionary tales in the English (and often in other) languages: for example, in Ted Hughes' poems in *Meet My Folks* (1961). Hughes' poems blend the human-ordered world with the animal imagination in a 'queer but extremely polite' manner (Hughes 2008, 39).

Our interest here is to re-examine apparent didacticism, as it concerns power and especially gender relations, human-animal relations and adult-child relations. In Edward Lear's rambling bird-obsessed bestiary (2010), and in the cautionary tone we find in Hilaire Belloc's 'Jim, Who ran away from his Nurse, and was eaten by a Lion', and like works, we find a creaturely didacticism that challenges received wisdom and common sense by stressing imagined animal voices, which plays with the indeterminacy of animal meaning.

Dipping into Bakhtin's carnival mode, childhood is also reckoned as a prime venue for turning things upside down or inside out, as we will see illustrated further in the Chapter 5, in the case of 'The Teddy Bears' Picnic'.

Cautionary Verses for Children: Horror or Humour?

Cautionary tales for children were epitomised in Heinrich Hoffmann's *Struwwelpeter* (1845/1890), an illustrated collection that features children who are punished due to misbehaviours, such as whipping dogs, sucking thumbs, not allowing the nails to be cut, and not watching the path ahead while walking. Of particular note in our investigation are anthropomorphic animals. Among other grotesque and comic figures, these are part and parcel of why this collection has lasting appeal to child readers. In 'Cruel Frederick', the dog Tray made a successful revenge against the boy who whipped him 'till he was sore, and kicked and whipped him more and more' (Hoffmann 1890, 5). After biting Frederick till he bled,

> He seats himself in Frederick's chair
> And laughs to see the nice things there:
> The soup he swallows, sup by sup—
> And eats the pies and puddings up.
> (Hoffmann 1890, 5)

Likewise, in 'The Story of the Man that went out Shooting', we find a little bespectacled hare turning herself from the target into the hunter and shooting the human hunter, although she missed her mark. Animals also serve as an amused chorus. In 'The Story of Johnny Head-in-Air', three fishes caught sight of how Johnny fell off while he was walking to the brink of the river with his eyes on the sky. After he was timely pulled from the river and all wet, the fishes came to 'enjoy the fun and laughter':

> Each popp'd out his little head,
> And, to tease poor Johnny, said:

> 'Silly little Johnny, look,
> You have lost your writing-book!'
>   (Hoffmann 1890, 23)

Animals, symbolically, can be interpreted as adults or parents in disguise. Just as in 'The Dreadful Story about Harriet and the Matches', the two cats warned the girl not to play with the fire, and the girl, as a good reader might expect, disregarded the warning and burnt herself to death. The portentous cats, endowed with speech capacity and human sentience, mourned over the little girl:

> And when the good cats sat beside
> The smoking ashes, how they cried!
> 'Me-ow, me-oo, me-ow, me-oo!!
> What will Mamma and Nursy do?'
> Their tears ran down their cheeks so fast;
> They made a little pond at last.
>   (Hoffmann 1890, 7)

There is, of course, a strain of human in every speaking animal depicted in the book. But a symbolic understanding of animals would be too earnest to spoil the fun of their presence. There is some truth in Peter Russell's observation that the retribution of children's misdemeanours depicted in *Struwwelpeter* occurs 'in the workings of natural justice parents (who are not strict, but indulgent, even neglectful) play only a minor role' (2016, 218). No doubt that animals, as in a web of human-nature relations, add a spin of comic innocence to these punishments.

The purpose of these warnings and punishments is not avowedly to scare children into submission. As the subtitle indicates, the book is supposed to be full of 'pretty stories and funny pictures'. Although Johnny was laughed at by the three fishes, his keen observation of the world around and his obsession with dreamy, other-worldly ideas would win more sympathy than admonition. The visualisation of animal characters, as in the dog wearing a napkin round his neck, the hare wearing spectacles, the cats weeping with handkerchiefs, also counterbalances the brutality of these stories' grim endings. It might then be argued that 'such imaginative rehearsals' characterised with 'a mixture of fascination and terror which constitutes their particular power' are 'not only unlikely to damage the infant psyche, but are actually conducive to healthy growth' (Russell 2016, 217).

Cautionary verses reach the apex in Hillarie Belloc's *Cautionary Tales for Children* (1907), which are also filled with the fun of terrible things. Belloc's cautionary verse is inspired by Hoffmann's book and continues the style of comic exaggeration, using disproportionate punishments for childish faults. As Styles describes it, 'The feature of the cautionary which stands out most strongly is extreme retribution meted out, usually to children, for smallish misdemeanours which are funny because they are so exaggerated' (1997, 150). Unlike Hoffmann's book, which targets children (3–6 years old), Belloc's cautionary verses are designed for the admonition of children between the ages of 8 and 14 years.

While Hoffmann's method of admonition resorts to 'natural justice', Belloc's denies any serious moral intent. This is made explicit in the opening, an address to a reader who might ask whether the verses were true:

> And is it True? It is not True.
> And if it were it wouldn't do,
> For people such as me and you
> Who pretty nearly all day long
> Are doing something rather wrong.
> Because if things were really so,
> You would have perished long ago,
> And I would not have lived to write
> The noble lines that meet your sight,
> Nor B.T.B. survived to draw
> The nicest things you ever saw.
> (Belloc 1941, 3)

As foreshadowed in this introduction, Belloc's cautionary verses are an attempt to mainly ridicule the didactic messages customarily given within the moralistic children's stories of the Victorian period. The method of admonition is, therefore, more parodic than that in Hoffmann's *Struwwelpeter* not only because it takes the story quickly to the humorously disproportionate punitive measures for common childish faults, such as the famous instances of 'Jim, Who ran away from his Nurse, and was eaten by a Lion', 'Maltida, Who told lies and was Burned to Death', and 'Rebecca, Who slammed Doors for Fun and Perished Miserably', but also because these severe punishments are parodic of generic Victorian customary warnings.

Jim, Who Ran Away from His Nurse, and Was Eaten by a Lion
There was a Boy whose name was Jim;
His Friends were very good to him.
They gave him Tea, and Cakes, and Jam,
And slices of delicious Ham,
And Chocolate with pink inside,
And little Tricycles to ride,
And read him Stories through and through,
And even took him to the Zoo –
But there it was the dreadful Fate
Befell him, which I now relate.

You know – at least you ought to know.
For I have often told you so –
That Children never are allowed
To leave their Nurses in a Crowd;

Now this was Jim's especial Foible,
He ran away when he was able,
And on this inauspicious day
He slipped his hand and ran away!
He hadn't gone a yard when – Bang!
With open Jaws, a Lion sprang,
And hungrily began to eat
The Boy: beginning at his feet.

Now just imagine how it feels
When first your toes and then your heels,
And then by gradual degrees,
Your shins and ankles, calves and knees,
Are slowly eaten, bit by bit.

No wonder Jim detested it!
No wonder that he shouted 'Hi!'
The Honest Keeper heard his cry,
Though very fat he almost ran
To help the little gentleman.
'Ponto!' he ordered as he came
(For Ponto was the Lion's name),
'Ponto!' he cried, with angry Frown.
'Let go, Sir! Down, Sir! Put it down!'

The Lion made a sudden Stop,
He let the Dainty Morsel drop,
And slunk reluctant to his Cage,
Snarling with Disappointed Rage
But when he bent him over Jim,
The Honest Keeper's eyes were dim.
The Lion having reached his Head,
The Miserable Boy was dead!

When Nurse informed his Parents, they
Were more Concerned than I can say: –
His Mother, as She dried her eyes,
Said, 'Well – it gives me no surprise,
He would not do as he was told!'
His Father, who was self-controlled,
Bade all the children round attend

To James' miserable end,
And always keep a-hold of Nurse
For fear of finding something worse.
(Belloc 1941, 5–10)

If one notes a little of the misogyny of 'The Spider and the Fly' here in the casual disparaging of the nurse, then this matches other racist/imperialist angles on the matter, all of which confirm the text as of its time. These poems deal with life and death situations in which the naturalness of animal instincts are to the fore. The key difference between these poems is that the moralism of 'The Spider and the Fly' is subverted by humour in Belloc's poem, and in the end, it is automatised moralism that is the funniest thing of all, as revealed in the lessons Jim's thoughtful parents have passed on.

The mock moral is clear and final, as fitting in Belloc's sly and predictable model of cautionary tales, that children should be obedient to their keepers. Jim's running away from the nurse is a naughty behaviour, not a crime at all, so his sudden and untimely death is as delightfully gory as it is implausibly funny because of the arbitrary nature of such punishment as well as the reactions of the adults in the piece. Such ambivalence in Belloc's tales, as Jennifer Sattaur notes, oscillates between 'moral and irreverent, terrifying and invitingly fun' (2011, 143). These tales, she insists, are carnivalesque as through the Bakhtin's lens of carnival, presenting

> a world in which everyone and everything is engaged in a grand and very serious game of nonsense – a game which undermines the 'ready-made and completed' adult world into which the children in *Cautionary Tales* must be initiated, by destabilizing the relationships between crime and punishment, morals and rewards, the normal and the ridiculous.
>
> (140)

This verse plays on the fashion of taking children to the zoo through the latter part of the nineteenth century when the institution serves as a venue of colonial exhibitions of wild species (Ritvo 1987). This motif is salient in Belloc's earlier works *The Bad Child's Book of Beasts* (1896) and *More Beasts for Worse Children* (1897), both containing a wide array of animals arranged for moral purposes: dromedary, hippopotamus, dodo, baboon, rhinoceros, python, chamois, and marmozet. In the disguise of their exotic and, therefore, comic appearance, a note of sadness can be detected in their collective fate as victims of humans' voyeuristic impulses. Like the ambivalence of Belloc's cautionary verses, animals are pervasively funny too. There is the baboon 'dressed respectably', the frog who 'is just sensitive to epithets', and the Indian elephant who reads *The Times*. Belloc's works paradoxically entertain, challenge, and subvert symbolic associations that come with adult responsibility, childish obedience, and assumptions as to nature/culture boundaries. Child-animal analogies along such lines are clearly spelt out in the Introduction to *The Bad Child's Book of Beasts*:

> I call you bad, my little child,
> Upon the title page,
> Because a manner rude and wild
> Is common at your age.
>
> The moral of this priceless work
> (if rightly understood)
> Will make you-from a little Turk-
> Unnaturally good.
>
> Do not as evil children do,
> Who on the slightest grounds
> Will imitate the kangaroo,
> With wild unmeaning bounds:
>
> Do not as children badly bred,
> Who eat like little hogs,
> And when they have to go to bed
> Will whine like Puppy Dogs:
>
> Who take their manners from the Ape,
> Their habits from the Bear,
> Indulge the loud unseemly jape,
> And never brush their hair.
>
> But so control your actions that
> Your friends may all repeat.
> 'This child is dainty as the Cat,
> And as the Owl discreet'.
>   (Belloc 1941, 157–160)

Cautionary tales for children, as we can see from Hoffmann to Belloc, seek to balance didacticism and entertainment, two impulses that often tussle in children's literature. Nonsensical verses, as we have seen, are drawn to account for the universally affective dimension of the fantastic and the precarious, from which a jovial ruthlessness springs. A comparison of the two writers draws Peter Russell to conclude that 'both nimbly tread a tightrope between earnest moralising and light-hearted comedy, Hoffmann leaning further to the former side, Belloc to the latter' (224). Will it be sufficient to say that 'cautionary tales' is a chameleon genre? Although the name itself seems to suggest the function of admonishing children on adults' behalf, the content, quite often, caters to the attitudes of children who always rebel against tedious warnings from sermonizing adults. And so we see that the name of the genre itself has come to be taken ironically.

The cautionary verse is, therefore, less an enforcement of decorum and obedience than a flirtation with dis/order. Hovering between warning and comedy, this genre converts children's potential fright, with all its exaggeration, into laughter. These characteristics, when integrated with nonsense, are brought out to the full in 'Jabberwocky'. This quintessential piece of nonsense verse, as we will soon elaborate, has influenced contemporary nonsensical cautionary poems, such as Dennis Lee's poem 'I Eat Kids Yum Yum' in *Garbage Delight* (1977). In this poem, a girl bumped into a mighty monster who roared a mighty song attempting to eat her up, leaving only her teeth and clothes. But the girl was not amused nor cowed; instead, she confronted the monster singing to rhyme a way out of it: 'It's time to chomp and take a chew/And what I'll chew is you' (37). Her hunger was so vigorously felt that the monster fled in a wink and the girl went skipping home and 'ate her brothers model train' (37). Here we find the tables turned in what might be read as a child-empowering cautionary tale for monsters, one which, if one gives it a moment's thought, certainly owes a debt to 'Jabberwocky'.

Into the Tulgey Wood

We can easily find precursor works for Lewis Carroll's 'Jabberwocky' especially in an Old English text like *Beowulf*, but 'Jabberwocky' is certainly the precursor of texts, like those of Hillaire Belloc and Dennis Lee, above.

Creatures that do not exist, spoken of in words that do not exist – there is in this arrangement a delighted nostalgia for a wider world where less was known and so more was possible. That nostalgia is, though knowingly deployed, as suggested by the uncanniness of the text. We have been in such woods as these before, and we will come again.

> 'Twas brillig, and the slithy toves
> Did gyre and gimble in the wabe:
> All mimsy were the borogroves,
> And the mome raths outgrabe.
>
> 'Beware the Jabberwock, my son!
> The jaws that bite, the claws that catch!
> Beware the Jubjub bird, and shun
> The frumious Bandersnatch!'
>
> He took his vorpal sword in hand:
> Long time the manxome foe he sought –

> So rested he by the Tumtum tree,
> And stood awhile in thought.
>
> And, as in uffish thought he stood,
> The Jabberwock, with eyes of flame,
> Came whiffling through the tulgey wood,
> And burbled as it came!
>
> One, two! One, two! And through and through
> The vorpal blade went snicker-snack!
> He left it dead, and with its head
> He went galumphing back.
>
> 'And, hast thou slain the Jabberwock?
> Come to my arms, my beamish boy!
> O frabjous day! Callooh! Callay!'
> He chortled in his joy.
>
> (Carroll 2009, 134–136)

The tale is instructive; it is told to instruct. This is one of the almost-too-obvious ways to receive the genre of the text. The beamish boy who is both the poem's addressee and the subject of its action presents, in either case, as an illustrative ideal. Inside the frame of the story told by the poem, we see the triumphant success of one beamish boy, and as well, this rite-of-passage is exemplary for the beamish boy or girl (an Alice, for instance) who is the text's putative listener – the listening subject whom one must imagine will have questions for the tale's teller, questions without which the poem's meaning will remain opaque. Like so much in the Carrollian oeuvre, the text here suggests the performance and the dialogic encounter necessary to the exegesis the text demands. But, just as there is an outside in the poem to the story it contains, so there is an outside of the poem in Alice's first encounter with it – it is in a book and on a page she merely happens upon. Again, as with so much in Lewis Carroll, the ambivalence between the spoken and written confounds the exegesis the text demands as per Humpty dumpty's explanations, which we will look at shortly.

To introduce the text this way ignores its most conspicuous feature and the most straightforward means of generic classification for it – namely, that this is nonsense. And again, it is worth noting here that there is, in this, a continuity with texts of Carroll's day intended for children. It is noteworthy that 'the Owl and the Pussycat' and 'Jabberwocky' were both first published in 1871. The ideas of nonsense, topsey-turveydom, and misrule for the poetic entertainment of children were certainly well established in Victorian England. Consider William Brighty Rands 'Topsey-Turvey World':

If the butterfly courted the bee,
And the owl the porcupine;
If churches were built in the sea,
And three times one was nine;
If the pony rode his master.
    (Opie and Opie 1973, 232)

Nonsense is intended to delight children, and there is behind this, for the adult poet, a notional affinity between the not-yet-adult mind and the mock-able arbitrariness of how the sensible world has to be. In William Howitt's 'The Wind in a Frolic', we read an invitation for the child to identify with forms of chaos:

The wind one morning sprung up from sleep,
Saying, 'Now for a frolic! now for a leap!
Now for a mad-cap, galloping chase!
I'll make a commotion in every place!'
    (Opie and Opie 1973, 162)

The frolic here is at the expense of, for instance, the aged; it is also at the expense of a hapless schoolboy 'who panted and struggled in vain' and ends up with 'his hat in a pool, and his shoe in the mud' (Opie and Opie 1973, 163). If the celebration of naughtiness marks a break with the child-controlling verse of earlier centuries, Howitt's and Rand's examples seem pale and tame beside Lear's 'Owl and the Pussycat' (and many other efforts of Lear's and Carroll's). Lear and Carroll provide a model for the celebration of misrule for the appreciation of children – a structural innovation from mid- to late-Victorian literature, of which *The Cat in the Hat*, eighty years later, may be the peak product.

    The impossible nonsense of anthropomorphism in 'The Owl and the Pussycat' is a starting point and a staple in entertaining children with poetry and with what it inspires.[3] In 'Jabberwocky', the nonsense is shallower and deeper than in Lear's poem. Allow us to indulge this claim by way of a set of questions: where precisely *is* the nonsense in 'Jabberwocky'? Why is this poem so enduringly and uniquely interesting? Why has it been such a touchstone text for so many disciplines? Have these things to do with the incongruity of actions or actors in the story? There is nothing anthropomorphic happening here unless it is the case that whiffling and burbling are human notions of sound production. These creatures are neither real nor explicitly anthropomorphic but framed to be fantastic foes of humans.

    Surely, they are not human sounds, but clearly, they are human perceptions of sound – perceptions drawing attention to the necessary stretches the imagination makes in an effort of getting the world out there into words to exchange by mouth or on paper. There is no doubt the apt sounding neologism draws attention to the idea of perception as language and so as a human attribute. The landscape is alive and even if we cannot recognise the words, the readers will recognise that the landscape is made by the way of words. Yes, there are pictures in the book, but the words are the authority here for what the reader should be able to see.

The humour of the poem is on the surface in the words, which are not words at all. We do not have to dig down very far to find out how those words mean though. As parodied in Humpty Dumpty's mock critical practice with the poem, this is nonsense that becomes more meaningful as we spend more time with it. The process so many have undertaken of attempting to translate is particularly enlightening of the poem. The effort to understand the intention of the poem in another language leads us to see more of its means of meaning.

'Jabberwocky', in telling its story, parodies the idea of the rite of passage to adulthood; it reflexively parodies the verbal rituals which represent and perhaps entail that rite of passage and the genre in which it is lauded or fragment thereof, perhaps Anglo-Saxon poetry. Approaching the text from the point of view of genre draws attention to the form/content aspect of how the parody works. The way in is through understanding what can and cannot be understood through context clues. Most of the grammar and the grammatical words can be understood this way – that is to say, what is incomprehensible in the poem is the invented lexicon and its narrative role. By a word-by-word analysis of what can be known, one progresses fairly directly to the question of genre: what kind of a text/story is this?

If genre is the deep structure of a text and denotation of a single lexeme is the shallow apparent surface, then in this poem, those roles appear to be reversed. The story is simple; it has a simple structure. What delays us from getting near to that structure is the resistance of words and their refusal to mean for us. Yet those words, with a little attention, come to suggest what little they need to mean for us. Reversal is the key here, and a reversal is, of course, the first reflexive clue we are given with this poem; the text is presented to Alice as mirror writing, and the problem-posing method starts with Alice – she has to work out that it is mirror writing. Knowing this is the way to begin to understand. In this 'thinking out loud' sense, Alice has to perform the necessary reversal; she has to perform 'Jabberwocky' into the possibility of meaning anything at all. But we will not get much of a sense of this until the exegetic encounter with Humpty Dumpty in his chapter, where we exercise the notion of words meaning 'simply' what they are meant to mean, an idea reflection revealed to be *hubris* Humpty Dumpty style.

Reversals, borders, other sidedness, and wrong sidedness – these are the thematic core of *Through the Looking-Glass* and they are what Looking-Glass Land is all about. The oneiric aspect of the experience, for Alice and for the reader, is consonant with what Freud will soon say of dreams – that they are wish fulfilments. In any case, if dreaming is a reverse side of waking, then dreaming and waking are reverse sides of the one material – the material one may think of as life or experience. This is the arrangement Maurice Merleau-Ponty suggests by means of analogy for language, in general, with the process of weaving; the trope at stake is *wrong-sidedness*:

> It goes without saying that language is oblique and autonomous, and that its ability to signify a thought or a thing directly is only a secondary power derived from the inner life of language. Like the weaver, the writer works on the wrong side of his material. He has to do only with language, and it is thus that he suddenly finds himself surrounded by meaning.
>
> (1964, 44–45)

'Jabberwocky' is a text which makes this kind of revelation palpable for the reader. The Tenniel pictures may help a little, but it is Carroll's words (words *his* to an unusual degree) that create for the readers the scene in which they find themselves. For Alice in particular, 'Somehow it seems to fill my head with ideas – only I don't exactly know what they are!' (Carroll 2009, 136).

In both Alice books, so many of our protagonist's make-believes are true performatives. Alice not only dreams but, more importantly, wishes her way into Looking-Glass Land. The Looking-Glass frame suggests that everything in it needs to be read reflexively. And everything needs to be read dialogically, even contrariwise, as well. It is not only the encounter with Humpty Dumpty that shows us exegesis requires conversation; our every encounter with Alice and with her thinking suggests a dialogue with our assumptions, with what we, as readers, thought we might have been able to take for granted – about little girls and about words and the world.

'Jabberwocky' draws our attention to the mystery and difficulty associated with working out what things are about. Once we have a sense of the poem's genre, we know what it is about in a fundamental sense: it is about a boy-and-beast battle as a rite of passage circumscribed by convention as to what is desirable, what needs to be done, and so it is about becoming adult. Consonant with the novel's broader progression towards our protagonist's becoming Queen Alice, Alice's reading of the poem reveals that becoming an adult and its dialogical entailments go on inside and beyond the text, with and without a mirror. So 'Jabberwocky' is part of Alice's course in becoming an adult. This is a course in seeing, if not understanding, the craziness of the world in which adults hold power, a course in the giddiness of coming to that power, a course in vertigo as sometimes accompanied by falling. As readers, our course in all this as much as it is Alice's; her interaction with the text and her exegetic performance teach us. And while it may be unfair to assert that the limited understanding Alice claims is disingenuous – certainly when Alice tells us, 'However, *somebody* killed *something*, that's clear, at any rate' (136, emphasis in the original) – we, of course, by now know much more of the story.

With Alice, we encounter the unexpectedness of experience and the dreaminess of growing up and this is the fundamental problem for the reader who hopes for a conventional plot in the Alice books. The plot is of its nature crazy, mazy and inconsistent, which fails to sustain suspense because scenes dissolve into each other the way scenes do in dreams and especially in our recollection of them. And yet, as in dreams, there is suspense. Constant reframing brings us up against irony because the point of view that was operational moments ago has now been superseded. One irony leads to another as text is constantly recontextualised. The process witnessed is, of its nature, reflexive.

Irony is where meaning lies opposite to what a surface reading seems to say. Of 'Jabberwocky' and our first encounter with it, we may say it is ironic that a mirror should be needed to make readable a text found in a book, in the book we are reading. This irony applies to much of what Alice meets in Looking-Glass Land. It is of the nature of the place. In Tweedledum and Tweedledee, we meet this irony's nth degree. The anthropomorphism of enantiomorphs yields an irony in the paradoxical form: the disagreement of the same. In 'Jabberwocky', it is ironic that the simplest of stories subsists in this most arduous of poetry – the encounter with which is not unlike the encounter with a text like *Beowulf*. In fact, of course, it is modelled on that kind of encounter, the difference here being that attention is drawn to the fact by the nature of the encounter, so conversely reading Old English is like reading mirror writing: not hard once one has the knack. Therefore, one can say that reading 'Jabberwocky' one understands an irony when one makes the genre recognition entailed in seeing the story, something like that Victorian affection for a picture which reads another way. Seeing the story, one knows where one is; as per Merleau-Ponty's statement, 'one suddenly finds oneself surrounded by meaning'. Certainly, it is ironic that it is words we do not know that allow us to see a world that is alien to us. As we observe in shallower and deeper readings of the poem, in 'Jabberwocky', other words welcome us to a world we already know because it is ours because of historical and literary compatibility for the genre in which we intuit meaning.

The place known already where we have never been – nowhere better than in 'Jabberwocky' is the nature of the dreamer's experience captured as a literary artefact. Alice's dismissal of the rich content with which she has been presented is one with the waking subject's immediate progression to the pressing business of the day. Every frame leads onto a next and so one is wary of saying it is ironic that in the effort to interpret 'Jabberwocky', humour arises from generically serious subject matter delivered in language that is apparently opaque. Humour is in the deeps of the poem and it comes from absolutely novel language showing us the place and the actions we understand and already know – not because we have been there but because we are acculturated to their conventionality; that is to say, because we recognise a frame.

Each of the interacting layers of irony one reads from the encounter with 'Jabberwocky' is possible precisely because there are layers because of the reframing acts that are necessary to *any* understanding of the text. From a pedagogic point of view, we think this explains the exceptional value of this particular text: once tricked into understanding anything of it, whoever stays with the text will be carried on by a process of reframing the act of reading *requires* the reader to perform.

Irony is mobile metonymy; it is the portal trope. And portality – in fiction, as for the dreamer – derives its case-by-case quality from the nature of worlds entered into, displaced, or juxtaposed. In Carroll–Dodgson worlds, we can say hermeneutics meet mathematical certainty; of course, the meeting must generate ironies (of the kind to which an apocryphal Queen Victoria was subject when provided by Dodgson with a mathematical treatise when hoping for a new story).[4] Deleuze writes of irony that it is 'itself a multiplicity – or rather the art of multiplicities: the art of grasping the Ideas and the problems they incarnate in things, and of grasping things as incarnations, as cases of solution for the problems of Ideas' (1994, 182).

For Linda Hutcheon, as for Deleuze, irony is a trope of multiplicity involving 'an oscillating yet simultaneous perception of plural and different meanings' (1994, 66). The perception here entails participation in a text and the performance it demands is specifically in Judith Butler's sense of exercising 'that reiterative power of discourse to produce the phenomena that it regulates and constrains' (Butler 1992, 2). Those reframings through which Alice guides us are identity-making and world-altering not only for Alice but for readers as well. Play with the symbols makes the world inside the text Alice reads, and (in the dream without the dream of the poem) it makes Alice, the reader she is. It also makes the world through which Alice makes her way, that world in which it would be unwise to wake the Red King who is dreaming us. The reframing play in the story, commencing with and never far from the mirror motif, reaches an infuriating pitch in Chapter VIII when Alice encounters the Knight's Peircean play with the naming of a song. Naming, we see, is an endless activity.

Poetry Re-framed Through a Looking-Glass

Outside of Looking-Glass Land and the book which contains it, the exegetic encounter entailed in and inspired by this play transforms the world in which poetry is read. To read and to understand are to perform an identity – to read is to become someone. If this is the general case, so then it is through a text like *Through the Looking-Glass*, we come to the frame in which this particular truth is to the fore. Hutcheon writes that 'irony is an inevitable consequence of the distance between addresser and addressee' (57). This can be taken to mean that in a world of perfect understanding, there could be no irony nor any need for acts of interpretation. The interpretation would be meaningless in the solipsistic world Humpty Dumpty proposes, that world the existence of which his acts of interpretation contradict. In the terms laid out for genre and convention above, in coming to understand 'Jabberwocky', we understand it as a norm-asserting text. Ironically, it is the apparent opacity of that text that reveals the fact of its asserting norms. In other words, if we, as readers, were not pressed to see what we can and cannot understand in the text, then we would not have noticed the text's core structure of meaning, as disclosed by our understanding of the genre (the text here presupposing heterogeneous readerships, some of which will know the genre better, and some perhaps worse, than Alice).

Humpty Dumpty's claims provide a proving contrast with the reader's general circumstances. His attempts to take charge of the poem's meaning are another kind of performance, a performance of that character's arrogance, further, a crude effort to escape the inescapable – that is, the fact of participation in the text. Here is a character claiming to sit in judgement outside of the work, but we know that he is just one more of the cast we can expect to go out like a candle, should the Red King leave off dreaming. By the end of the book, we will know that the only character for whom this truth might be doubted is Alice herself; she is and is not the Alice who went through the Looking-Glass at the beginning of the story and yet she is the one who survives her dream. Still, all of Alice's characters (Humpty Dumpty included) survive to us, beyond her dream and beyond Carroll's book; it is only forgetting that wears away the meaning of signs or gets them off the merry-go-round. As Umberto Eco writes in his essay on Peirce, 'Semiosis explains itself by itself: this continual circularity is the normal process of signification' (98).

Reading 'Jabberwocky' is norm-setting in all sorts of ways. We understand this world from the outside; we understand that we bring our understanding with us and that this is something we already know how to do. Perhaps the most immediate effect of 'Jabberwocky' on Alice is revealed in her gliding down the handrail to get out of the house to see the garden. However, little Alice claims to know, the experience has been a revelation for her; in the giddy state in which she finds herself, she has to arrest her progress by grabbing hold of the door-post in order to be able to walk normally. A moment later (at the beginning of Chapter 3 'Looking-Glass Insects'), Alice will be inexplicably elsewhere, though with the same motive remaining to her of seeing the garden, and like a good dreamer, she will ask no question of this changed circumstance.

One of the curious ironies of Alice's situation, and perhaps of the child's, more generally, is that while the asking of, perhaps, annoying questions keeps her squarely in the domain of childhood, still the asking of questions is her means of gaining the knowledge that will allow her to become an adult. But perhaps it will be interesting to note the many places in her stories where Alice might have asked a question but did not. For the pre-Romantic authors we have mentioned earlier in this chapter, citizenship of adulthood or a possible right of adulthood is posited on the transcendence of childishness. This idea certainly persists in the child-directed verse of the nineteenth century, as we saw with the anonymous dictum about children being seen and not heard. With the influence of the Enlightenment and Romanticism, however, we begin to get a critique or at least some cynicism creeping in. There might be some false steps on the path to the getting beyond of childishness, as suggested in Robert Louis Stevenson's 'Looking Forward':

> When I am grown to man's estate
> I shall be very proud and great,
> And tell the other girls and boys
> Not to meddle with my toys.
>   (Opie and Opie 1973, 294)

This putative transcendence of childhood is imagined for children by adults. What we see in the Stevenson epigram above is a kind of hailing. If, as a youngster, you get what is funny in this poem, then you are being hailed as an adult-on-the-way, at least because you understand what is childish about the protestation of adulthood here. Of course, on another level, we read the poem as mocking the self-important pretensions of adults; the mocking is done both for the benefit of children who are big enough to see into the hypocrisy of adult superiority and it is for the benefit of adults who remember childhood, see what is childish in adult behaviour, and also witness the potential for hypocrisy there. The good reader has quite a challenging, if pleasant, puzzle here about the nature of child/adult power relations. There is solidarity built between the adult and the child who share a critique of assumptions and pretensions about the nature of adulthood. And the moral of the poem is perhaps that what is derided as childishness in childhood is never really transcended, least of all by those who claim the transcendence. 'Jabberwocky', like 'Looking Forward', is a text which anticipates a performance context involving heterogeneous readerships, which nevertheless has a prospect of solidarity in the act of reading together. Perhaps, it is worth mentioning here that in the case of 'Jabberwocky', one such putative segment of audience would be those who understand the language of the poem, not in the sense that Humpty Dumpty pretends to, but in the sense – of being native speakers – of what we would then take not to be nonsense.

    For poetry and for childhood and for their interaction, 'Jabberwocky' is the rite of passage – transcendence to adulthood – reduced to rote mock-heroic gibberish, gibberish of the kind which becomes more cleverly meaning the more closely we look at it. Like Stevenson's 'Looking Forward', 'Jabberwocky' is a compromise text – one which on 'another level' bears a critique of its face value assertion; here, the adult lauded passage to adulthood is made absurd by the mode of its delivery:

> And, hast thou slain the Jabberwock?
> Come to my arms, my beamish boy
> O frabjous day! Callooh! Callay!
> (Carroll 2009, 136)

And there is a chortle for joy, there is the resting by the tum tum tree, there is the uffishness of thought. All of this meaning nonsense is suggestive of Julia Kristeva's pre-thetic semiotic chora in *Revolution in Poetic Language* (1984); that is to say, in this case, it suggests a poetic struggle to recover innocence in the form of sound before the sense, in the 'pre-sense' of an unrecoverably foreign and ancient language.

Every way we turn with this text brings us to an ironic reframing – sense out of nonsense, depth from the surface, or content (the moral of the genre) where there seemed to be only form and the structure of a story. It is as if we, as readers, must always jump because there is always an earthquake going on in these lines. The jumping is between reading positions, or points-of-view, and it is largely between positions inside and outside of the text. It is that involuntary inside-out dance on the part of the reader – and the ambivalence that goes with it – to which we will now draw attention.

Nonsense is not simply fun to be with; it presses us to make sense of it and that is work even if it is fun to do. In the case of 'Jabberwocky', what this means is that the poem needs readers to be aware of their heterogeneity (as readers) in order to make, for themselves, parodies from the text. Parodies of what? Parodies of worlds, of texts, already known and already the subject of at least a minimally dialogic exchange (worlds written and read). In other words, finding 'Jabberwocky' funny (or even simply intelligible) has to do with understanding that you are not the first or the last or the only one looking into this world. One is, at the very least, looking over Alice's shoulder at her discovery. To understand the poem does not necessarily entail portal awareness, but we think it probably does necessitate some portal induced dysphoria. That is because the interpretive work entailed in getting any reading out of the poem means that we have to be outside to be inside, and vice versa. Portal-induced dysphoria is useful for modelling both the experience of the non-native entering a culture and the experience of the child progressing towards adulthood. 'Jabberwocky' is a text that gives its reader that kind of experience of having to learn from materials that appear to be foreign. Ambivalence here takes on the uncanny feeling of belonging and not, of knowing and not.

We read from the outside because we only read by means of our own contextual investments (the skills we bring to bear); we read from somewhere. This is true of every text, but it is reflexively true of this one – this text draws our attention to the fact. These are the particular words of apparent nonsense to show us this truth. As a camera captures light from the outside, so 'Jabberwocky' explains its reader's world by way of materials apparently alien to that world, by means of new and alien technology. Can we see anything by peering into a camera? Simply the outside world. There is nothing to read in the photograph unless an image of the world is captured. Is it any different with a book? Something of the outer (the 'real') world must be developed; otherwise, it will not make sense for a reader. Is nonsense foreign to us? The epic efforts of enthusiasts the world over to translate 'Jabberwocky' would seem to say no. Still, the most significant 'outside-ness' we experience with 'Jabberwocky' and in Alice's adventures more generally is that of foreignness. Looking-Glass Land is foreign to Alice and it is foreign to us as readers. These feelings of foreignness are interestingly related: it is not our dream, it is Alice's. Then again, as with literature for children more generally, take one step back from the frame we occupied to read and we recognise that we are reading the story told by Carroll–Dodgson not *to* Alice this time, but *of* her – a story told to us if we happen to be there reading. 'Jabberwocky' is alien to Alice, but she manages to get into it and she takes us with her. Looking-glass land is alien to her, but she carries us with her through it and manages through her journey to assert the ultimate right of possession, one beyond citizenship – that of sovereignty. Of course, this is consonant with the British experience of the world in the late nineteenth century, at the height of the empire. Child sovereignty dissolves like the carnivalesque dream it turns out to be. And in the century to come, British world dominance likewise dissolves. We might say childhood dissolves into adult life, past into present and future. More immediately, however, Alice's experience serves to show us the place where everyone gets to write the tale – the world one makes oneself in dreams, an inner world made from outer world materials?

That is the kind of place 'Jabberwocky' reveals to us. And it is the inside-out-ness of dream experience as recounted for the benefit of the waking that best accounts for the feelings of foreignness and uncanniness crystallised in our experiencing 'Jabberwocky' with Alice. Other worlds are a moment away; they are with us in waking, in dreaming, in reading, and in conversation. This seems more true by virtue of everyday technology today than it was when Carroll wrote. Do other worlds make sense or nonsense of each other? The question and the answer here have to be read to be understood from the outside but can only be read from inside the world the text produces – in which case (a reflexive consequence of thought), the outside is the inside and so vice versa.

This brings me back to irony: the ironic view is always from elsewhere because it is a performance of reframing. The adult frames the text for the child, the child's text frames adult reflections, and so on. What 'Jabberwocky' teaches is that if you start digging for irony, you not only find it everywhere, but you find you are not where you started digging.

You are down in the hole you are looking into. And you are looking up, too. The irony is the trope of being in two places and two minds at once. And – in fiction, as for the dreamer – the figure properly adequate to these circumstances and the vertiginous portality of 'Jabberwocky' is not the Möbius strip but rather its 3-D counterpart, the Fortunatus purse[5] we will meet in *Sylvie and Bruno,* the value of which Lewis Carroll will explain for us in the following terms:

> 'But why do you call it Fortunatus's Purse, Mein Herr?'
> The dear old man beamed upon her, with a jolly smile, looking more exactly like the Professor than ever. 'Don't you see, my child—I should say Miladi? Whatever is *inside* that Purse, is *outside* it; and whatever is *outside* it, is *inside* it. So you have all the wealth of the world in that leetle purse!'
> (Carroll 1982, 494)

If we read the Alice books as, ultimately, texts about identity and growth then – as later in the woods where things have no names and also in 'Jabberwocky' – we learn that de-familiarising is a way to get to know yourself and to get to know your differences. It may not seem that way at the time, but after the experience of puzzling out meaning where there first appeared to be none, one has a better idea both of one's potentials and of where one might actually be or not.

Only the absolutely other can instruct us? Was ever a monster made that could pass such a test of character? In the case of 'Jabberwocky', any understanding of the self to which it gives rise has to do with violent, murderous opposition to a creature almost entirely of human making. Let us be clear, the Jabberwock is, as the dragon (its prototype and genus to its species) and as with other man-made monsters, the product of a little natural science and a lot of human imagination. How does this jabberwocky match up with robot monsters, zombies, Frankenstein's monster, and the like? Clearly, they have much in common.

One may well ask – might the Jabberwock be, in another context, more of a lost thing? Go after a monster with a vorpal sword and the experience is transformative for everyone involved.

If only the absolutely other can instruct us, then in the encounter with the Jabberwock, such an opportunity is permanently foregone. And, one notes, it is ironically foregone because the monster is merely ourselves in the mirror, as told in a poem seen through a mirror, revealed in a story full of mirrors and named, almost disingenuously, for one. Humans cannot say monster without speaking of themselves, and no one else is allowed to say monster. No one else can say boo to a goose.

Carroll's texts serve to radically re-negotiate forms and genres of poetry and narrative, literatures for children and the meaning and gendering of childhood itself. 'Jabberwocky' feels to be the dense core of such an effort; it bears in it the DNA of the whole enterprise. We find in Alice, a protagonist who models ways of being with animal others and ways of seeing animal others that are not necessarily anthropomorphic. We could say, perhaps, that they are, in the main, more hallucinatory than anthropomorphic.

One Carrollian animal creation that is conspicuously anthropomorphic, but in an inscrutable way is the Cheshire-Cat of *Alice's Adventures in Wonderland*. Yes, this cat speaks, but attention is drawn to another, less expected, anthropomorphic feature, its grin. The reversal of expectation appears to be straightforward. Alice declares, 'Well! I've often seen a cat without a grin', thought Alice, 'but a grin without a cat! It's the most curious thing I ever saw in all my life!' (59). The image of the Cheshire-Cat seems prescient of the evanescence of other-than-human animality. Animals are vanishing from our world and the safaris of Victorian imperialists (one must be William Cornwallis Harris) read as pioneering in that enterprise. The Cheshire-Cat is not a big game cat threatened with extinction. So the image of animal evanescence is ironically delivered in the figure of the animal-with-us who will survive if we do. This disdainful companion is another, for the purposes of this story, very practical cat. Still, this cat is a potentially sinister and a dangerous other.

> The Cat only grinned when it saw Alice. It looked good-natured, she thought: still it had very long claws and a great many teeth, so she felt it ought to be treated with respect.
> (Carroll 2009, 56)

The Cheshire-Cat is shown to be unpredictable both by its nonsense talk (in common with other denizens of Wonderland and Looking-Glass Land, it refuses common sense) and, more corporeally, by its evanescence, its potential not to be (cf. Les Murray's fox). There is something uncannily credible, both in its contrariness and its being hard to spot, to tie down; its being hard to hang onto. Are animals in general not like that in being not like us? They won't behave according to sensible rules. Are animals not like children in this respect?

The Jabberwock is fearsome, but it is a death waiting to happen; likewise, the Jubjub bird and the frumious Bandersnatch. These are creatures with little in the way of human characteristics, available to the story for the purposes of demonstrating human mastery over animal others. They are avatars of alterity, showing otherness to be a frightful and dangerous thing, against which measures would be wise to take.

In the evanescence of the Cheshire-Cat, we find what we could be called a failing anthropomorphism. Here is a creature with our characteristics who, in languaged, as in corporeal senses, cannot hold on to reality. What Alice – and so we – sees last of this animal is its least unconvincing and most inscrutable anthropomorphic trait – its grin. Reducing the depicted animal to its physical anthropomorphism shows us that, in the process of anthropomorphism, what we humans have done with words and with pictures, is to vanish the animal. In the Chapter 5, we will meet more carnivalesque creatures, also evanescent, doubtful equally in their ferocity and in their humanity – these are the teddy bears of the picnic.

Notes

1 Caroll's parody of the first line catches the rollicking metre of Howitt's poem, along with the motif of conversation between two speakers:

> Will you walk a little faster? said a whiting to a snail,
> There's a porpoise close behind us, and he's treading on my tail.
> (Carroll 2009, 90)

2 Hoskyns (also Hoskins) was himself expelled from Oxford for too much satire and was imprisoned in the Tower of London for a year for speaking his mind, so we can say he knew what he was talking about on this particular topic.
3 It is interesting to speculate here about the nonsense genre as a challenge to the fable. From Aesop to La Fontaine and on, there seems to be nothing absurd per se, in the fact of anthropomorphism. One might ask then what the advent of Romanticism and/or the Industrial Revolution had to with making human-animal or animal-animal transformation funny. Nor has the fable been abandoned in modernity: what is funny in Dr Seuss's *The Cat in the Hat* has nothing to do with the absurdity of the human actor in the story taking the shape of a cat.
4 Popular lore suggested that Queen Victoria was a fan and had wished Carroll to dedicate a book to her but was shocked when presented with Dodgson's *An Elementary Treatise on Determinants*. The tale is almost certainly apocryphal and was strongly denied by Dodgson (Wikipedia, 'Lewis Carroll').
5 The Fortunatus story appears to date to the sixteenth century story, as published by Johann Otmar in Augsburg in 1509. Andrew Lang also employed the story in his "Fortunatus and his Purse" (Wikipedia, 'Fortunatus (book)').

References

Ariès, Philippe. *Centuries of Childhood: A Social History of Family Life*. Trans. Robert Baldick. New York: Alfred A. Knopf, 1962.
Belloc, Hilaire. *The Bad Child's Book of Beasts*. Illus. Basil Temple Blackwood. London: Camelot Press, 1896.
Belloc, Hilaire. *More Beasts for Worse Children*. Illus. Basil Temple Blackwood. London: Edward Arnold, 1897.
Belloc, Hillarie. *Cautionary Tales for Children*. London: Eveleigh Nash, 1907.
Belloc, Hilaire. *Hilaire Belloc's Cautionary Verses*. Illus. Album Edition with the Original Pictures by B.T.B. and Nicolas Bentley. New York: Alfred. A. Knopf, 1941.
Blake, William. *Collected Poems*. Ed. W.B. Yeats. New York: Routledge, 2002.
Butler, Judith. *Bodies that Matter. On the Discursive Limits of Sex*. London and New York: Routledge, 1992.
Carroll, Lewis. *Alice's Adventures in Wonderland and Through the Looking-Glass and What Alice Found There*. Oxford: Oxford University Press, 2009.

Carroll, Lewis. *Sylvie and Bruno – The Complete Illustrated Works of Lewis Carroll*. London: Chancellor Press, 1982.
Chaucer, Geoffrey. *Canterbury Tales* by J. Saunders. London: Charles Knight & Co., 1845.
Deleuze, Gilles. (1969). *The Logic of Sense*. London: Athlone Press, 1990.
Deleuze, Gilles. *Difference and Repetition*. London: Athlone Press, 1994.
Hoffmann, Heinrich. (1845). *Struwwelpeter*. Routledge, 1890.
Howitt, Mary. (1829). *Sketches from Natural History*. Boston: Weeks, Jordan & Co., 1839.
Hughes, Ted. *Meet My Folks!* Illus. George Adamson. London: Faber and Faber, 1961.
Hughes, Ted. *Collected Poems for Children*. London: Faber & Faber, 2008.
Hutcheon, Linda. *Irony's Edge*. London: Routledge, 1994.
Ireson, Barbara and George Adamson. 1958. *The Faber Book of Nursery Verse*. London: Faber & Faber, 1983.
Kristeva, Julia. *Revolution in Poetic Language*. Trans. Margaret Waller. New York: Columbia University Press, 1984.
Lear, Edward. *The Complete Verse and Other Nonsense*. Harmondsworth: Penguin, 2001.
Lecercle, Jean-Jacques. *Philosophy of Nonsense: The Intuitions of Victorian Nonsense Literature*. London: Routledge, 1994.
Lecercle, Jean-Jacques. "Translate it, translate it not". *Translation Studies* 1(1) (2008): 90–102.
Lee, Dennis. *Garbage Delight*. Illus. Frank Newfeld. New York: Macmillan of Canada, 1977.
Merleau-Ponty, Maurice. *Signs*. Trans. Richard C. McCleary. Evanston: Northwestern University Press, 1964.
Natov, Roni. *The Poetics of Childhood*. New York: Routledge, 2003.
Opie, Iona and Peter Opie. eds. *The Oxford Book of Children's Verse*. Oxford: Oxford University Press, 1973.
Ritvo, Harriet. *The Animal Estate: The English and Other Creatures in the Victorian Age*. Cambridge, Massachusetts: Harvard University Press, 1987.
Robinson, Peter. *Poetry & Translation: The Art of the Impossible*. Cambridge: Liverpool University Press, 2010.
Russell, Peter. "Mixing the Useful and the Sweet, or: The Delights of Admonition. An Essay in Comparative Literature". *Otago German Studies* 1 (2016): 214–225.
Sattaur, Jennifer. *Perceptions of Childhood in the Victorian Fin-de-siècle*. Cambridge Scholars Publishing, 2011.
Sendak, Maurice. *Where the Wild Things Are*. New York: Harper and Row, 1963.
Seuss, Dr. *The Cat in the Hat*. New York: Random House, 1957.
Shelley, Percy Bysshe. "A Defence of Poetry". *The Harvard Classics*, Vol. 27. New York: Collier, 1910.
Shi, Zhecun. *Shi Zhecun's Collection of Selected Proses*. Beijing: Baihua Wenyi, 1986.
Styles, Morag. "Poetry for Children". *International Companion Encyclopedia of Children's Literature*. Ed. Peter Hunt. London: Routledge, 1996. 187–203,
Styles, Morag. *From the Garden to the Street: Three Hundred Years of Poetry for Children*. London: Bloomsbury Publishing, 1997.

Toy Story. Dir. John Lasseter. Pixar Animation Studios, 1995. Film.
Wikipedia. "Fortunatus (book)". http://en.wikipedia.org/wiki/Fortunatus, accessed on 1 July 2021.
Wikipedia. "Lewis Carroll". http://en.wikipedia.org/wiki/Lewis_Carroll, accessed on 1 July 2021.
Wordsworth, Williams. *The Poetical Works of William Wordsworth*. Vol. 2. Ed. William Knight. Edinburgh: W. Paterson, 1882.

5 If You Go Down to the Woods Today
Wild and Domestic Textuality

Zanni Louise's and David Macintosh's (2017) picture book *Archie and the Bear* models a case of representing ambivalent humanimal identity through anthropomorphism. Archie is a boy in a bear suit who insists on the reality of his bear-ness: 'It's not a suit', Archie would growl, 'I AM a bear!' Fed up with having his imaginative reality denied, Archie goes off to the forest, behaving on his way as much like a bear as he possibly can (bear sack, honey sandwiches). He sharpens his bear eyes and knows not to be afraid because he knows that bears are not afraid. Then, of course, a bear appears, a creature massively larger than Archie. This bear, it quickly transpires, believes himself to be a boy. Archie offers a honey sandwich and their friendship is now assured because boys like sandwiches and bears like honey. After various engaging activities, the bear shows Archie how to read and then Archie reads to the bear. Archie teaches the bear how to get honey out of a log and so the bear gets Archie some honey. Night settles, it gets cold and Archie offers the bear his bear suit for warmth. Of course, this leaves Archie cold and now there's nothing for it but for the two of them to go back to Archie's place, be by the fire under a warm quilt together, nibbling honey sandwiches.

How happy we humans and animals are, together in this reciprocity of beautiful confusions, where despite extraordinary and exaggerated differences in size, the animal and the animal who is human are able to find cosy and companionable solutions to any doubts there might have been as to who they each were, vis-à-vis the other. The solutions are all by way of conversation and pictures as able to be read from the page by both of these characters *in* the book, doing perhaps what an adult and child reader outside of the book would be doing, notwithstanding, in either case, differences in power as caricatured by way of size.

This text recalls specific antecedents, perhaps the most obvious of which is Maurice Sendak's *Where the Wild Things Are* (1963).

> The night Max wore his wolf suit and made mischief of one kind and another his mother called him 'WILD THING!' and Max said 'I'LL EAT YOU UP!' so he was sent to bed without eating anything.

DOI: 10.4324/9781003219330-6

Sendak's Max is also a boy in an animal costume – in fact, a boy in wolf's clothing. Another case of prosopopoeia. This whole-body mask that Max wears is, we hypothesise, a magic charm with very specific effects.

> That very night in Max's room a forest grew and grew and grew – until his ceiling hung with vines and the walls became the world all around and an ocean tumbled by with a private boat for Max and he sailed off through night and day and in and out of weeks and almost over a year to where the wild things are.

His journey, though solitary, is not unlike that of a certain owl and a certain pussycat we have met. Max's wolf suit – and the wildness he exhibits under its influence – bring him to the place where that wildness is at home. It further allows him security and even mastery in this special place (one not without its dangers).

> And when he came to the place where the wild things are they roared their terrible roars and gnashed their terrible teeth and rolled their terrible eyes and showed their terrible claws till Max said 'BE STILL!' and tamed them with the magic trick of staring into all their yellow eyes without blinking once and they were frightened and called him the most wild thing of all and made him king of all wild things.

Like Alice (and like the Pevensie children in Narnia), Max is now an all-powerful ruler of the magical place he has come to inhabit. And so, a carnivalesque role reversal is affected.

> 'And now,' cried Max, 'let the wild rumpus start!'
> 'Now stop!' Max said and sent the wild things off to bed without their supper.

The tables are turned: the wild and rebellious one, who had been subject to the whims of adult control himself, now subjects the wildest of all possible creatures to *his* will. By wearing the carnival mask, the underling becomes the king for a time, outside of time. But it is lonely at the top. The new arrangements are not meant to last.

> And Max the king of all wild things was lonely and wanted to be where someone loved him best of all. Then all around from far away across the world he smelled good things to eat so he gave up being king of where the wild things are.

Max now wishes for the tame and familiar world where his dinner might be waiting.

> But the wild things cried, 'Oh please don't go – we'll eat you up–we love you so!' And Max said, 'No!' The wild things roared their terrible roars and gnashed their terrible teeth and rolled their terrible eyes and showed their terrible claws but Max stepped into his private boat and waved good-bye and sailed back over a year and in and out of weeks and through a day and into the night of his very own room where he found his supper waiting for him and it was still hot.

The happy ending shows a mastery, perhaps some wisdom, retained for Max from his adventure. He defies the danger of the creatures who would express their love for him by eating him, and he gets to have his own hot dinner, just where he left it. The control he exercises as ruler of a fantasy world enables him to achieve some self-control. In this story, mastery, of self and over others, is the mechanism for growth and though empathy is not apparent to the fore in these considerations, it is nevertheless implied in the role reversals involved.

The interpretation of Max's journeying to the wild jungle and back home is clearly amenable to colonial analysis, from which angle there are resonant in his adventure 'numerous uncanny echoes of narrative patterns, events, psychologies, and structures that can be seen as typically-even archetypally-colonial' (Ball 1997, 168). Among the Freudian, (post)colonial, and cultural perspectives of understanding Sendak's book (Stephens 1992, Shaddock 1997, Kidd 2011), how Max manages his emotions through the journey is a locus of discussion. According to Sendak himself, he attempted to explore 'how children's various feelings – anger, boredom, fear, frustration, jealousy – and manage to come to grips with the realities of their lives' (qtd in Abate 2013, 140). Sendak's use of fantasy, of becoming a wild thing, as an empowering mode is well noted in 'enabling children to tame "ungovernable" and "dangerous" emotions by providing a healthy catharsis' (Tatar 1993, 210). The journey in catharsis leads to self-understanding and maturity (Nikolajeva 2010, 169–170). His journey, as with Alice in Looking-Glass Land, is one towards maturity. The dream is, of its nature, evanescent. As is so often so in cases of portality, no time has elapsed in the wider world or the world that is real while the adventure and epiphany took place. In the blink of an eye, one is changed; in the blink of an eye, one is home again.

Archie and Max are human children in picture books, created for the entertainment and improvement of human children outside of picture books. They have an obvious common progenitor in *Winnie-the-Pooh*, a story series that conspicuously crosses boundaries, on the one hand between human and nonhuman animal others, on the other hand between subject and object, animate and inanimate. *Winnie-the-Pooh* is a story to vividly demonstrate the bringing to life of lifeless objects that is characteristic of childhood and its imagination.

Transitional Objects and a Reciprocal Vision

What does it mean when a toy in a story evinces sentience? Who effects this 'bringing to life'? And how is the magic done? The traditional spookiness of dolls has perhaps to do with the emptiness of masks that no one wears. Here is the representation of the animate, brought to life by whoever believes in the life behind the mask. Toys and dolls are phenomenal opposites of the girl or the boy in the bear or the monster suit – not humans pretending to be someone else but no one pretending to be someone. The softest toys demand the closest haunting. They smell just like the child who believes in them, who dutifully ensouls the shreds and patches. But the child is not the maker, no more of the doll with the little sister than s/he is of Santa Claus.

In his analysis of toys, Roland Barthes notes that

> All the toys one commonly sees are essentially a microcosm of the adult world; they are all reduced copies of human objects, as if in the eyes of the public the child was, all told, nothing but a smaller man, a homunculus to whom must be supplied objects of his own size.
> (2003, 220)

In toys, Barthes sees the power differential between adults and children, that children's toyland is a miniature world of adults' fantasy. Despite this, Barthes also insists on adults' emotional attachment to childhoods rich with the creative possibility that comes from reproducing a playworld. Within this miniaturised simulacrum world, Barthes tells us, 'the child can only identify himself as owner, as user, never as creator; he does not invent the world, he uses it: there are, prepared for him, actions without adventure, without wonder, without joy' (1973, 53–54). We might regard Barthes as pessimistic about the affective efficacy for children of adult created and manufactured, of adult gifted, toys. Just as the speaking animal is a human invention, so toys for children are as much a product of the adult human mind as are beast fables or books for children more generally.

Gaston Bachelard proposes what we might consider a counter to this view in his romantically inflected idea of a poetic retreat of adulthood. When adults recall their childhood, the 'oneiric house of dream-memory ... lost in the shadow of a beyond of the real past', they turn into imagined children (1994, 15). It is the adults producing toys and other cultural works for children who make an effort to keep childhood alive and full of fun and wonder. Whether this is simply the imposition of adult wishful thinking on the gullible remains an open question. The point – on which Philippe Ariès concurs with his invention of childhood (1962) – is that it is fanciful to think of childhood as an eternal flame able to be kept alive by efforts at innocence. Rather, adults have an essential role in the creation of all we understand of childhood as a stage in life. For better and for worse, childhood is something inflicted by adults on children, and perhaps much in the manner of the putative language sentient humans impose on animals.

Somewhat in the ambiguous spirit of eighteenth-century object narratives, both Barthes and Bachelard write of toys in material culture as prefiguring the world of adulthood. Object narratives are written from nostalgic adult eyes dwelling upon childhood and innocence. By way of nostalgia, objects in the stories assume narrative agency while non-human narrators spell out human ethical concerns for the sake of human business rather than, of course, for themselves. However, the social materialist aspect does not lead to a close paralleling of toy narrators with toy products in the world of everyday life. As Susan Stewart notes, 'the inanimate toy repeats the still life's theme of arrested life, the life of the tableau. But once the toy becomes animated, it imitates another world, the world of the daydream' (1993, 57).

Once toys are romanticised or fictionalised, they serve not less as objects with instrumental power than as markers of social relations and emotional connections. Objects' metonymic values are pushed to the forefront in narratives where they are experienced as selves who speak out their roles of play, desires, companionship, or rites-of-passage in one's life. According to Jane Bennett, 'found objects … can become vibrant things with a certain effectivity of their own, a perhaps small but irreducible degree of independence from the words, images, and feelings they provoke in us' (2009, xvi). The 'thing-powers' of which she writes has, in relation to its materiality, the ability to 'act as quasi agents or forces with trajectories, propensities, or tendencies of their own' (viii) and therefore registers a special effect in human beings.

Through encounters with inanimate objects and 'silent' animals, these things exercise their invisible influence upon humans while humans tend to project their feelings and habitual ways of thinking to relate onto these at least partly unwitting creations. In Jean Piaget's theory, anthropomorphism is seen as a sub-species of animism and as an 'ubiquitous evolutionary strategy' (cited in Harvey 2006, 15). Here, animism and anthropomorphism are viewed as interrelated modes of thinking, generating rich investments of nature and of the other-than-human in children's stories.

In Donald Winnicott's terms, these articles of child's play (such as teddy bears or security blankets) are 'transitional objects'. Winnicott illuminates the manner in which play – and the objects of play – provide the opportunity for the child to move from dependence to autonomy. All these toys, dolls, and stuffed animals are considered comfort objects – objects of affection and attachment. They serve as substitutes for the mother to appease the child's anxiety after his or her separation from the mother's breast. Playing with these transitional objects can compensate for the child's loss and help establish an I-It sense of the world. Winnicott claims the mental/psychological space these objects occupy is 'neither subjective nor objective but partakes of both' (1951, 231). The 'in between' space created by a transitional object develops into a generalised intermediate area of experience, with all kinds of applications and analogies in the life the child grows into – between the dream and the reality, internal life and external life, family and strangers, fiction and fact, the made world and the world-as-given. Immersed in experience, children thus come to possess, if fleetingly, an external world of 'magical omnipotent control' (1971, 12).

The child's autonomous identification with self and others is also theorised by Jacques Lacan and Maurice Merleau-Ponty. In Jacques Lacan's famous formulation of the 'mirror stage' in child development from 6 to 18 months, the point at which children recognise themselves in the mirror (or other symbolic contraption which induces reflection) is taken as a critical moment in the emergence of an independent sense of self. It is a matter of identification, 'to know the transformation produced in the subject when he takes on an image' (cited in Merleau-Ponty 2010, 253). Merleau-Ponty affirms that the mirror image 'permits the subject to isolate himself and to establish a reciprocal system – to facilitate the other's interference' (2010, 87). He writes, 'the child becomes capable of being a spectator of himself. He is no longer a sensing ego, but a spectacle; he is this someone that we can see' (2010, 254). Reciprocity, dialogism, and a rejection of traditional dualisms are themes throughout the philosophy of Merleau-Ponty. They go to the nature of the life in the flesh, only lived – only known – in relation to others: others demanding empathy, others of whom we demand empathy.

> Whether speaking or listening, I project myself into the other person, I introduce him into my own self. Our conversation resembles a struggle between two athletes in a tug-of-war. The speaking 'I' abides in its body. Rather than imprisoning it, language is like a magic machine for transporting the 'I' into the other person's perspective.
>
> (1974, 19)

The otherness of the encounter and of community implies an always other-sidedness to our work with meaning, the means of which must never be fully known. In *Signs*, Merleau-Ponty writes:

> It goes without saying that language is oblique and autonomous, and that its ability to signify a thought or a thing directly is only a secondary power derived from the inner life of language. Like the weaver, the writer works on the wrong side of his material. He has to do only with language, and it is thus that he suddenly finds himself surrounded by meaning.
>
> (1964, 44–45)

This observation of wrong-sidedness has profound implications for how we understand the nature of meaning and of the child's active entry into a world of others for whose benefit meanings are made. The idea of meaning made where we cannot quite see it, from materials given by custom and tradition (e.g. natural language and its gestural accompaniments), touches on the ideological construction of reality. Or one might say it pertains to the make-believe children and adults, equally, have no other life but to live.

Child-Like Sentience, Wild or Domesticated

After an introduction to *Winnie-the-Pooh*, in part interrogating attitudes to zoos and their inmates ('the nicest people go straight to the animal they love the most, and stay there'), consider how our protagonist comes into the story. The conventional narrative structure is abandoned, in favour of a more childish (and more poetic) diegesis.

Consider our introduction of Winnie-the-Pooh himself:

> Here is Edward Bear, coming downstairs now, bump, bump, bump, on the back of his head, behind Christopher Robin. It is, as far as he knows, the only way of coming downstairs, but sometimes he feels that there really is another way, if only he could stop bumping for a moment and think of it. And then he feels that perhaps there isn't. Anyhow, here he is at the bottom, and ready to be introduced to you. Winnie-the-Pooh.
>
> (Milne 1926, 1)

This paragraph is, we think, extraordinary for the manner in which it brings us so immediately into the ambivalence of this 'character' who is, at once, bear we might meet in the wilds or the zoo, anthropomorphic (so human) sentience in the shape of a bear, a child's toy teddy, a Winnicottian 'transitional object', brought to life by the imagination of the child, in this case, Christopher Robin. We note here that considering the place of transitional phenomena in the life of the child, Winnicott insisted that 'one must recognize the central position of Winnie the Pooh' (1971, xvi). If Pooh's experience of life in transitional space is less than salubrious then one is reminded of the philosopher, Martha Nussbaum's description (vis à vis transitional space) of 'the highly particular transactions that constitute love between two imperfect people' (2012, 282.)

The bear is named to begin; he is Edward Bear – an appellation suggesting a Victorian/Edwardian properness and formality. We have a name suggesting an animal – and at once, social class, gender, epoch – before we have anyone to meet. Somehow the giving of this name at the outset suggests not only human sentience and feeling (a character aware of what is happening to him), but an ambivalence as well between what might be the name of an older man (name from an older age) and what might be the name to which a child is becoming accustomed. How old is a teddy bear? How wise? How naive? We are soon to find out some of these things, but at this stage in the story, we don't yet know what kind of a character it is that is now receiving the bumps on the head, coming down the stairs. Ouch! The word is not there in the text, but we feel it. Bump, bump, bump. We feel the pain experienced by Edward Bear before we know who he is. The suffering inflicted upon him is his introduction; his introspection concerning it certainly suggests a character older than his owner/tormentor. He is a character abused by being dragged downstairs. With this knowledge, we almost immediately adopt a mirror-ambivalence for Christopher Robin – a possible friend of real and imagined bears, one likewise growing into his name-as-given, and yet a kind of careless torturer of innocent teddy bears. But Christopher Robin is, of course, the real, sentient creature in the piece or the one coming to sentience. And he is the real innocent too. His carelessness is of his nature as a child, and it reflects his relationship with the teddy bear, that is thing, and friend, and animal-other. Yes, Christopher Robin is the real sentient human here, except that, of course, he too is a character in a book. He too, demands of the child's imagination just in order to be.

From here we proceed, still on the first page of the story, into a further confusion of names and namelessness – a kind of garbling of relationships that is entirely credible because it so resembles the child-thought-speech on which it is modelled and which has been recognisable, as such, by readers for almost a century.

> When I first heard his name, I said, just as you are going to say,
> 'But I thought he was a boy?'
> 'So did I,' said Christopher Robin.
> 'Then you can't call him Winnie?'
> 'I don't.'
> 'But you said—'
> "He's Winnie-ther-Pooh. Don't you know what 'ther' means?"
> 'Ah, yes, now I do,' I said quickly; and I hope you do too, because it is all the explanation you are going to get.
>
> (Milne 1926, 2)

Things are confused coming into the story. Names are shown to be doubtful from the outset. It is hard to know who is who, what kinship might be involved, to whom or what pronouns might refer. But one guesses that here there is an adult and there is a child, and there is an imagined anthropomorphic entity. Why are names as they are in this book? How do systems of reference work in the text? Not by way of conventional adult logic.

Now this bear's name is Winnie, which shows what a good name for bears it is, but the funny thing is that we can't remember whether Winnie is called after Pooh or Pooh after Winnie. We did know once, but we have forgotten. There is a lot of plot-convenient forgetting going on in this book and there is a lot of invention proceeding on a basis we could not call commonsensical. This diegetic process is characteristic of 'a bear of little brain', whose qualities are characteristic of child logic (Tremper 1977). Pooh says, 'I do remember, and then when I try to remember, I forget' (Milne 1926, 17).

Pooh's is a child-like sentience and he is a character of impressive imagination, of insight. He is likewise impressive as a poet and songster. Able to think tangentially (herein the nature of his surprises), in rhetorical terms, Pooh typically proceeds metonymically with ideas.

> 'Aha!' said Pooh. (*Rum-tum-tiddle-um-tum.*)
> 'If I know anything about anything, that hole means Rabbit,' he said, 'and Rabbit means Company,' he said, 'and Company means Food and Listening-to-Me-Humming and such like. *Rum-tum-tum-tiddle-um.*'
> So he bent down, put his head into the hole, and called out: 'Is anybody at home?' There was a sudden scuffling noise from inside the hole, and then silence.
>
> (Milne 1926, 21)

Pooh looks sideways at things to understand them, which is a little like understanding who to be by understanding another animal, like understanding how an animal is by bringing a doll to life. *Winnie-the-Pooh*, as a phenomenon, is a poetics in its own right. Playing with the pretend-animality of the child entering the culture, this figure embodied in that 'Bear of Very Little Brain' whom 'long words Bother' (1926, 45), couples distraction with invention in order to progress through an endless series of crises, many, if not most of them, self-generated.

Pooh, a character of extraordinary, and perhaps even now growing, popularity, was to begin a bear of 1926. The poetics of the transitional object we find embodied in the 'person' of Pooh are enabled, in part, by an earlier and also popular collection of bears. The charm of Pooh and his friends, as Ellen Tremper reminds us, 'depends upon the fact that the stuffed animals have been transformed into seemingly breathing ones with complicated lives of their own, while Christopher Robin, and all children to whom they are read, wait, round-eyed and passive, for the grown-up magician to perform this miraculous life-giving metamorphosis' (1977, 35).

In the child-animal-primitive association, the animal is taken as a figurative child, waiting to be 'naturalised' and nurtured. A juvenile adventure, an animal fantasy, or a 'domestic fantasy' (Hunt 1992), the story of Christopher Robin and Winnie the Pooh implies a childhood that is, beyond a surface ambivalence for nature and society, nevertheless civilised. The nature-nurture dynamics work here, pointing to a bestial and gendered imagination concerning childhood (Stanger 1987, Nelson 1990).

If we accept some narrative equivalence between becoming literate and domestication, then it is easier to understand why texts directed at children are so frequently contingent upon a 'naturalised' domestic landscape, one that nurtures wild sensibilities while recognising their temporal and spatial limits as limits of the imagination. The 'wild' is in this sense where children are coming from and this point of origin is quite distinct from their destination as adults, but then conterminous with the domesticated. So the story starts with Christopher's 'oneness with Pooh' as the little boy carries the bear with him everywhere and ends with Christopher starting school; the author leaving them in an enchanted place where 'a little boy and his Bear will always be playing' (Milne 1928/2004, 176).

Domestication can be seen as the opposite of wildness in the way of gained literacy, as Layla AbdelRahim argues in her book *Children's Literature, Domestication, and Social Foundation* (2014). To concretise her contention against 'domesticated logic' in children's book, she sees Winnie-the-Pooh as another subject to Christopher's language as 'grammar of ordered reality'. Underlying that is a 'logical predictability of a controlled reality and time' (99). Travelling through Christopher Robin's Hundred Acre Wood, we learn that the conceptual vitality lies in curbing the human impulse to domesticate the wild so that the wild, with its connotations of freedom, illiteracy, and play can thrive on its own terms, regardless of whether being the wild within or without. Identity formation, as Michael T. Taussig suggests, is not so much about staying the same as 'in imitation of resistance to an often imagined Other' (1993, 27). Milne's Christopher Robin and Sendak's Max both imagined their wild otherness and eventually resisted such imagined otherness and returned to the world of civilisation as ambiguously tamed. This is a tale of finding the golden mean between the wild and the civilised. Although it is the civilisation that generally gets the upper hand, we cannot forget that the ontological process has, to a certain extent, replaced the conventional cross-species separateness and effaced aggression. Although the stories both end with a return to civilisation, the 'wild rumpus' is still heard.

The civilisational logic normalises human interventions in the wilderness, regardless of inflictions caused on wild places or figures in allegorical stories. Despite the socially constructed civilisational logic, storytellers often make attempts to trifle with the rigid human-wild animal relations. To nurture a good story with wild animals, the balance between distance and engagement should be well kept. Such a motif leads us to examine stories and poems in which child-wild animal distinctions are totally erased, proliferated and redefined.

The Wood Where Things Have No Names

Where is language – where is meaning, where are sense and nonsense – in transitional spaces? In the case of *Winnie-the-Pooh,* we find ourselves – much as in the opening paragraph of James Joyce's *The Portrait of the*

Artist as a Young Man (2004) – in the ambiguous territory of an adult remembering child speech or of the adult attempting to meet the child halfway in meaning.

> Once upon a time and a very good time it was there a moocow coming down along the road and this moocow that was down along the road meet a nicens little boy named baby tuckoo.
>
> (Joyce, 3)

Our persona, in this case, is adult-in-child's-mind, a kind of prosopopoeia akin, one might argue, to anthropomorphism. The readership here is similarly ambiguous. The text is at once an induction into language and reading and being with others and being in a story. Like the Japanese *furigana* superscript, which sounds out characters, the text is equally efficient in leading the reader to or from literacy, to or from the adult world of common sense and narrative strategy. Nostalgia for childhood is, since childhood's invention, Romanticism or perhaps the Garden, is a longing not only for a missing time but also for a desirable place. Slipping back into the namelessness of the Kristevan semiotic chora (Kristeva 1984)– reverting to transitional space – suggests all the comfort of not needing to know or understand, suggests for the adult mind an unattainable openness. Dorothy Gale asks her transitional creature, Toto, if he supposes there is such a place as 'over the rainbow' – 'where troubles melt like lemon drops'(cited in Nathanson 1991, 212) . What do we suppose such a place would be like? The Carroll's 'wood where things have no name' resurface, in which Alice and the talking fawn are, for a blessed little while, to each other just dear fellow travellers. The putative affinity among living things is perceived and cherished, conjuring up an imagined land where nonhumans and humans live outside the pale of anthropocentrism.

In relation to the Carrollian topos as also sketched in the Introduction, this chapter further investigates a popular cultural text of the early twentieth century – "The Teddy Bears' Picnic" (cited in Boulton and Ackroyd 2004, 17), a song consisting of John Walter Bratton's melody composed in 1907 and Jimmy Kennedy's lyrics written in 1932 . To first contextualise the idea of the teddy bears picnicking, we look to Donna Varga's article 'Babes in the Woods: Wilderness Aesthetics in Children's Stories and Toys, 1830–1915' (2009). Varga contends that:

> Representations of nonhuman wild animals in children's stories and toys underwent dramatic transformation over the years 1830–1915. During the earlier part of that period, wild animals were presented to children as being savage and dangerous, and that it was necessary for them to be killed or brutally constrained. In the 1890s, an animalcentric discourse emerged in Nature writing, along with an animal-human symbiosis in scientific child study that highlighted

childhood innocence, resulting in a valuing of wild animals based upon their similarity to humans.

(188)

The effects of Darwin's writings and, equally, Alice's encounter with the Fawn in the wood where things have no names might be seen as presaging a space for a more reciprocal, less anthropocentric approach to animal-human relations. However, it seems that the child-animal nexus is most to the fore in Jimmy Kennedy's lyrics for 'The Teddy Bear Picnic' (cited in Boulton and Ackroyd 2004, 17). The idea of analogies and affinities between animals and children is very ancient. In Book Eight of his *History of Animals*, Aristotle aligns 'psychical qualities' of animals with 'the phenomena of childhood':

> for in children may be observed the traces and seeds of what will one day be settled psychological habits, though psychologically a child hardly differs for the time being from an animal; so that one is quite justified in saying that, as regards man and animals, certain psychical qualities are identical with one another, whilst others resemble, and others are analogous to, each other.

On the question of whether the picnic of bears ought to be considered as an entertainment for adult or child, Varga offers the following insight: describing a toy mechanical bear produced around 1900, she tells us, 'Objects such as these were probably intended for adult manipulation, but they nevertheless taught children that their own animal toys were not just childish things that would later need to be abandoned but were juvenile forms of acceptable adult entertainment' (195). For Varga, it was 'the uniting of the sublime wild aesthetic with that of innocent childhood' that 'created, by the cusp of the twentieth century, a belief in a natural kinship between animals, especially young animals, and children, who in their naïveté and guilelessness were superior to adult humans' (197). The effect of the transformation amounts to the saving of animals 'from the tragedy of wilderness' (Varga, 203). By means of this transformation, she posits, 'The hunting ethos is reversed, and it is the animals who become the great white hope wherein it is they – in signifying childhood innocence and its protection – who are responsible for redeeming humankind' (203). We can easily read Kennedy's lyrics in terms of this kind of apology and a hope of re-admission of humans – via childhood innocence – to the domain of natural animality. Kennedy's lyrics play on the received animal nature of childhood, on the putative childishness of animals.

A paean to libidinous excess, 'The Teddy Bears' Picnic' is focused on one Rabelaisian moment – a debauch, a Saturnalia of bears – the day of the picnic. It may be objected that the sense of debauchery is vitiated and ironised by the fact that this is a lyric about and for children – the children are bears and the bears are children. Mediating between these dangerously animated creatures, whom we learn through the song have so much in common is their avatar-in-common – The Teddy Bear – the stuffed toy dating with the tune to almost the turn of last century, named for the US President of that era, Teddy Roosevelt. It is neither the child *per se* nor the wild animal *per se* but rather the Teddy Bear to whom the picnic belongs.

The lyrics and music of 'The Teddy Bears' Picnic' present the listener (who may also well be singing) with a series of idylls: the woods, the secret thing seen there, which is the picnic, the ceremony of the treats, the hide-and-seek, the dance, the wild rumpus of the play and shout, and the taking home to bed of the tired little teddy bears. The series of places which are events (the moments of and around the moment of the day, the picnic) coax the reader/performer into the story – a story in which one's reading position shifts as ambiguously as do the *dramatis personae*. Bear? Toy? Child? Transitional object? Allegorical character?

Peer a little further into these 'woods' and we see that these bears are the animal avatars of the children put to bed by the mummies and daddies. But the bears are the toys belonging to the children as well, and at once anthropomorphically and zoomorphically invested, they lie in the place of children in relation to the children who play with them – in that place, they are lifeless things, soft, harmless objects brought to life by creatures who are somewhere ambiguously on the continuum between the animal and the human adult, between the instinctual and the rational. Note that much of this observation will be applicable in general in the case of anthropomorphic/zoomorphic toys, so for instance, in the recent case of the *Toy Story* film series.

What does a real bear do at a picnic? Presumably, a real bear would scatter the terrified picnickers and wreck what it could not scoff down. And then? 'A fed bear is a dead bear', the park signs remind us. A real bear at a real picnic is probably not a happy ending. So there is real humour of the incongruous under the surface of the anthropomorphism on which the whole story of the Teddy Bears' Picnic depends: the delicate Edwardian comedy of manners meets the wild and untamed thing.

It is precisely the analogy between bears and children, the anthropomorphic-zoomorphic reciprocity at the core of this lyric, which places us in the woods of libidinous excess. 'Beneath the trees where nobody sees', how long will they hide and seek? Just as long as they please. Because, of course, time in the adult calendrical sense is as meaningless for infants as it is for bears. The adult world, of music and of lyric making, is the essential framing context for the little story in the song. We are interested in this song because of the way it plays on the animal nature of childhood, on the putative childishness of animals, those who substantially or altogether lack the languaged sentience of adults, for the fine balances it establishes in illustrating a reciprocity between child and animal subjects and objects (these equal others of adult self-consciousness) and for the way it generates a continually surprising ambivalence with regard to the cute cosiness and the vicious wilfulness of children on the one hand and animals on the other. Where the children play and the woods where we find the bears of the picnic may be lovely places and have their lovely moments, but it is safer to be at home. And what if such a place of terror is in the home? Of course, this is the mundane reality of parenthood. And is not this song a kind of comic release valve for those adults who orchestrate its singing by their offspring, who more or less perform a confession when they participate in the show?

Just how scared should we be? Let us not underestimate the dangers. 'Every bear that ever there was will gather there for certain' – Kodiaks, little Malay sun bears, perhaps the odd koala will sneak in; but, more to the point, there will be grizzlies, black bears, brown bears, polar bears – all of them will be there! We should be very afraid. But then, should we really be? A Jekyll and Hyde transformation defuses the situation, makes them, after all, 'tired little teddy bears'.

As in Lewis Carroll's wood where things have no names, this is a fantasy world with an apparent portal ('if you go down to the woods'), but that portal keeps slipping away as we approach it. In the case of the wood where things have no names, the mere effort to name the place would prove the point: we are there, but we do not know where that is in relation to anywhere else because we are already there. It is like this at the teddy bears' picnic, too – if the singing is happening, then we are always already there. And this sits strangely with the tense-and-aspect setup of the lyric: 'if you go down', 'you're sure of', 'you'd better go'. The description of apparent real-time events is delivered as a travel advisory. But the presaged picnic is all that we see in these lyrics. Temporally, as well as spatially then, we think that here, as in the wood where things have no names, the outside is the inside. In this lyric, as in that wood, we experience the *unheimlich* 'Fortunatus Purse feeling' that if you are there, you are not and if you are not, then you are there. We are interested in how these picnic woods are foreshadowed in Looking-Glass Land, both by the action and scene in 'Jabberwocky' and in the wood where things have no names.

Alice ends Chapter Two of her adventures in the Looking-Glass Land with the recognition that she is a pawn and that she must soon move. Pawns in chess, we must remind ourselves, are generally moved rather than self-moving, but as good readers, we overlook this nicety of life on our side of the mirror in order to keep up with Carroll's plot. Volition, and its grammatical counterpart, agency, are at stake here in a manner typical of Alice's predicament. It is the oneiric logic of Alice's ever-shifting situation which finds her next surveying a landscape in which bees turn into elephants and in which Alice finds herself running down hills and jumping over brooks and then travelling on a train that likewise, despite some trepidation on the part of the passengers, jumps brooks. After her train journey, Alice converses with the Looking-Glass Insects for whom the chapter is named. The companionable and chicken-sized gnat with whom she speaks regards Alice as one of them, just as the live flowers had in the previous chapter, just as the Cheshire-Cat in Wonderland had taken it for granted that Alice was mad too. After the tearful gnat sighs himself away, Alice presses on through an open field with a dark wood on the other side of it. This is the wood, foreshadowed by the Gnat (Carroll 2009, 152), where things have no names.

How do we know where we are? We know from the outside, as Alice herself does as she enters and, when she remembers what things are, as she leaves the wood. Haecceity is to the fore when every particularity – when all of the 'thisness' – of experience as lived needs to be, but cannot be, named. We think of the world as named outward from a subjective centre (by a biblical Adam, for instance), but here as in an Alzheimer's space, it is as if the entire world were named but for this pocket closest to subjectivity, now no longer a centre but the mobile site of a de-centring. The outer world of names embraces the here-and-now lived space of the un-nameable. The encounter in such a place – of sentient beings for whom these essential facts must equally apply – provides a practical instance of Levinas' dictum, 'the absolutely foreign alone can instruct us' (73). That is how it is for Alice and for the Fawn whom she meets, each of whom is and is not herself/himself for the purposes of the encounter.

> It's a great huge game of chess that's being played – all over the world – if this *is* the world at all, you know. Oh what fun it is! How I *wish* I was one of them. I wouldn't mind being a Pawn, if only I might join – though of course I should *like* to be Queen, best.
>
> (Carroll 2009, 144)

Suggested in Alice's surmise is both the unreality of the world beyond the familiar and the desire to participate in it. The desire for innocent participation slides unnoticed into a desire for mastery. The connection between these and the violence implied has been foreshadowed on the other side of the mirror in Alice's Queen fantasies and by her viciousness: 'once she had really frightened her old nurse by shouting suddenly in her ear, "Nurse! Do let's pretend that I'm a hungry hyaena, and you're a bone!"' (Carroll, 126).

This imperious outlook makes the wood where things have no names suggestive of the unmapped territory of the Victorian mind – the kind of space in which a Livingstone and a Stanley might meet, the dark woods of a dark unknown continent. Alice's sojourn through apparently a-semiotic space is brief and its outline is quickly recounted. After much name-based banter, the Gnat vanishes and Alice walks on:

> She very soon came to an open field, with a wood on the other side of it: it looked much darker than the last wood, and Alice felt a *little* timid about going into it. However, on second thoughts, she made

up her mind to go on: 'for I certainly won't go *back*', she thought to herself, and this was the only way to the Eighth Square.

(Carroll, 144)

It is just at this point Alice recognises that she is entering the wood where things have no names. As a pawn, she has no choice but to go on and it is through fearful territory she must travel if she wishes to realise her ambition of becoming a queen. This is a winter's tale and, though notionally aboveground, much darker than the summer spirited wonderland adventures. Entering the woods, Alice ponders the danger of losing her name; she worries that if she is given a new one, it will be ugly. Her mind wanders on the theme of answering to a name in the manner of a dog. By the time she is in the forest proper, she is tired and ready to appreciate the shade offered; but by now, she can no longer think of the words 'wood' or 'tree', and so paradoxically, she is able to place herself with certainty in the space where things cannot be named. In the midst of Alice's determined yet futile efforts to remember who she is, a Fawn wanders by. There is immediate rapport via eye contact between these creatures who can name neither themselves nor each other. Pressed by Alice to divulge his identity, the Fawn promises to do so if Alice will come along with him a little further. 'I ca'n't remember *here*', he says (Carroll, 156). The two progress together lovingly, Alice's arms around the soft neck of the Fawn, until they come out of the woods and, in the moment of recognition, the Fawn flees as quickly as he can. Alice is saddened by his departure but comforted to remember who she is once more.

Returning to the ambiguity of subject and reading positions in 'The Teddy Bears' Picnic', we would like to argue that the picnic woods and those where things have no names share a magic by means of which we are conjured to forget who we are and so that we may make our own guesses on that topic. This, we would argue, is the ideal space of poetry today.

In their *Dictionary of Imaginary Places* (2000), Alberto Manguel and Gianni Guadalupi write that 'Looking-Glass Land is the tangible proof of Zeno's refutation of space' (382). The paradox of the arrow is obviated because in Carroll's creation, 'visitors proceed from one point to another without the unnecessary and infinite bother of covering intermediate space' (Manguel and Guadalupi, 382). National borders in the modern world, dividing languages, currencies, and customs from each other might be conceived in just these terms. The unknown world, on the other side, makes as little sense to its non-native as any of the world's random corners might make to a child. In the a-semiotic space of the forest where everything forgets its own name, we find an apt metaphor for the situation of the foreigner who, entering a new culture, has lost the name for everything he/she knows. Yet there might be something Edenic in just such a loss. In 'The Balance of Brillig', Elizabeth Sewell notes the suggestion that "to lose your name is to gain freedom in some way, since the nameless one would no longer be under control" and that "the loss of language brings with it an increase in loving unity with living things' (1992, 387). Alice's dialogic encounter with the world she negotiates is suggestive of larger concerns for culture's novitiate and for the manner in which the experience of those entering culture might be exemplary for (adult) others to whom culture's conditions have become invisible because automatised. Alice's conversations with those she meets, and particularly with the Gnat, involve the reader in a train of thought recalling the *physis-nomos* debate in the *Cratylus* of Plato (and which perhaps foreshadows the symbolic logic of the century to come). The contention over nature and convention in the *Cratylus* signals the beginning of an ongoing debate in the Western world about the great undecidables of signification:

> *Hermogenes.* I should explain to you, Socrates, that our friend Cratylus here has been arguing about names; he says that they are natural and not conventional; not a portion of the human voice which men agree to use; but that there is a truth or correctness in them, which is the same for Hellenes as for barbarians.
> (1952, 85)

Socrates in the *Cratylus* says that trusting names and the givers of names condemn us to 'an unhealthy state of unreality' (114). Consider the Fawn Alice meets in the wood. This creature only becomes scared of Alice and only runs off in fear when names have returned because the two of them (Alice's arms around the Fawn's neck) have now passed beyond the wood.

> 'I'm a Fawn!' it cried out in a voice of delight, 'and, dear me! You're a human child!' A sudden look of alarm came into its beautiful brown eyes, and in another moment it had already darted away at full speed.
> (Carroll 2009, 58)

Alice almost cries with vexation at having lost this new friend before she had really found him, before she had found out who he was, just at the moment when she had discovered *what* he was. In the manner of a child's innocence, we see, on both the Fawn's part and on Alice's part, an openness and a welcome to the unknown other. Reminding us of an Edenic expulsion, the openness and the welcome are dissolved by fear born of knowledge. This fearful knowledge – like that of the non-native entering the new culture – is born of the world of already named entities.

In the picnic woods, these Goldilocks bears are an ambiguous collectivity and one to generate ambivalence. They are numerous, various, even spectral, and ghostly ('every bear that ever there was'). And their presence at the picnic is likewise open to interpretation. Is it appetite or ceremony that draws them? Each is there in equal proportion; all we know for certain is that 'today's the day the teddy bears have their picnic'.

Is it the naming of them that prevents their seeing us? Let us return to this question but meanwhile ask, is it their lifelessness that makes them characters we cannot meet? And then, returning to our dramatis personae and the idea of the picnic as performance, must we not ask which is the mask and which face lies under it? Are these creatures coming to life (the animation of the toy shop, the resurrection of the dead)? Are these humans made animal or vice versa? As in the wood where things have no names, here we are bound not to know. In his essay 'Blessed Rage: Lewis Carroll and the Modern Quest for Order', Donald Rackin writes,

> There can be no telos, no final goal or ultimate 'meaning' within Alice's biological nature or her natural surroundings: Her natural curiosity and her human need for what she calls the 'the meaning of it all' make her, like us, a permanent stranger to her natural environment. She will never attain that Eden she calls 'the loveliest garden you ever saw'.
>
> (1992, 400)

As in Zeno's paradox, in Looking-Glass Land: everything up to and including the subjective de-centring is where it is, but it cannot have got there.

And in the picnic woods? It is also the case that you would have to be somewhere else in order to be here. Animals and secrecy, in another words, animality and unknown motives, have us in this place in which it is apparent adults cannot rule. Or need this be apparent? Outside of the woods, outside of the story, who is it watching, following? Who is it singing to let us know? The question is difficult to answer because the border is mobile. Is the story in the song, even in the tune itself? Or is the song in the story? As with the Red King and the text he appears to inhabit, so with the habitable text more generally. The trope that rules here is metonymy, *glissement*. An identity that binds bear, teddy and child alike, as we have seen, slips away. Equally, time slips away. We are always in the future of the picnic and six o'clock will usher in the dream world of sleep. But were we not already there? And in the same measure, the place slips away – the woods are as easily in the home, in the book, and in the dream as they pertain to any lived reality of adult, of child, of toy, of bear. Metonymy is the dreamer's trope, and equally the child's: it is the work of one thing leading to another. It can be poetry.

It is fearful work. Children are fearsome – hence, as per Aristotle's observation, the analogy with bears. Safety is a theme. The child's world should be safe; it is the duty of adults to make it so. But is it safe at home when the wild rumpus could begin before any self-respecting dinner gong or alarm clock might ring? Then again, where are these woods? Are they simply downstairs in the Edwardian nursery? Are they in the dreaming child's mind? Isn't that where the real bears roam?

In the play-scape of the child's space, there is much ambiguity and ambivalence. The adult effort to render it intelligible – in this case, to make of it a poetic experience that works for children and adults – is bound to drift. Things become what they touch; things are brought to life – a toy is a bear is a child is asleep and could wake to be anything. Nor is wakefulness protection from the vicissitudes of play; here is Johan Huizinga's *homo ludens* unfettered (1949). Play is performance and as with 'Jabberwocky', the play and performance take place on various interacting planes – some more textual, others more or less practical. We sing to play to be ourselves in order to know who we are. There is the personal significance for one of us, on account of having performed in it, having, in the early sixties, made the first of his very rare stage appearances as a teddy bear in this particular picnic. There on the stage, which was the forest floor, glitter brought tears to the eyes.

The Teddy Bears' Picnic

In this song which adults have children sing, a fearful other world of child/animal rule is posited, 'beneath the trees where nobody sees'. The carnival place of the picnic exists, as childhood does, temporally apart from, though framed by, time in the adult clock-and-calendar conception, time which is as meaningless for infants as it is for bears. The whole story can easily be read as an adult wish that there were a place and time, beyond the pale of the home, where the animality of children might be safely contained and might act out safely. Such a place would be a paradoxical construction because it would depend on adults allowing the authority of an evanescent subject, one with whom relations of control are in ambivalent flux.

That is why the idea of the picnic is funny: the bears are no longer animals or even children; through the metonymic chain, they are reduced from being toy avatars of either to being tokens of all these possibilities, in a story in a song. The adult world frames away its fears of otherness and of difference; these felt as per Romantic myth to be immanent in the human world. Like the canon's reasonable appropriation and containment of the ambivalent logic of poetry, the bears have been sent to their picnic, the beauty of which is that it is unknown and inscrutable. The thing that is certain there is 'a big surprise … where nobody sees'. To parents, the terror of the bears at home appears as perpetual until clock time is invoked to save the day: 'At six o'clock their mummies and daddies will take them home to bed'. The Republic of the Playpen is where the games continue, but now in a context safe for the adults watching over, whose onerous duty is to make a world safe for all participants.

'The Teddy Bears' Picnic' offers a poetry of the carnival place out of time. In this song, the music in and around words situates a reversal of the Wordsworthian counter-intuition we read in the idea of the child as 'father of the Man' (Wordsworth 1950). Adults, the unseen servants in the piece, supervise and make safe all of the symbolic arrangements of which they merely pretend to be in awe. 'The Teddy Bears' Picnic' is the kind of republic where we glimpse the rule of poetry's ambivalent logic. We savour the vision in the song before it dissolves in the image of the dreaming child, that 'tired little teddy bear'. But the glimpse we get here is much as we might imagine of Zeno's in famous lost republic, as accounted by Kristeva in *Strangers to Ourselves*:

> Love prevails over men and women who freely belong to one another, dressed in the same manner, having abolished marriage, schools, courts, money, and even temples – only the inner god of the Spirit was revered. Cannibalism, incest, prostitution, pederasty, and of course, the destruction of the family are also accepted among the features of that ideal State.
>
> (1991, 60)[1]

Animals and Secrecy

In 'The Teddy Bears' Picnic', animals and secrecy lead us to the place beyond the rule of law or adult rationality, a place that exists because it is performed, a place that is known because it is seen, if only in some mind's eye, a place that is able to be seen because the gaze is not returned (since no retribution has been enacted), a place that is fearful on account of the unknown consequences that would come of being seen seeing, a place – and here is the suspense in the story – that one must therefore dare to see, if only with the mind's eye. It is important to recognise the transaction lacking here – that is to say, the extent to which we are presented with events that are not dialogic, which do not amount to an encounter. Inside this universe, the bears perform because they do not see out. We, who sing, perform them there, performing our unseen seeing of the bears. The bears perform for themselves but only because we have performed them there. More certainly than with any Red King, when we stop singing, those bears go out like a light. Six o'clock, they are tired little teddy bears. They hide and seek as long as they please. And what are they now? And where? We cannot know. It cannot be recalled. Come along with them further, out of the woods. We may ask them later when they wake. But they cannot remember here. Is not the whole of this lyric an effort, despite the dismay of anthropocentrism, to remember such a place and such a manner of being in the world, in such a world?

As where, more generally, metonymy slips into power, trope infests trope: the Fortunatus' Purse here is a carnival paragon. Apparent equivalence, as a basis for meaning, dissolves in doubt into a next space. It is the victory of the syntagmatic over the axis of selection. The carnival embellishes the performance which frames it. The frame of voices sings those ambivalent antics of a mind's eye and its symbolic woods. Dreaming and waking: worlds frame and contain each other, and in so doing, they show us the other-sidedness of language – language which is ours as it is Humpty Dumpty's, which precedes us and survives us and belongs to the conversation if we are a part.

192   *If You Go Down to the Woods Today*

> 'I don't know what you mean by your way,' said the Queen: 'all the ways about here belong to me – but why did you come out here at all?' she added in a kinder tone. 'Curtsey while you're thinking what to say, it saves time'.
>
> (37)

In the wood where things have no names, we do not merely not know where we are; neither can we know who we are. Namelessness is the reverse of the apparent madness in 'Jabberwocky', the circumstance in which names appear to have no meaning. In both cases, we read under the spell of knowing and not because we only understand from the outside. It is a similarly ambivalent place the bears inhabit in 'The Teddy Bears' Picnic'. We do not know where they are, beyond the echoes we appreciate of, for instance, Lewis Carroll or of Dante's *selva oscura* (dark wood). We do know what sorts of things they are beyond, though – in their carnival, they are in a Carrollian kind of space: beyond (but understood by means of) common sense, beyond adult control or advice (yet sung into being through the work of adults), beyond (and yet not beyond) the parental gaze. Our not knowing in relation to the bears places them in a wood where things have no names. Certainly, the bears are not given names in this fragment of a song, the text, which remains to us. Do the bears have names for anything? Does their playing games imply any naming? As we have seen, there are several dimensions to our not knowing who these characters are. Children? Animals? Stuffed toys come to life? The adult imagination or any or all of these things? Symbols for the same? Each an avatar for any or all of the others? Each the apotheosis? If we do not know who the bears are, then can we know ourselves? Can we know what kind of vantage privileges our seeing? In his essay, 'Why Look at Animals'(1980), John Berger writes:

> The eyes of an animal when they consider a man are attentive and wary. The same animal may well look at other species in the same way. He does not reserve a special look for man. But by no other species but man will the animal's look be recognized as familiar. Other animals are held by the look. Man becomes aware of himself returning the look.
>
> (4–5)

Can we know who we are when we encounter animals when we meet our bears (even as vaguely as we do here)? Ambivalence, like irony, is catching. The encounter with the inscrutable other returns us to leitmotif in Levinas' dictum: these absolute others are here to instruct. Far from mentioning animals in the passage of *Totality and Infinity* (1969) in question, Levinas insists it is only man who could be absolutely foreign to me: 'Free beings alone can be strangers to one another' (73). For Levinas, freedom common to human others is precisely what separates them (73–74). In the picnic woods, shall we presume that the look is never returned, that our voyeurism remains just that? And yet the animals here, more foreign than foreigners, turn out to be familiar because, of course, they are us, dressed up in bear suits for a song. Voyeurism turns out to be narcissism.

Nevertheless, let us ask what we are meant to ask of this wild rumpus. Who are we to see over the picnic, to see where we must not be seen, equipped as we are with a knowledge of 'marvelous things to eat and wonderful games to play'? These things are known to us because we have been there. We have been the bears and we have been *with* the teddy bears. We have worn the same cloth; we may have been cut from it. We have been the children of the picnic and we now peer in as if from the future, knowing it is our past selves we see. Is it not all pretending, all adult fantasy, to be bears, to be children, to be toys? And, of course, the function of the picnic is to teach and model pretending. How is it we catch unaware? Surely, these are the parent's hands on the child, the child's hands on the teddy? In either case, the terror dissolving in that clutch is the real terror of the animal other (the rending bear of the wilds confronted, the hunter's decisive strike, the beast going down like a sack of potatoes).

We are here in this song, singing for the hide and seek, hiding from and seeking ourselves in those others by whom we must not be seen, as if a time traveller's fatal paradox would be invoked were we to be recognised in this place beyond the pale. Fort! Da! We are there and not. *We* sing this – children and adults – a unison across the generations of those learning to be there and not: learning to be naked and seen, learning to be clothed and seeing. What does a teddy bear wear? Will a teddy bear tell what it has seen? The effigy we make is a secret of both sides.

In *The Animal that Therefore I am*, Derrida writes of '*the passion of the animal*': '*my* passion *of* the animal, my passion of the animal other: seeing oneself seen naked under a gaze behind which there remains a bottomlessness, at the same time innocent and cruel perhaps, perhaps sensitive and impassive, good and bad, uninterpretable, unreadable, undecidable, abyssal and secret' (2008, 12). Nakedness is at stake here for Derrida:

> Before the cat that looks at me naked, would I be ashamed *like* a beast that no longer has the sense of its nudity? Or, on the contrary, *like* a man who retains the sense of his nudity? Who am I, therefore? Who is it that I am (following)? Whom should this be asked of if not of the other? And perhaps of the cat itself?
>
> I must immediately make it clear, the cat I am talking about is a real cat, truly, believe me, *a little cat*. It isn't the *figure* of a cat.
>
> (5–6)

The quiddity of Derrida's real cat has to be insisted upon. Alice's fawn is, by contrast, one of us even when he does not know who or what or where he is. Nor does his rediscovery of these things deprive him of language. Pretending for a moment that our bears are not us, they are nevertheless anthropomorphic. They are from somewhere; they are where we have put them or allowed them.

In 'Why Look at Animals', Berger links the post-industrial disappearance of animals from the daily lives of humans to a range of modern phenomena, including the zoo, the cultural marginalisation of animals and the universal presence of zoomorphic toys in contemporary childhood. All this is, for Berger, symptomatic of a nostalgia for animals and their putative child-like innocence, a nostalgia that can be dated to the eighteenth century (12). The promotion of animal characters and imagery in and through childhood is thus inextricably linked to the fate of real animals: 'The animal has been emptied of experience and secrets, and this newly invented "innocence" begins to provoke in man a kind of nostalgia. For the first time, animals are placed in a *receding* past' (12).

Then how do we see animals? Do we see them? Berger writes of the disappearance of 'the animals transformed into a spectacle':

> In the windows of bookshops at Christmas, a third of the volumes on display are animal picture books. Baby owls or giraffes, the camera fixes them in a domain which, although entirely visible to the camera, will never be entered by the spectator. All animals appear like fish seen through the plate glass of an aquarium. The reasons for this are both technical and ideological: Technically the devices used to obtain ever more arresting images – hidden cameras, telescopic lenses, flashlights, remote controls and so on – combine to produce pictures which carry with them numerous indications of their normal *invisibility*. The images exist thanks only to the existence of a technical clairvoyance.
>
> (16)

Let us return to the question of the look and the possibility of its being returned. Derrida turns the gaze of his individual house cat onto himself, and ponders, at the moment of 'naked' encounter, his human-animal nature,

> As with every bottomless gaze, as with the eyes of the other, the gaze called 'animal' offers to my sight the abyssal limit of the human: the inhuman or the ahuman, the ends of man, that is to say, the bordercrossing from which vantage man dares to announce himself to himself, thereby calling himself by the name that he believes he gives himself.
>
> (12)

Of the zoo experience, Berger writes,

> However you look at these animals, even if the animal is up against the bars, less than a foot from you, looking outwards in the public direction, *you are looking at something that has been rendered absolutely marginal*; and all the concentration you can muster will never be enough to centralise it … Within limits, the animals are free, but both they themselves, and their spectators, presume on their close confinement … In all cases the environment is illusory. Nothing surrounds them except their own lethargy or hyperactivity.
>
> (24–25)

Lethargy or hyperactivity (alternate conditions to which the zoo animal is doomed) in 'The Teddy Bears' Picnic' model the child-animal analogy: the wild rumpus of the picnic on the one hand and the putting to bed of the tired little teddy bears on the other. Derrida asks, 'Can one speak of the animal? Can one approach?' (21). The picnic, as much as the zoo, shows us that acts of framing and of representation occlude actual others. In every frame, there is a mirror. To speak of the other is to violate the freedom Levinas lauds, that freedom which is held in common but makes separate and which allows the absolute other to instruct.

On the idea of deprivation of language being responsible for 'the great sorrow of nature' ('audible lament through sensuous sighing and even rustling of plants'), Derrida writes, 'there must be a reversal … in the essence of nature', according to which 'nature (and animality within it) isn't sad because it is mute … On the contrary, it is nature's sadness of mourning that renders it mute and aphasic, that leaves it without words' (19). If sadness for the animals is the result of muteness, then is this idea not overturned with the picnic carnival of the bears? And how convincing can this overturning be? It is true these animals do not speak when we might have plausibly entertained that option for them. Doubt is cast because these subjects whom we encounter in the woods are neither convincingly bears nor convincingly subjects; they are merely figments of an imagination conjured up by our singing.

Is it our privilege to write then, just because we say so, of a real cat which is not also the figure of a cat? Again one must ask, who catches whom unawares? What kind of catch do we deal with here? Is it the case, as Derrida supposes, that they would not be naked because they are naked? As with the bears, so Derrida too finds his encounter with the cat and the question of reciprocity such that he is left wondering who he is (5). What is the danger here? 'You'd better not be alone'! Is it fear of one's self, fear of the conversation ending? 'It's safer to stay at home'. At home, where the make-believe and the wild rumpus mostly go on out of the weather? Fear of the return of the gaze, fear of seeing one's self in those innocent eyes (fear that one's innocence will be recovered?) – these are fears we carry with us wherever we go. Are there among us those of us who know what we sing because we have already seen ourselves in the place which is not one but where one thing has led to another. Neither the bears nor their woods can be over-read.

Who are we when our fears dissolve into laughter, into song, when we sing together? How easily a minor chord rekindles fears laughter has dissolved. All this from the giddy subject shifting, from the not knowing who. This is the *glissement* – the slipped grip – of ambivalence.

The Space in Which Poetry Is Possible

This is a book about poetry; perhaps, more particularly, about how poetry is inhabited and to what ends. What are children and animals doing in this almost entirely adult human-made world of meaning? How do they survive, if they do, at the cutting edge of what humans are able to mean for each other?

If poetry has had an affinity with foreignness, then poetry has been conceived as a community of foreigners or even of strangers to themselves. The position of the poet in the modernist, and later, conception is like that of the foreigner in a new culture – one we might see as foreshadowed by Carroll's Alice in her experience of the wood where things have no names. Yet the poet finds names in this space beyond and names the things of one world as if they were in and of another. Innocence recovered, the poet's world is one being named again, re-named as if for the first time. There are long continuities inherent in this position. Invoking Zeus' power as god of borders and strangers, one acknowledges the difficulty of prayer where the words will not be right for the place. Washed ashore in the land of the Phaecians, Odysseus prays to the unknown god of the stream:

> Hear me Lord, whoever you are. I come to you as many others have come, with a prayer. I am a fugitive from the sea and from Poseidon's malice. Any poor wanderer who comes in supplication is given respect, especially by the immortal gods. I am such a man, and I now turn to you after much suffering and seek the sanctuary of your stream. Take pity on me, Master, I am your supplicant.
>
> (Homer 1991, 83)

Because of an ambivalence for words and belonging, poetry today aspires to the condition of a foreign language. At the least, it exercises a dutiful ambivalence towards that prospect of ambivalence. This is what a middle path between obviousness and obscurity entails. Poetry is keeping on that way. We believe it is in large part the discovery of childhood that has made this circumstance possible. Poetry past Modernism is characterised by an ambivalence for belonging foreshadowed in Plato's expulsion and enabled by Romanticism's prizing of a recovery of innocence, of not knowing, of Keatsian negative capability. There are pagan and Christian readings, apology and redemption, which might be applied to the situation, but in either case, the space in which poetry is possible today is a space in which the truth of the unknowable is avowed. Lewis Carroll's 'Jabberwocky' and his woods where things have no names provide the reader with practical examples of how words may bring us to the place beyond words.

This poetry-after-Romanticism of which we write is something very different from poetry that had been practised before. For Barthes, modern poetry is a 'language which resists myth as much as it can' (1973, 133). Myth and poetry are attempting to do exactly the opposite: 'Whereas myth aims at ultra-signification, at the amplification of a first system, poetry ... tries to transform the sign back into its meaning: its ideal ultimately, would be to reach not the meaning of words, but the meaning of things themselves' (Barthes, 133). Ambivalence towards questions of identity and belonging is again to the fore here. Poetry, as we know it now, is perhaps somewhere in the gulf which Jacques Maritain alerts us exists between Rimbaud's *'Je est un autre'* and Lautréamont's *'Si j'existe, je ne suis pas un autre'* (1954, 169). Poetry travels in gaps and contradictions and rather than embrace faith which entails ambivalence, poetic modernity embraces ambivalence itself; or we may say, it places its faith (in the sense of investing its cultural capital) in ambivalent (as opposed to be bivalent) logic. Here is what Kristeva (via Bakhtin and the French symbolists) sees as definitive of modernity in her thesis on poetic language. Poetry is the adventuring logic of trickster language, of Odysseus as *anthropos polytropos* (complex and multifaceted). There is an affinity here for the idea of a literature for children, generally conceived, in the post-Carrollian context. The surprise of a challenge in the substance of saying – this is what poetry and literature for children have both made their business. A poetry for children redoubles the commitment.

From Bakhtin, Kristeva borrows the true *and* false logic of carnival ambivalence and contrasts this with the true *or* false logic of identity. Kristeva's ambivalence entails the contradictory nature of a poetic language that always includes its own negation: speech and non-speech, real and non-real, norm and transgression (1984, 116–126). For Kristeva, the carnival in poetic language is invisible and unobservable because it is the movement of language itself and unable to be contained by the conventional logic of language (16). Kristeva coins the term 'orthocomplementarity' to make more subtle the difference between true and false, which a poetry need not accept as finality. Kristeva is interested in a truth which 'consists in the ability to participate in the process of contradiction which, logically and historically, both includes and goes beyond' (222).

Mindful of the fact that we have not discussed here any texts created by children, we nevertheless wish to close this chapter by asking if poetry has become a universe in which the thinking of children has a legislative authority of the unacknowledged kind Shelley imagined – an authority which is neither present in poetry before Romanticism and Modernism nor in society more generally today. To properly historicise this question would be a worthy question for another work. We hope here to have at least joined some dots between texts that would be worth discussing in the presence of such a question.

Thinking back to our fawn fleeing the putative 'level woods' of namelessness, thinking of our picnic bears as tired or wild as the song requires, one observes in either case that it is no more children ruling the world or literature than it is animals ruling the zoo today. In either case, we witness the ideological disappearance to which Berger alerts us. The difference between the zoo and the world of animals adults have made for children is that, for the time being at least, there are ever more children to replace themselves and to take up the vision offered. In this vision, children are empowered, and likewise, a high value has been placed on the poetry of chaos children have come to represent. The animals cannot replace themselves so easily. Perhaps that is because their chaos is not so easily subsumed in adult means of meaning and in the making of this world.

In C.S. Lewis' Narnia, fauna is classified in a few ways, but the most important of these recognises that there are two kinds of other-than-human animals: 'talking beasts' and 'dumb beasts'(cited in Bassham 2005); you might say, sentient and non-sentient; or you might say, more and less anthropomorphised creatures. The key difference between them from a human's moral perspective (i.e. to say, from the perspective of the Pevensie children) is that it is permissible to eat dumb beasts, but it is not permissible to eat talking beasts. Eating talking beasts is akin to cannibalism.

As we know that, in the real world, there are no animals who speak, we may take it as read that the particular Christian ethics C.S. Lewis invented for Narnia allow the eating of anyone who does not answer back. But of course, that would not be an 'anyone', that would be an 'anything'. What effect does it have on the child to think that there is a story world, in a book, in which a certain kind of animal must be treated differently from other animals because it has been anthropomorphised, because it is a speaking character, and in this sense human – an animal made human for our entertainment? Does this rhetorical strategy, implicit (perhaps even emblematic), we feel, in many fantastic narratives for children, teach empathy and compassion for other-than-human animals? Or does it cultivate a callousness towards other-than-human others, and perhaps towards others more generally? This is a theme to which we shall return in Chapter 7. In Chapter 6, we will focus our attention on texts in which our dinner does indeed speak in dealing with the issue of food anthropomorphism.

Note

1 Kristeva comments on what we are able to reconstruct of Zeno's cosmopolitanism, that it emerges from the core of a global movement that makes a clean sweep of laws, differences, and prohibitions; and that by defying the polis and its jurisdiction, one implicitly challenges the founding prohibitions

of established society and perhaps of sociality itself; that by abolished state-controlled borders one assumes, logically and beforehand, an overstepping of the prohibitions that guarantee sexual, individual, and family identity. A challenge to the very principle of *human association* is what is involved in cosmopolitan utopia: the rules governing exchanges with the other having been abolished (no more State, no more family, no more sexual difference) – is it possible to live without constraints – without limits, without borders – other than individual borders? (1991, 60) Zeno's Republic would appear to present just the sort of challenge to *everything sacred* which the poets will be accused by Socrates and Plato of unwittingly posing.

References

Abate, Michelle Ann. "'Mischief of One Kind and Another': Nostalgia in Where the Wild Things are as Text and Film". *Portrayals of Children in Popular Culture: Fleeing Images*. Eds. Vibiana Bowman Cvetkovic and Debbie Olson. New York: Lexington Books, 2013. 139–152.

AbdelRahim, Layla. *Children's Literature, Domestication, and Social Foundation: Narratives of Civilization and Wilderness*. New York: Routledge, 2014.

Ariès, Philippe. *Centuries of Childhood*. Harmondsworth: Penguin, 1962.

Aristotle. *The History of Animals*. Trans. D'Arcy Wentworth Thompson. http://classics.mit.edu/Aristotle/history_anim.html, accessed on 1 March 2021.

Bachelard, Gaston. *The Poetics of Space*. Boston: Beacon Press, 1994.

Ball, John Clement. "Max's Colonial Fantasy: Rereading Sendak's 'Where the Wild Things Are'". *ARIEL: A Review of International English Literature* 28(1) (1997): 167–179.

Barthes, Roland. "Acts of Cultural Criticism". *Close Reading: The Reader*. Eds. Frank Lentricchia and Andrew DuBois. Durham: Duke University Press, 2003. 216–225.

Barthes, Roland. *Mythologies*. Trans. Annette Lavers. New York: Hill and Wang, 1973.

Bassham, Gregory. "Some Dogs Go to Heaven: Lewis on Animal Salvation". *The Chronicles of Narnia and Philosophy: The Lion, the Witch, and the Worldview*. Eds. Basham, Gregory and Jerry L. Walls. Chicago: Open Court, 2005. 273–285.

Bennett, Jane. *Vibrant Matter: A Political Ecology of Things*. Durham: Duke University Press, 2009.

Berger, John. *About Looking*. New York: Vintage, 1980.

Boulton, Jo and Judith Ackroyd. *The Teddy Bears' Picnic and other Stories*. London: David Fulton, 2004.

Carroll, Lewis. *Alice's Adventures in Wonderland and Through the Looking-Glass and What Alice Found There*. Oxford: Oxford University Press, 2009.

Derrida, Jacques. *The Animal that therefore I am*. Trans. David Wills. New York: Fordham University Press, 2008.

Harvey, Graham. *Animism: Respecting the Living World*. New York: Columbia University Press, 2006.

Homer. *The Odyssey*. Trans. E.V. Rieu. Harmondsworth: Penguin, 1991.

Huizinga, Johan. *Homo Ludens – A Study of the Play Element in Culture*. London: Routledge and Kegan Paul, 1949.

Hunt, Peter. "Winnie-the-Pooh and Domestic Fantasy". *Stories and Society*. London: Palgrave Macmillan, 1992, 112–124.
Joyce, James. *A Portrait of the Artist as a Young Man and Dubliners*. New York: Barnes & Noble Classics, 2004.
Kennedy, Jimmy. "The Teddy Bears' Picnic". 1932. http://www.tapirebook.org/7ti4s.pdf, accessed on 9 November 2014.
Kidd, Kenneth B. *Freud in Oz: At the Intersections of Psychoanalysis and Children's Literature*. Minneapolis: University of Minnesota Press, 2011.
Kristeva, Julia. *Revolution in Poetic Language*. Trans. Margaret Waller. New York: Columbia University Press, 1984.
Kristeva, Julia. *Strangers to Ourselves*. Trans. Leon S. Roudiez. New York: Columbia University Press, 1991.
Levinas, Emmanuel. *Totality and Infinity*. Trans. Alphonso Lingus. The Hague: Martinus Hijhoff, 1969.
Louise, Zanni. *Archie and the Bear*. Illus. David Mackintosh. Sydney: Little Hare, 2017.
Manguel, Alberto and Gianni Guadalupi. *The Dictionary of Imaginary Places*. San Diego: Harcourt, 2000.
Maritain, Jacques. *Creative Intuition in Art and Poetry*. Cleveland: Meridian Books, 1954.
Merleau-Ponty, Maurice. *Signs*. Trans. Richard C. McCleary, Evanston: Northwestern University Press, 1964.
Merleau-Ponty, Maurice. *The Prose of the World*. Trans. John O'Neill. London: Heinemann, 1974.
Merleau-Ponty, Maurice. *Child Psychology and Pedagogy: The Sorbonne Lectures 1949–1952*. Trans. Talia Welsh. Evanston, Illinois: Northwestern University Press, 2010.
Milne, A.A. *The House at Pooh Corner*. (1928). Illus. E.H. Shepard. London: Egmont, 2004.
Milne, A.A. *Winnie-the-Pooh*. (1926). Illus. E.H. Shepard. London: Egmont, 2013.
Nathanson, Paul. *Over the Rainbow: The Wizard of Oz as a Secular Myth of America*. Albany: State University of New York press, 1991.
Nelson, Claudia. "The Beast Within: Winnie-the-Pooh Reassessed". *Children's Literature in Education* 21(1) (1990): 17–22.
Nikolajeva, Maria. *Power, Voice and Subjectivity in Literature for Young Readers*. New York: Routledge, 2010.
Nussbaum, Martha M.C. *Philosophical Interventions: Reviews 1986–2011*. US: Oxford University Press, 2012.
Plato. *The Dialogues of Plato*. Trans. Benjamin Jowett. Chicago: Encyclopaedia Britannica, 1952.
Rackin, Donald. "Blessed Rage: Lewis Carroll and the Modern Quest for Order". *Lewis Carroll. Alice in Wonderland: Authoritative Texts of Alice's Adventures in Wonderland, Through the Looking-Glass, The Hunting of the Snark*. Ed. Gray, Donald J. New York: Norton, 1992. 398–404.
Sendak, Maurice. *Where the Wild Things Are*. New York: Harper and Row, 1963.
Sewell, Elizabeth. "The Balance of Brillig". *Lewis Carroll. Alice in Wonderland: Authoritative Texts of Alice's Adventures in Wonderland, Through the Looking-Glass, The Hunting of the Snark*. Ed. Gray, Donald J. New York: Norton, 1992. 380–388.

Shaddock, Jennifer. "Where the Wild Things Are: Sendak's Journey into the Heart of Darkness". *Children's Literature Association Quarterly* 22(4) (1997): 155–159.

Stanger, Carol A. "Winnie the Pooh through a Feminist Lens". *The Lion and the Unicorn* 11(2) (1987): 34–50.

Stephens, John. *Language and Ideology in Children's Literature*. London: Longman, 1992.

Stewart, Susan. *On Longing: Narratives of the Miniature, the Gigantic, the Souvenir, the Collection*. Durham, NC: Duke University Press, 1993.

Tatar, Maria, Wilhelm Grimm and Maurice Sendak. "Dear Mili and the Literary Culture of Childhood". *The Reception of Grimms' Fairy Tales: Responses, Reactions, Revisions*. Ed. Donald Haase. Detroit: Wayne State University Press, 1993. 207–229.

Taussig, Michael T. *Mimesis and Alterity: A Particular History of the Senses*. New York: Routledge, 1993.

Tremper, Ellen. "Instigorating Winnie the Pooh". *The Lion and the Unicorn* 1(1) (1977): 33–46.

Varga, Donna. "Babes in the Woods: Wilderness Aesthetics in Children's Stories and Toys, 1830–1915". *Society and Animals* 17(3) (2009): 187–205.

Winnicott, Donald. *Playing and Reality*. London: Routledge, 1971.

Winnicott, Donald. "Transitional Objects and Transitional Phenomena" (1951). *Through Paediatrics to Psycho-Analysis*. Cambridge: Harvard University Press, 1997.

Wordsworth, William. *Selected Poetry*. Ed. Mark van Doren. New York: The Modern Library, 1950.

6 Carnivorous Companions
Anthropomorphic Food in 'The Walrus and the Carpenter' and Elsewhere

The oysters in 'The Walrus and the Carpenter' are far from being the only anthropomorphic food in the Carrollian oeuvre, but courtesy of the Tweedledum-Tweedledee dialectic, they bring to Alice's attention key ethical dilemmas in terms of human intentions and appetites as these impact animal-others. The polite deportment of these two unlikely carnivorous companions reminds us of Brecht's famous lines 'From a German War Primer' (1987, 286): 'Amongst the highly placed/it is considered low to talk about food. /The fact is: they have/already eaten'. The Walrus and the Carpenter talk with those who will be their dinner, but never speak with them of this fact. They lure their prey to their deaths through polite conversation, the conversation of a very English kind.

Following the recitation of 'The Walrus and the Carpenter', Alice's interpretive discussion with the Brothers Tweedle immediately re-frames the ethical dilemma of eating (in this case, sentient speaking) animal-others, in the context of a larger ontological enquiry, one that puts Alice's own existence in doubt: dreamt by the Red King, she might go out like a candle, if the Red King wakes. Thus the relationship of humans with others is to be understood as on a par with questions as to the relationship between fiction (and dream) and reality. A question of power relations may be regarded as implicit in this 'who gets to be God (?)' scenario. Before ascertaining that what sounded to her like the 'loud puffing of a large steam-engine' was the Red King's snoring, Alice had worried that it was a wild beast, like a lion or a tiger. So raw as well as reasoned power is at play here, and there is without doubt an eat-or-be-eaten imperative to the poem's context. Alice is quite prepared to make moral judgements about the Walrus' and the Carpenter's intentions and conduct, but is frustrated in her efforts to do so by further contradictory information the Tweedles supply.

As is so commonly the case in the Carrollian oeuvre, Alice and the reader find themselves forced to weigh up what is odd and what is not, what is good form and what is impolite. It is not only nature and convention (*physis* and *nomos*) that are at stake in this interrogation of taken-for-grantedness; it is important also to consider at which point things get personal. One may read the episode as a parody of sentimentalism,

DOI: 10.4324/9781003219330-7

likewise as a cautionary tale suggesting one is well advised to be wary of those larger and more powerful than oneself. Importantly though, this scene asks us to examine the relationship between euphemism and atrocity in our own dealings with the less powerful others.

Although a substantial part of literature is concerned with the reflections of nineteenth-century European imperialist ideology at large (Hooper and Kearins 2008; Webb 2010), social Darwinism that was in the full swing then (Straley 2016; White 2017), natural history (Lovell-Smith 2003; 2007; 2020; White 2017), and a non-anthropocentric approach, that is, the strategic intervention of speciesist supremacy of human over an animal in 'The Walrus and the Carpenter' (Jaques 2016; Kerchy 2020), scant attention has been paid to the aesthetics and ethics of food anthropomorphism in this poem. Commonly accepted as a literary trope that de-familiarises and dissolves human-animal certainties, anthropomorphism, as in the Alice books, is also considered as Carroll's response to Darwinism and the impossible ethics of care it entails (Straley 2016; White 2017). The illustrated poem enacts a dark comedy of survival, a parody of sentimentalism, in which food, as frequently anthropomorphised, possesses a sort of schadenfreude or baffling fascination. Along with an ethical turn, however, Jane Bennett affirms a positive identification of anthropomorphism as capable of 'uncover[ing] a whole world of resonances and resemblances -sounds and sights that echo and bounce far more than would be possible were the universe to have a hierarchical structure' (99). Michael Parrish Lee, to add to the scholarship, proposes that anthropomorphic fantasy could be a part of 'coinventions with animals – modes of "becoming with" that remain rooted in bodily needs and pleasures and that shape the identities of human and animal inventors together' (2014, 508). The ethical dilemmas are gradually presented, conflated with contemporary concerns of sustainable eating, as anthropomorphism does make oysters being eaten by their predators, walruses and human beings, 'a scene of guilty and hypocritical murder' (White, 134).

To what extent is the empathic imagination enlisted in writing and reading characters, who are in fact, food anthropomorphised? We consider this question by engaging Joseph W. Meeker's 'play ethic' and also the idea of 'creaturely' ethics,[1] and through an effort to understand the implications of these in the reading of texts where anthropomorphism is to the fore. Endowing our food with voice and consciousness provides a perspective, which, though outlandish (and so often a source of humour), encourages us to reconsider the ethics of what/who we eat and how/why such choices impact humans, animals, and the environment.

Aesthetics and Ethics Meet

In 'The Walrus and the Carpenter', aesthetics and ethics meet in considerations of form and courtesy as these impact the lives of anthropomorphised entities that are, or are in danger of becoming, food. Contradictions between good 'form' and appetite are a source of frustration for Alice. This is most clearly shown in the case of the wild kitchen scene that closes the inside story in *Through the Looking-Glass*. Here Alice cannot eat the leg of mutton because it's rude to 'cut' someone to whom you have been introduced.

> 'You look a little shy; let me introduce you to that leg of mutton,' said the Red Queen. 'Alice – Mutton: Mutton – Alice'. The leg of mutton got up in the dish and made a little bow to Alice; and Alice returned the bow, not knowing whether to be frightened or amused.
> 'May I give you a slice?' she said, taking up the knife and fork, and looking from one Queen to the other.
> 'Certainly not,' the Red Queen, very decidedly: 'it isn't etiquette to cut any one you've been introduced to. Remove the joint!' And the waiters carried it off, and brought a large plum-pudding in its place.
> 'I wo'n't be introduced to the pudding, please,' Alice said rather hastily, 'or shall we get no dinner at all. May I give you some?'
>
> (234–235)

How much ruder it would be to eat them alive (or otherwise)! Food that speaks is indeed fearsome!

Although our focus in this chapter is on a specific instance of anthropomorphised food in the Carrollian oeuvre, it is worthwhile noting some more recent comparable instances, including one inspired directly by *Through the Looking-Glass*. Norman Lindsay's (1918/1990) Australian classic *The Magic Pudding* was penned with the chaos of Chapter 9 of *Through the Looking-Glass* in mind and in particular, the pudding passage.

> 'What impertinence!' said the Pudding. 'I wonder how you'd like it, if I were to cut a slice out of *you*, you creature!'
> It spoke in a thick, suety sort of voice, and Alice hadn't a word to say in reply: she could only sit and look at it and gasp.
> 'Make a remark,' said the Red Queen: 'it's ridiculous to leave all the conversation to the pudding!'
>
> (235)

Norman Lindsay's Pudding, though taciturn at times, nevertheless does a fair amount of the talking in his eponymous work. This Puddin' is not merely a portable and inexhaustible food source; he is also a naughty boy named Albert, who, by virtue of the power of his own two legs, is always about to abscond. As in Alice's adventures, food, anthropomorphised here in the form of Albert, provides a focus for contradictions between form and appetite. The contradictions and their apparent easy resolution are expressed in a manner that is, or has come to be, seen as characteristically

Australian, particularly noting the national icon and proverbial status of the work.

> They had a pudding in a basin, and the smell that arose from it was so delightful that Bunyip Bluegum was quite unable to pass on.
> 'Pardon me,' he said, raising his hat, 'but am I right in supposing that this is a steak-and- kidney pudding?'
> 'At present it is,' said Bill Barnacle.
> 'It smells delightful,' said Bunyip Bluegum.
> 'It is delightful,' said Bill, eating a large mouthful.
> Bunyip Bluegum was too much of a gentleman to invite himself to lunch, but he said carelessly, 'Am I right in supposing that there are onions in this pudding?'
> Before Bill could reply, a thick, angry voice came out of the pudding, saying—
> 'Onions, bunions, corns and crabs,
> Whiskers, wheels and hansom cabs,
> Beef and bottles, beer and bones,
> Give him a feed and end his groans'.
> 'Albert, Albert,' said Bill to the Puddin', 'where' s your manners?'
> (15–16)

Through *The Magic Pudding*, Lindsay is responsible for the creation of what is arguably the most optimistic fantasy object in world literature: plenty personified and made portable; more particularly, the fantastic idea or wish fulfilment that the child, instead of being a burden in times and in places of want, could function as a portable cornucopia. A moment's reflection brings us to the dark side of the fantasy. It will be fair to say that the puddin' as a possession (slave and cannibal commodity) has provided an apt palimpsest for wishful thinking of the Australian kind, likewise for Australian styles of cynicism with regard to such wishfulness.

A similarly optimistic and darkly ambivalent object is found in Al Capp's comic strip *The Short Life and Happy Times of the Shmoo* (2003), the Shmoo – an animal who just loves to be eaten, as long as s/he's eaten with love. Kill a shmoo with evil intentions (an interesting distinction in the circumstances) and it will not taste good. Unlike Albert, one cannot doubt the shmoos' desire to be killed and eaten; this is really what they live for. If one considers anthropomorphised food on a continuum according to its complacency in the face of human appetite, then the Shmoo would be at the opposite end of the scale from the chickens in Peter Lord and Nic Park's (2000) *Chicken Run*, those creatures whose anthropomorphic qualities, in particular volition and ingenuity, are wholly directed to the project of not becoming food.

Just in case the shmoo's motives seem too inscrutable to credit, in Douglas Adams' (1981) *The Restaurant at the End of the Universe*, we meet the definitive animal-wanting-to-be eaten and able to cogently and coherently say so, for the simple reason that – in order to contend with perhaps irrational human scruples – it had bred itself specifically for the purpose, not only of being eaten, but of being able to declare itself in just these terms to the diner.

> A large dairy animal approached Zaphod Beeblebrox's table, a large fat meaty quadruped of the bovine type with large watery eyes, small horns and what might almost have been an ingratiating smile on its lips.
> 'Good evening,' it lowed and sat back heavily on its haunches, 'I am the main Dish of the Day. May I interest you in parts of my body?' It harrumphed and gurgled a bit, wriggled its hind quarters into a more comfortable position and gazed peacefully at them.
> (120)

If cruel irony tugs here at the reader's moral heartstrings, then perhaps this is because Adams' cow reveals to us a *reductio ad absurdum* of the much taken-for-granted rhetorical pleasure of anthropomorphism. How is that pleasure related to the pleasure of eating? A cow wishes to aestheticise its demise by gracing a menu for the benefit of the human appetite. This cow goes to shoot itself, but humanely.

> 'Don't worry, sir,' he said, 'I'll be very humane'.
> It waddled unhurriedly off into the kitchen.
> A matter of minutes later the waiter arrived with four huge steaming steaks. Zaphod and Ford wolfed straight into them without a second's hesitation. Trillian paused, then shrugged and started into hers.
> (121)

In this case, the effort to allay the squeamishness of those with doubts about the eating of other animals fails: 'Arthur stared at his feeling slightly ill'. But it fails only for the twentieth-century Englishman, whose scruples these tailored circumstances ironically, given the work's provenance, cannot successfully address. It is the scruples of nineteenth-century English diners and conversationalists with which we will be more concerned in this chapter.

Questions of Courtesy in Life and Death

Life and death questions and questions of courtesy seem a playful juxtaposition and one typical of the oneiric predicaments in which Alice frequently finds herself. What is serious inside the story may be comical to those looking into the frame. On the world-historical scale, we recognise affinities of Alice's circumstances with those of the British national/imperial context she and her author and readers inhabited. A number of critics have noted the imperialist impulse (and reflections of nineteenth-century European imperialist ideology) and justifying social Darwinism in the Alice texts. Daniel Bivona argues that 'Like any good imperialist... Alice assumes that because she comes to play a role in the creatures' drama by virtue of her undismissible presence, she can thereby dominate it, and successful domination must be the inevitable reward of 'comprehension' (1986, 158). The knowledge that comes of the chaotic or mimetic Looking-Glass Land is a baffling yet useful means to Alice's empowerment. Bivona argues that to fulfil an imperialist vision, Alice 'must reestablish "precedence" in all its senses for herself – temporal, spatial, political, and interpretive' (161). It is through such means Alice is able to retain her own position, 'as, impossibly, both master in the master/slave drama and Hegelian "Wise Man", who lives beyond a point of closure outside of the "game"' (161).

The imperialist subtext, therefore, cannot go unnoticed. The desire of retaining a meaning-making but an unmediated encounter with the mirror world, an 'imperial land' in Greeman Richard's words (2007), or a 'fantasy world of great fluidity' (Morgentaler 2000, 91), gradually transforms Alice from a curious and well-mannered girl to a young woman entitled to wear a crown. Critics such as Sarah Minslow (2009) and Caroline Webb (2010) have also observed that Alice is paradoxically an imperialist subject and a colonised child, one who has internalised the power structures of British culture.

Richard Greeman's (2007) essay 'Alice in Imperialand' refers particularly to the political satire of 'The Walrus and the Carpenter' and interprets the 'imperialist rivalry' between a 'British Walrus' and the 'French Carpenter' (as this may have appeared circa 1870) while the oysters are 'the newly subjugated peoples of the colonies' (67). In recent interdisciplinary investigations of the politics of the nonsense poem, the oysters have been claimed to represent the Maoris, and the Walrus and the Carpenter as imperial avatars (Hooper and Kearins 2008; MacLachlan 2013). Despite the developing body of scholarship contained within the discussion of the imperialist context of the Alice texts, scant attention has been paid to the particular contradiction of interest to us: that is the underlying contradiction between form and appetite, and the suggestion of atrocity and cannibalism, in view of the anthropomorphised status of the oysters.

The manners with which the masters of the empire managed the society they kept were dramatically at variance with the gory work of ruling more of the world than anyone else. There were cannibals (cannibal-subjects) to contend with in various parts of the globe over which the sun never set. Some other fresh subjects of the crown may have been more easily disposed of than the cannibals. This *realpolitik* contrasted dramatically with the niceties of Victorian manners and social mores at home: those codes of conduct comprising what we might think of as a social aesthetic, habits making society itself an art event. The wilder the empire became in its bizarre inclusions, the more rarified the air of the hill stations, the more domesticated at least upper-class British civilisation became at home (Kenny 1995; Kennedy 1996).[2] And so the empire, in its endless riches and variety, came to ornament the British nation's ruling class as it preened in the mirror at home.[3] In Europe's most peaceful century at home, the aesthetics of reasonable order were apparent in war and in battle where these did occur and in the pomp of foreign courts too, however woeful their decay might presently be. Beautiful order was, often however, to the Victorian sensibility, conspicuously missing in the barbaric deportment of those – like cannibals – who clearly needed conquering and civilising. Richard Hakluyt had written in the sixteenth century, 'For nothing more glorious...can be handed down to the future than to tame the barbarian, to bring back the savage...to the fellowship of civil existence' (cited in Armitage 2000, 76). In *Taming Cannibals: Race and the Victorians*, Patrick Brantlinger shows how cannibalistic life was, in Victorian society, thought to be 'criminally insane' and the 'nadir of savagery' (2011, 66), without any consideration of systematic beliefs that might have made such practices normative for particular circumstances of culture. By the end of the nineteenth century, it was quite apparent to the average European that everywhere other than home in the European sense did indeed need civilising – hence 'manifest destiny'[4] in the United States, hence doctrines of vacant possession in a new Europe like Australia, doctrines that would later come to be called 'terra nullius'.[5]

The completion of the world map in colours provided by Europe was an encyclopaedic project, one enabled as much by Enlightenment thinking as by modern industrial muscle. Discovering, cataloguing, comprehending the conquered world was exciting, but these were not tasks for the faint hearted. The oddities of the specimen box were thankfully shut up when observation was not required. But they would peer out fearfully, unexpectedly, like the return of the repressed Freud was soon to discover, in dreams and out of the mouths of babes. Before we even enter Looking-Glass Land, we are told that Alice once really frightened her old nurse by shouting in her ear, 'Nurse! Do let's pretend that I' m a hungry hyæna, and you' re a bone!' (124). Like the lion and the unicorn, characters Carroll brings to life later in the book, we see from Alice's threat that the dangers of the far-flung outposts (here Africa and India) invade even the imagination of the nursery. We see that it is a particular feature of Alice's generation that the civilising British nation, and likewise empire, are empowered by the savage forces they subsume and whether or not those forces are real or imaginary, dreamt up in myths or known in daylight.

Margaret Boe Birns notes that outlandish creatures in Wonderland are 'relentless carnivores' who 'save for some outer physical differences, are very like themselves, united, in fact, by a common "humanity"' (1984, 457). This view is later echoed by Rose Lovell-Smith in her exploration of the 'eat or not to eat' motif in Alice stories (2003). Perhaps this is what the world is coming to. The expansion of the British Empire, cannibals and all, shows the world 'curiouser and curiouser'.

If Romanticism had left a legacy of awe for the sublime as perceived in nature, what Victorian society recovered from that project and its Enlightenment antecedents was a duty to order, to organise, the world of inscrutable others that British conquest revealed. The 'dark' continent, home of hyenas amid myriad other terrors, was so named because of its being a place of danger, specifically in that various lights of civilisation (for instance Christianity, advanced capitalist technologies of production and consumption) were yet to shine upon it. Who was there in Victorian England to be offended by the racist implications here for the inhabitants of the dark continent? We should not forget how recently Kant had discussed the inhabitants of Africa without any reference to his own categorical imperative.[6] The world beyond, to the colonising mind of nineteenth-century Europe, needed waking to modern reality and its pre-eminent truths. So to politician and to missionary alike, the scramble for Africa could be rhetorically justified without reference to raw materials and markets; rather, it was about *bringing to light*, about waking primitive people from a dream, because they had no way to wake themselves. For better and for worse, we might view this effort at self-justification as an early stage of a process that would come to be called globalisation. As with the sublime, awe has been a key to the aesthetic quality of a world newly discovered, appreciated, understood. But unlike the Romantic's awe of the natural world, the awe in the case of the empire was for the effort, the prowess, of a particular human, one clearly distinguished by class, by race, by gender, and by the possession of cultural – among other forms of – capital.

The point to press about the rhetorical-ideological event bringing the British Empire to its peak in the run-up to the Great War is that it was, for those on the winning team, a beautiful thing: a thing of beauty along the lines of Augustus finding Rome in brick, but leaving it in marble. The Alice books participate spectacularly in this aesthetic enterprise, precisely by their revelling in the absurd differences the empire brought into the home and into common knowledge, even into the nursery.

When the world, as received through evolving communication channels, is so overwhelming in its multiplicity and contradiction that it no longer makes sense, what better to make of this than non-sense? There can be no more appropriate subject vehicle for that nonsense than the inquisitive child, the child who seeks to reconcile the sensual world of what is becoming known with the domestic and social spaces in which one must learn how to be and who to be. A child like Alice. And one should note that while Alice's constant questioning is understandable in her circumstances (in the circumstances that is, of one participating, almost always unequally, in a chaotic plot), it is also comforting for the reader, child, or adult, who can in one sense at least be always a step ahead of Alice. One stays a step ahead, though only because Alice is a character in a book and we are readers looking in.

The empire for England is a chaotic, often dream-like, collection of odd facts and persons with which to contend, from which to make order. And for the British Empire and the evolving British nation at home, we can say that the aestheticisation of its own order depended on the contrast an empire provided. It depended likewise on a consciousness of superiority: that European, better Anglo-Saxon English-speaking, better British mastery was a sign that all was right with the world. The Looking-Glass Land is in many ways an apt metaphor for the relation of those at home to the colonies and to the empire 'out there', 'a great huge game of chess being played-all over the world' (144). But a hungry hyaena can even reach the inner sanctum of the nursery. And a girl like Alice can go on great adventures, hunting nonsense one might say. However serious and dangerous it might seem for Alice at the time, we, the readers, know it is all happening in a book with pictures and with conversation – a comfortable place to be.

How to stave off understandable fears in a world we cannot understand? As Joseph W. Meeker reminds us, 'Human beings are the Earth's only literary creatures' (4). When our world will not make sense, we empower ourselves by making nonsense with it, from it, of it. We amuse ourselves through a form of distraction that takes us away from serious considerations of power, of world-historical thinking or of our own place in the great scheme of things.

And yet the great schemes are there, along the lines of the method Polonius has an inkling of in Hamlet's madness. In Elizabeth Sewell's classic (1952) study *The Field of Nonsense*, we are told that nonsense as practised by Carroll (and also by Lear) 'does not, even on a slight acquaintance, give the impression of being something without laws and subject to chance, or something without limits, tending towards infinity' (5).[7] Sewell goes on to contend that nonsense is an art of words and not of things: 'In Nonsense all the world is paper and all the seas are ink. This may seem cramping, but it has one great advantage: one need not discuss the so-called unreality or reality of the Nonsense world. The scope of enquiry is limited to what goes on inside a mind' (17). We do not intend to dwell upon this last, puzzling assertion, beyond insisting that, like all literary artefacts, nonsense poetry is composed and read in real-world contexts, in relation to which its not-uncommon function is to poke fun, to make nonsense, to play.

Jospeh Meeker proposes a 'play ethic' as an antithesis of the Western work ethic, one that facilitates biological diversity in an open-ended rather than an aggressively-fetishised productive way. Following Meeker's thesis, comedy not only 'moderates healthy relations among people' but, more significantly, is a catalyst for conflicts 'between people and the Earth's natural processes' (1997, 11). Whether in terms of humanistic culture or biological stability, 'comedy is a contributor to survival' (Meeker, 11).

In the case of nonsense, through what could be called 'play ethic', we replace what cannot be made sense of. Paradoxically, this process has powerful revelatory effects, even if, at the time, these are only suggestive. Why else all this endless scholarly chatter about Alice?

In his monograph *Philosophy of Nonsense: The Intuitions of Victorian Nonsense Literature*, Jean-Jacques Lecercle argues that the genre of nonsense in the Victorian period is an 'attempt to solve by imaginary means a real contradiction in the historical conjuncture' (2002, 2). Contradiction, as noted by Lecercle, is structured and maintained in a dialectic of 'subversion and support', 'excess and lack'. The nonsense text is a 'verbal asylum' within which the 'madmen' can speak within the rhetorical, linguistic, and philosophical limits of a text, which functions to phrase 'both the discourse of madness and the discourse on madness' (208). 'The Walrus and the Carpenter' opens with just such revelations of madness, framed through contradiction (or contrariwise, we could say, of contradiction, framed by mad speech), whose confluence of "madness, doubt, simulacrum", as Alan Lopez articulates, puts the status of 'critical subject within Alice' in question (103). The sun shining in the night, the boiling sea, the question of whether to debate the putative wingedness of pigs; such non-sequiturs and their ontological, temporal-spatial and speech-action contradictions provide a setting for the main nonsense of the poem – that of a polite conversation with one's dinner.

Nonsense is a powerful means of aestheticising contradictions. When things don't make sense – they are funny, as in, for instance, that hybrid monster of poetry Horace imagines for us at the beginning of the *Ars Poetica*. The two senses of 'funny' in English coalesce here: the world doesn't make sense so let's see how it's funny; also, let's see what fun we can have with it. This kind of making things funny turns out to be a kind of making sense. One contradiction attended, amused, leads to another. This is, however erratically, the manner in which Alice's adventures proceed and the manner in which tension rises as the stakes rise in *Through the Looking-Glass*. As we come to the climax, we recognise the dangerous moment of empowerment at which Alice, an unwitting player in a Great Game, is to become herself an aesthetic power *par excellence* – a queen. For credibility here, one notes that the monarch of the day had certainly not, at Alice's age, expected she would ascend the throne. This final rite of passage for Alice, at the border of dreaming and waking, is symbolically apt in the growth narrative we read here. The children will inherit the empire so that they will require its concomitant graces, social and otherwise.

To return to the human-animal dimension of Alice's unfolding predicament, one observes that the story she inhabits is one full of strange as well as familiar creatures. We might say that Alice's story – the book in which she finds herself – is as full of weird and incomprehensible creatures as is the empire of which England now finds herself, mistress. That the animals met generally engage Alice in conversation may be taken as nothing more than presence to the genre. Our interest is in the *kind* of conversation and in how Alice participates. As regards the anthropomorphism, our interest is in the persons of the story (and of whom they might represent). Acknowledging that anthropomorphism itself is a species of nonsense (i.e., animals do not talk in the real world), our interest is in how this nonsense works and where the method is in this madness. In the case of 'The Walrus and the Carpenter' as in the case of 'Jabberwocky', a reflexive textuality is to the fore.

Alice is not a participant in the story of the Walrus and the Carpenter. She is – as we, her readers are – looking in on the tale, overseeing the nonsense, as a serious, if often perplexed, reader. And yet, she will, in the world of her story, be called upon to make moral sense of what has gone on and to evaluate the relative moral worth of the two carnivores in questions. Like the white man with the rifle under the pith helmet, Alice's understanding of her wild surrounds may be woefully incomplete, it is nevertheless the moral centre and compass of the tale as it is available to us.

In this case, it is Alice who casts the first stone even before brothers Tweedle begin on their moral exegesis. The poems in *Through the Looking-Glass* serve in each case as object lessons. They suggest problems of interpretation and they suggest moral issues. More explicitly, they suggest that moral problems are problems requiring interpretation; contrariwise, that problems of interpretation must be ethical problems. Understanding the poem helps Alice to apportion her disapprobation for the Walrus and the Carpenter. Understanding those characters and their motivations helps Alice through the moral dilemma the poem presents to her.

Rhetorically, whatever is received as nonsense draws our attention to a contradiction. A contradiction, as embodied in the enantiomorph status of the contrariwise Tweedles, demands resolution. The resolution entails moral exegesis – that is to say, a unified effort at ethics and at interpretation. Rhetoric and ethics are among the most beautiful of civilisation's endowments. In our day-to-day deportment as civilised beings, these amount to form. Like the cow pointing out its best cuts to the diner at the restaurant at the end of the universe, it is only because of our civilisation that we have been able to cultivate those scruples that make us squeamish because we are able to see that we could be a cow, that any large mammal could feel what we feel.

And so when Alice, near the top of the story, comes to regret having been introduced to an animal or part thereof that she would nevertheless have liked to eat, surely these are for her, as a human, higher moral stakes than the eating of oysters should be in the case of a walrus? At this stage in our involvement, what we read as nonsense we nevertheless cannot dismiss as such. It is only because of a conversation that could not have happened that we are able to consider a moral question as to the consumption of oysters by walruses, or more importantly, of other moral questions to which this scene might point, by analogy.

If ethics are a rhetorical effort, then nonsense must always be ethically invested. To say that nonsense is the key aesthetic in Alice's adventures is to acknowledge that she travels with and among contradictions, always of a moral complexion. Carroll's Alice is uncannily drawn to participate in contradictions between aesthetic forms of society and the grisly truth of power relations among animals (not to say nations and their others), and especially of the powers of humans over other animals and over human others. 'The Walrus and the Carpenter' is, among Alice's adventures, only the most sustained meditation on such an illustrative event. If there is a putative play ethic, as per Meeker's contention (1997), it must be embedded in what Thomas Samson describes as 'a social order in which the dominant categories of perception of human relationship are those of "exploiter" and "exploited"' (2015, 52).

Whether 'The Walrus and the Carpenter' – and its 'mock' moral conundrum – was merely a joke to Carroll and Tenniel and contemporaries is somewhat beside the point. The business seems somewhat more serious in the world of the twenty-first century, that world in which seven-billion humans eat sixty-billion plus vertebrate animals a year (not to count the fish). The moral questions seem more urgent when we are instantly witnessing deficiencies in the way humans treat each other at any moment, at many points on the globe. Instances of literary anthropomorphism help us to consider how and why personhood is attributed, discarded, and denied.

Aesthetics and ethics meet in every instance of anthropomorphism; that is to say, the social forms involved in the depiction of other-than-humans in our particular human terms will always entail self-description. There is no avoiding mirror images. There is no not seeing ourselves. Such are the lessons of Looking-Glass Land.

Time for a Pleasant Run

Now the time has come for a pleasant stanza-by-stanza saunter through this poem, beginning with some of the most memorable lines in the history of nonsense.

> The sun was shining on the sea,
> Shining with all his might:
> He did his very best to make
> The billows smooth and bright —
> And this was odd, because it was
> The middle of the night.
> (Carroll 2009, 162)

Here, in the poem's scenic establishment, dimensions of this nonsense-in-particular are evoked, as if they were archetypal. The poem is a place of nth degree impossibilities, on the grandest, on the cosmic scale.

Notwithstanding the possibility that a century and a half on, thanks to global warming, the midsummer sun may soon be shining on an ice-free midnight sea (at least at the North Pole), to be in this picture is to inhabit a lie of a kind that precludes what we take to be fundamental realities of our world. Yet, already we uncannily feel that the paradox is all surface.

In *The Logic of Sense* (1990), in many ways an extended meditation on Alice and her predicaments, Deleuze tells us, 'Paradox appears as a dismissal of depth, a display of events at the surface, and a deployment of language along this limit. Humor is the art of the surface, which is opposed to the old irony, the art of depths and heights' (9).

A sun shining on the sea in the middle of the night? Is night's middle not when the great archetypes are dreamt? The oneiric suggestion gives the impression of a theatrically constructed world, one in which the normal rules of the cosmos may be dismissed at will, should theatricality require it. The surface, as opposed to depth here, pertains to this self-conscious staginess.

How can we characterise this kind of nonsense? First, perhaps by the fact that it is already several kinds of nonsense. The setting of the scene is not merely physical; we are presented with a rhetorical map with which to begin the exploration. Although we deal in surfaces, there are several – the physical/impossible, the rhetoric implied, and (stood upright) the proscenium arch – the framing for the tableau of the tale. Contradictions are accomplished in the fact of paradox, indispensable to our remaining in the tale as readers. What is impossible is delivered as matter of fact (the sun cannot shine in the middle of the night). The anthropomorphism is nonsense (the sun, though no doubt mighty, is not able to do things 'with all *his* might', nor can *he* do his best at anything).

The opening stanza likewise establishes the easy flow of the language, to be accomplished in the lulling of the listeners and oysters alike into a false sense of security. The alternating tetrametre and trimetre, the end-stops and the masculine rhymes are the means of delivering us absurdity as if it were common sense, common knowledge.

The façadism of the staged setting is confirmed as an allegory in the second stanza, where we encounter the moon as a feminine character balancing the masculine sun already met. Now we know that we are in some kind of morality play. We suspect that ethics may be the topic. Equally, we know, and much more quickly than in the case of 'Jabberwocky', that all of this is a parody. But parody of what precisely?

> The moon was shining sulkily,
> Because she thought the sun
> Had got no business to be there
> After the day was done —
> 'It's very rude of him,' she said,
> 'To come and spoil the fun!'
> (Carroll 2009, 162)

Here the nonsense is interpersonal, much in the manner of Alice's own conversational interventions. Now we are invested in the social, if not moral, dimensions of the nonsense. It is all about manners, about what is right or wrong to do in the social sense. Our attention here is on the aestheticisation of contradictions. What do contradictions do to the social order, to the sense of comfort or harmony on which a reader might rely? The indignation of the moon, which only participates in the absurdity of anthropomorphism, is a sport for the reader. The moon is the figure of fun here. And what's not funny to the moon, exercising her cosmic responsibilities, is funny to us. What business can an impossible sentience have being upset about an impossible event involving another impossible sentience? And yet, by means of an anthropomorphism, the setting here establishes male privilege and power, likewise female peevishness, as mere facts of nature.

> The sea was wet as wet could be,
> The sands were dry as dry.
> You could not see a cloud, because
> No cloud was in the sky:
> No birds were flying overhead —
> There were no birds to fly.
> (Carroll 2009, 162)

With the third stanza, a new kind of nonsense is introduced. Until now, it has appeared that the inattention of the reader might determine whether or not the nonsense was picked up. It all sounds reasonable until, in this stanza, it appears that the source of nonsense must be the speaker's inattention, as expressed in repeated truisms and tautologies (sea wet, sand dry; no cloud, cloudless sky; no birds flying, no birds to fly). How funny it can be to say nothing new! And this might be what language does when one is not paying attention. Tautology slips off the tongue as if something new *had been* said. The repetition of the already known here has an almost hypnotic effect on the reader, whose expectations of novelty or event are eroding at this point. Nothing much happening here. It is just language play. Another lulling into a false sense of security. And until now, we are still in the setting, a behavioural stage setting that already shows the leading characters' feelings as 'sham sympathy' (Scheman 1979, 320). Entropy sets in before the plot, before our first meeting with our protagonists, in the fourth stanza.

> The Walrus and the Carpenter
> Were walking close at hand:
> They wept like anything to see
> Such quantities of sand:
> 'If this were only cleared away,'
> They said, 'it would be grand!'
> (Carroll 2009, 162)

If the moon's sulky indignation, in the second stanza, seemed at least sincere, here faux sentiment ality and bogus emotion are introduced. It is at this point that we can say affective presence in the poem is established as fake. This is a kind of *prosopopoeia* – the apparent protagonist characters are introduced as wearing masks, as disingenuous. We meet them as characters dissembling their emotions. And now, when we think back to the sun and moon, we realise that their pretensions to masculine vigour on the one hand and feminine decorum on the other were, of course, nonsense. We see that that nonsense has yet another surface we could not have seen before. It is not that the masks are removed, rather simply that we see that there are masks. We are in the presence of cosmic powers that we would be unwise to trust. Already the fate of the oysters is foreshadowed.

The scene is set for further trickery to come. The tautologies of the third stanza now press the good reader (the one who has accepted the nonsense so far received) to doubt within-the-frame the veracity of what is spoken over it. It is interesting to note here, in terms of Alice's later conundrum as to the ethics of intention versus action, that in the fourth stanza, the Walrus and the Carpenter are of one mind. Are they are a chorus? Or does their conversation amount to the meaning paraphrased here? They have come to agree that it would be grand if the sand were cleared away? We do not know. What we know is that they have large designs on this environment and that their only qualms about destroying it relate, as we see in the next stanza, to the fact that those designs might be impractical, from what appears to be an economic point of view.

> 'If seven maids with seven mops
> Swept it for half a year,
> Do you suppose,' the Walrus said,
> 'That they could get it clear?'
> 'I doubt it,' said the Carpenter,
> And shed a bitter tear.
> (Carroll 2009, 162)

In this stanza, authority is sought in an earlier generic form. 'Seven maids with seven mops' suggests a biblically inclined proverb, or nursery rhyme, or cautionary tale. Nonsense is sustained by an ongoing confusion as to genre. This confusion helps to ensure that the elements of the story continue not to fit (in the *non-sequitur* type of nonsense).

In this fifth stanza, we first glimpse a temperamental contrast between the companions: the tearful taciturnity of the carpenter, as opposed to the inquisitive forward thinking of the Walrus. The melodramatic sentiment is easily disposed of in favour of a progress-at-all-costs boosterism. Sweeping sand with a mop is, on the face of things, stupid and so funny; but when we realise it is a beach's worth of sand needing to be removed, we approach a new nth degree of absurdity: using the wrong tool to remove an apparently infinite quantity of something infinitely small, when there could be no sensible motive for doing so. When we see that it is young women who will be put to this impossible task for six months, merely to test a hypothesis, we get an inkling of the imperiousness, and lack of empathy, of these co-conspirators. Further, what we might have taken for a marked gender bias in the opening construction of the sun and the moon, now begins to suggest a full-blown misogyny. The Carpenter's bitter tear is shed not for the imagined workers but for the impracticality of an exploitative design, of which only this little is known. Nevertheless, the scene is now set for the hypocrisy, at least the Walrus will seem to demonstrate, in the final stanza. The focus here is on intention, and note that, at this time, the Carpenter does not weep for the consequences (actual or foreseen) for any creature, only for an undisclosed scheme gone awry.

The bitterness of the crocodile tear, outside of the quotation marks, might be taken as indicating the narrator's complicity with the Carpenter's apparent dissembling. In fact, we would argue that lack of sincerity cannot be positively established for the Carpenter at any point in the poem. All that is factually established about the setting up to this point is that these probably sarcastic characters are on a beach, where beyond the absurd anthropomorphics in which they take part, such fundamentals of life on Earth, as sun and moon and day and night, cannot be taken for granted.

Aside from all this speculation, one notes that the delivery here is so deadpan that it is plausible these two are simply mad. Mad characters inhabiting a mad world where the sun shines in the middle of the night. Or is it that the mad setting shows that the world has been presented from a madman's point of view? Or it could be that the Walrus' emerging hypocrisy reveals him to be the sane one of the two. It may simply be that the Carpenter is empathically challenged to the degree that he is not capable of hypocrisy. The reader should, at this point, perhaps assume that, unless these two are a comedy act, they are either mad or bad or both. But of course, we know that they are a comedy act because they are *in* the nonsense. The framing of the tale as an ethical problem encourages us to wonder about the nature of the method in their madness/es.

And now the innocent oysters come into the story:

> 'O Oysters, come and walk with us!'
> The Walrus did beseech.
> 'A pleasant walk, a pleasant talk,
> Along the briny beach:
> We cannot do with more than four,
> To give a hand to each'.
> (Carroll 2009, 163)

Cary Wolfe proposes that within the Western tradition, we need to think in terms, not of human/animal, but in terms of humanised human, animalised human, humanised animal, animalised animal: 'animalized humans, perhaps the most troubling category of all, since all manner of brutalizations carried out by cultural prescription can serve to animalize humans, as can reminders of human beings' mammalian, or even merely bodily, organic existence' (2003, 101). Consider the array of human-animal characters gathered around the text we are examining: the author/narrator/persona, the human-human, the Carpenter (perhaps an allegorical type), the human-animal Walrus, the subaltern human-animal oysters, and the human readers outside of the text.

We know that the Walrus and the Carpenter would have been happy to exploit seven nameless female humans without much consideration. Perhaps the seven maids are merely illustrative and so not to be taken as characters in the story? If glancing reference deprives those young women of agency and humanity, these are given in bucketloads to very unlikely characters, the oysters. Notch up a point for the Walrus-as-hypocrite hypothesis here. The Walrus does the beseeching. So the animal-other of the piece – the big one – invites the little animal-others to be among those who will show themselves presently as higher up the food chain. Karl Steel argues for the 'helplessness, this absolute passivity of the oyster's flesh' (2015, 81) and points out that the eating of oysters is never ethically problematic, even for some vegetarians. Peter Singer notes that in the Cartesian conception, oysters would represent a certain kind of 'imperfect' creature whose capacity for pain must be in doubt (Singer 2009, 174). Descartes' doubts as to the thinking capacity of some animals (1970, 207–208) led him to conclude that no animals have souls (because if some did, then all would), a notion to be countered, in a later century, by David Hume's claim that 'the life of a man is of no greater importance in the universe than that of an oyster' (1998, 100).[8] Singer's doubts as to the pain capacity of oysters led him to stop eating them.

As we learn later in the poem, the oysters are introduced into the story in order to be conned. Though endowed with speech and the mental capacity to choose, the young oysters are portrayed as failing to act in their own interests. Much as mobs or voters are frequently portrayed, they follow blindly where they are led (as per a common analogy with lemmings). This failure, like their capacity for speech and decision, is of a very human quality. We should stress, at this point, in any case, that our interest in the oysters as oysters are limited, particularly because oysterhood seems to be such a small part of the subjectivity they present in this text.

The question of culpability for the ultimate demise of the oysters comes back to this stanza. The Walrus cons the oysters with soft soap. Hindsight shows his intention to have been dark. The Carpenter does not declare himself but is complicit in his action; he goes along with the plan. Exactly whose, we cannot say.

In the sixth stanza, things may seem non-threatening, but we later discover that the oysters are about to make life-and-death decisions at just this point in the narrative. The Walrus and the Carpenter, hindsight will show us, have already made *their* life-and-death decisions for the oysters.

A number of ethical questions are to the fore for those of us privileged to oversee this conduct, to survive the interaction and to ponder its meaning. In *Our Aesthetic Categories*, Sianne Ngai calls attention to the aesthetic exploitation of animals in the market by 'giving face' in cuteness, which 'seems to amount to denying speech' (2015, 91). Making a creature appear to be cute may be to ascribe it with familiar, manipulatable and unthreatening qualities, and further, to diminish its actuality as an animal. Here, we observe a characteristic paradox of anthropomorphism as a rhetorical event – the more familiar the animal becomes to us, the less animal it is. That is to say, the illusion of knowing the animal comes from its having been given qualities to which we can relate as humans, qualities, for instance, sentience, speech, a range of emotions and rational choices the animal-other does not, in fact, have. With making-cute, we observe a like phenomenon. The character made cute feels familiar, in an unthreatening sense. The more cute, the less volition that character has. Conversely, dissent from expected norms or actions would have the effect of eroding the apparent cuteness of the character in question. The Japanese logo Hello Kitty,[9] a character whose name interestingly derives from that of the one actual out-of-the-story-frame animal in *Through the Looking-Glass*, i.e., Kitty, represents perhaps an nth degree of the phenomenon. Hello Kitty, as a logo, has no mouth and so nothing to say for herself; she can only be described by others. We can say then that cute anthropomorphic characters are overdetermined as lacking power. And yet, the oysters of our poem are not at all lacking in agency – they have voices after all. Some decide to stay and some decide to go. If they act against their own interest and on the basis of lies or disinformation, then this situates them squarely in the human predicament here on Planet Earth.

So, in the prelude to the Walrus' and the Carpenter's feast, the young anthropomorphised oysters are depicted as going to their slaughter obligingly, even enthusiastically. Note that their age has nothing to do with their oyster-hood and everything to do with their function as characters in the story. Elder = possessing the human qualities of experience and so wisdom; to be young is to be lacking these virtues. It is true that this could be the case also for members of some other species, other mammals, for instance; but there is no reason for thinking that something akin to experience should make oysters either more virtuous or more likely to survive. Of course, neither the young oysters on their exhausting beach trek nor the first-time reader know where they are going. The Walrus' tricking of the oysters is by way of an Althusserian act of interpellation:[10] like working-class children of colour who consider themselves lucky to be included in a mainly white middle-class Disney world, the Walrus hails the oysters as potential participants in a conversation it would be a privilege for them to take part in. In a classic Marxist sense, let us say, the young oysters, seduced with the soft soap, are victims of false consciousness: their world is ideologically other than they imagine it to be.

It appears John Lennon was struck by this notion: 'It never dawned on me that Lewis Carroll was commenting on the capitalist system' (cited in Patterson 1998, 82).

Cabbages and Kings: Appetite, Distraction, and Nonsense

Appetite is central to the plot, to the dialogue, and to whatever ethics underlie these mechanisms of the 'The Walrus and the Carpenter'. Different from the conventional food plot, as Michael Parrish Lee describes it, 'a sort of shadow plot, shifting and fleeting' (2016, 7), the poem makes visible the human need to eat and keep on eating, which would necessarily drive some animal others to death. What makes this foot plot even more unsettling is the depiction of the young oysters as humanized, "all eager for the treat" that is promised by their predators, the Walrus and the Carpenter. Rhetorically, one might observe at this point that Darwinism and Social Darwinism meet in such an instance of anthropomorphism.

Carrollian scholarship notices that Darwin's theory has a great impact on the Alice books, with its central themes of variation amongst species, the struggle for existence, and natural selection echoed in the plots of change, death, and anthropomorphism (Auerbach 1973; Straley 2016; White 2017). For instance, Jessica Straley highlights the ambiguity of how Carroll toys with anthropomorphic figures as 'the promise of parody, not the destructiveness of Darwinism' (87), while Laura White argues that the nonsense of anthropomorphism is 'part of Carroll's satiric response to [the Darwinian] incipient blurring of lines' (110). As for Carroll, although he was a proponent for animal rights and wrote that 'the prevention of suffering to a human being does not justify the infliction of a greater amount of suffering on an animal' (quoted in Jaques, 44), his nonsense about eating anthropomorphic oysters, according to White, affirms that 'oysters can in fact be eaten without a twinge of conscience', partly because they, growing in an extraordinary scale, were a common staple in the Victorian diet and partly because the main purpose of this poem is a satirical anti-Darwinian critique (White, 26). These interpretive insights, mostly concerned with aesthetics, nevertheless compel us to consider not only the long-established but also the developing ethical positions regarding oysters for a renewed interpretation that possibly resonates with human perceptions of the worldwide ethical predicament that faces the animal world.

The 'hailing' of the oysters for the apparent purpose of conversation suggests a normalising ideology is embedded in the unequal interspecies communication of the poem. As Deleuze has noted, 'At Alice's coronation dinner, you either eat what is presented to you or you are presented to what you eat' (23). The ideological inversion at work here is simply that what appears to be about funny animals who cannot talk is about perhaps not-always-so-funny animals who can talk.

By this stage in the text, the characters are well established. The Walrus is the initiator of talk, of ideas and of feelings. The Carpenter, if taciturn, is unequivocal. Being with the two protagonists of the poem is shown to be a privilege for their subalterns and one in demand (they can only handle four oysters at a time). But not everyone needs to read the situation in this manner. Not every oyster will be taken in.

> The eldest Oyster looked at him,
> But never a word he said:
> The eldest Oyster winked his eye,
> And shook his heavy head —
> Meaning to say he did not choose
> To leave the oyster-bed.
> (Carroll 2009, 163)

Here we see taciturnity, lower down the food chain, revealed as an instinct for self-preservation. The party-pooping eldest oyster, interestingly, in shying from human company, likewise shuns the rhetorical trap of anthropomorphism. Of course, oysters do not wink or shake their heavy heads; however, these antics are somewhat more oyster-credible (and so less amusing) than those the footloose youngster-oysters shall presently evince. Staying close to the place nature intended, declining the pleasure of conversation with humans – hindsight shows these decisions in the light of wisdom, through which the eldest oyster probably avoids the fate of the subaltern others in the poem. One can say the eldest oyster likewise avoids subalternity by remaining in the oyster bed. The metonymic implication here is that the more like an oyster the likelier one is to survive as an oyster; conversely, the closer enthusiasm (mania) brings oysters to humans, the lower their chances of survival. At this point, it is difficult to resist the parable of capitalism/imperialism Lennon seems to have read into the poem (cited in Patterson, 82), though one might as easily read the allegory as being about race in the colonial context. Later in the poem, the eldest oyster's wink will be more meaningful for us as we come to an understanding of how it may have been that certain oysters reached an advanced age while certain others did not. In any case, the reticence of the elder oysters is a proof of agency for the oysters in the poem, in general.

> But four young Oysters hurried up,
> All eager for the treat:
> Their coats were brushed, their faces washed,
> Their shoes were clean and neat —
> And this was odd, because, you know,
> They hadn't any feet.
> (Carroll 2009, 163)

To supply a perhaps more plausible zoomorphic analogy, the youngsters go like lemmings to what sounds uncannily like a job interview. Aren't they all trying too hard, making the maximum effort to be victims of a system we could read, as Lennon does, as capitalist and imperialist? This is the point in the poem where we reach the highest absurdity in anthropomorphism. Clean shoes – no feet. Perhaps a spectral analogy is suggested? The attention drawn to the stretch of the imagination here parallels the oddity declared in the first stanza. But that oddity was physical/cosmological; this one has the effect of breaking the rhetorical spell of anthropomorphism that runs through the whole poem. We are more or less told not to believe what we read. This witnessing within the text asks the reader to recognise, while in the story, that the terms of the story are impossible. And yet we read on! The rhetorical strategy here – as with the midnight sun earlier – is the simple assertion that things are funny as they are because they are not possible.

What kinds of consequence are there for such an aside? This reflexive moment could be taken as a reminder that there cannot be an ethics of the impossible; that any feeling we might have for the situation of the oysters would be a misplaced feeling, one based on our indulging a sentiment with no practical basis. Ruskin's pathetic fallacy comes to mind here (1918).[11] It is fair to assert that the witnessing of the challenges to the pedal extremities of the young oysters calls into question the apparent ethical frame of the poem *in toto*. Is it the case that there is no moral problem with eating oysters; rather, is there a moral problem with anthropomorphising the un-anthropomorphisable? That is to say, that evincing empathy for entities incapable of receiving it will be an unhealthy thing – from an ethical/aesthetic perspective. And yet we roll along with the truth-in-the-tale of the oysters as actors in their own world, 'eager for the treat'.

'Eager for the treat' establishes the series of bitter ironies in the poem (foreshadowed by the earlier 'bitter tear' of the aggressors) – the victims of oppression are eager to rush to the doom made attractive by the apparent selectiveness of those much more powerful than their own kind. Note also that, at the same time, what makes impossible the ambulatory meal-to-be is also what makes it cute and funny.

> Four other Oysters followed them,
> And yet another four;
> And thick and fast they came at last,
> And more, and more, and more —
> All hopping through the frothy waves,
> And scrambling to the shore.
> (Carroll 2009, 164)

Who is watching the event unfolding here? Are we the readers more like oysters (albeit the kind with shoes but no feet), or are we more like oyster eaters, of the human or the anthropomorphised kind? Others – beyond the pale of empathy – take the form of hordes and so they lack dignity, though speech will perhaps recover for them some empathy and some dignity, but only at last when these are too late to help them. Not too late, though, for the reader to know that, in the end, the oysters knew that they were tricked. They went to their deaths knowing.

> The Walrus and the Carpenter
> Walked on a mile or so,
> And then they rested on a rock
> Conveniently low:
> And all the little Oysters stood
> And waited in a row.
> (Carroll 2009, 164)

Perhaps this is the most macabre stanza of the poem, as we learn later that the oysters are awaiting their execution. And now the oysters need, not merely, as we will see in the following stanza, to regain their breath from their mile-long exertions, but also to be distracted, perhaps even entertained. Otherwise, why should they not, despite their tiredness, simply wander off and so save themselves? Is it really too late to go back?

> 'The time has come,' the Walrus said,
> 'To talk of many things:
> Of shoes — and ships — and sealing-wax —
> Of cabbages — and kings —
> And why the sea is boiling hot —
> And whether pigs have wings'.
> (Carroll 2009, 164)

It is nonsense that will distract or entertain them, perhaps hypnotically engage them, as it does the reader watching and reading on. And the nonsense here consists again, of non-sequiturs, non-possibilities, and lies. This is a post-truth text, *avant le lettre*. It seems here that the soon-to-be victims are billed as privileged eavesdroppers, as gullible children might be in the case of adult conversation apparently not intended for (but in fact crafted for the benefit of) young ears. But now we learn that the oysters do indeed expect to participate in the conversation.

> 'But wait a bit,' the Oysters cried,
> 'Before we have our chat;
> For some of us are out of breath,
> And all of us are fat!'
> 'No hurry!' said the Carpenter.
> They thanked him much for that.
> (Carroll 2009, 164)

The oysters' own admission that they are fat is the next in the series of ambiguous and bitter ironies for the to-be-duped in the piece. The physical defect of which a sentient able body complains is, from another point of view, the desirable quality of an edible animal.

Levinas explains in his ethics of otherness that what is seen in a face is its invisibility and absolute alterity: 'The Other precisely reveals himself in his alterity, not in a shock negating the I, but as the primordial phenomenon of gentleness' (1969, 150). Francois Raffoul further ruminates on Levinasian defacement in an encounter, '*The face is above all exposure to death*. This radical exposure of the face is radically stripped of protection, defenseless: the face is defenselessness itself' (2016, 137). Is it the oysters' naked exposure of their 'faces' that invites their oppressors to slaughter them? Is the prohibition of murder situated in the face-to-face encounter or does it originate in the fact that the encounter with the other *could be* face-to-face?

Hindsight will shortly tell us that the oysters are protesting for the wrong reasons and the Walrus and the Carpenter have manipulated their 'forces of encounter' in a wicked way. It is interesting to note that at this point, in a first reading of the poem, the reader's knowledge of circumstances is with the oysters. There is plenty of subtle foreshadowing, but it is the Walrus and the Carpenter who already know with certainty what the rest of us do not know – namely, the fate of the oysters.

>'A loaf of bread,' the Walrus said,
>'Is what we chiefly need:
>Pepper and vinegar besides
>Are very good indeed —
>Now if you' re ready, Oysters dear,
>We can begin to feed'.
>   (Carroll 2009, 164)

The foreshadowing of the oysters' fate continues by metonymic means. This stanza is about what goes with your victims to make your victims more delicious. Note the clear, simple, evaluative language: 'Pepper and vinegar besides/Are very good indeed'. If we trace that kind of expression back through the poem, we find the sun doing his best to shine unnaturally, the idea that the clearing of the beach (for some unknown development purpose) would be grand, and that the footless oysters are clean and neat in the shoe department. Everything declared positive in the poem, either by the narrator or speaking characters, is to do with trickery and with exploitation.

The next lines show us that it was in the previous stanza (here in this conversation apparently not for their ears) that the penny finally dropped for the oysters.

>'But not on us!' the Oysters cried,
>Turning a little blue.

'After such kindness, that would be
A dismal thing to do!'
'The night is fine,' the Walrus said.
'Do you admire the view?'
(Carroll 2009, 165)

The oysters now know they are to be victims; they now know that they have been tricked and they know that they have been complicit in their own destruction. Their agency has worked against them, and in a very particular way – they have sealed their fate to the extent that they engaged with humans and pretended to human qualities, as in this case, walking and talking. The Walrus deflects their realisation, which has come in the form of a directly addressed reproach – 'a dismal thing to do!' This is the oysters' moment of the witness of the atrocity to be perpetrated against them. That distasteful topic is ignored by the simple tactic of changing the subject. As earlier suggested, the polite deportment of these two carnivorous companions reminds us of Brecht's famous lines about food and low talk (286). And, of course, something else is probably already happening while the conversation of the oysters is being ignored.

The apparent hypocrisy of the Walrus will come into sharper focus from here. The following disingenuous lines provide readers with a picture of the mental state in which one pretends to care about a consequence of benefit to the speaker ahead of the action by the speaker that will bring about the suffering for which one professes to be affected. Planning for some *schadenfreude*?

'It was so kind of you to come!
And you are very nice!'
The Carpenter said nothing but
'Cut us another slice:
I wish you were not quite so deaf —
I've had to ask you twice!'
(Carroll 2009, 165)

It is curious that the Carpenter does not say much at all throughout, but at this point, claims to not be heard. Is that because he is so single-mindedly bent on the task at hand (i.e., putting the oysters away), or is it because the cloying disingenuous sentimentalism of the Walrus is tedious, even irritating, to his companion? As if the Walrus were having lunch with Ruskin. Or perhaps the poem we have is a biased report, and we are not privileged to know all that the Carpenter may have said? The Carpenter just wants to get on with it and the Walrus is concerned with conversational form. Is it the case, that as with the young oysters, the animal-other tries too hard to justify his/her interpellation as anthropomorphic sentience? If that is so, we once again remind ourselves that this (as all spoken fantasies) is of human manufacture.

The other curious thing in this stanza is that we cannot quite be sure to whom the Walrus is speaking when he says, 'It was so kind of you to come! /And you are very nice!' (more evaluative language presaging imminent doom). Is the Walrus thanking the victims or only the carpenter? Is there an implied hierarchy of deference here? In that case, might we read this as Carpenter – fully human – to be thanked by the humanimal Walrus; oysters to be ignored as not worthy of anthropomorphism, or of being no longer worthy of anthropomorphism, having served their very specific purpose (to be dinner)? But then it might be that the Walrus is thanking the victims? 'So nice' = so delicious? Addressed to a sentient victim, one who understands, at least denotatively, the language addressed, these read like the words of a psychopath. If, as is more likely, the Walrus is not here talking to the oysters, then we can identify this place as the point of de-humanisation in the poem. That is to say, the moment at which the oysters become food is the moment they are deprived of humanity and become unambiguously unworthy of conversation. Is it the case then that the Carpenter has been so absent until now because, until now, his conversation might have been taken as intended for the oysters? Is it that he speaks now because he now believes there can be no confusion as to whom his interlocutor must be?

Carol Adams refers to the act of human meat eating as endorsing a structure of 'the absent referent' (2015, 20–22), especially by transforming nonhuman subjects into nonhuman objects. Behind every meal, Adams suggests, is not only a definitional and metaphorical absence but also a literal one: 'the death of the nonhuman animal whose place the meat takes' (2007, 23). Thus in making animals absent or in de-humanising them, we fail to sense anything disturbing in the violence that is part of the routinisation of human exploitation of nonhuman others. In the case of this poem, it is noteworthy that the rhetorical work now in question (whether absenting or de-humanising) is not done by the human in the picture, but by the humanimal, subaltern servant of the imperial power – that subaltern whose speech is the exercise of the rule on behalf of a class of persons mainly absent from the scene. Consider in this light the bureaucratic efficiency of the Raj.[12] One is particularly mindful here of how colonial masters have organised colonial subjects to do most of the 'grunt work' of oppressing the colonised subalterns further down the food chain. To take the ethics out of the picture in the poem, one might ask if the function of anthropomorphism is to have animals justify the manner in which humans think of, and treat, animals.

But perhaps the verb tense is the key to the interpretation here. 'Cut us another slice' from the Carpenter suggests that at this point, dinner is already well underway. So we may read 'you are very nice' as suggesting that as long as the Walrus still has the taste in his mouth, the oysters, suggested by the pronoun, remain anthropomorphic entities. This reading puts the Carpenter on a psychopathic par with the Walrus.

And now the Walrus' sentimentalism, or hypocrisy, comes to the fore.

> 'It seems a shame,' the Walrus said,
> 'To play them such a trick,
> After we've brought them out so far,
> And made them trot so quick!'
> The Carpenter said nothing but
> 'The butter's spread too thick!'
>   (Carroll 2009,165)

Here we have what seems like genuine empathy – perhaps redeeming – on the Walrus' part. Naomi Scheman observes, 'It is not an empirical generalization that deception and betrayal are incompatible with genuine sympathy; rather, not even the acutest pangs of identification and commiserative sorrow will do if they serve to hide or disguise from the Walrus what his actions come to' (323). For what ethical purpose? And from whose point of view will these feelings open up new spaces for thought and action? If we hold, as animal standpoint theorists do (Best 2016; Donovan 2016), that 'genuine' empathy and sensory experience can act as the foundation of one's moral values and behaviours in promoting the emancipation of oppressed or consumed animals, then what will Walrus' possibly sham feelings lead us to? Are we tempted to fall into his trap of language deception or glean more important lessons regarding the origin of power, language, and speciesist identity?

Although it seems likely the feast is well progressed at this stage of the poem, we cannot tell whether the action implied in this stanza is before or after or during the eating of the oysters – and it might make a moral difference if we could know. The Carpenter appears disinvested in the question of whether empathy is relevant here. It is the dining experience that concerns him. The Walrus ramps up the melodrama now.

> 'I weep for you,' the Walrus said:
> 'I deeply sympathize'.
> With sobs and tears he sorted out
> Those of the largest size,
> Holding his pocket-handkerchief
> Before his streaming eyes.
>   (Carroll 2009,166)

We see at this point that execution is still impending, at least for some of the oysters. The Walrus' empathy is now shown to be pantomimic and yet the tears might not be crocodile tears. He might yet be convinced of his own goodness in having feeling for the oysters. In this case, we encounter a beautiful illustration of Sartrean bad faith. The ambivalence of a self-deception is at stake here, where the perpetrator of an oppressive act understands the lie they tell but at the same time believes it, at least in order to convince the one to whom the lie is directed. This makes the Walrus at once the perpetrator and victim of the lie ('victim', even though he is not immediately dinner). The circle of Sartrean *bad faith* is one in which 'I flee in order not to know, but I cannot avoid knowing that I am fleeing' (Sartre 1998, 43). The Walrus' self-regard as a sympathetic person, despite being a murderer, is characteristic of a bad lie, as Sartre puts it, 'The ideal description of the liar would be a cynical consciousness, affirming truth within himself, denying it in his words, and denying that negation as such' (50) and it is 'possible only because sincerity is conscious of missing its goal inevitably, due to its very nature' (66).

Then is the Walrus truly sorry for himself when he expresses what we take to be feeling for the oysters-as-victims of the plot in which he participates? Is it the case that the Walrus believes in the inevitability of oysters being eaten by him? Even if that were so, he nevertheless appears to believe in the genuineness of the conversation, at least to an extent we cannot ascertain in the case of the Carpenter.

We think it is because of precisely such doubts that this seems the most psychopathic moment of the poem. The humanimal weeps for those he is about to murder and eat. To add to the gruesomeness, perhaps, these are one and the same act. The fact that it is a speaking non-human animal acting and feeling towards other speaking non-human animals in this way makes the Walrus' conduct somehow more cannibalistic than that of the Carpenter.

> 'O Oysters,' said the Carpenter,
> 'You've had a pleasant run!
> Shall we be trotting home again?'
> But answer came there none —
> And this was scarcely odd, because
> They'd eaten every one.
> (Carroll 2009,166)

Only after dinner does the Carpenter acknowledge the lapsed personhood of those he has eaten. Only in death are the oysters entities for whom mock empathy can be expressed. Only now does the Carpenter acknowledge them as anything other than food, now that they are beyond the possibility of conversation. Or is the carpenter genuinely deluded, perhaps on account of madness? Does he believe he is talking to the oysters still/at last? If so, then his delusion is characteristic of a larger one and, we note that for the Carpenter, the oysters are now credited with having it alright (or having had it alright – 'You've had a pleasant run!'). It really was a privilege, so the Carpenter thinks, for the young oysters to have been able to spend their final moments in such elevated company. The final interpellation of the oysters, and the only one made by the Carpenter, comes when the oppressed are no longer capable of being called because they are no longer sentiences in the story.

Bad faith, in the sense that the Walrus expresses before the event, and that the Carpenter seems to express after the event, is what we think Lennon had in mind with his comments on the poem: in this case, the bad faith of the capitalist class who sees the oppressed as beneficiaries of a system that benefits the capitalist class.

Is it yet possible that the disconnect apparent in the Carpenter's conversing with the oysters he has already eaten is unconscious precisely by way of showing anthropomorphism to be a contradiction: one moment there were oysters to converse with, even if he had not bothered conversing with them up until this point, the next moment the Carpenter has had his dinner. Then how are these events connected? Perhaps the Carpenter is unable to see any connection along these lines? Is it the case that the Walrus (perhaps on account of being an animal) cannot help but connect knowledge of the eaten interlocutors, as interlocutors, with the fact of their having become dinner?

Considering the contrasting attitudes of the Walrus and the Carpenter, we might observe that empathy for animal-others is possible in this poem for the character who is partly animal, but not for the character who is fully and unambiguously human.

Point of View in Ethics and the Absent Final Frame

The ethical dimensions of any exegesis of 'The Walrus and the Carpenter' are established in the co-text of Looking Glass world. Take a step back from the poem and we find ourselves in the company of Alice and the Brothers Tweedle. The Brothers Tweedle claim a special knowledge of the text, a knowledge Alice would not presume to:

> 'I like the Walrus best,' said Alice: 'because you see he was a *little* sorry for the poor oysters.'
>
> 'He ate more than the Carpenter, though,' said Tweedledee. 'You see he held his handkerchief in front, so that the Carpenter couldn't count how many he took: contrariwise'.
>
> 'That was mean!' Alice said indignantly. 'Then I like the Carpenter best—if he didn't eat so many as the Walrus'.
>
> 'But he ate as many as he could get,' said Tweedledum.
>
> This was a puzzler. After a pause, Alice began, 'Well! They were *both* very unpleasant characters—'.
>
> (Carroll 2009, 166–167)

With Alice's comments, Beer aptly notes that the episode "disconcerts by its insouciance about treachery and consumption. It refuses to resolve or absolve" (2016, 233). As the ontological doubt is established in the heroine's mind, the problematic appetite of carnivorous companions is nevertheless left unresolved. Meetings of ethics and aesthetics are, therefore, ubiquitous in Alice's heuristic experience of Wonderland and Looking-Glass Land; in other words, she is always learning how to behave, to survive, to succeed. Absurdity is never far in this process, and the absurdity frequently boils down to confusion and contradiction between the arbitrary and motivated aspects of social interaction and of the physical world. Whether things are arguable or not, Alice's natural inclination *is* always to argue.

The obvious ethical stakes with which Alice contends in her shared exegetic efforts with 'The Walrus and the Carpenter' concern the distinction between action and intention. The Walrus is the less worse of two bad characters because he cared about those he was murdering; the Walrus is the worse of the two because he ate more? Bertrand Russell reflects on the Red King's dream that follows suit, 'A very instructive discussion from a philosophical point of view, but if it were not put so humorously, we should find it too painful' (cited in Carroll and Gardner 1965, 238). Pain is indeed at the pointy end of ethics and partly accounts for why children's stories use 'the distancing effect of anthropomorphism to circumvent a difficult experience' (Flynn 2004, 419). Although a once-popular tendency to make cruelty to animals amusing in writing was curbed in writing for Victorian children (Bump 2014, 70), the endowed personhood of creatures waiting to be eaten in this poem unsettles what Jerome Bump detects, despite cruelty witnessed in Wonderland and Looking-Glass Land, as 'a new ethics of compassion' in Alice's stories.

Let us return to the very different conclusions Descartes and Peter Singer have come to with not dissimilar evidence, concerning, in the first case, the question of the soul, and in the second, the question of suffering and our responsibility for it. If soul-less-ness is the criterion for making morally acceptable the industrial slaughter of any animal for human consumption, then it is difficult to see how one could morally conceive a limit to what should be allowable along these lines. Is that why it is now happening on an unprecedented scale? Then again, though the scale of mammal and bird slaughter is now unprecedented, safeguards against cruelty in animal killing have become *de rigeur* in at least the developed world. In terms of sheer numbers slaughtered and eaten though, it is difficult to imagine where the line would be drawn to signal excess.

If, on the other hand, pain is the criterion for establishing the moral goodness or otherwise of the party who would be the perpetrator of pain – ultimately this is the diner – then the eating of animals can never be justified because we can never know where to assert a threshold for the experience of pain. In particular, the psychopathic moments of 'The Walrus and the Carpenter' evoke images, for the twenty-first-century reader, of cannibalism and the Holocaust. J. M. Coetzee's fictional animal activist Elizabeth Costello speaks of the killing and eating of animals in reality as 'each day a fresh holocaust' (1999, 35). Even in the literature, she criticises the topological use of animals as schematic elements of human design. 'The life-cycle of the frog', she said, 'may sound allegorical, but to the frogs themselves it is no allegory, it is the thing itself, the only thing' (Coetzee 2003, 217). Linking these concerns about the aesthetic and physical exploitation of animals, Derrida claims that 'no one can deny...the *unprecedented* proportions of this subjection of the animal (2008, 25, emphasis the original). But almost no one denies the fact that we have organised 'on a global scale the forgetting or misunderstanding of this violence, which some would compare to the worst cases of genocide' (Derrida, 26).

If we are forgiven a moment's speech on behalf of the other, then it would be fair to say that it would be better for animals if either every human thought as Peter Singer does or at least if humans entertained his kinds of doubts, as opposed to Descartes' certainties. Human survival is predicated on the food choices, with backstories of consumption (e.g., the leg of mutton, eggs, puddings, oysters, lobsters, and the mock turtle in the Alice books). As White notes, 'Darwinian logic makes any seriously-conceived anthropomorphism very troubling' (112). By anthropomorphising these oysters as a part of our two-legged family and conducting a quasi-friendly chat with them, their consumption would identifiably project the consumers as cannibals: 'They'd eaten *every one*' (Carroll 2009, 166, our emphasis). Forget for the moment any (mock) horror that might adhere in the eating of oysters; in terms of representation, eating anthropomorphic food is cannibal business. The terms here are, we remind ourselves, of representation. This is the contradiction in which any reading of 'The Walrus and the Carpenter' and in which any reading of anthropomorphic and zoomorphic texts is inevitably caught. The text is about animals and the treatment of animals; the text is about humans and the treatment of humans.

To recognise genre is to see a frame. In this text, as throughout the Carrollian oeuvre, the frames fly thick and fast. Nonsense is poem is fable is satire. How not to read as an allegory? More fundamentally, how not to read as a parable? Surely the tale teaches? Assiduously avoiding the risk of intentionalism, we may nevertheless ask, what is the function of nonsense (of this particular nonsense, and of nonsense in general)? Let us be clear about the question – we wish to ask: what is the function of the text we laugh at precisely because it does not make sense, the text that makes fun just where sense would otherwise be?

Set aside the many rhetorical dimensions of the fun just in this one text (hyperbole, paradox, tautology) and the question of function boils down to two options: the world the text reveals to us is impossible, so funny; the world we live in is shown not to make sense, and so is funny. There is a reversible allegorical relationship between these options: seeing how an impossible world does not make sense is suggestive of the nonsensical aspects of the real, let us say of 'the wrongness of the real' (hence the slippage between utopias and dystopias); conversely, the wrongness of the real world we know suggests the parody. It is not over reading to see a critique as necessarily implied by the presence of nonsense. It is easy to track this rhetorically too: hyperbole suggests things have gone too far, paradox the impossible, tautology that repetition has gone undetected where things might have progressed. So what is the critique suggested by 'The Walrus and the Carpenter'? Already we have had no choice but to enter the killjoy's territory of explaining a joke. This cannot be done without context.

Perhaps Carroll's average contemporary would have read in the poem the parable of the nonsense of anthropomorphism, suggesting that empathy for creatures incapable of conversation with us is a misplaced empathy. Then what is funny in 'The Walrus and the Carpenter' is that oysters who cannot talk, though given the power of speech and so the ability to engender empathy, nevertheless meet the common fate of oysters in the company of humans. You cannot beat the natural order, the way of things, natural selection. When it comes to dinner, rhetorical tricks cannot prevail over appetite. It would appear then that what we have here is a meeting of the acceptance of Darwinism, social and otherwise, with Ruskin's critique of the pathetic fallacy and demolition of sentimentalism. There is something hard-nosed in the Victorian retreat from the overblown anthropomorphism in which the Romantics routinely engaged. Read this way 'The Walrus and the Carpenter' engages the peak-imperial *zeitgeist*, part of the territory where the sun never sets.

But, as per our comments above, every anthropomorphic entity is a character in a text, on a par in this sense, with any character intended for human. So the anthropomorphic poem is always also, whatever else, a poem about people, about relations between the persons of the story. Allegory won't be avoided. By analogy, read that those who are subaltern to the powerful in this story, i.e., the doomed oysters, would do better to know their place – at least they might survive a little longer that way.

So much for the readers Carroll might himself have imagined. Then how do *we* choose to read today? Stepping back from that frame in which the innocent oysters are interpellated for the dinner they will be, can we help but read them as a paradigm case of the subaltern who cannot speak, those whom we humans have lent a voice, even if only for the purpose of mockery, even if only to laugh at their credulity, the inevitability of their ill-treatment at the hands of our kind? Consider blackface as a comic device. *Schadenfreude* realized!

Was nonsense, of the kind we find in 'The Walrus and the Carpenter' a Barthesian inoculation[13] for the mid-and-later Victorian reader? Was it that little dose of acknowledged evil that allows us to fight off the full-blown disease? The evil, in this case, would be crediting subalterns with sentience on a par with our own. Where would that over-empathy logically lead? The full-blown disease would be the nonsense world in which oysters have as much say as we do. In practical terms, over-empathy would logically lead to going to bed with no supper. The way of the wicked world trumps the fantasy that those beneath are as we are and so deserve our empathy. And we learn that our getting dinner is in the nature of this recognition that such empathy would be misplaced.

One hundred and fifty years and much Lewis Carroll scholarship on, is this what we learn from 'The Walrus and the Carpenter'? We think that the poem confronts its twenty-first-century reader with the contradictions entailed in an anthropomorphic worldview. Comparing contemporary and Victorian cultures of animal treatment, White reckons that "our culture anthropomorphizes animals as readily as Victorian culture did, but we do so with much greater self-identification and guilt" and "we look to real animals more closely for indications of subjectivity or even consciousness" (2017, 113). As for Alice, our conundrum concerns ethics contrasting the primacy of action as opposed to intention. We intend to be in conversation with our dinner, and oops, there go our partners in conversation.

In *Creaturely Poetics* Anat Pick canvasses (2011), 'the ramifications (for thought and also for action) of being oriented toward vulnerability as a universal mode of exposure' for all humans, animals, and other nonhumans (5). In Pick's proposal of 'creaturely ethics', its source 'lies in the recognition of the materiality and vulnerability of all living bodies, whether human or not, and in the absolute primacy of obligations over rights' (193). The anthropomorphic oysters, in this sense, while revealing a shared and enhanced human-animal vulnerability, expose the endowment of and from 'higher' species as problematic. No hierarchy is recognised without a point of view implied.

We have argued that nonsense is a powerful means of aestheticising contradictions. Then where does the aestheticisation of contradictions lead? Perhaps the best answer is that it leads to different places for different persons in the drama of reading. For many, that will be a comfortable place – as if the grit in the oyster shell had allowed the creation of a pearl and one ought to be satisfied with that result. For others of us though, the grit stays, and the contradiction, however beautifully posed or disguised, nevertheless remains short of resolution or transcendence, and so requires further contemplation.

Alice cannot immediately come to a definite conclusion with regard to the ethical priorities set by the parable she has just heard, but the faces of the oysters are encountered and the loud protest from the pudding in the final feast scene is heard: "What impertinence! ... I wonder how you'd like it, if I were to cut a slice out of *you*, you creature!" (235). This far into the story, the girl whom all experience empowers sits comfortably in the judgement seat, "could only sit and look at it and gasp" (235). Of course, Alice has a further frame to step back from or to step through yet, to her putative waking world, where she is the god-like shaker of kittens. We immediately see how human-animal relations stand then in the world where animals do not converse.

Step back out of the text altogether, we are the humans reading and discussing the story. We are the ones whose lives go on from here, fresh from our book with conversation and pictures; we with our empire stranger than fiction (though no longer proudly declared as such), with creatures one could hardly credit (even if they lack speaking parts), we with our oysters for dinner as well. Is there a 'real' point of vantage from which to view the manner in which ethics are generically determined? That would be a God's-eye view. We are as likely to arrive at that as we are to find Bertrand Russell's famous orbiting teapot (cited in Dawkins 2006, 52). If we cannot avoid finding our own image in the mirror Alice's adventures hold up to us as readers, then it will also be fair to say that none of us who have been through the Looking-Glass can comfortably deny or predict what might happen if those who are dreaming should wake.

Notes

1. The 'creaturely' is a critical term gaining more prominence in recent years. In *The Animal That Therefore I am* (2008), Derrida proposes a new French word animot (rather than l'animal or les animaux) to suggest the heterogeneous elements of 'plural animals heard in the singular' to "envisage the existence of 'living creatures' "(47). Along similar lines, Eric Santer's *On Creaturely Life* (2006) locates the idea of 'creaturely life' in the 'writings of a series of twentieth-century German Jewish writers'(xiv). He connects an uncanny interplay, of the natural and the human as 'creaturely', to post-Holocaust literary expression. The formulation 'creaturely' is further explained in Anat Pick's *Creaturely Poetics* (2011) to foreground the shared animality, vulnerability and contiguity between humans and animals as a contemporary occasion for ethical solicitation.
2. The particular aesthetics of the hill station in colonial history are dealt with in-depth in Judith Kenny's (1995) essay 'Climate, Race, and Imperial Authority: the Symbolic Landscape of the British Hill Station in India', and also in Dane Keith Kennedy's *The Magic Mountains: Hill stations and the British Raj* (1996).
3. In *Ornamentalism: How the British Saw Their Empire* (2002), David Cannadine argues that the British empire developed an essentially ornamental mode of rule by referring to architectural style, ceremonial display, royal travels, and the distribution of honors.
4. The phrase was coined by Democratic politician, publicist and historian, John L. O' Sullivan to describe the process and 'divine' mission of American expansion.
5. Terra nullius is a Latin term deriving from Roman law that means that land belonging to one as 'nobody's land'. For the benefit of English colonists in Carolina, John Locke had developed, in these terms, the self-justifying ethical basis of the terra nullius doctrine, the idea that Europeans had a right to occupy land that they could not see as having heretofore been cultivated.

6 In his essay 'On the Different Races of Man' (1977), Kant's views on race – although perhaps typical of the anthropology of his time – demonstrate a powerful conviction that the white race was superior to the other three races Kant imagined as encompassing the human types. Kant particularly viewed black people as inferior and unintelligent.
7 In fact, Sewell canvasses a relationship between nonsense and infinity in her 'Seven Maids with Seven Mops' chapter. We believe that there might be what one could describe as a natural relationship between nonsense and that which the mind cannot compass (infinity being possibly the best example of this). Recognition that presented infinities, e.g. the sands that cannot be mopped, are only apparent further complicates the picture and leads us to wonder whether every crossing of the abstract/concrete boundary provides a potential site for the practice of nonsense.
8 Hume also writes that, 'all animals are entrusted to their own prudence and skill for their conduct in the world, and have full authority, as far as their power extends, to alter all the operations of nature' (1998, 100).
9 Hello Kitty's lack of a mouth has been claimed to enable fans/readers to 'project their feelings onto the character' (Herskovitz 1999, 3) and to liberate from language constraints and speak to viewers 'from the heart' (Walker 2008).
10 In an account of interpellation, Althusser describes a situation in which a policeman in the street shouts, 'Hey, you there!' The hailed individual 'will turn around. By this mere one-hundred-and-eighty-degree physical conversion, he becomes a subject. Why? Because he was recognized that the hail was 'really' addressed to him' (1971:163). Such 'hailing' constitutes the subjectification of the hailed individual or a way to lead the hailed one to actively construct a subject position not subject to such disciplinary call.
11 John Ruskin once dismissed such 'romantic' or 'naive' wandering caused by anthropomorphic thinking as a 'pathetic fallacy'. He spoke of the anthropomorphic tendency derisively, "it is only the basest writer who cannot speak of the sea without talking of 'raging waves,' 'remorseless floods,' 'ravenous billows,' etc." (Ruskin, 1918/2013:122). Ruskin's criticism is a sharp denial of the overabundant use of anthropomorphism in Western poetry at certain times (particularly the poetry of the late 18th century) when Romantic poets attributed much human effect to entities that could not possess it.
12 See Niall Ferguson's various works about civilization and the British empire, such as *Empire: The Rise and Demise of the British World Order and the Lessons for Global Power* (2008) and *Empire: How Britain Made the Modern World* (2015).
13 Roland Barthes uses the term 'inoculation' to suggest that an institution covers its bad nature by admitting a little bit of evil therein. The inoculating figure recognizes publicly 'the accidental evil of a class-bound institution' only to 'conceal its principle evil' (1983, 150).

References

Adams, Carol J. "The War on Compassion". *The Feminist Care Tradition in Animal Ethics: A Reader.* Eds. J. Donovan and C. J. Adams. New York: Columbia University, 2007, 21–36.

Adams, Carol J. *Sexual Politics of Meat.* New York: Bloomsbury, 2015.

Adams, Douglas. *The Restaurant at the End of the Universe*. New York: Harmony, 1981.
Althusser, Louis. *Lenin and Philosophy and Other Essays*. Trans. Ben Brewster. London: New Left Books, 1971.
Armitage, David. *The Ideological Origins of the British Empire*. Cambridge: Cambridge University Press, 2000.
Auerbach, Nina. "Alice and Wonderland: A Curious Child". *Victorian Studies* 17(1) (1973): 31–47.
Barthes, Roland. "Myth Today". *The Barthes Reader*. Ed. Susan Sontag. New York: Hill and Wang, 1983, 93–149.
Beer, Gillian. *Alice in Space: The Sideways Victorian World of Lewis Carroll*. Chicago: University of Chicago Press, 2016.
Best, Steven. *Politics of Total Liberation: Revolution for the 21st Century*. Place of Publication Not Identified: Palgrave Macmillan, 2016.
Birns, Margaret Boe. "Solving the Mad Hatter's Riddle". *Massachusetts Review* 25(3) (1984): 457–468.
Bivona, D. "Alice the child-imperialist and the games of Wonderland". *Nineteenth-century literature* 41(2) (1986): 143–171.
Brantlinger, Patrick. *Taming Cannibals: Race and the Victorians*. Cornell University Press, 2011.
Brecht, Bertolt. *Poems 1913–1956*. Eds. John Willett and Ralph Manheim. London: Methuen Inc, 1987.
Bump, Jerome. "Biophilia and Emotive Ethics: Derrida, Alice, and Animals". *Ethics & the Environment* 19(2) (2014): 57–89.
Cannadine, David. *Ornamentalism: How the British Saw Their Empire*. Oxford: Oxford University Press, 2002.
Capp, Al. *The Short Life and Happy Times of the Shmoo*. New York: Overlook Press, 2003.
Carroll, Lewis. *Alice's Adventures in Wonderland and Through the Looking-Glass and What Alice Found There*. Oxford: Oxford University Press, 2009.
Carroll, Lewis and Martin Gardner. *The Annotated Alice*. London: Penguin Books, 1965.
Coetzee, J. M. *The Lives of Animals*. Princeton, NJ: Princeton University Press, 1999.
Coetzee, J. M. *Elizabeth Costello*. London: Secker & Warburg, 2003.
Dawkins, Richard. *The God Delusion*. London: Transworld, 2006.
Deleuze, Gilles. *The Logic of Sense*. Trans. Mark Lester and Charles Stivale. Ed. Constantin V. Boundas. London: Athlone Press, 1990.
Derrida, Jacques. *The Animal That Therefore I Am*. New York: Fordham University Press, 2008.
Descartes, René. *Philosophical Letters*. Oxford: Oxford University Press, 1970.
Donovan, Josephine. *The Aesthetics of Care: On the Literary Treatment of Animals*. New York: Bloomsbury, 2016.
Ferguson, Niall. *Empire: The Rise and Demise of the British World Order and the Lessons for Global Power*. New York: Basic, 2008.
Ferguson, Niall. *Empire: How Britain Made the Modern World*. London: Penguin, 2015.
Flynn, Simon. "Animal Stories". *International Companion Encyclopedia of Children's Literature*. Ed. Peter Hunt. London: Routledge, 2004.

Greeman, Richard. "Alice in Imperialand". *New Politics* 11(3) (2007): 67–73.
Herskovitz, Jon "Itty-bitty Merchandise Hawker Leads Sanrio's World Conquest". *Japan Times* (1999) 5 February.
Hooper, Keith, and Kate Kearins. "The Walrus, Carpenter and Oysters: Liberal Reform, Hypocrisy and Expertocracy in Maori Land Loss in New Zealand 1885–1911". *Critical Perspectives on Accounting* 19(8) (2008): 1239–1262.
Hume, David. *Dialogue Concerning Natural Religion*. Ed. Richard H. Popkin. Indianapolis/Cambridge: Hackett Publishing, 1998.
Jaques, Zoe. *Children's Literature and the Posthuman: Animal, Environment, Cyborg*. London: Routledge, 2016.
Kant, Immanuel. "On the Different Races of Man". *Race and Enlightenment*. Ed. Emmanuel Chuckwudi Eze. Oxford: Blackwell, 1977, 38–48.
Kérchy, Anna. "The Acoustics of Nonsense in Lewis Carroll's Alice Tales". *International Research in Children's Literature* 13, Supplement (2020): 175–190.
Kennedy, Dane Keith. *The Magic Mountains: Hill Stations and the British Raj*. Berkeley: University of California Press, 1996.
Kenny, Judith T. "Climate, Race, and Imperial Authority: The Symbolic Landscape of the British Hill Station in India". *Annals of the Association of American Geographers* 85(4) (1995): 694–714.
Lecercle, Jean-Jacques. Philosophy of Nonsense: The Intuitions of Victorian Nonsense Literature. New York: Routledge, 2002.
Lee, Michael Parrish. "Eating Things: Food, Animals, and Other Life Forms in Lewis Carroll's Alice Books". *Nineteenth-Century Literature* 68(4) (2014): 484–512.
Lee, Michael Parrish. *The Food Plot in the Nineteenth-Century British Novel*. New York: Palgrave Macmillan, 2016.
Levinas, Emmanuel. *Totality and Infinity: An Essay on Exteriority*. Trans. A. Lingis. Pittsburgh, PA: Duquesne University Press, 1969.
Lindsay, Norman. *The Magic Pudding*. Australia: Angus & Robertson, 1918/1990.
Lopez, Alan. "Deleuze with Carroll: Schizophrenia and Simulacrum and the Philosophy of Lewis Carroll's nonsense 1". *Angelaki: Journal of the Theoretical Humanities* 9(3) (2004): 101–120.
Lord, Peter and Nick Park. *Chicken Run*. Aardman Animations, 2000. DVD.
Lovell-Smith, Rose. "The Animals of Wonderland: Tenniel as Carroll's Reader". *Criticism* 45(4) (2003): 383–415.
Lovell-Smith, Rose. "Eggs and Serpents: Natural History Reference in Lewis Carroll's Scene of Alice and the Pigeon". *Children's Literature* 35(1) (2007): 27–53.
Lovell-Smith, Rose H. "'The Walrus and the Carpenter': Lewis Carroll, Margaret Getty, and Natural History for Children". *Australasian Journal of Victorian Studies* 10(1) (2020): 43–69.
MacLachlan, Alice. "Government apologies to indigenous peoples". *Justice, Responsibility and Reconciliation in the Wake of Conflict*. Springer Netherlands, 2013, 183–203.
Meeker, Joseph W. *The Comedy of Survival: Literary Ecology and a Play Ethic*. Tucson, AZ: University of Arizona, 1997.
Minslow, S. G. *Can Children's Literature be Non-Colonizing? A Dialogic Approach to Nonsense*. PhD thesis, University of Newcastle, Australia. 2009. Available from: http://hdl.handle.net/1959.13/802970.

Morgentaler, Goldie. "The Long and the Short of Oliver and Alice: The Changing Size of the Victorian Child". *Dickens Studies Annual* 29 (2000): 83–98.

Ngai, Sianne. *Our Aesthetic Categories: Zany, Cute, Interesting.* Cambridge, MA: Harvard University Press, 2015.

Patterson, R. Gary. *The Walrus Was Paul: The Great Beatle Death Clues.* New York: Simon & Schuster, 1998.

Pick, Anat. *Creaturely Poetics: Animality and Vulnerability in Literature and Film.* New York: Columbia University Press, 2011.

Raffoul, François. "Responsibility for a Secret: Heidegger and Levinas". *Heidegger, Levinas, Derrida: The Question of Difference.* Cham, Switzerland: Springer International Publishing, 2016. 133–147.

Ruskin, John. 1918. *Selections and Essays*, ed. William Roe Frederick. New York, Chicago: C. Scribner's Sons, 2013.

Santner, Eric L. *On Creaturely Life Rilke, Benjamin, Sebald.* Chicago: University of Chicago, 2006.

Sartre, Jean-Paul. *Being and Nothingness: An Essay on Phenomenological Ontology*, Trans. H. E. Barnes. London: Routledge, 1943/1998.

Scheman, Naomi. "On Sympathy". *The Monist* 62(3) (1979): 320–330.

Sewell, Elizabeth. 1952. *Field of Nonsense.* Illinois: Dalkey Archive Press, 2015.

Singer, Peter. *Animal Liberation.* New York: HarperCollins, 2009.

Steel, Karl. "Insensate Oysters and Our Nonconsensual Existence". Ed. Steve Mentz. Oceanic. New York: Punctum Books, 2015, 79–91.

Straley, Jessica. *Evolution and Imagination in Victorian Children's Literature.* Vol. 103. Cambridge: Cambridge University Press, 2016.

Thomas, Samson. "Alice in Wonderland and Through the Looking Glass: Heterocosm as a Mimetic Device". *New Review of Children's Literature and Librarianship* 21(1) (2015): 42–58.

Walker, Esther. "Top Cat: How 'Hello Kitty' Conquered the World". London: The Independent. 21 May 2008.

Webb, Caroline. "'I'll Be Judge, I'll Be Jury': 'Tail'-Telling, Imperialism and the Other in 'Alice in Wonderland'". *Papers: Explorations into Children's Literature* 20(2) (2010): 1–9.

White, Laura. *The Alice Books and the Contested Ground of the Natural World.* Vol. 20. New York: Routledge, 2017.

Wolfe, Cary. *Animal Rites: American Culture, the Discourse of Species, and Posthumanist Theory.* Chicago: University of Chicago, 2003.

7 This Little Piggie Went to Market
A New Humanimal Politics for Poetry

Pressed to identify the most common rhetorical feature of Children's Literature, we would name the devices anthropomorphism and prosopopoeia. These tropes – the subject of this book – undoubtedly dominate the field of children's literature, and the younger the readership aimed at, the more they appear to the fore. These two terms are overlapping means of mainly describing the same phenomena. Specifically, we are dealing here with the fantastic idea that other-than-human animals speak, to each other and perhaps also to humans.

In the twenty-first century children habitually encounter animals, in forms ranging from anthropomorphic images of animals in picture books, video games, and animations, to displays of living animals in zoos, aquariums, and natural reserves under constant human (or machine) surveillance. Children encounter virtual animals in such settings far more than they encounter real animals in the wild or other natural settings. Concomitant of the formative reality of contemporary childhood – characterised by a general lack of contact with the natural environment – is the advent of the Anthropocene, an epoch where the human influence on the geology, flora, fauna, and climate of the planet is such that it has culminated in a series of emergencies, ranging from climate change and human overpopulation to the sixth mass extinction of species, spanning numerous families of plants and animals in highly degraded biodiverse habitats (Latour 2017; Zalasiewicz et al. 2019). As implied by the name 'Anthropocene', we know that humans are the principal cause of the degradation of environment worldwide and its apocalyptic consequences for other than humans on the planet. We know that species are becoming extinct daily at an accelerating rate, and we know that many of these disappearances forever are of species that have not yet been recorded. One thing we do know about such 'unknowns' is that we humans are the main reason things are going so badly for other-than-humans in general.

As threats to so many forms of life ramp up, questions arise as to the place of nature in human affairs. Indeed, we need to question the 'nature' of 'nature' itself. We mean to say, questions need to be asked about how nature is socially constructed in language and culture, and

DOI: 10.4324/9781003219330-8

what purposes that construction serves. 'Naturalness' has served as a cloak for ideological construction since one might say time immemorial, but in an age of extinctions this rhetorical flourish takes on a more sinister aspect. In, and since, the catastrophic Australian bushfires of 2019–2020 (in which 71 humans and billions of other animals died), it has been a commonplace for the fires to be referred to as a 'natural' disaster. This is – apart from legalistic insurance jargon – a way of diminishing responsibility for what science tells us conclusively is now, in its scale and ferocity, something of human making, something, in that sense, *un*natural.

It will be fair to speculate that an inverse proportional relationship obtains today between the prevalence of culturally produced animals for children and the paucity of real animals encountered by children in nature. Conversely, while there must be plenty of overlap, it will be safe to assume that the more children are associated in real life with real animals the less likely they are to be meeting the creatures we have mentioned – in the books, on the screen, in the game, and so on.

It is in this socio-historical context that the present study has investigated the ethics of an aesthetic: that of anthropomorphism in children's literature. In these pages, we have looked at various ways of approaching the investigation. Thus far into our enquiry, a number of big questions occur to us. The most obvious of the largely unasked questions here is – Why anthropomorphise? Why zoomorphise? Why put these masks on humans and animals so that one might seem to be the other, so that we confuse them with each other? Why put words in the mouths of those who cannot speak? And why, specifically, do this for the (putative) benefit of children? At one level this speculation points to a question we might frame for rhetoric as a whole, or a question we might direct at metaphor in particular.

The most obvious answers to the questions offer apparent contradictions. On the one hand to anthopomorphise/zoomorphise is to acknowledge the animal nature of humans (a common animality), on the other hand it is to disguise human activity as 'natural activity'. One may progress from these broad questions to more specifically directed enquiries. Is anthropomorphism integrally bound up with an anthropocentric worldview in contemporary children's literature? What forms of anthropomorphic representation could serve to imagine constructive interspecies bonds that take us beyond anthropocentrism – or, one could say, 'human chauvinism?' Is there any moral ground on which anthropomorphic poetry should be based to balance creative insights and ecological concerns for those of tender years living through an unnatural history?

We began this book by talking about a long established affinity of children for animals and animals for children. This nexus, celebrated since Romanticism, appears as coextensive with the idea of literature for children and of childhood as the state in which youngest people exist. There seems to be a 'naturalness' to this connection and affinity between children and animals; the kind of naturalness of which scholars should naturally be wary.

In the absence of any avowed ideological commitment for or against the idea of anthropomorphism (on the part of players in the field), it might be better to ask – why has this rhetorical move been so hard to avoid? And it may well be that anthropomorphic and allegorical tendencies are simply unavoidable. We see the world in human terms by telling stories full of necessarily human characters. Perhaps reading, or more broadly, language, is allegorical by nature, being 'such a lopsided, referentially indirect mode' (de Man 1996, 52). As with anthropomorphism, so with the impulse of allegorisation, of carrying in language all manner of referential doubts and epistemological ambiguities. These appear to be hardboiled features of children's literature in general. Often these are intertwined to generate anthropocentric narratives that serve fabulist pedagogical purposes, a point affirmed by Derrida, who warns young readers to 'avoid fables' in the sense that 'the history of fabulization ... remains an anthropomorphic taming, a moralizing subjection, a domestication. Always a discourse of man, on man, indeed on the animality of man, but for and in man' (2008, 37). It nevertheless makes sense, as noted in previous chapters, that forms of representation simply cannot shun human self-depiction and anthropomorphism; nevertheless, on a positive construction, they shape the nonhuman animals that become literary characters for creative compassion. And one notes that an allegorical strategy, applicable to reading and writing, is susceptible to a heuristic urge to find meaning in the personalities and actions of animals.

One might suppose then that an obvious animal–child affinity here is simply irresistible: that young children, like animals, lack to begin with the ability to speak. Children, like 'higher' animals (mammals for instance), further resemble adult humans in many physical and feeling ways. In some senses, children might seem to adults as a kind of 'missing link' or proof of human animality. Adults may not be able 'to talk to the animals', but they are able to communicate with little animals of their own kind, in the shape of human children. Part of the process of raising them is bringing them into language, equipping them, over time, with the means of adult communication. By making the effort to communicate with those who are coming into language, adults address and they commune with the animal side of humanity. Flipside of this identification is the prosopopoeia practised when humans speak *for* the animals, an activity uncannily similar to speaking *for* languageless children or others. Consider the parent/owner of a mute creature in the piece telling all who will listen: 'my pet/my child is telling you this'.

Lest we delve too deeply into the 'phoniness' of anthropomorphism as a habit, perhaps we should pause to consider how the world would be without it. Would the world be worse off, would children be worse off, would animals be worse off, would there be less empathy in the world, if children were not exposed to literature in which the animals speak?

Our Part in the Anthropocene Extinction

At the time of writing, in the world today, 1 million species are facing extinction. This is as a result of human activity. The worldwide crisis currently underway is coming to be known as the Anthropocene Extinction (the Sixth Great Extinction) – an event in which all humans living on Planet Earth in some way participate. In the geological timeframe, homo sapiens are a species that has been on the planet only for a few hundred thousand years. Unique among species and unique among extinction events, humans have collective awareness that this is taking place, that they are together responsible for this, and that collectively we are – in terms of knowledge, skills, and technology – uniquely positioned to do something about it. We humans may be the cause of the problem, we are also (bar the vanishing of our species altogether) the only possible source of a solution. Along such lines, one might say that the disease may also be the cure in this case, if indeed there is to be a cure. The most obvious cure would of course be an 'extinction swap' – where 7 billion humans make a conscious collective decision to leave the scene so that all other forms of life have a chance without us. Beyond the ethical and narrative value of considering such a solution, there is no plausibility to such extreme approaches to the problem. One might argue that this fact demonstrates the extremes of anthropocentrism. Do humans believe that human life is more or less important than all other life together? If we answer that humans must generally believe themselves more important than everyone else put together, but that any other species would feel the same way given the opportunity, then we should be alert to the logical quandary in which we find ourselves. To think of the other-than-human others as volitional sentiences in this way is to anthropomorphise. To attribute our motives and hunches and feelings to them is to anthropomorphise. To see ourselves exonerated on the basis of just doing what any animal would do (to vote for self-interest), is also to anthropomorphise (or to zoomorphise ourselves). And this last approach is particularly disingenuous. We might not know all that the dolphins, whales, sea turtles and clonal colonies of aspen know, but we understand at least a proportion of what we know; we have means every other animal lacks; and we know it is through our knowledge and means the current crisis has come. We have in all human cultures such concepts as duty, responsibility, culpability, amends. The lengths, to which humans have gone to ignore these moral imperatives, are in the case of human–animal relations, truly extraordinary.

Of course, not all humans are aware of the scale or the scope of the current worldwide ecological crisis. Perhaps in fact some of the humans who are themselves suffering the worst effects of climate change, environmental degradation, and species loss, are the least aware of the global picture. On our planet today – and note that it is the only one, at the time of writing, with humans or with animals or with any life we know – perhaps things are simply so bad already, and it is so obvious that they will soon be worse, that the only sensible thing to do is to bury one's head in the sand, or make hay while the sun shines, or burn coal while there is still some air left, whichever way one wants to look at it, depending on the point of view or vested interest. Is it a call to arms or a motive to escape reality, to, for instance, seek refuge in a poem or a picture book; to escape into a story, perhaps a better one, one with a nicer ending?

It is a fascinating fact that while more and more species are vanishing from the Earth and while more and more domesticated (considered conveniently edible) animals are being slaughtered and scoffed down by more and more humans (7 billion humans roughly eating 70 billion other animals a year at last count [if we leave out the fish]), the growth in the number of literary animals (largely anthropomorphised animals) who have taken up residence in books and picture books continues unabated. Have the animals taken refuge in pictures and texts because this is the only safe place for them now?

Of course this poetic kind of speculation is in itself a kind of fairytale thinking, a story to justify how things are, perhaps to justify how we humans believe we cannot help but be. We note also that suggesting the animals might take refuge in our books is simply a euphemism for the fact that it is we who have put them in the picture books, and the other books, in just the way we put animals in a zoo; just as it is a euphemism to call a prison for animals a zoo.

Where does fairytale thinking of this kind lead us? One must be reluctant to assign simple cause and effect in the case of cultural products and events. Nevertheless, it is difficult, in view of the available facts, to resist the conclusion that this kind of thinking leads to more and more animal death at human hands, and to more and more species extinctions. Still humans go on with the fantasy of putting words in the dumb creatures' mouths. We ramp it up! We have so much for them to say; much more than we have to say to save them. Some of it fearful, some of it reassuring. The more of them we eat, the more we make them speak. We make them speak from the script we have prepared especially for the purpose.

Consider, in terms of volition, the objective conditions of animals in the world today. They do not have a vote. They do not write poems or picture books, however much they are featured. Perhaps the birds have taught us but if *they* sing, it is without a song we would understand as such. Every day there are less *kinds* of animals. Pockets of care aside, we humans are less kind to them. The only way to be more, to be safe, as a species, is to be edible, delicious. The extraordinary success of chickens as a species has come at a cost to chickens (who may well soon be grown in vats for human convenience and so, in a way, transcend the cruelty concomitant with their success as a species). Those few kinds of animals whom we regard as our companions, or those who are protected (in those places on the Earth where there is effective protection for animals), thrive. Nine hundred million dogs in the world. Six hundred million cats. Their domestication allows us to understand what they mean, when, beyond some simple, however heartfelt, expressions, they can't mean in our language. Perhaps one day we will give them the vote? But the feral are many.

Other-than-human animals today fall into these four categories: those threatened with extinction because they are wild, those notionally 'protected', those few kinds ever more numerous because we want to kill and eat more and more of them, and those whom we cherish as pets (and to whom we generally feed other animals, because most of our pets – cats and dogs particularly – are carnivores, in fact mostly they are more consistently carnivorous than we humans are.) Such are the objective conditions in which we may consider the nexus *poetry-animals-children* today, conditions comparable to those suggested in Adorno's much debated and revised provocation that it is barbaric to write poetry after Auschwitz (1983, 34).

The Hundred-Acre Wood Where a Hundred Scenes and Creatures Contend

In these last observations we revisit some of the characters (the many humanimal creatures) and contexts, themes and ways of seeing that have brought us this far in the investigation. We consider how these and some new players and scenes, new perspectives, cast light on current global/local crises as reflected in the problematics of the child–animal–poetry nexus.

The foxes and cats and tigers we met, the fish and bears and frogs and birds, even the cicada and the thing that was ambiguously lost – they were all *us* at least largely, much as in the manner of that old playwright's *dictum* – all your characters are *you*. Had they not been us in disguise we might not have recognised them at all. Prospopoeia is to this extent perhaps necessary, not to say unavoidable.

And – where have we been? In the cage with a little bird, and outside looking in. In the Bible. Under the microscope. On the paper in which the poem appears. In and out of hats with cats. Fishing in the river. On a long sea voyage with strange companions. In Oz briefly. And where the wild things are. In a rumpus. Now and then in what appears to be real life, with real creatures. We have been at the picnic with the bears, in the wood where things have no name. We were on that beach where the chatty oysters are eventually eaten. And all of these places have been a kind of wallpaper in the nursery where the rumpus ebbs and flows from sleep to dream and wake to play. We were there in all these places and in our own heads all the while. We saw where we were sent. These wilds of the imagination are palimpsests each containing and concealing all others, much in the manner Freud imagined for all the cities that were Rome, in his seminal book *Civilization and Its Discontents* (1930/2016).

Dreamy, and more canonic than not, how well do the 'people' and 'places' we have visited provide for the ethical *mise-en-scène* needed to understand and act in the current crises we face? As we witness the vanishing of the real and the proliferation of the story book creature, gone-ness is a key thematic and a mainstream concern today in culture produced for and concerning children and young adults. One might consider allegorical readings of a text like *Shrek* (purportedly about 'fairytale creatures'), along these lines. Ideas of mourning and loss have been well established in poetry concerning nature. This is part of the legacy of Romanticism and its relation to industrialisation and the loss of habitat and species that has gone along with it. Consider Carl Sandburg's poem, 'Buffalo Dusk':

> The buffaloes are gone.
> And those who saw the buffaloes are gone.
> Those who saw the buffaloes by thousands and how they
> pawed the prairie sod into dust with their hoofs, their
> great heads down pawing on in a great pageant of dusk,
> Those who saw the buffaloes are gone.
> And the buffaloes are gone.
>
> (1970, 256)

There is nothing anthropomorphic about the buffaloes of this poem, who, one might say at the time of the poem's composition had vanished from the prairies onto the buffalo nickel (1913–1938). On the coin, the buffalo (reverse) is an awe-inspiring singular entity, one coupled with the equally vanishing native American (obverse). The respective mottos: 'liberty' and '*e pluribus unum*' cannot but be read ironically. In Sandburg's poem the buffalo is – as its native American witness – an absence *en masse*, alien and unknowable as the gone often are.

The broader category to which such poems belong is that of witness. And so we are bound to ask – how easily does a poetry of witness – presumably the telling of how things actually are – accommodate the rhetorical strategies we know as anthropomorphism and prosopopoeia? Consider Alfonsina Storni's little bird in the cage speaking to a captor, pleading for freedom. How else can such cases be made unless a human voice is bestowed upon the one who needs the help of humans?

The converse question then will be, without the masks and without the speaking for, the throwing of voices, how is empathy to be achieved. Sandburg's poem saddens but it provides no prospect of hope for the buffalo. How, that is, does a poem achieve the kind of empathy that gets beyond the sadness of loss and leads to action – an action such as perhaps the opening of a cage (symbolically or otherwise), or the conservation of a species?

What does it mean to situate the child between the speechless creature and the adult whose world is all worded, in the manner Ludwig Wittgenstein suggested with 'the limits of my language mean the limits of my world.' (1971, 115)?

Rilke brings together children and animals in the eighth Duino Elegy. His animals are creatures who 'look into the Open/with their whole eyes' (1922/1977, 55), because their view is not obstructed by self-consciousness.

> We know what's out there only from an animal's
> face: for we take even the youngest child
> turn him around and force him to look
> at the past as formation, not that openness
> so deep within an animal's face. Free from death.
> (55)

Rilke's child is a creature being trained out of its native animality into the languaged self-consciousness of adults. The animal imagined here does not see or know us as others and will not know death: These aspects of animality are a kind of teaching. Rilke shows us 'an animal' that is 'infinite, incomprehensible, and blind' to his condition (57). Perhaps most humans see human-ness everywhere they look and cannot see past themselves? The politics (if we may call it that) of every other animal is to survive, to resist, to be, or for Les Murray's fox in 'The Gods', sometimes not to be. Terrible things are done, *not* in the names of these things, because there are no names. *We* give all the names on Earth.

Our old accommodations of labour versus capital seem today to be dissolving into a new alignment of interests one could call, on the one hand national and nostalgic (identified group self-interested), on the other hand cosmopolitan and altruistic: the national/tribal interest versus the local/planetary/interspecies interest. Avatars of the two extremes we might see in vegans on the one hand and survivalists on the other.

Rilke's animals of the eighth elegy are free in the sense of being free of death, because this abstraction has no meaning for them. Where humans see a future, these creatures see endless completion. Rilke's child, in this scheme, 'may lose himself in silence' (55). But the child is 'shaken out of it' (55). Then death is to be the place. To look beyond death is 'with the wide eyes of animals' (55). With that knowledge, we remember we are in a poem, that poem is an elegy; the reader has not transcended self-consciousness. Death remains. An art of words is a leave taking then:

> Who's turned us around like this,
> So that whatever we do, we always have

> The look of someone going away? Just as a man
> On the last hill showing him his whole valley
> One last time, turns, and stops, and lingers –
> So we live, and are forever leaving.
>
> (59)

One might describe the extremes of an equation here, involving those who are, in principle, however reluctantly, okay with humans being survived, so that the planet goes on being inhabited by everyone else; and on the other had those who are happy for humans to survive everyone else. Both are fantasies of course; we think, very unpleasant fantasies. But which of the two is nastier? Which is the more morally bankrupt? A last word here to Rilke:

> Since near to death one no longer sees death,
> and stares ahead, perhaps with the large gaze of the creature.

Our human business-as-usual on Planet Earth is a big problem for those who have no say in making the problem – those who have no words, no vote, no poem to write, no picture books to make. Not that they can know much (other than very directly and often too late) about their problems, or even express to our satisfaction who they are. Ignorance of the law may be no defence in the face of the law but the collective understanding of humans for what they are collectively doing to their world, for the scale of the crisis, for the scale of response required, brings our species into a zone of culpability never before known. What is involved in motivating the change that will mean survival to those who are threatened by the current human-engineered crisis? How may that motivating change manifest itself, in books for children, in books for scholars about them, in culture more popularly? A large part of the answer in each of these cases must be to tell the truth, to insist on the truth, to not walk past it or let it be swept aside. Witness! Provisionally then, we find ourselves saying that the truth about anthropomorphism is that, like humans, and because of humans, we cannot be sure whether anthropomorphism is more of a problem or more of a solution. We must therefore insist it is both!

In Those Picnic Woods Where Things Have No Name

What does Rilke's animal in the wild (or his panther in the zoo) have to do with the animals of the picture book or the poem for children more generally? Quite a lot, we will argue, and particularly as it concerns questions of time and consciousness. Wild and tame are places in mind as much as elsewhere. There is an other-sidedness to what is read or pictured, of the waking, of the dream, of the ambiguous view from the other side of the mirror. Into the woods of a vanishing, as if we never were.

Let us return briefly to those bears of the picnic and their eternity of play, rest and play again. These *described* creatures, benign and equally sinister in aspect, never speak for themselves in their song. Their animality and ontology are, as with those creatures with whom Rilke deals, as are perhaps all other-than-human animals at close quarters, *tabula rasa* objects for the projection of human hopes, fears and, in short, awareness. They shine with the light of a bible of sorts. This picnic is a complex semiotic event – as we have said, a carnival, a Bachannal, an upending of civilised adult norms (though at least partly for the entertainment of civilised adults). It takes place in a kind of myth-light, the same light that we find somewhere in Pooh's Hundred Acre Wood, and in Alice's wood where things have no names. In such a place, only imaginatively reached, what do the bears of the picnic teach us about children, about their toys, about the masks children put on or are given, about pets and wild animals, about parents and guardians and the relationships between all of these characters and putative sentiences in the world of the child?

Like Rilke's creature just above they live in a moment the same as eternity, in which death has no relevance because it is an unknown thing. Yes, sleep comes but what do the tired little teddy bears know of it? The teddies – who are children, who are creatures of the wild – are ambiguously ruled by and yet outside of the adult world in which the picnic woods are merely a kind of wallpaper for the nursery. Rilke has alerted us to the possibility that the opposite is true – that's to say, that the nursery and its activities are merely what adult consciousness has limited the adult mind to make of the picnic woods, which are indeed a place of forgetting, a place where things have lost their names, or never had them to begin with. And what of death then? Death is 'to be the place'. A knowledge that shuts the gates of Eden on all who understand where they are. Call this the participant's paradox of consciousness, what makes us, for Rilke, 'spectators, always, everywhere / looking *at* everything and never *from*!' (59).

If human consciousness is unavoidably projected on to all creatures in close quarters with humans, and perhaps more particularly on those creatures made literary artefacts, then this can be no more true than in the case of those creatures who have become our pets, who have been given names and places to sleep and feed and play alongside us. Hence so much poetry concerning dogs, cats, caged birds, horses and cows of the home paddock.

Pre-historically, one might say, humans have gone from being at the mercy of those creatures with whom they found themselves at close quarters, to deciding which creatures would be kept near. The taming of animals to human interest and requirement is thus the taming of the world more generally, to the human will and ways. That process of bringing into our orbit and of subjecting to our language ('here boy, down girl, roll over, good now') is of its nature, an anthropomorphic process and it involves putting a human mask on the wild creature that was. Taming is the creation of a new class of creature – the one we wish close enough to ourselves, to accept in our homes and our hearts. If the teddy bear is a transitional object then we may think of domestic animals (pets of the home and the beasts of our home paddock) as 'transitional creatures'. They have been bred for purposes of specified nearness – for companionship, for their soft fur, complacency, loyalty, protection, indifference, and sometimes dinner too. Children learn from interactions with pets (and likewise familiar animals of the farmyard) all kinds of human values – empathy, kindness, the need to satisfy hunger and thirst, to understand those who are different but with whom we can commune – into whose eyes we see to imagine a soul, who see into our eyes.

While it is easy to see household pets in this light, the industrial scale of animal agriculture has created a new class of creature still – those domesticated for our most sinister purpose (that is for the purpose of dinner or pelt or medical experiment), those from whom the names have been taken. Those of this new class are increasing exponentially in number as they become more hidden from the general human gaze. Most of the 70 billion land animals slaughtered for food in the world annually too are far less visible to those who dine upon them than were those oysters to the walrus and the carpenter.

With pets and to a less extent with the slaughter class of animal there is also the 'problem' of reversion to type, in other words of return from the domesticated transitional state to animality, to wild nature – going feral. So we have half a billion feral cats in the world compared with the 200 million or so kept as pets at home. The damage they wreak on the never-domesticated population represents the greatest single extinction threat. In Australia, for instance, 2.8 million feral cats each kill an average of 740 animals a year (Web 2019). How does that match up with the toll we 7 billion humans are taking on the animals we breed to feed on, on the untamed world that shrinks by the day? Those we have made or let go feral – they too are part of the anthropocentrism, part of an ever-more-human world. Death to the wild where our emissaries go, even when they have abandoned us or when we have abandoned them!

Poetry has been one of the places we have tried to see ourselves in this big picture, one of the places we have made the effort to feel for other-than-human others. Anthropomorphism has perhaps been a barrier to such attempts to understand and to be instructed by otherness.

Sandburg's gone buffaloes trigger a deep sadness, but one that does not connect us to encounter with any animal. Rilke's engagements have us reflect on great abstractions that may define us, and even shame us into action. But these seem attempts at cerebration – at understanding what the animal knows, in terms of how and what we know. Is there a poetry that goes to the question of the feeling of other-than-human creatures, and that does this without projecting how humans feel onto them? Is that even a possibility? For poetry or for humans more generally?

The Nameless We Keep Hidden Among Us, for Purposes of Dinner

Alice Fulton's 'feminist experimentalism', as Lynn Keller notes (1999), puts her poetry at the intersection of science and language. Fulton admits that she has a devotional attraction to 'make a language commensurate to feeling, impossible as that is' (1999, 327). Her insistence on treating feeling as 'a foreign language' allows her to call unsettling ethical issues into question through play with language. Inspired by the Fractal Theory of mathematician Benoit Mandelbrot, Fulton strives to apply 'fractal poetics' in her poetry to achieve 'a dynamic, turbulent form between perfect chaos and perfect order' (2005, 323). Her poetry is playfully allusive and richly texualised but possessed at once of its own structural integrity. Fulton frequently makes exploratory efforts to consider ethical dimensions of human action and experience as these related to animal welfare. Delving into ethical contradictions embedded in 'felt' experience, emotion is experienced to call attention to human/nonhuman interconnectedness as 'a fabric of entanglement' with reciprocated consciousness (Fulton, 161).

Fulton's 'Some Cool' deals with human conceptions of animal predicaments, as they are generally ignored in today's consumer society. This is a poem of witness, about the experience of the minor and the unnoticed quotidian, with an attempt to understand feeling as a power and condition humans have in common with other animals, those for whom we have learned to feel nothing.

> Animals are the latest decorating craze.
> This little piggie went to market.
> This little piggie stayed home.
> It's a matter of taste.
>
> (2004, 111)

The opening verse is a collage of nursery rhymes, animal consumption, and interior decoration, as well as an allusion to the child/animal bond. The child's room decorated with cute piggies has multi-dimensional connotations. It suggests domestic space that could be familiar to a child, a safe space. It also addresses putative primordial relations between humans and animals as told in nursery rhymes, implying ways of understanding animals as part of home education for children. We learn that 'It's a matter of taste', a highly ambiguous construction in the context of this poem. Does 'taste' suggest – a room decorated with cute animals, the slaughter of animals who are yearning for life, or what the pork *tastes* like. Ambiguity reigns in the text as Fulton goes on with the synonym, 'hog':

> I have string of pig lights for the tree.
> each hog is rendered into darlingness,

rendered in the nerve-dense rose
of lips, tongue, palm, sole. Of the inside
of the eyes and nose.
They were green bows.

(2004, 111)

'Nerve-dense rose' feels like an automatised metaphorical expression to conceive of well-known mammalian nervous system phenomena. Perhaps there are scientists for whom this phrase might go without saying, but, in this poem, the metaphor for the pig's physical means of feeling arrests the reader. There is something beautiful (rose-like) about the whole-animal connectedness by means of which pigs, like Fulton's human readers, are sensate. What then of the hog-pig continuum or contrast?

In American English, hog suggests dead animal bodies which are processed as a commodity, as opposed to the living animal (pig) or the animating piggie image in the nursery rhyme. A circle of apparent synonyms – pig, piggie, and hog – make subtle the otherwise blunt assumptions of equivalence on which today's consumer society unthinkingly depends. If 'piggie' connotes lively innocence for the facilitation of children's play, then hog connotes commercially available animals used to satisfy human appetites. As the body with 'lips, tongue, palm, sole' must be the whole body that has been slaughtered, we can also be reminded of the similar body parts in the pork eater, the human who is also an animal.

The scene of 'intrusion into the body, the pain, the looking away, the unfeelingness', on which Fulton elaborates in an interview (Fulton and Miller 1997, 603), is woven through subtle punning. Stress is laid on the numb feelings of producers, consumers, and onlookers to generate a pervasive and tragic sense of what Dianna Taylor calls 'percepticide', a psychic numbing and distancing of affect, a cultural disorder characterised by the percipients' failure to enact what they have seen (1997, 123–124). Fulton does this by depicting animal slaughter in a manner that bears resemblance to scenes of the Holocaust, as these would be known to her highly literate readership. Seeing without the possibility of admitting the happening of the violence is a blinding, or even killing of senses. Such a tendency of cold affect, as indicated from Fulton's 'fractal poetics', reveals a human process of dissociation, objectification, and manipulating others.

In this poem, the total control of pigs-as-objects by humans is foregrounded in the happenings of the slaughter house and the packing house and in the homes of humans in which meat and the cuteness of piggies are consumed. Tension and empathy build steadily following the movements and gaze of the pig as these are witnessed by an imagined human observer, one somehow more objective than 'the man' in the poem or than the average unthinking consumer of pork. For such an observer, it is the feelings of pigs that are to the fore in what is observed.

> Pigs are so emotional. They look at the man
> who'll stun them, the man
> who'll hang them upside down in chains.
> they smell extinction and try to climb
> the chute's sides as it moves.
> At the top, the captive bolt guy
> puts electrodes on their heads
> and sends a current through.
> (2004, 113)

Man and pig – victim and tormenter, in the terms of the poem, each is equally object and subject – are seen by the persona as exercising what volition is available. But it is the pigs – as victims – who have something to feel here.

In the poem 'Call the Mainland', Fulton writes, 'Emotion // makes its presence felt in flesh' (2001, 64). For whose benefit does Fulton's persona encounter a pig-to-be-slaughtered, for whom is its affective state elaborated? The persona makes that identity clear:

> I write
>
> for the born-again infidels
> whose skepticism begins at the soles
> of the feet and climbs the body,
> nerve by nerve.
> (Fulton 2004, 114)

'Nerve-by-nerve' presents an apposite analogy – the body of the self-blinding, objectifying, dissociated sceptical human is a body full of feeling, just as is a pig's. The voice and point-of-view in this poem are nuanced, wry, cynical; but they tell a consistent story – they urge the reader to feel what the real pig feels, to get through the grammar and rhetoric and symbolic business, in order to understand what a human can ultimately understand of a 'real' pig – that is, embodied feeling. By using different formulations of pig symbolism and reality – piggie, pork, hog, slaughtered pigs, emotional pigs, this poem addresses the question of human understanding of nonhuman others in the contemporary context where wild animals become spectralised and diminished (in Berger's words) and countless mammals are raised for intensive large-scale meat production. Part of the context for this industrial scale of slaughter, and for this absolute dominion, is training in desensitisation for consumers.

Poetry, in Adorno's view (34), at least at some points, cannot bridge the gap between aesthetics and atrocity. Does this philosopher's pronouncement still apply to this distressing and tragic situation of other-than-human animals in the world today? Fulton's 'Some cool' provides a reflective observation by reconsidering relations of values and meanings of objects and subjects we routinely encounter. This poem, as if uttered by the fictionalised activist Elizabeth Costello from J.M. Coetzee's academic novel *The Lives of Animals* (1999), calls on a reassessment of ethical attitudes towards those who suffer. As with Elizabeth Costello, linking the slaughter of animals that have a 'massive physical wish to live' with the human-to-human atrocities we know as the Holocaust, locates animal suffering as a result of de-humanising acts:

> I return [...] to the places of death all around us, the places of slaughter to which, in a huge communal effort, we close our hearts. Each day a fresh holocaust, yet as far as I can see our moral being is untouched. We do not feel tainted. We can do anything, it seems, and come away clean.
>
> (Coetzee, 35)

Empathy for animals in Fulton's poems resists any such definitive moral judgment. A sense of the non-binarising prevails: the peripheral that Lynn Keller has called, following Fulton's lead, the 'then some inbetween' (311). Fulton has claimed an enchantment with the space of possibility, 'the space of between, where meaning is neither completely revealed nor completely concealed' (1999, 15). Here again, we are in the familiar territory of logic of yes *and* no – beyond the reach, that is, of bivalent logic (Kristeva 1984). A sense of 'betweenness' in Fulton's work obscures any definite species border. We who read have understood what her animals feel because we too are embodied creatures, creatures of a context, in which subjects may be objects, but in which sensate experience remains retrievable because it is felt by readers, as by other animals. Ultimately, in Fulton's work, what the spirit of reciprocity demands is empathy for selves other than but such as *our*selves.

When Fulton proposes her aesthetics of 'felt' in 'The Permeable Past Tense of Feel', she expresses her ambition to structure human affect through her construction and refiguring of language and its meaning:

> I know
> there must be ways to concentrate
> the meanings of felt in one
>
> just place. Just as this flame
> assumes the shape of the flesh it covers.
> I like to prepare the heart
> by stuffing it with the brain.
>
> (2001, 71)

The poem demands of its explication a dialogic reflexivity. Is 'just' as an adjective with the connotations of fairness or rather a dead metaphor that becomes a sentence-initial conjunction? By juxtaposing ambiguous uses of 'just', the poet suggests justice as something humans risk losing sight of; rather humans are obliged to view their world in a larger-than-human context. Implied here can be an appeal to environmental justice against the cosmopolitan backdrop of human injustice taking place on an industrial scale. The image conjured up by 'Just as this flame/assumes the shape of the flesh it covers' not only ironically implies the act of barbecue or cooking of slaughtered animals. It also refers to devotion to the sacred heart of Jesus in Catholic tradition (so often depicted with flame within). The religious metaphor in 'Some Cool' (e.g. 'vestment') invites reflection on the sacredness of the concentrated image of human affect embodied by the dying God; if God feels what we feel and what we inflict on each other, can we not feel what we inflict on animals other-than-us? Do we not know of such an empathic God precisely because of our own like empathic capacity?

The last lines of this poem 'I like to prepare the heart/by stuffing it with the brain' bring us to consider what can and/or must be felt by sentient animals such as ourselves, and also to consider what poems/words can do for us or to us in relation to these questions of thinking and feeling. The poem as a whole invokes a strong appeal to empathy for these animals-to-be-slaughtered. Where are 'we' as human agents and where are other-than-human others in 'The Permeable Past Tense of Feel', 'Our presence is a double-dwelling' we are told:

> Why must I say they are like
> us whenever I say let them live? Speak eco-speak
> like eat not flesh and save the watershed, like
> maybe the whole blue-green.
> (Fulton 2001, 70)

The 'doubleness' here is multiple: we speaking humans and our mute others, what I say and what I do, what I wonder about and what I must say. Thus, among other things, anthropocentric projection is acknowledged and the possibility of reciprocal relations with our un-languaged others is brought into question. The possibility of reciprocity is brought into a question as to the limits of our ability to represent others.

Poetry is a recipe, as we learn in the last lines of the poem, and what is cooking in the poem addresses both language issues and environmental problems. Fulton's work calls for a reconfiguring of the heart/head dualism. These two last enigmatic lines allude not only to culturally inscribed tension between heart and mind, emotions and intellect, but also to the habitual acts of cooking and eating dead animals: again, 'this flame/assumes the shape of the flesh it covers' (71). The key question suggested here concerns how feeling, thinking, and knowing might furnish means for proposing an alternative rhetoric for animal ethics. The ethical doubts might lead to a tail-chase for many readers, but this train of thought need not be self-defeating. Certainly, the stakes are high. They concern, as indicated, 'maybe the whole blue-green' (the planet, the biosphere). We are reminded of the world-embracing scale of the twenty-first century struggle between the powerful and disempowered, between those highly placed, whom Brecht tells us have already eaten, and those less fortunate with whom they dine.

Knowing What We Know, We Ask What Is to Be Done

The border between aesthetics and ethics is a place of the hypothetical, not to say the impossible. Wherever we find fiction we must have entered a parallel universe, a world of 'what if' and 'what else could be'. Between the possible and its infinite others lies the land of what we know. We know, for instance, how tiny and far our place in the cosmos, and our place, in time is. We know, for instance, that our star is somewhere near the halfway mark of its life. And so it must be for our world as well. Awareness of where and when and how we are – *understanding* – points to extinction. We, with our human consciousness, are, as various religions acknowledge, the creatures who know death. Though this is only now coming to light, thus far in the Anthropocene, we are the bringers of death and extinction on a scale our planet – the only one known to have life – has never before seen.

Can we do better than simply say goodbye to the ones who are gone because of us? Here we come to the limits of imagination. The limits of our imagination show the limits of our empathy. What would it mean to picture a world without us? Are we able to do that imagining? Is it a healthy or necessary thing to do? And then where does the story go? Will it be in an other-than-human genre, or will we, assuredly, anthropomorphise the creatures who will have survived us? Or not do that? Is it possible to not anthropomorphise? What would it mean to not anthropomorphise? For whose benefit would that be done?

But is this not the nature of literature, of cultural expression more generally? We were always in impossible places – places dreamt, wished for, willed, places long forgotten, places that never will be. And so perhaps there is not so much difference between making fiction as we have been accustomed and imagining a world in which we are gone? But can we go with kindness now? Can we go with feeling for the others? Or will it simply be more about ourselves because that is as far as we go. If we imagine a world which only we survive, a moment's reflection shows that too is impossible. Imagine rather a world we help to heal and make whole again. The point is that we have choices in what we imagine. And those choices are at least one of the beginnings of the future. Shall we go to the limits of the imagination? Let's see what we can see from there.

Perhaps the only way to save the species we wittingly or otherwise doom will be to splice their DNA with ours so that our offspring will be humanimal? Or imagine a short-circuit in the general scheme of karma and reincarnations, such that all those whom we've eaten return to judge, to haunt us, to do unto us what we've done to them. Imagine every human life tied to the life of an animal other, so that one will not survive without the other. Imagine lives lived in other bodies, other bodies in ours. And who will exorcise the other? Imagine the clock of the Earth run back so that life becomes harmless again. Imagine a year and every insect has its day – to rule, to feast on all others. Or every year we choose again which creature we will be. Imagine an alien force will come and set the world to rights. Imagine if all of the animals came out of the books – the picture books and the rest – and spoke for themselves at last.

We humans are, as all creatures, of many aspects: upright with opposable thumb, conscious of our consciousness. The human is a knower and maker, and this despite astounding ignorance and stupidities that keep on repeating again and again. Creatures of unlimited global spread, we are the everywhere animal. And as we have said, the human is bringer of death. Perhaps above humans we are creatures of the imagination. This is how we come to be in a book like this, about the kinds of books we are about.

And though fiction and experiment are the beginnings of what may be, it is nevertheless the case that these are tools enlisted in the quest for truth and in the quest for what *should* be. Now that the world is just beginning to recover from the Trump experiment, one might well conclude from it that, outside of a book or off the screen, there is nothing worthwhile *after* truth. It really will help us all – humans and everyone/everything else – if we have some idea of where we are and what is actually happening. We necessarily rely on all sorts of expert knowledge.

So what do fiction and poetry have to do with a quest for truth? We return to the voices of our introduction in suggesting a poetry that does not speak over animals, that is wary of speaking for them, that is, rather, interested in speaking with or to or objectively or feelingly about animal others. Indicated here is a poetry of witness and of what is to be done. That would be a poetry of truth telling, a poetry telling the truth on behalf of those others whose means of presence to us is simply in being themselves. If the poem in the book is where we and the children meet the animals, have we the means of allowing the creatures there to be themselves?

There is no gainsaying what literature – what any instance of art – may teach, may reveal to us. For all of its ideological investment – and as worthy as this is of analysis – art (and perhaps especially the art of poetry) remains very much a province of mystery. Why do people make it? Why do people consume it? How does it bring pleasure? And how do the pleasures it brings relate to the reality of the world and relate to action (or the possibility of action) in the world. These questions are fundamental to the framing terms of this work – poetics and ethics. What are the poetics and ethics of anthropomorphism? What have they been? What can they be? What potential do we have as – as children, as parents, as readers, as writers, as illustrators, as translators – to decide these things?

In his *The Company We Keep* (1988), Wayne Booth investigates the ethical consequences of literature and defends ethical criticism, or in his words, the ethics of the power of story worlds in adding 'life' upon 'life' (14). Of relevance here is his reminder that different actual ethical outcomes become assimilated to human experience in the act of reading: 'the load of values carried away from the [reading] experience, can often be most substantial when the reader has been least conscious of anything other than "aesthetic" involvement' (14). In a similar vein of championing ethical awareness, Jane Bennett (2010, xvi) calls for an emphasis on 'the agentic contributions of nonhuman forces (operating in nature, in the human body and in human artifacts) in an attempt to counter the narcissistic reflex of human language and thought'. As more scholars extol the virtues of anthropomorphism to the advantage of animals (Baker 1993; Simons 2002; McHugh 2011), the question on this topic is not how can one evade the impending ethical issue, but as Timothy Clark puts it, 'how to represent animal lives in human language and culture without illusion or injustice?' (2014, 179). We are in the realm of duty here. The duty of humans must now be care. A responsible future for us, in and with our biosphere, is only if we care to understand, only if we understand to care.

New Humanimal Sensibility

Outside of the pages of children's texts, momentum gathers as more children are involved in street demonstrations in the context of, and in opposition to, a seemingly irreversible global environmental crisis. In 2019, child activists, led by Greta Thunberg, mobilised global youth to participate in the 'climate strike for the future' with an open letter (Youth-Led Climate Strike 2019). Viewing themselves a 'voiceless future of humanity', the school children made an appeal for responsible action, demanding justice for 'all past, current and future victims' of the environmental crisis. The international youth-led movement, bolstered by children's immediate concerns over the social and political reality facing the wounded planet, subverts those that inform a conventional childhood education based on an apolitical protocol of innocence. Feeling 'betrayed' by adults over the Anthropocene realities, an increasing number of young people have dispensed with the idea of growing into 'adults of tomorrow', those who relentlessly continue the onslaught on Earth's web of life without guilty conscience; instead, they call for the construction of a renewed ecological community that benefits all beings. The global COVID pandemic of 2019 has added impetus to agitation for a significant re-set of human priorities concerning the planet.

And what about the adults in the story, the ones who have been with and listening to these kids? We who have – one way or another – been in the poems and picture books, expecting always more to come, have done our fair share of imagining. Is a further duty for us then to imagine – to facilitate – a poetry to motivate the kind of movement

Greta Thunberg represents – to involve those coming into poetry in the necessary work of witness – to understand the needful truths, to envisage better futures? To begin the undoing of the human damage to everyone and everything else?

If convention places such speculation beyond the scope of a volume such as this, then one will be justified in asking how a book like this should in fact conclude. Certainly, the work thus far points to new investigations and future projects in the ethics and aesthetics of cultural production (poetry or other), as it involves children and animals. Equally it suggests further speculation concerning the key mysteries of the study so far – why anthropomorphism, why the masks? What do these tell us about humans as animals, their place, and the place, of culture in the world?

We do know that these related phenomena of anthropomorphism and prosopopoeia are ancient. Perhaps they are present at the wellspring of human culture – with shamanism, with painting and with figurines, the oldest survivors of what may have been the first recognisable material expressions of human imagination. In so saying, we return to Stewart Guthrie's claim that anthropomorphism is both the key too and at once something more fundamental than religion (1993). It may be the basis of human culture. Maybe then the key defining characteristic of the human species is that it does this business we call culture in the broadest sense – entailing the circulation of masks, pretending to be creatures other than we know we are, the asking of questions in the form of stories, all kinds of tropic activity in and out of language. Perhaps it is necessary that culture involves pretending, dissembling. It may be that pretending is always in large part about who we are or think we are, about how we are in relation to others whom we see as the same or different, about others with whom we align ourselves or from whom we assert a distance. It may be that the human-as-a-problem-for-everyone-else is largely to do with the human pretending to not be a creature at all, pretending to be other than animal.

Is the purpose of culture, likewise of religion, to come to terms with the recognition, however stridently denied, that we too are animal, despite all the differences we see and imagine to separate us from animal others? Does that recognition of human animality persist, even at times as a dirty secret, despite the extraordinary degree to which we have dominated other species and placed ourselves and our sense of self at the centre of all that is able to be known?

Somehow central to the species' story is that deep down we always knew we were animals. We invented gods in all shapes and sizes, largely animals to begin, and then in our own image. There was a lot of pretending that we were other than animal but was Darwinian evolution such a revelation? Or more of a reversion to earlier doctrine? Theories of evolution were a victory of common sense over wishful thinking, of empirical observation over the power of illusion and the convenience for religions to justify the idea of human exceptionalism.

We humans have understood ourselves as being conscious and so separate from the universe of entities we see as lacking consciousness. Any part of this arrangement might be an illusion, but despite the decreasing viability of such illusions, they have been very difficult to shake. Anthropomorphism and prosopopoeia may merely be vain efforts to come to terms with a frustration that consciousness of consciousness makes its possessor no less animal, though it brings the animal closer to the knowledge of death.

Also true is that, being animal, we have in some sense worn no mask at all. Or we have no more worn a mask than has the chameleon, or the lyre bird pretending to be another bird, or the stick insect pretending to be part of the tree. In a way, humans – this *we* of the story must speak for all animals simply because we are the ones who speak. The way the parrot must repeat, the way the lyre bird has to imitate, as many other creatures (and indeed plants) do. We humans are the ones who write, who reflect. Exceptionalism yet persists, however we try to cure ourselves of it. The world is our responsibility in a way that cannot be said of any other creature. We know this because, if we open our eyes, we are able to understand the damage we have done, the damage we are doing. At this point, in *the* story, we do not seem to handling responsibility very well. Perhaps we know also, deep down, that this may all be meaningless to say, if our cosmos has no meaning. Our feeling for self and other – however well or poorly developed – has us cling to this last and inviolable illusion: that even if there is no purpose, we ourselves are purposeful. We humans – for good and ill – make difference, and the differences we make are evident everywhere.

The only future worth living – perhaps the only live-able future – is the one in which humans collectively have brought care to the fore, and have cast the circle of care wide enough to include, not only all creatures and all life, but everything humans touch. Some might say that this has long been advocated by some religions or by branches of some religions. This may be so but, if so, this enlightened doctrine has had limited success, and has been typically overshadowed by the less palatable motives and associations of religion: fear, wishful thinking, and the will to power over others (human and otherwise). These deplorables have, of course, plenty of currency outside of religious circles. If in the generalised struggle for survival, at present, many if not most species-teams are doing poorly, it may yet be the apparent winner will be a loser with and like the rest because that is the only way this struggle to the death can end. What would be the lesson for no one to learn from that? Simply that consciousness was a power that finally defeated itself, that consciousness was some seed of doom.

But things may well be otherwise. And we humans, typical of our more general *hybris*, may have been quite wrong about consciousness and its being our exclusive intellectual property. Consider the anthropomorphism operational in Sandburg's famous little fog poem:

> The fog comes
> on little cat feet.
>
> It sits looking
> over harbor and city
> on silent haunches
> and then moves on.
> (1970, 33)

Who can say that the rain on its way is not a conscious thing, or a tiny part of some larger awareness, of which human awareness has thus far been limited, but not so far limited as to prevent Sandburg's fantastic speculation? Where science has left us without any answers and religion has been ready to claim mysteries as its own, might we not be better off with the questions art offers in showing us possibilities we had not previously considered?

As per Strawson's negatively framed claim that there is no evidence for believing that consciousness is not a fundamental property of matter (2008), the panpsychist thesis dispenses with perhaps the last bastion of human exceptionalism. It looks onto an ethos of either absolute nihilism or total care. Consider:

> It's okay to eat animals because they don't think.
> It's okay to eat plants because they don't feel.
> It's okay to do anything to anything that's not alive because it's
>   not alive.

Consider where this kind of thinking has got us so far. Facing a great extinction the great questions must concern survival – and not only ours. Despite the valiant efforts of so many – in and out of the poems and picture books – the attitudes and actions of the human race are not yet convincingly turning towards survival.

The viable middle way between dualism and physicalism suggests, not mind over matter, not that consciousness 'emerged' as property of a species of animal, but that mind and matter are ultimately indistinguishable, that mind is actually everything and everywhere – that consciousness is a universal property. Of course we may be entering a hall of mirrors here, it being far from inconceivable that panpsychism is itself simply another anthropomorphism – the creature is only able to deny its exceptionalism by imagining itself and its qualities everywhere and in everything. More human *hybris* still? More exceptionalism?

Then, on the other hand, if anthropomorphism is indeed inescapable, there would be no alternative theory not likewise afflicted. In which case, applying Ockham's razor, panpsychism retains some attraction – as (however counter-intuitively) the simplest theory with the most explanatory power.

What if all of these efforts we call anthropomorphism or prosopopoeia – or more broadly culture – were simply an effort to connect with a greater consciousness of which it seems we must logically be a part... or, more likely a part than not? Science provides some knowledge of what we know and what we do not know, of what we might be able to find out through observation, through thought and hypothesis, and the fashioning and testing of theories. Science helps us to see where the black boxes are. But when we come to questions so close to the heart – why masks? why metaphor? why art? – any definite speculation leads either to fiction or to religion or both (if we don't like it we call it superstition or unconvincing, if we do like the speculation then it might firm up – become canonical or an article of faith or both).

However stolid the dogma, we live with genuine mysteries, with questions we cannot help but ask, even as the multitude may shy from enquiry. These circumstances inspire awe, reverence, enquiry, mania, criminal intentions, crusades to save, genocidal and ecocidal intention, and any combination of any or all of the above. But what if the deep reason we have the creatures speak in poems and in picture books were nothing more than a yearning towards the prospect (or the recognition) of a fully conscious cosmos? At issue then would be not the truth or otherwise of the panpsychist hypothesis, but rather that such a hypothesis is irresistible to that possession we humans call consciousness. What if it were merely that such thinking had led us thus far through the maze to the perilous place where we find ourselves at present? Then the function of anthropomorphism in poetry for children may simply be to comprehend the mystery of that of which we are part.

Or it may be a proof of something as flimsy as the fact that humans are a silly species, and with an inkling that they are. We cannot help putting on costumes and masks and pretending and throwing our voices about.

Once again we are perhaps beyond the remit of *a book like this*. It will be wiser in our circumstances to seek our provisional answers in poetry. What poems can offer us in relation to topics so large is largely a question of temperament. But then perhaps that is precisely what we seek through poetry – to find the right temperament to deal with our time and place and circumstances.

What our times require are redemption, grace and restitution, some kind of human treaty with the rest of life and the rest of the world – the making of amends. A time for stewardship has come, true stewardship as opposed to pretending. As with the imperialist's *terra nullius* dream, it is time to abandon all fantasies of anything given humans by deities of human invention. These fantasies of right may help tribes to survive other tribes in an age of tribal warfare. The word nation may well fit as aptly here. Such fantasies of might-made-right cannot save the planet.

Part of the temperament these times require is the ability to bear witness to ourselves, to our past and present actions, and to our plans. We need to be able to see and to show and to say how we have been wrong. As is perhaps demonstrated in Wordsworth's poem 'To a Butterfly', which ends:

> Oh! pleasant, pleasant were the days,
> The time, when, in our childish plays,
> My sister Emmeline and I
> Together chased the butterfly!
> A very hunter did I rush
> Upon the prey:—with leaps and springs
> I followed on from brake to bush;
> But she, God love her, feared to brush
> The dust from off its wings.
> (1870, 45)

And there are many other choices, of temperament of attitude. There are many ways, in word and image, the healing might begin. We make choices of a politicised – of an ideological – nature every time we exercise our imaginations. We can mourn, as with Sandburg's gone buffaloes. We can see the animal not there, or the invisible spirit imagined, as with Sandburg's fog.

We can more make things more personal and perhaps hypocritical, like the weeping walrus with the gone oysters. Another temperamental approach for the silly species is found in a text to which we have devoted much time and attention in this book (particularly in Chapter 4). The 'point' of 'Jabberwocky', if such may be claimed, is perhaps not so much to anthropomorphise or conduct fantastic othering, but rather to make fun of our arranging ourselves so seriously among these objects and creatures we have only imagined as so different from ourselves. And what does 'Jabberwocky' teach in the end? Not that imaginary animals have origins, though of course they do. Rather that imagination has structure, that apparently inscrutable texts make meaning the way meaning is made in our world. That for all our stylised and fanciful, our triumphant (even murderous) intervention in the world, the creatures of our imagination obey the rules of the story in which we put them, and things are at the end as they were in the beginning. That it is *hybris* to think otherwise. If that was a viable message for the comical clergyman-mathematician to deliver in 1871, is it still viable now? Certainly, the taking-the-piss-out-of-ourselves part is. Such pauses to consider where we are, even in relation to the least plausible of others, may be where we begin the healing. Seeing ourselves is a way to be better. So Alice grows through the looking glass.

None of this work of being, of bettering, ourselves and our world, can ever be complete. As Wordsworth shows with his butterfly chase, we can reflect and come to new understandings of ourselves and our past and potential. And perhaps another tack we can take – another spur to action – will be the straightforward apology of the kind we find in Robert Burns' poem, 'To a Mouse'

> I'm truly sorry Man's dominion
> Has broken Nature's social union,
> An' justifies that ill opinion
> Which makes thee startle
> At me, thy poor, earth-born companion
> An' fellow-mortal.
> (1838, 34)

References

Adorno, Theodor. "Cultural Criticism and Society". *Prisms*. Trans. Samuel Weber and Shierry Weber. Cambridge: MIT Press, 1983. 17–84.

Baker, Steve. *Picturing the Beast: Animals, Identity, and Representation*. Manchester: Manchester University Press, 1993.

Bennett, Jane. *Vibrant Matter: A Political Ecology of Things*. Durham: Duke University Press, 2010.

Booth, Wayne. *The Company We Keep: An Ethics of Fiction*. Berkeley: University of California Press, 1988.

Burns, Robert. *The Poetic Works of Robert Burns*. Edinburgh: William and Robert Chambers, 1838.

Clark, Timothy. *The Cambridge Introduction to Literature and the Environment*. Cambridge: Cambridge University Press, 2014.

Coetzee, J.M. *The Lives of Animals*. Princeton: Princeton University Press, 1999.

de Man, Paul. *Aesthetic Ideology*. Minneapolis: University of Minnesota Press, 1996.

Derrida, Jacques. *The Animal That Therefore I Am*. New York: Fordham University Press, 2008.

Freud, Sigmund. *Civilization and Its Discontents*. Peterborough, Ontario: Broadview Press, 1930/2016.

Fulton, Alice. *Feeling as a Foreign Language: The Good Strangeness of Poetry*. St. Paul: Graywolf, 1999.

Fulton, Alice. *Felt: Poems*. New York: Norton, 2001.

Fulton, Alice. *Cascade Experiment: Selected Poems*. New York: Norton, 2004.

Fulton, Alice. "Fractal Poetics: Adaptation and Complexity". *Interdisciplinary Science Reviews* 30(4) (2005): 323–330.

Fulton, Alice, and Cristanne Miller. "An Interview with Alice Fulton". *Contemporary Literature* 38(4) (1997): 585–615.

Guthrie, Stewart E. *Faces in the Clouds: A New Theory of Religion*. New York: Oxford University Press, 1993.

Keller, Lynn. "The 'Then Some Inbetween': Alice Fulton's Feminist Experimentalism". *American Literature* 71(2) (1999): 311–340.

Kristeva, Julia. *Revolution in Poetic Language*. 1974. Trans. Margaret Waller. New York: Columbia University Press, 1984.

Latour, Bruno. *Down to Earth: Politics in the New Climatic Regime*. Cambridge: Polity Press, 2017.

McHugh, Susan. *Animal Stories: Narrating Across Species Lines*. Minneapolis: University of Minnesota Press, 2011.

Rilke, Rainer Maria. *Duino Elegies and The Sonnets to Orpheus*. Trans. A. Poulin, Jr. Boston: Houghton Mifflin, 1922/1977.

Sandburg, Carl. *The Complete Poems of Carl Sandburg*. Revised and Expanded Edition. London: Harcourt, 1920/1970.

Simons, John. *Animal Rights and the Politics of Literary Representation*. London: Palgrave, 2002.

Strawson, Galen. *Real Materialism and Other Essays*. Oxford: Oxford University Press, 2008.

Taylor, Diana. *Disappearing Acts: Spectacles of Gender and Nationalism in Argentina's "Dirty War"*. Durham: Duke University Press, 1997.

Web. "Cats Kill More than 1.5 Billion Native Animals per Year". 9 July 2019. www.anu.edu.au/news/all-news/cats-kill-more-than-15-billion-native-animals-per-year#:~:text=Pet%20and%20feral%20cats%20together,of%20Australia's%20leading%20environmental%20scientists, accessed on 26 December 2020.

Wittgenstein, Ludwig. *Tractatus Logico-Philosophicus*. Second Edition of New Translation. London: Routledge & Kegan Paul, 1971.

Wordsworth, William. *The Poetical Works of William Wordsworth*. Ed. William Michael Rossetti. London: E. Moxon, 1870.

Youth-Led Climate Strike. "Climate Crisis and a Betrayed Generation". *The Guardian*. www.theguardian.com/environment/2019/mar/01/youth-climate-change-strikers-open-letter-to-world-leaders, 2019, accessed on 2 July 2021.

Zalasiewicz, Jan, et al., eds. *The Anthropocene as a Geological Time Unit: A Guide to the Scientific Evidence and Current Debate*. Cambridge: Cambridge University Press, 2019.

Index

AbdelRahim, L. 181
Adams, C. 226
Adams, D. 205–206
Adorno, T. 20, 244, 252
aesthetics and ethics 203–206, 212–213, 255
Agamben, P. 18
agency 2, 7, 19, 42–43, 63, 105, 176, 185, 218–219, 221, 225
'Alice in Imperialand' 207
Alice's Adventures in Wonderland 168
allegory 40, 128, 214
Anatomy of Literary Nonsense, An 60
Anderson, C. C. 59
animal archetypes 43–48
Animal Claim, The 19
animal communication 4–5
Animal Farm 120
animality 5, 12, 19, 189, 240, 241, 248–249, 258; animetaphor and 95; of cats 71, 168; of children 190, 246; contradictions in 65; crimes against 35; human-animal encounters and 97; human-imagined 84, 94; humans admitting their 26, 27, 28; hybrid human- 76; morality denying 33; natural 183; of nature 195; perceiving self and 27; pretend- 180; relationship between creativity and 41, 50; shared 30, 33, 234
animal poetry 4, 5–9; feminist experimentalism and 250; quest for truth and 256; as recipe 254–255; space for 196–198
animal presence 93–94
animals in poetry: given capacity to speak 17; as non-entities 17–18
Animal that Therefore I Am, The 193
animal voices 3–6

animal zodiac, Chinese 110–115
animetaphor 34, 95
animism 176
'animot' 5
Anthropocene, the 2, 17, 239; Sixth Great Extinction 28, 242–244
anthropocentrism 4, 20, 22, 31, 40, 58, 77, 128, 182, 191, 240, 242, 249
anthropomorphism 5, 9, 20, 239–240; of abstractions in nursery rhymes 107–110, 124; antidotes for 40–41; fairytale thinking and reifying power of 77–83; food (*see* food anthropomorphism); human understanding of animals and 31–35; as inescapable 260–261; nonsense and (*see* nonsense); representing ambivalent humanimal identity through 172; as rhetorical strategy 35–43; as sub-species of animism 176; as trope 20, 39; un/consciousness of 20–25
'Anthropomorphism and Trope in the Lyric' 39
anthropos polytropos 37
Apseloff, M. F. 59
Apuleius 76
Archie and the Bear 172
Archy and Mehitabel 7, 72–77, 87
Archy Does His Part 72–77
Archy's Life of Mehitabel 72–77
Ariès, P. 175
Aristotle 36
Ars Poetica 58, 211
Arthur, G. 118
Asquith, P. J. 36
'As the World Turns' 124
atrocity 13, 35, 203, 207, 225, 252
Attar, F. u.-D. 7, 133

Index

Auden, W. H. 6
avant-garde poetry 73

'Babes in the Woods: Wilderness Aesthetics in Children's Stories and Toys, 1830–1915' 182–183
Bachelard, G. 175–176
Bad Child's Book of Beasts, The 154–155
bad faith 35, 228–229
Bakhtin, M. 60, 106, 130, 150, 197
'Balance of Brillig, The' 187
Barai, A. 68
Barthes, R. 130, 175–176
'Bat, The' 23–25, 28
Becker, J. E. 27
becoming-animal 5, 18
Beer, G. 229–230
Belloc, H. 150, 151–156
Bennett, J. 18–19, 176, 257
Beowulf 156, 161
Berger, J. 40, 47, 81, 192, 194–195, 198
Berryman, J. 28
Bettelheim, B. 79
Beyond the Pleasure Principle 115
Bible, the 22
Birkerts, S. 25
Birns, M. B. 208
Bivona, D. 207
Blake, W. 107, 143, 146, 147
'Blessed Rage: Lewis Carroll and the Modern Quest for Order' 189
Bloom, H. 30
Bojack Horseman 7
Booth, W. 257
Braidotti, R. 20
Brantlinger, P. 208
Bratton, J. W. 182
Breaking the Magic Spell-Radical Theories of Folk and Fairy Tales 79
Brecht, B. 202
British Empire 208–210
Buber, M. 20, 125
Buddhism 20
'Buffalo Dusk' 245
Bump, J. 230
Burns, R. 263
'Bye Baby Bunting' 119

'Call the Mainland' 252
Cammaerts, E. 104, 112–113
Campbell, J. 70
cannibalism 230, 232

Capp, A. 205
carnival 12, 59–60, 63, 73, 130, 150; characters of 91; lens of 154; performance framed by 191–192; place of 190; Romanticism and 146; as site of resistance 92–93; subversion and 105; true and false logic of 197
carnivalesque texts 12, 59–60, 92, 146, 154, 166
'Carrion crow sat on an oak, A' 118
Carroll, L. 1, 2, 6, 64, 197; cautionary tales by 156–169; on Fortunatus purse 167; nursery rhymes and nonsense by 104–107; as proponent for animal rights 220; re-negotiation of forms and genres by 167–168; *see also* 'Jabberwocky'; *Through the Looking-Glass*; 'Walrus and the Carpenter, The'
Cat and the Cuckoo, The 6
'Cat as Cat, The' 93, 95–97, 125
Cat in the Hat, The 8, 67, 91–93, 147, 158
Cats 67
cautionary tales: horror or humour in 150–156; nursery rhyme 140–143; untranslatability in 147–150
Cautionary Tales for Children 151
Chaucer, G. 105, 133, 144
Chicken Run 205
child-animal relationships 2–3
childhood, poetics of 63–64, 257; fairytale thinking in 77–83; idea of childhood and 143–147; transcendence of childhood and 163–166
Children's Literature, Domestication, and Social Foundation 181
Chinese zodiac 110–115
Cicada 49–53, 62
Civilization and Its Discontents 245
Clark, T. 257
clear conscience 31–35
'Clod and the Pebble, The' 107
Coetzee, J. M. 230, 253
Collected Poems for Children 6
Comedy of Survival: Literary Ecology and a Play Ethic, The 62
'Come into Animal Presence' 93
Company We Keep, The 257
Cone, T. 97
Conference of the Birds 7, 133
conscience, animal-like lack of 32–33

consciousness: in anthropomorphism 20–25, 33–34; seeking of forgiveness and 25–28
constitutive phenomenology 94
contact zones 5, 94–95
contradiction 31, 53, 93, 121, 197, 211, 229–231, 240; aestheticisation of 215; in *Bojack Horsemen* 7; between chaos and order 91; ethical 250; expression of empathy and 20; food anthropomorphism and 13, 204, 207; human-like animality and animal-like humanity 65; humans learning from animals 82, 94; between meaning and lack of meaning 106; between nature and culture 77; nonsense and 60–61, 143, 211–212, 233; in nursery rhymes 123; paradox and 214; participation in process of 197; performative 144
'Controlling the Tongue' 144
Cooper, M. 18
Copernicus 2
Costello, E. 230, 253
courtesy 206–213
COVID-19 pandemic 24, 257
Creaturely Poetics 233
'Creaturely Rhetorics' 19
creaturely sensibility 47, 50
Creed, B. 30
Cronin, M. 43
'Crows' 148
'Cruel Frederick' 150
Cummings, E. E. 72–73
cyborgs 5

Dahl, R. 130
Daoism 20, 96–97
Darwin, C. 2, 36–37, 220
Darwinian observations/critique 37, 220, 231, 258
Darwinism 203, 207, 220, 232
Davidson, A. 66
Davis, D. 19
Davis, H. 20
death 246–247, 248, 255–256
Deleuze, G. 5, 18, 60, 142–143, 162, 214, 220
de Man, P. 39
Derrida, J. 5, 37, 44, 70, 95, 193–195, 231, 241
Descartes, R. 96, 230
Dickinson, E. 17
Dictionary of Imaginary Places 187

didacticism 62–63, 150, 152, 155
Diterlizzi, T. 142
domesticated animals 82, 178–181, 207, 243, 249
domestication 12–13, 28–29, 181, 241, 244
Donne, J. 7
Donovan, J. 20
Douglass, P. 71
Doyle, R. 18
'Dreadful Story about Harriet and the Matches,' The' 151

Eco, U. 163
eco-phobia 11, 103
Edward Lear: Landscape Painter and Nonsense Poet 66
Eliot, T. S. 67–72, 73, 80, 87, 147
Embree, L. 94
empathy 49–50, 120, 128–133, 227–229, 245–246
ethical awareness 257, 258–259
Ethics 22
ethics and aesthetics 203–206, 212–213, 255
ethics in nursery rhymes 124–127
Expression of the Emotions in Man and Animals, The 36–37

'Fabling Beasts: Traces in Memory' 78
Faces in the Clouds: A New Theory of Religion 5, 23
fairytale thinking 77–83
Fantastic Beasts and Where to Find Them 47
Fantastic Mr Fox 130
Farmer Duck 120
fate 121–122
feminist experimentalism 250
'Fern Hill' 40
Field of Nonsense, The 60, 210
Fiut, A. 25
'Floods of Autumn, The' 97
food anthropomorphism 202–203, 220; aesthetics and ethics in 203–206; Alice Fulton and 250–255; questions of courtesy in life and death of 206–213
Forché, C. 93
forgiveness 25–28
Fortunatus purse 167, 185, 191
'Fox jumped up one winter's night, A' 128–130
fractal poetics 250
Freud, S. 115, 159

268   Index

'Frog He Would a-Wooing Go, A' 130, 132–133
'From a German War Primer' 202
From Tongue to Text: A New Reading of Children's Poetry 106
Frost, R. 85
Fulton, A. 250–255

Gaia hypothesis 5, 37
Garbage Delight 156
Gay Science, The 33
genre 9, 79, 149, 160, 161, 163, 255; cautionary tales 140–141, 155–156; comedy 92, 105; crossover 11, 104, 114–115; fairytale 77, 81, 122; flight from 52; as frame 231; literary nonsense 106; nonsense 60, 106, 143, 147, 211–212, 216; nursery rhymes 113, 114–115, 136; points of view and 8, 159
Gibson, L. 40–41
'Goats' 40–41
'Gods, The' 25, 27, 43–46, 246
Golden Ass, The 76
'Goldilocks and the Three Bears' 79–80
Goldthwaite, J. 105
Gross, H. 39
Guadalupi, G. 187
Guattari, F. 5, 18
Guthrie, S. 5, 23, 38, 40, 58
Gutzschhahn, U.-M. 148

Hale, S. J. 125
Haraway, D. 5, 18–20, 94–96
harmony and reconciliation 121
Harris, W. C. 168
Hart, H. 68
Hawhee, D. 19
Hawk in the Rain, The 41
Hello Kitty 219
Herbert, A. P. 140–141
'Hey Diddle Diddle' 104, 105
Heyman, M. 106
Hoffmann, H. 150, 152, 155
Holocaust, the 13, 230–231, 251, 253
Holquist, M. 97
Holub, M. 37–38
'Hombre pequeñito' 17
Homer 37, 196
Horace 58, 72
Hoskyns, J. 105, 144
Howe, N. 78
Howitt, M. 141–142
Howitt, W. 158

Hughes, T. 6, 7, 41–43, 45, 48, 50, 149–150
Huizinga, J. 190
human-animal relations 18–19; contact zones of 94–95; current global/local crises and 244–247; empathy in 49–50, 120, 128–133, 227–229, 245–246; ethical awareness in 257, 258–259, 263; expression of emotions by animals and 36–37; future of 259–263; household pets 249; human consciousness projected onto animals in 248; human self-regard and superiority in 33–35; human understanding of animals and 31–35; naturalness of 240–242; in nursery rhymes 115–124; punishment in 126–127; re-negotiating animal archetypes 43–48; uncanny encounters in world where nothing is still 28–31
human exceptionalism 259–260
humanimal 8, 11–14, 41, 76, 103, 172, 226, 228, 244, 255, 257
humanimality 76
human solipsism 32
Hume, D. 22
'Humpty Dumpty' 121–122, 160, 163
'Hundesprache' 149
Husserl, E. 94
Hutcheon, L. 162–163
hypocrisy 217

'I caught a fish' 61–64
'I Eat Kids Yum Yum' 156
'If I had a donkey that wouldn't go' 120
'I-It relationship' 97–98, 125
I-It sense of the world 176–177
imaginary creatures 83–87
Imaginary Menagerie: A Book of Curious Creatures 85
'I'm Nobody! Who are you?' 17
imperialism 20, 221
imperialist context 13, 48, 154, 168, 203, 206–207, 222, 261
'In Praise of Self-Deprecation' 32, 34, 35, 41
'In the Microscope' 37–38
irony 11, 63, 149, 161–164, 165, 166–167, 192; as art of depths and heights 214; of extinction 81; nonsense and 59; tugging at heartstrings 206
'I-Thou' relationship 20, 97–98, 125

'Jabberwocky' 64, 140, 144, 156–162, 190, 197, 212; faux foreignness of 149; genre of 161, 163; humour of 159; irony in 161–162, 166–167; parody in 165; tongue in cheek fun of 146; transcendence of childhood in 163–166; translations into other languages 148; *see also Through the Looking-Glass*
Jenkins, H. 92
'Jim, Who Ran Away from His Nurse, and Was Eaten by a Lion' 152–154
Joyce, J. 181–182

Kandinsky, V. 21
Katrovas, R. 30
Keats, J. 6
Keller, L. 250, 253
Kennedy, G. A. 5, 19
Kennedy, J. 144, 182–183
Kennedy, J. S. 5, 23
Konrad, K. 21
Kostkowska, J. 34
Kristeva, J. 165, 191, 197
Krüss, J. 86–87, 149

Lacan, J. 177
'Ladybird, ladybird' 122
'Language as Sensuous Action: Sir Richard Paget, Kenneth Burke, and Gesture- Speech Theory' 19
Larios, J. 84–85
Lear, E. 64–67, 85, 105–107, 130, 150, 158
Lecercle, J.-J. 60–61, 105, 106, 148, 211
Le Doeuff, M. 37, 38
Lee, D. 156
Lee, M. P. 203, 220
Le Guin, U. K. 62–63
Lennon, J. 220
Levertov, D. 90, 93–96, 124–125
Levinas, M. 5, 20, 97, 224
Lewis, C. S. 198
liminal encounters 12, 20, 84, 95
Lindsay, N. 204–205
Lippit, A. 34, 81–82, 95
'Little Bo-peep' 126, 135
'Little Miss Muffet' 117
Lives of Animals, The 253
Logic of Sense, The 142–143, 214
'Looking Forward' 164
Lord, P. 205
Lost Thing, The 86, 87, 90, 108, 125
Louise, Z. 172

Lovell-Smith, R. 208–209
Lovelock, J. 5, 37

MacDonald, R. K. 92
Macintosh, D. 172
Magic Pudding, The 205
Malay, M. 46–47
Malcolm, N. 105
Mandelbrot, B. 250
Manguel, A. 187
Maritain, J. 197
Marquis, D. 7, 72–77, 87
'Marriage of the Frogge and the Mouse, The' 130–131
'Martian Sends a Postcard Home, A' 44–45
'Mary had a little lamb' 125
McGillis, R. 59
'Meadow Mouse, The' 28–29, 31, 35, 41, 42
Meditations 96
Meeker, J. 52, 62, 203, 210, 213
Meet My Folks 149–150
Menely, T. 19
Menninghaus, W. 81
Merleau-Ponty, M. 160, 161, 177
metonymy 39–40, 162, 189, 191–192
microscopic world 37–38
Milne, A. A. 180
Milosz, C. 25–28, 35
Minear, R. H. 92
Minslow, S. 207
Moe, A. M. 19
monsters 59, 84, 156, 167, 175, 211
More Beasts for Worse Children 154
Morgenstern, C. 83
Morgenstern, J. 3
Morton, T. 109–110
Mother Goose 110–115
Murphy, P. 20
Murray, B. 61–62
Murray, L. 25, 27, 43–46, 246

Nagel, T. 24
nakedness of animals 193
'Nasobame, The' 83–84
Natov, R. 63
Natural History of Religion, The 22
naturalness of affinity between children and animals 240–242
nature, social construction of 239–240
Nel, P. 92
Neruda, P. 6
Newberry, T. 145
Ngai, S. 219

270   *Index*

Nietzsche, F. 33–34, 38, 39, 42, 77
Nikolajeva, M. 63
nonsense: anthropomorphism and 58–61; in *Archy and Mehitabel* 72–77; in *The Cat in the Hat* 91–93; contradiction in 211; fairytale thinking and 77–83; in 'I caught a fish' 61–64; Mother Goose as 110–115; nursery rhymes and 104–107; objects and subjects lost in action and 87–91; in *Old Possum's Book of Practical Cats* 67–72; in 'Owl and the Pussy-cat, The' 64–67; paradoxes and 142–143; in 'The Walrus and the Carpenter' 213–220, 231–233; unreal creatures, spouting 83–87; untranslatable 147–150
nursery rhymes 103–104; ambivalent oscillation in 127–128; anthropomorphism of abstractions in 107–110, 124; as cautionary tales 140–143; complex negotiations of identity in 133–137; ethics in 124–127; human-animal relations in 115–124; Mother Goose as nonsense practice 110–115; nonsense and 104–107; warnings in 122–123; wisdom in 136–137

object narratives 176
Odyssey, The 37
Oerlemans, O. 19, 40
Ohrem, D. 105
'Old Mother Goose' 116
Old Possum's Book of Practical Cats 67–72, 80, 87
On the Parts of Animals 36
'On Truth and Lies in an Nonmoral Sense' 34
Opie, I. 103, 112
Opie, P. 103, 112
'Orchard' 38–39
orthocomplementarity 197
otherness: ethics of 224; wild 181
Our Aesthetic Categories 219
'Owl and the Pussy-cat, The' 64–67, 130, 158
Oxenbury, H. 120
Oxford Dictionary of Nursery Rhymes, The 103, 114

'Panther' 47–48
paradox 59, 61, 187, 189, 193, 214, 219, 232; of animal being 27; animality-humanity 97; of consciousness 248; contradictions and 214; observer's 32; of one without language testifying against language 25; of presence 14; size and power 128; theory of sense 143
paradoxical form 142–143, 161, 187, 190, 207, 211
Park, N. 205
Parliament of Fowls 133
parody 165, 214, 232; in cautionary tales 141; Darwinism and 220; form/content aspect of 159; in nursery rhymes 105; of sentimentalism 202–203
Paschkis, J. 84–85
passion of the animal 193–194
pathetic fallacy 38–39, 81, 109, 222, 232
pathos 29
percepticide 251
'Permeable Past Tense of Feel, The' 253–254
Philosophical Imaginary, The 37
Philosophy of Nonsense: The Intuitions of Victorian Nonsense Literature 211
Piaget, J. 176
Pick, A. 233
Plato 196
play ethic 210–211
Poetry and Animals: Blurring the Boundaries with the Human 19
Poetry and the Fate of the Senses 18
Poetry of Nonsense, The 104
poetry of witness 93
Portrait of the Artist as a Young Man, The 181–182
posthuman 5, 14, 20, 45
prejudice 49–50
prosopopoeia 5, 59, 96, 173, 216, 239, 241, 245, 258, 259, 261; adult-in-child's-mind 182; allegory and 127, 128; defined 6; ventriloquism and 74; wearing of masks 216
Ptolemy 2
Pullinger, D. 106, 134
'Punch and Judy' 114

'Quangle Wangle's Hat, The' 85–86

Rackin, D. 189
Raffoul, F. 224
Raine, C. 44–45
Rands, W. B. 157–158

reciprocal vision 175–178
Reesman, J. 70
Reid, H. 104
religion, anthropomorphism in 22–23
Restaurant at the End of the Universe, The 205–206
revenge by animals 120
Revolution in Poetic Language 165
rhetorical strategy, anthropomorphism as 35–43
Rhodes, H. 144–145
Richards, G. 207
Rilke, R. M. 47–48, 246, 247–248
'Rising in the Morning' 144–145
Roethke, T. 23–24, 28, 30–31, 35, 41, 42
Romanticism 18, 143–144, 146, 164, 182, 240, 245
Root and Herbal Classics 21
Roth, R. 92
Rowling, J. K. 47
Rukeyser, M. 93
Rule, S. 71
Ruskin 38, 81
Russell, B. 230, 234
Russell, P. 151

Sagar, K. 41
Samsa, G. 50
Samson, T. 213
Sandburg, C. 245, 249, 260
Santner, E. L. 18
Sartrean bad faith 35, 228–229
Sattaur, J. 154
Sax, B. 84
Scheman, N. 227
Schneiderman, L. 59
Scott, W. 113
secrecy 191–196
self-deprecation 32, 34, 49
Sendak, M. 6, 8, 147, 172–174, 181
sentience 25, 26, 29, 41, 45, 75, 91, 215, 219, 225, 229, 232, 248; aesthetic-recreational environmentalism and 34; of animals 108, 125, 133, 151; child-like 122, 178–181; of toys 175
sentimentalism 202–203
Seuss, Dr. 8, 67, 87, 91–93, 147
Sewell, E. 60, 70, 105, 187, 210
Shakespeare, W. 105
Shelley, P. B. 6, 146
Shepard, P. 65
Shi, Z. 147–148

Short Life and Happy Times of the Shmoo, The 205
Shortsleeve, K. 92
Signs 177
'Sing a Song of Sixpence' 127–128
Singer, P. 230, 231
Sixth Great Extinction 28, 242–244
social Darwinism 203, 207, 220
'Some Cool' 250–255
Songs of Experience 146
Songs of Innocence 146
'Spatzen Internationale' 86, 149
'Spider, The' 140–141
'Spider and the Fly, The' 141–142, 154
Spinoza, B. 22
'Star, The' 108–110, 124–125
Stephens, J. 60
Stevenson, R. L. 164
Stewart, S. 18
Stone, R. 38–39
Storni, A. 17
storybook lands 1–2
'Story of Johnny Head-in-Air, The' 150–151
'Story of the Man that went out Shooting, The' 150
Strachery, E. 121
Straley, J. 220
Strangers to Ourselves 191
Strawson, G. 260
stray creatures 30
Struwwelpeter 150, 151, 152
Stuart, S. 105
Styles, M. 112–113, 146, 151
Swift, J. 124
Sylvie and Bruno 167
Szymborska, W. 7, 32, 33–34, 35, 41

'Table Rules for Little Folk' 145
Taming Cannibals: Race and the Victorians 208
Tan, S. 48, 49–53, 62, 86, 87, 89, 91, 108, 125
Tao, H. 21
tautology 215, 216
Taylor, D. 251
Taylor, J. 105, 108–110, 125
'Teddy Bears' Picnic, The' 144, 150, 182–184; animals and secrecy of 191–196; song of 190–191
'There were three jovial Welshmen' 116
'This Little Piggie Went to Market' 127, 134–135
Thomas, D. 40, 46–47

Thomas, L. 5, 37–38
'Thought Fox' 41, 42–43, 45, 50
'Three Blind Mice' 119
'Three Young Rats' 59–60
Through the Looking-Glass 104; anthropomorphic food in 202–203; British Empire and 208–210; courtesy in 207; creatures encountered by Alice in 188–189, 211–212; ethics in 203–206, 212–213; food anthropomorphism in 202–204; irony in 161–162; poetry re-framed in 162–169; reversals, borders, other sidedness, and wrong sidedness of 159–160; shifting landscapes in 185–188; themes of 159–161; *see also* 'Jabberwocky'; 'Walrus and the Carpenter, The'
Thunberg, G. 257, 258
Tigges, W. 105, 106
Tinsley, M. B. 69
'To a Butterfly' 262
'To a Mouse' 263
'To his little Son Benedict from the Tower of London' 144
'Topsy-Turvey World' 157–158
toys brought to life 175–178, 182–183
Toy Story 147, 184
transitional objects 175–178, 249; in *Winnie-the-Pooh* 178–180
Translations from the Natural World 43, 46
Tremper, E. 180
Tucker, N. 113
'"Twinkle, Twinkle, Litter Star" as an Ambient Poem; a Study of a Dialectical Image' 109–110

uncanny, the 1, 24, 28–31, 119, 165, 174
un/consciousness of anthropomorphism 20–25
'Unhappy Schoolboy, The' 145
unheimlich 30, 185
untranslatability 147–150

Varga, D. 182–183
Victorian period 161, 186; anthropomorphism in 232–233;

diet of 220; ethics of compassion in children's literature of 230; imperialism of 168; manners and society 178, 207–209; moralistic stories of 152; nonsense, topsy-turveydom, and misrule in children's entertainment 157–158, 211
voyeurism towards animals 192–195

Waddell, M. 120
'Walrus and the Carpenter, The' 202–203, 207, 212; aesthetics and ethics in 203–206, 212–213; appetite, distraction, and nonsense in 220–229; bad faith in 228–229; empathy in 227–229; innocent victims in 217–225; nonsense in 213–220, 231–233; poetic structure of 213–216, 224–225; point of view in ethics and absent final frame of 229–234; psychopathy and pain illustrated in 230–231
Waste Land, The 67
Webb, C. 207
Webb, L. 41
Weil, S. 42–43
Wells, C. 105
Wells, P. 7, 76
'What Is It Like to Be a Bat' 24
When Species Meet 19
Where the Wild Things Are 6, 8, 147, 172–174
White, E. B. 76
White, L. 220, 231
'Why Look at Animals' 47, 192, 194
wilderness 13, 42, 124, 181, 182–183
'Wind in a Frolic, The' 158
Winnicott, D. 176–177
Winnie-the-Pooh 174, 178–180, 248
'With Trumpets and Zithers' 25–28
Wittgenstein, L. 32, 246
Wolf, C. 20
Wolfe, C. 217–218
Wordsworth, W. 146–147, 262
wrong-sidedness 160, 178
Wu, F.-L. 59

Zhuangzi 96–97
Zipes, J. 77, 79
zoomorphism 5, 22, 31, 33, 40, 49
zoopoetics 19, 44

Printed in the United States
by Baker & Taylor Publisher Services